Acclaim for LEON WIESELTIER's

KADDISH

"I have never read a book like this. No one has. It is something new in the world, and at the same time something very old. One feels this work—in its depth, idiosyncrasy, moral intellect, and stupendous range—to be an extension (dare I say it?) of the Talmud, and also its modern opposite. It seems hardly enough to say that Leon Wieseltier's *Kaddish* is beautiful, wise, amazing." —Cynthia Ozick

"The most beautiful book written this decade."

—Andre Aciman, *Slate*

"Read this extraordinary book and you will be both intellectually enriched and deeply moved. . . . [Wieseltier's] exploration of the Jewish laws of mourning . . . is among the best I have ever read. His *Kaddish* is not only for his father; it is for all fathers for whom no kaddish has been said."

—Elie Wiesel

"Stunning. . . . Wieseltier plunges us into the sea of rabbinical sources in which he swims with astounding cultural confidence. Soon, his sense of duty and ours transmute into fascination as the son's seemingly simple quest becomes a detective story of the spirit. . . . At its center are the most important questions about the nature and exercise of freedom, about whether aristocracy can be earned, about the obligations of love." —*Los Angeles Times Book Review*

"[An] astonishing book . . . meticulously learned yet intensely personal and impassioned . . . a demonstration of the power of an ancient tradition to engage a contemporary intellectual through the urgency of its concerns even if he or she cannot accept all its tenets." —*The New York Times*

"*Kaddish* inspires a sense of awe at the sheer magnitude, depth and wisdom of a tradition that attempts to provide both a practical framework and a moral explanation for the deepest and most ungovernable human impulses."

—*Newsday*

"Everything is [here] for the reader of any, or no, religion: the quick and the dead, the spiritual and the material, passion and duty . . . moral fables, ludicrous myths, piercing insights, transmitted by a committed but humorous and often exasperated twentieth-century American."

—*The New York Review of Books*

"[A] profound work not *about* Judaism but *of* Judaism: The inner life of the faith mediated through the sensibility of a wise, deeply learned, and reliable guide. I cannot point to another piece of writing in the English language that accomplishes within—and for—Judaism what Wieseltier has achieved."

—*National Review*

"Readers from all religious backgrounds will conclude this remarkable book at once harrowed and renewed."

—*Booklist*

"Profound. . . . [*Kaddish*] is much more than a personal memoir; it is an examination of the nature of ritual and of tradition. . . . [It] speaks so wisely and unsanctimoniously about the most important things."

—*Times Literary Supplement* (London)

"Extraordinary . . . an epigrammatic thinker of Pascalian concision and luminosity . . . a superb writer. . . . [*Kaddish*] is a fine book, no, more: It may well be destined to become an American Jewish classic."

—*Forward*

LEON WIESELTIER

KADDISH

Leon Wieseltier was born in Brooklyn in 1952. He is the literary editor of *The New Republic*.

KADDISH

LEON WIESELTIER

VINTAGE BOOKS
A Division of Random House, Inc. *New York*

KADDISH

FIRST VINTAGE BOOKS EDITION, FEBRUARY 2000

 Published in the United States by Vintage Books, a division of Random House, Inc., New York, and simultaneously in Canada by Random House of Canada Limited, Toronto. Originally published in hardcover in the United States by Alfred A. Knopf, a division of Random House, Inc., New York, in 1998.

The Library of Congress has cataloged the Knopf edition as follows:
Wieseltier, Leon.
Kaddish / by Leon Wieseltier. — 1st ed.
p. cm.
Includes bibliographical references and index.
ISBN 0-375-40389-2 (hc).
1. Kaddish. 2. Judaism—Liturgy. 3. Jewish mourning customs.
4. Wieseltier, Leon—Religion. I. Title.
BM670.K3W54 1998
296.4'45—dc21 98-15881
CIP

Vintage ISBN: 0-375-70362-4

www.vintagebooks.com

Printed in the United States of America
10 9 8 7 6 5 4 3 2 1

PREFACE

TO THE MEMORY
OF
MARK WIESELTIER,
MY FATHER

לזכר נשמת אבי
מרדכי בן שלמה זלמן
הריני כפרת משכבו

On March 24, 1996, which was Nisan 5, 5756, my father died. In the year that followed, I said the prayer known as the mourner's kaddish three times daily, during the morning service, the afternoon service, and the evening service, in a synagogue in Washington and, when I was away from home, in synagogues elsewhere. It was my duty to say it, for reasons that will become clear in this book.

I was struck almost immediately by the poverty of my knowledge about the ritual that I was performing with such unexpected fidelity. And it was not long before I understood that I would not succeed in insulating the rest of my existence from the impact of this obscure and arduous practice. The symbols were seeping into everything. A season of sorrow became a season of soul-renovation, for which I was not at all prepared.

Since I am so inclined, and to assist myself against my inadequacy, I began to study. I was bred for bookishness. I set out in search of the history of the mourner's kaddish, and I kept a journal in which I recorded the ancient, medieval, and modern sources that I found, and the speculations that they provoked. This volume is that journal. It is not exactly a work of scholarship. About this I wish to be clear. My inquiry into the origins and the meanings of the mourner's kaddish was the opposite of systematic study. I did not approach the sources or arrange the sources according to a plan. I did not submit the sources to a larger historical or linguistic or conceptual analysis. And I did not aspire to comprehensiveness. There were more sources, but there was not more time. I was not capable of the composure that a really rigorous investigation required. My researches were somewhat wracked.

I was fixed in my obligation, but I was a rover in my tradition. The texts led me around, pointing me in many directions, establishing lines of filiation, referring to each other in a great chain of custom and consciousness. The rabbis were passing me down, in accordance with my need and my curiosity. It would be arid to describe my experience as "intertextuality." It was more vivifying than that. The texts were like tracks in a garden. A little vertiginously, I followed where they led. Sometimes I paused before what was revealed, sometimes I hurried past. For a year, I never roamed beyond the garden wall. I saw the garden from many points of regard. I never saw it whole.

Many years ago, in an essay by Coomaraswamy on the aesthetics of Buddhism, I read about the Pali word *samvega,* which was "often used to denote the shock or wonder that may be felt when the perception of a work of art becomes a serious experience." The aim of Coomaraswamy's essay was to establish the legitimacy of a form of contemplation that is not disinterested. In the Buddhist sources that he cited, the artistic object is described as a "support for contemplation." And the natural object, too: one Pali work tells of a prince who "used as a support of contemplation simply a dewdrop," by the sight of which he was moved to intellection, to philosophical reflection. The prince was rewarded for the work of cognition not with the apprehension of the dewdrop, but with the idea that was suggested to him by the apprehension of the dewdrop.

I see no reason why the careful cognition of a text cannot provide a similar stimulation, a similar suggestiveness. During my year in mourning, certainly, I employed the texts of Judaism as supports for contemplation. That is to say, I scrutinized these laws and these legends to the best of my ability, and then I turned them to my own purposes, to my own severities. I consulted the thoughts of my precursors so as to attain to my own thoughts. My contemplation was not disinterested. I worked in haste, and I do not doubt that I made mistakes, for which I am sorry. But I was impatient. I was the mourner in the garden, rising to recite the kaddish and then seeking (in the words of a Pali authority) "contentment with the flavor of the chosen support of contemplation that has been grasped."

All the translations in this book are my own, except for translations of Scripture, for which I have relied upon the King James translation. (Occasionally I have altered it to correct for grammatical or Christological awkwardness.) The mourner's kaddish that I have translated is the version in the Ashkenazic rite. In this book, the Jewish house of worship is not referred to as the synagogue. I have always disliked that term. It is a cold word, a Greek word. (It derives from the Greek word that means "to assemble," and it appears in the Septuagint, the Greek translation of the Bible produced in Alexandria in the third century B.C.E., as the translation for the Hebrew word *edah,* or "assembly." The Jewish house of worship, as opposed to the Temple, which was a center of cultic sacrifice, does not appear in the Bible.) Worse, the term "synagogue" became a linguistic and iconographic abbreviation for the degradation of the Jews. In my own mind, I have never been able to divest the term of the connotations that were conferred upon it by the centuries-long conflict between *ecclesia* and *synagoga*, in which the latter was represented, with varying degrees of crudity and refinement, as an old and defeated woman, mocked, trampled, blinded by a snake, run through by a sword, ridden by the devil, her staff broken, her law turned upside down. I prefer to call the house of worship a shul. "Shul" is a Yiddish term, originating by way of the old German *scuola* from the Latin *scola*, and it denotes what is, for me, the significant and saving feature of the house of worship as it developed in Jewish life: it is a place of study as well as a place of prayer. "Shul" is a warm word, a Jewish word. I have always found it to be the friendliest of Jewish words, even when I have spurned its friendship.

A word about the dedication of this book. In its discussion of the obligations of children to parents, the Talmud remarks that "one must honor him in life and one must honor him in death." (Him or her: it is not the intention of the rabbis to make a distinction between the father and the mother.) How to honor one's father in death? "When he reports what his father told him, he must not say, 'This was said by my father.' He must say, 'This was said by my father, and I am the atonement for where he rests.'" Those startling Hebrew words—"I am the atonement for where he rests"—appear in the dedication of this book. They appear here, I should add, in technical violation of Jewish law. For the passage in the Talmud hastens to add that this peroration should be spoken only during the year of mourning, it is the mourner's peroration; but my year of mourning has now passed. Since this book is my journal of that year, however, I have permitted myself to attach the words to my father's name.

And when grief is gone? Still one may not speak of one's parents baldly. After the twelve months of mourning, the rabbis continue, one must accompany the mention of one's dead father or one's dead mother with the words, "May his memory be a blessing for life in the world to come." Modern Jews have abridged this locution of piety. They speak of their dead and say "May his memory be a blessing," and they mean a blessing here, upon us. But the rabbis mean a blessing there, upon him. It is a beautiful proposition, and an outrageous one. I can believe that the memory of our dead is a blessing here, upon us. Can I believe that it is a blessing there, upon them? This was the argument of my father's kaddish, and the subject of these investigations by his diligent and doubting son.

THE MOURNER'S KADDISH

Magnified and sanctified
may His great Name be
in the world that He created,
as He wills,
and may His kingdom come
in your lives and in your days
and in the lives of all the house of Israel,
swiftly and soon,
and say all Amen!

Amen!
May His great Name be blessed
always and forever!

Blessed
and praised
and glorified
and raised
and exalted
and honored
and uplifted
and lauded
be the Name of the Holy One
(He is blessed!)
above all blessings
and hymns and praises and consolations
that are uttered in the world,
and say all Amen!

May a great peace from heaven—
and life!—
be upon us and upon all Israel,
and say all Amen!

May He who makes peace in His high places
make peace upon us and upon all Israel,
and say all Amen!

KADDISH

I

Everything struck hard. The door slamming behind me in the black car. The shovel stabbing the mound of soil. The wooden box hitting the floor of the pit.

I stood and I swayed and I said what I was told to say. I was presented with the words that justify the judgment, and I justified the judgment. "He is the Rock, His work is perfect, for all His ways are judgment . . ." I was presented with the words of the kaddish, the long one for the funeral, the one about the world that will be made new, the one that I had never said before, and I uttered it. "Magnified and sanctified may His great Name be . . ."

"Magnified and sanctified . . ." Sounds, not words. Words that were nothing but sounds. The words spilled into the pit and smashed upon my father's coffin. I watched the words disperse across the surface of the wood like the clods of dirt that were falling upon it. I saw them there, the shattering words. I saw the letters and their shades. Finally they vanished into the earth. They were buried with him.

"He is the Rock." And the Rock struck hard. And I struck hard against the Rock.

Justify the judgment, but judge the judgment, too. Bring the judgment to judgment!

Out of tears, thoughts.

Magnified and sanctified . . . Magnified and sanctified . . . Magnified and sanctified . . .

Sorrow, feed me.

May His great Name be blessed . . . May His great Name be blessed . . . May His great Name be blessed . . .

It is in the hall of study that we pray. The beauty of the room is owed to its homeliness. It is decorated only with books. When I stand by the wall of books, I feel as if I am standing on the shore of an immensity.

The spines of books. Books and spines. Books are spines.

Magnified and sanctified . . . Magnified and sanctified . . . Magnified and sanctified . . .

The shul feels so worn. A red velvet cloth is thrown over the rostrum at the front of the room, directly before the ark in which the Torah scrolls are housed. Here stands the precentor, that is, the leader of the service, that is, the mourner; and as I place my hands on this cloth, which is the color of wine, I see the traces of the hands that preceded mine. There are stains in the velvet. In places it is threadbare. This is an exquisite erosion. It is not neglect that thins these instruments. Quite the contrary. The more threadbare, the better. The thinner, the thicker.

May His great Name be blessed . . . May His great Name be blessed . . . May His great Name be blessed . . .

A black river.

Magnified and sanctified . . . Magnified and sanctified . . . Magnified and sanctified . . .

I don't know what to do. No, I know what to do. I will open a book.

The most influential work on dying and mourning in the Jewish tradition was composed by Nahmanides, the religious genius of Spanish Jewry in the thirteenth century. It is known as *Torat Ha'Adam*, or *The Law of Man.* It is a vast compilation of laws and customs, drawn from ancient and medieval sources, and its treatment of the practices of mourning served as the model for the great medieval and early modern codes of law. It concludes with a great essay on eschatology called "The Gate of Recompense," a detailed explication of the system of rewards and punishments. But I begin at the beginning, with the introduction to the work. It is a philosophical reflection on mortality, written largely in a rhyming (and somewhat maddening) pastiche of Biblical and rabbinical phrases. "Every individual knows melancholy and joy," Nahmanides declares. Yet there are many ways to interpret human vicissitudes. "There is the man who is happy with his lot. He rejoices in the fullness of his sufficiency, in his rising star. He puts tomorrow out of mind, and drinks to forget his misery and his toil." (The "rising star" refers to the astrological sign that, in the words of one medieval Hebrew writer, "rises at the end of the eastern sky every hour and minute.") And there is also "the wise individual who rejects pleasure and recoils from his time and from every precious thing that he sees. On days of delight he thinks of mourning, and of despair on days of hope. He prefers weeping to happiness, and he scatters joy before sorrow and sighing. He foresees nothing but evil." The man who lives in the present, and the man who refuses to live in the present. Nahmanides disapproves of them both. "The two of them have diseased their hearts." The optimist "errs intellectually"; he does not grasp that no star always rises, for "the sphere is round," and the sign that ascends today descends tomorrow. The pessimist, though he is not mistaken intellectually (Nahmanides has described him as "the wise individual"), "is too clever, and he drinks with cynics." The cynics seek "to make the precious world tedious." Their enigmatic discourses are "a calumny against time." But time, Nahmanides observes, is "a truthful witness and a faithful judge." Time uses "proper weights and measures." It "never treats a man unfairly and never interferes with his deserts." In the consideration of mortality, certainly, the stars have nothing to teach. "The stars and the signs do not have the power to make people die or to make people live, so do not look to them, for they will neither harm you nor help you." No, "it is from the Lord of All that all comes." But the difference between theology and astrology is not only that God is powerful. It is also that God is just. "He acquits the righteous and convicts the wicked, and He makes everything right in its time. And in His ways there are hidden secrets (as the few have agreed, for the many will never be wise), things that are too exalted for creaturely knowledge, such as the distant future and the deep past. What, then, is there for poor, tempted man to do, when he comes before the king, except to justify the judgment and to verify the verdict?"

But I do not wish to justify the judgment and to verify the verdict! Count me, then, among the many who will never be wise. (Or try me another time.)

Help me, Nahmanides. Help me.

And this brings Nahmanides to the matter of mourning. More precisely, to the absurdity of mourning. "I want now to say what my heart believes and what my mind has proven." And what is that? He begins with a perplexity: "Since man is destined to die, and deserves to lie down in the shadow of death, why should we torture ourselves over somebody's death, and weep for the dead, and bemoan him? After all, the living know that they will die. It is puzzling that those who know what will come to pass should then mourn, and call others to lamentation." Nahmanides is describing a collision of the heart and the mind. (No wonder he began with "what my heart believes and what my mind has proven.") He is suggesting that what one knows must have an effect upon what one feels. This seems perfectly true. Did I expect my father not to die? Of course not! But still I wail. What good is philosophy, if there is pain?

Yet Nahmanides does not believe that mourning is absurd. He has answers to his question. This is his first answer: "It was the destiny of man to live forever, but as a consequence of that ancient sin, human beings have gone down to the slaughter. Therefore they tremble, because they are being separated from their true nature." Nahmanides is referring to the sin in paradise, to the consequences of Eve's apple. He is proposing that we do not mourn over death, we mourn over mortality. This is an interesting idea, though it has little to do with the real mourning of real people, who do not have their heads in their hands because they know that they will not live forever. And Nahmanides continues: "Moreover, I have searched and I have reflected, and in the entire Torah there is no prohibition against mourning and there is no commandment to be consoled. All that was prohibited [in Deuteronomy] was that mourners should cut themselves or shave their foreheads for the dead. But do not put off weeping and do not loathe sighing." Thus Nahmanides has established the Scriptural legitimacy of sorrow. Indeed, mourning is a primary religious activity: "It is important for us to understand that mourning is a service of the Lord, which enables us in grief and in belief to contemplate our true end and to know the location of our true home. In accordance with this, it is written [in Ecclesiastes] that 'it is better to go to the house of mourning than to go to the house of feasting, for that is the end of all men, and the living will lay it to his heart.'"

"There is no commandment to be consoled," said the giant of Gerona. I will remember that.

Magnified and sanctified . . . May His great Name be blessed . . . Magnified and sanctified . . . May His great Name be blessed . . .

And Nahmanides has a second answer to his question. Why mourn, if we know that we will die? "So that we may grieve for the sins of one who has died before his time. Or if a terrible thing befell him in one of his children, it is fitting to weep and to wail over this." Mourning is the proper response to the fate of those who die in sin. Nahmanides offers a reading (which is, again, a partial pastiche) of some verses from the third chapter of Lamentations. "If you repent, and you seek God out, then He will have compassion, according to the multitude of His mercies. For God does not wish to torment men, and He does not desire to bring them grief; nor to crush under His feet all the prisoners of the earth, to show that they are His prisoners and He has dominion over them; nor to turn aside the right of a man or to subvert a man in his cause—that is, when they are sinners before Him. Of all this He does not approve. But since He does not will such a wrong to come to pass, He also said: Do not believe that the many sufferings that befall you are accidental and do not come from Him, for who is he that saith and cometh to pass, when the Lord commandeth it not? Everything comes from Him. He commanded and all the deeds were created, and there is nothing evil or good that does not proceed from

Him. . . . And if everything proceeds from His mouth and from Him, and He has no desire to see evil done, since He acts justly, then wherefore doth a living man mourn and complain? It is for his own sins that he must mourn and complain." Nahmanides concludes, concretely: "Therefore, if a man dies earlier than most people die, or if a man's child dies, it is fitting that he, and those who love him, grieve and mourn—but their mourning must be such that it is a service of the Lord, in the sense that they mourn over the sins that were the cause of their suffering, and repent of the sins of which they are aware, and atone for the sins of which they are not aware. For the individual in pain to fortify himself with despair and to harden his heart in this regard—that is absolutely wrong."

A primeval glow in the city at dawn. As I drove to shul, everything was chaste. In the old, old light the buildings paled, the monuments dissolved. The city slipped back into the soil. I drove down to the river, where I observed the fading of human purposes. I saw the light of ancient Washington. A morning without civilization.

Nahmanides appreciates that an acquaintance with death can ruin an appetite for life. And so he seeks to secure the mourner against such ruin—to describe an ideal of mourning that is not despair, that honors the encounter with death but does not succumb to it. The rabbi wishes to harness the power of morbidity, to turn it to good use. I wish him luck.

So the mourner must not think metaphysically about death, says Nahmanides. The mourner must think morally about it. Death is not terrible. Sin is terrible. The death of my father was not a tragedy. It was a criticism.

My father died, so I must improve myself? I cannot follow the rabbi into this. The moralistic interpretation of death repels me.

Death, a reproach?

—He is guilty.
—No, he is dead.

It is ridiculous to suggest that death should not be a reason for despair.

Death is moralized because it is feared. But the moralist does not have the decency to admit that he is afraid.

The fear of death may be mastered, of course. But mastered by good works? I do not comprehend this. What has ethics to do with extinction? The inevitability of extinction lends a certain urgency to ethics, I guess. It is a boon to earnestness. (Live every day as if it is your last, and so on.) Still, a good man will die as surely as a bad man. Death is amoral, indifferent, mechanical; chop, chop, chop. It is a fact, and a value cannot unmake a fact.

God is just, but death is neutral.

I do not intend to be inconsolable, but I do not intend to be deceived.

In shul this Sabbath, we read the Song of Songs. There were gazelles in Georgetown.

"For love is strong as death, jealousy is cruel as the grave. . . ." Those words! They mark the discovery of finitude in the experience of desire. But in shul I took down from the shelves an edition of the Song of Songs that comes with the commentary of Elijah ben Shlomo Zalman, the Gaon of Vilna, the scholar and ascetic in Lithuania in the eighteenth century who has inspired more awe than any rabbi in modernity; and the Gaon glosses those words much less abstractly: "Love is strong as death, because at the hour of a man's death the parting of the soul from the body is difficult, for there is no love and no attachment and no mixture like that of the soul and the body; and jealousy is cruel as the grave, because there is no jealousy in the world like that of the man who goes to his grave and sees that the world still lives." The Gaon's gloss cuts me. It takes me back to the final days in the hospital when my father knew that the world still lived, and he was jealous.

I told a friend that I had returned to shul. So the circle is unbroken, he said. Maybe a little too unbroken, I thought. I like broken circles. I break circles.

Magnified and sanctified . . . May His great Name be blessed . . . Magnified and sanctified . . . May His great Name be blessed . . .

Back to Nahmanides. He concludes the introduction to his work on death with an admonition to his son. "My son! If sinners entice thee, consent thou not. For you will discover many sayings of the Greek philosophers and those who think as they do, sayings that harden the heart and stiffen the mind. They rejoice in a thing of nought, and are miserable comforters. They deny the future and they despair of the past. Who chooses them is an abomination—and a heretic. For Socrates, one of their wise men, is recorded as having decreed: 'They asked me, "Why have we never seen you sad?" And I replied, "Because I have nothing whose loss would make me sad."' He also said: 'He who knows the world will not rejoice over his good fortune and will not sorrow over his bad fortune.' They also said: 'The unhappy man is the man who cares.' They also said: 'He is deceived, who knows that he is on his way out of the world but seeks to cultivate it.' He and his friends the philosophers said many such things." I expect Nahmanides to denounce these Greeks and their philosophy of detachment, but he has a more intricate temper. "To be sure," he writes, "it is appropriate for them, and for all thinkers, to regard all the activities of the world as less than nothing, as vain, as devoid of purpose." Indeed, there is no need to stray among the Greeks for this wisdom. "After all, King Solomon exceeded them all [in Ecclesiastes] when, inspired by the holy spirit, he compared everything to vanity and declared that man hath no preeminence above a beast." Yet there was a difference between the alienation of Solomon and the alienation of Socrates. "Still, Solomon gave good heed and inquired strictly, and distinguished between good and bad, and between true and false. And so he instructed that in the day of prosperity be joyful but in the day of adversity shed a tear, that there is a time to weep and a time to mourn." That is to say, there is also a time *not* to weep and a time *not* to mourn.

I see what Nahmanides is up to. He is conceding the truth of pessimism, and then circumscribing it. Thus he proceeds to an ancient reading of God's observation, in the first chapter of the Bible, that the work of the sixth day of creation was "very good." According to the rabbis, "good" refers to the good impulse in man's nature, and "very" refers to the evil impulse in man's nature. "But is the evil impulse really very good? Only insofar as a man, in the absence of the evil impulse, would not build a house and take a wife and sire sons and daughters." Those are the deep, disabused words of the ancient rabbis. Nahmanides enlarges on their point:

"They penetrated far into the matter, and when they rendered the cultivation of the world null and vain, it was because the cultivation of the world cannot be sustained by anything except the service of the Creator, and in this way the world is indeed very good to those that be good and upright in their hearts. For it is a part of the service of the Lord to attend to the affairs of the world, and to the survival of all the species, so that God will forever look with favor upon His creation of us. . . . It is beyond doubt and it goes without saying that, from the standpoint of the mind, it is sheer idiocy to be angry or astonished at anything that happens; and it is also a sin and an iniquity, from the standpoint of God's justice, against which such individuals have revolted. Consider Job, and the story of his great and awful tribulations. How did he respond to what befell him? He rent his garments, and wept, and observed all the practices of mourning, and blessed his judge, saying: 'The Lord gave and the Lord hath taken away, blessed be the Name of the Lord!' And this should be the rule, concerning the future and the past: fury and fear lead to foolishness and falsehood. If one surrenders to despair and in this way finds solace, or if one's heart is not keen and one attributes what befalls one to accident or to custom—then one will drive wildly [and not mourn properly]."

And Nahmanides concludes with a consoling peroration: "May the Lord whose fury we fear, but whose will is our shield and our buckler, show us soon the restoration of the Temple, and fulfill in us and in our company the verse that declares, 'He will swallow up death in victory, and the Lord God will wipe away tears from all faces, and the rebuke of his people shall He take away from off all the earth, for the Lord hath spoken it.'" Look again at that verse. "He will swallow up death in victory . . . and the rebuke of his people shall

He take away from off all the earth." Isaiah could not have been clearer. For the prophet, and for the medieval commentator, death is a rebuke.

"It is a part of the service of the Lord to attend to the affairs of the world." A splendid sentence. Yet Nahmanides' affirmation is a complicated one. He wants to bite into the bitter fruit and to not taste the bitterness. To work in the world and to have no love for the world.

Nahmanides' quarrel is with Stoicism. (It is the Stoic version of Socrates that he presents, I think.) He does not believe that Stoicism is completely false. He admires its disdain for the material world, its ideal of inner freedom, its composure, its disenchantment. The Stoic's analysis of the world is right; but he does not grasp what is beyond the world, the remainder of reality. He is like a man who has backed out of a room but will not turn around. And behind his back is God.

God is what stands between Stoicism and despair, says the rabbi. (He is unfair to Stoicism, which is a theory of courage.)

The medieval Jew agrees with the ancient Greek that virtue is happiness. The difference is that the Greek will settle for less happiness than the Jew. (Or so the Jew thinks.)

Socrates, improved by Solomon. Stoicism, improved by Judaism.

The Stoic gives up on the world because it is an unjust world. But the unjust world and the just world are the same world. It is the unjust world that must be made the just world. For this reason, one must not secede from the world.

In the ideal of indifference, spirituality comes into contradiction with morality. (A spiritual victory is sometimes a moral defeat.)

Duty is a kind of passion, isn't it? A joyless kind.

Stoicism in the service of God, or an enchanted disenchantment.

"One will drive wildly." Nahmanides refers to the avenging Jehu, the son of Jehoshaphat, who overthrew the evil kings of Israel and Judah in an orgy of blood in the ninth century B.C.E. (He destroyed the House of Ahab and himself trampled Jezebel to death.) The Bible reports that Jehu was known for driving his chariot wildly, thoughtlessly, in a disordered state. He did the Lord's work, but he was a prince of instability. And what Nahmanides seeks for the mourner is stability, an unextreme attitude toward extremity.

Such wisdom is surely to be wished. But *this* mourner wants to drive his chariot wildly. Unphilosophically, unreligiously, wildly.

Magnified and sanctified . . . May His great Name be blessed . . . Magnified and sanctified . . . May His great Name be blessed . . .

I have to give a speech at the Holocaust Museum. A speech in the evening, which means that I cannot make it to shul. Yet I must do my duty; and so my friends arrange a prayer quorum for me, in the vestibule outside the auditorium. There I lead the worship, and there I say the kaddish for my father, who cherished this place. He sat in the rain with my mother on the day that the museum opened, marveling that it had risen. Now the words of his kaddish float high into the concentrationary ether of the atrium, and fly past the glass on which the name of his burned birthplace in Poland is carved, and drift into the halls that show the pictures of what was done to his world; and the syllables of my father's kaddish cling to those images like spit.

Magnified and sanctified . . . Magnified and sanctified . . . Magnified and sanctified . . . Or, the problem of repetition. It quickens. It dulls.

Years ago, when I stopped praying, the disappearance of the religious structure seemed to bring with it the promise of possibility: every day would begin differently. The adventure of self-creation! But really, was every day begun differently? I did not create myself. I merely acceded to other platitudes and other habits. It is not only religion that lives by repetition.

Every morning, a few minutes before seven o'clock, a yellow school bus passes me as I turn onto Massachusetts Avenue on my way to shul. Bless the sameness of the days!

In shul, on a swampy morning. A young man in shorts wants to know whether a certain prayer is said with a blessing or without a blessing. "With pants," he is told.

A friend calls to see if I have on my shelf the writings of Elijah Capsali of Crete, the sixteenth-century rabbi and historian. Capsali's chronicles of his time are among the most vivacious Jewish writings that I know, and I do have them, and I am glad to check a reference for my friend. Especially glad because I bump into an account of the death of the great rabbi Judah Minz in Padua in 1506, and the election of his son Abraham Minz to succeed him as head of the academy. The narrative includes this detail: "From the day of the death of his father, our teacher Rabbi Judah Minz, may his memory be a blessing, would lead the prayers in the synagogue, evening, morning, and afternoon, and he was wrapped in a black prayer shawl." A black prayer shawl! Where can I find one? It sounds exquisite. The garment was, no doubt, a version of the crepe that the Italians hung in their own hours of mourning; but lamentation, too, has a sumptuary aspect, and this Italianate indulgence would not deflect me from my spiritual purpose, I promise. Capsali notes also that "it was his intention to pray in this manner for a full year after his father's death, but he was expelled from his home." Abraham Minz was banished from Padua by the Venetian authorities because he presented a gift to the conquering German army. He fled for his life to Ferrara. I wonder if he left his black shawl behind.

Friday night. The Sabbath arrives in splendor. The rabbi introduces me to two men. They are brothers and they buried their father this morning. They have come to say kaddish, but they are not familiar with the words and the customs of the prayer. They are helpless. The rabbi asks me to help. At the moment in the worship when the mourners are supposed to be brought in, I bring the mourners in. (The unblind leading the unblind.) As soon as the brothers enter, the congregation breaks into a melancholy greeting: "May He who is everywhere console you among the other mourners of Zion and Jerusalem!" Soon it is time to recite the kaddish. The brothers rise with me. They read a transliteration of the prayer. "We're the dunces," one of them says. "No," I reply, "the dunces are the ones who don't try." I didn't like the sound of what I said, exactly; it reminded me of the smugness in which I was schooled. Yet what I said was right. As I watched the brothers struggle with the transliterated prayer, I admired them. The sounds that they uttered made no sense to them. But there was so much fidelity, so much humility, in their gibberish.

The golden bricks of the shul in the light of the summer morning. I arrived early and was filled with love for the sight.

The shul is losing its strangeness for me. This worries me. In a strange place, solitariness is possible. Sociability poses a threat to spirituality. Now I'm coming to know my fellow petitioners. They are no longer strangers, they are becoming friends. How do you pray with friends? How do you pray with anybody? Prayer is a throb of individuation, at least for me. And yet the congregation is one of the conditions of my kaddish.

I used to stay away from shul in part because I was too easily influenced by it. I wanted so much to be like the people with whom I prayed. This troubled me. One should not wish to be influenced. One should wish to be convinced.

It is more than twenty years since I stopped living according to Jewish law—since I threw off the yoke of the commandments, as the rabbis would say. Alas, I cannot say that my reasons were purely philosophical. I was governed also by my appetites. But one of the reasons for my failure was my experience of prayer. It was a disaster. Thinkingly and unthinkingly, in shuls and in schools and in forests and in fields, I had been praying for decades, and not once in those decades, not once, did I ever have the confidence that the cosmos in which I prayed was like the cosmos that my prayer described. I never had an intimation of objectivity. My prayers were increasingly frantic exertions of subjectivity, nothing more; and I could not persuade myself that the intensity of my feeling about what I said had any bearing upon its truth.

It was not within my power to provide the proof. Indeed, any proof that I provided would not be proof. The proof had to come from outside. I was sick of interiority. I dreamed of exteriority; of its certainty and its majesty. But I never found it. And so I came to consider my prayer a desolating and debasing form of utterance, and I stopped. And here I am, praying morning, noon, and night. The gorgeous, familiar, impotent words are tripping off my tongue. What am I doing?

Do not deny the invisible, but do not address it. The invisible may be inquired into, but it may not be importuned.

Today I thought that the best thing would be to throw myself into this completely, to have nothing but this. Let the tradition take it all! To surrender everything except the fathers: a terrible thought.

I feel like a copy. (Like an imperfect copy; and my imperfection is my salvation.)

I see the honor in withdrawing from the world. But to mourn?

This morning in shul I was assaulted by meanings. As I led the prayers, I understood certain words and phrases very sharply, with a startling force. Sometimes the sleep really does pass from one's eyes before prayer. And my wakefulness must have showed, because a few people remarked upon it.

I found a rip in my phylacteries. Hath heaven no more thunderbolts?

A man in our company rose to recite the kaddish. For whom, I wondered. When I asked him, he told me that he is a doctor, and he is saying the kaddish for a patient who died and left no children to say it for him.

I woke in the middle of the night and did not know where I was. A purple rash ran over my white walls. I felt a burning sensation in my throat. I worried about stifling myself. I was afraid. If only I can get to shul, I told myself, everything will be all right. I will tie myself to myself with my phylacteries, and the day will not harm me. At daybreak, I rushed to Georgetown.

There are days when there are just too many words in the liturgy. These are the skinless days. On such days I need to go slowly through the prayers. But I can't go slowly, because I'm the leader. I must get the entire company through this, to the kaddish and away. I must be spiritually efficient.

In Chicago. Kaddish on the road. A lovely little shul near the lake, with the separation of the women from the men cleverly accomplished by a row of plants. I say the kaddish and stroll along the silver shore. I am delighted to have done my duty. Tonight the fulfillment of my obligation does not oppress me, it refreshes me. It occurs to me that delinquency is such a waste of time: all those years spent extenuating, thinking, rethinking, apologizing, refusing to apologize, feeling guilt, hating the feeling of guilt. You can squander a lot of your soul not doing your duty.

In the morning I walked on Michigan Avenue and saw nothing but my father, who never set foot there.

In Brooklyn. On the afternoon of the Sabbath, the rabbi is discoursing about the blessing of the New Moon. He cites a law: "The blind are required to bless the moon." The blind, even though it is the sighting of the moon that is the occasion for the blessing. I think to myself: This is exactly the predicament of the mourner. He must bless what is wonderful even though he cannot see it.

The knowledge of a thing is more decisive than the sight of it.

A friend points me toward the modern career of the mourner's kaddish. In 1947, S. Y. Agnon composed a prayer to be said at military funerals, "as one follows the coffins of the fallen of the land of Israel." It is a preface to the mourner's kaddish. "When a king of flesh and blood goes to war against his enemies, he sends his soldiers to kill and to be killed. He may love his soldiers or he may not love them. He may have regard for them or he may not have regard for them. Even if he has regard for them, however, he regards them as dead, for the angel of death is close upon the heels of a man who goes to war, and accompanies him to kill him. When he is cut down and slain by an arrow or a sword or any of the other instruments of destruction, another man is put in his place. The king does not feel that someone is missing. After all, the nations are many and their troops are many. If one of them is killed, the king has many replacements. But our King, the King of Kings, the Holy One, Blessed Be He, wants life and loves peace and pursues peace and loves His people Israel. He chose us, and not because we are a large nation, for we are one of the smallest of nations. We are few, and owing to the love with which He loves us, each one of us is, for Him, an entire legion. He does not have many replacements for us. If one of us is missing, heaven forfend, then the king's forces are diminished, with the consequence that His kingdom is weakened, as it were. One of His legions is gone and His greatness is lessened. For this reason, it is our custom to recite the kaddish when a Jew dies." Agnon then proceeds to give a short commentary on the text of the mourner's kaddish, according to which God's Name will be "magnified in its power, so that there will be no loss of strength before Him . . . and sanctified so that we need not fear for ourselves, but only for the splendor and the pride of His holiness." But Agnon was not composing a general meditation on the mourner's kaddish. He was writing in Jerusalem when the city was under fire, and so he turns to address the harsh historical circumstances. "If this is what we pray and what we say for every individual who dies, how much more shall we pray it and say it for our brothers and our sisters, the lovely and pleasant and dear children of Zion who were slain for the land of Israel, whose blood was spilled for the honor of His blessed Name, for His people and His land and His heritage! Indeed, everyone who dwells in the land of Israel is one of the legions of the King of Kings, the Holy One, Blessed Be He, whom the King has appointed a watchman over His palace. When one of them is killed, He is bereft of others to put in his place. And so my brothers in the house of Israel, all of you who mourn in this mourning, let us direct our hearts to our Father in Heaven, the King of Israel and its Redeemer, and pray for ourselves and for Him, as it were: 'Magnified and sanctified may His great Name be . . .'"

It is a beautiful composition. It is also a little repugnant. The army of God: the metaphor has brought so much misery to the world! Surely military life is the antithesis of spiritual life. Surely the service of the Lord is not a war. As for the survival of the Jews in the land of Israel, I am inclined to extol the Jews in the land of Israel for it; to admire the legions, not the king.

In Brooklyn. A night with no sleep. I take a volume off the shelf in my old room and stumble upon the source of Agnon's interpretation of the mourner's kaddish. It is

Simhah Bunim of Przysucha, a hasidic master in Poland in the early nineteenth century who preferred philosophy to mysticism, the rational to the magical. (He was a pharmacist.) "The saying of Rabbi Bunim of Przysucha about the reason for the mourner's kaddish is well known," I read. "In the ordinary world, when a small unit of a large army is lost, the loss is not felt, and it is not until an entire division is missing that the depletion must be corrected and the army must be reinforced. It is otherwise, however, in the army of God. If only a single Jew is missing, then there is already a lack in the greatness and the holiness of God. Therefore we pray that His Name may be 'magnified and sanctified,' that is, that His blessed Name may be made complete for what it has lost with the disappearance of the deceased." And the passage concludes: "And in the instance of such a holy soul as Eliezer Abraham, may peace be upon him, it is especially true that such reinforcement is necessary." Eliezer Abraham was a young scholar who died in 1982, when he was twenty years old. He was my cousin. It was his father who cited the saint of Przysucha, in his introduction to a posthumous volume of his son's readings of Scripture that he published a few years later in Brooklyn. I did not know the son. The father taught me many things when I was a young man. I used to phone him whenever I was defeated by a discussion in the Talmud. I used to phone him often.

The time has come to make the arrangements for my father's tombstone. In accordance with the mortuary practice of American Jewry, there will be a "family stone" that will loom over the entire plot, and a "footstone" that will mark my father's grave and give his particulars. Many years ago my father asked us to arrange for the names of his brother and his sister to appear on his grave. They were murdered in Europe and there were no exequies. When the time comes, my mother says, she wants the same for her martyrs, too. She suggests that the family stone, too, should bear a sign of the scar. In this way, the Jewish experience of my father and my mother will be distinguished from the Jewish experience of the American brethren in whose company they will forever lie. Memory, memory, memory. She is right: there is a gulf between the Jews who saw what Hitler did and the Jews who did not see. I propose to find an appropriate verse from Psalms to engrave on the rock: the psalmist is always escaping his enemies and giving thanks for his escape. The gentleman whom we have retained to create this little monument says that he will need the verse in a few months.

Home after the morning prayers, a little before eight o'clock. A workman is standing outside the building. He smiles at me, with pity in his eyes. "Night shift, huh?" Well, yes.

Often I have kindled to the imagination of confinement. A contraction of experience seemed like a condition of real work. And now a contraction has occurred. I cannot stray the way I used to stray. Finally I have a measure of confinement. What will I do with it?

The evening prayer. It is almost sundown. I step up to the task. "Is it time?" I ask the young man in charge of the proceedings. He looks at his watch. "Another forty seconds," he replies. I have an antinomian fantasy. I will cause them all to sin! I will start in thirty seconds, and dupe my pious, hairsplitting comrades into praying a full ten seconds before the appointed hour! I resist the temptation, of course. I am here for them and they are here for me.

A friend asked why I am saying kaddish. A good question. These were my answers. Because it is my duty to my father.

Because it is my duty to my religion. (These are the strong reasons; the nonutilitarian, nontherapeutic reasons.) Because it would be harder for me not to say kaddish. (I would despise myself.) Because the fulfillment of my duty leaves my thoughts about my father unimpeded by regret and undistorted by guilt. On the subject of fathers and sons, my chore may keep me clear.

In Maimonides' code of law, a judgment: "Whoever does not mourn as the sages instructed is cruel."

—He is absent for me.
—Then he is present for you.

I am standing in my phylacteries at dawn, and suddenly they feel different. They do not bind me, they gird me. They seem (I know this is a little ridiculous) gladiatorial. The arm on which they are wrapped feels strong.

A Saturday night in July. The Sabbath ends irritatingly late. I feel as if I've been in shul all day. Driving around Dupont Circle, my senses amiably riot. Everything my eyes see is delicious. The cheesy marble fountain in the circle looks like a masterpiece of neoclassicism. There isn't a plain-looking woman on the street. In these months in shul, I sometimes fear for my senses. I remember a passage by Rabbi Joseph Soloveitchik, the master of my generation, its model of an intellectual in God. (But not my master or my model. I supped elsewhere.) It is a passage in a brilliant essay that has always bothered me. It gives Soloveitchik's account of the relation of "halakhic man," or the Jew who lives according to Jewish law, to the natural world. "There is no real phenomenon to which halakhic man does not possess a fixed relationship from the outset and a clear, definitive, a priori orientation," he wrote. When a religious Jew "comes across a spring bubbling quietly," he regards it for its fitness to serve as waters of expiation for a variety of human impurities. When he "looks to the western horizon and sees the fading rays of the setting sun or to the eastern horizon and sees the first light of dawn," he sees the obligations imposed by sunrise and sunset. When he "chances upon mighty mountains," he is put in mind of the legal measurements that determine, in the rabbinic law of torts, a private domain. And so on. I cannot accept this. It is dehumanizing. Surely the senses precede the commandments. If they do not, then the Jew is robbed not only of the pleasure in the physical world that is his or her natural right, but also of the opportunity to master that pleasure by infusing the physical world with metaphysical significance. Soloveitchik's analysis makes me want to bolt, to take back the physical world from its metaphysical significance. Anyway, no human being lives in a single domain. The choice between the physical and the metaphysical is the choice between air and water. The senses serve religion and the senses offer respite from religion. When I contemplate the dawn, I prefer not to think of my phylacteries. And if it all doesn't go together tidily, if there is a dissonance between the physical and the metaphysical, fine.

I don't like what I'm seeing in myself lately. I swing between a new irritability and a new lassitude. I feel harassed by time, and rush about between the pressure of my morning commitment and the pressure of my evening commitment; or I feel indifferent to time, and my eyes want to close and my limbs to go idle. I am angry or I am drowsy. In recent weeks I have been often visited by the image of my father in his hospital bed, dying and knowing it.

A shiny, breezy evening. Just as the prayers are starting, a troop of chubby, bratty boys from a yeshiva on the Jersey shore saunters in. The dust of a summer's day is upon them. I find myself a little annoyed at their rowdiness. (And a little embarrassed at my annoyance; when I was a boy I didn't like those old men who cared about nothing more than decorum.) Then it comes time for them to say amen, and they sing it out again and again; and with every little chorus I melt. It is almost impossible to think unsentimentally about continuity.

Where shall I start, in my search for the mourner's kaddish? —My search for the mourner's kaddish? But it has found me!

The search for what one already has found, or taking tradition seriously.

Until now, the mourner's kaddish used to be the least important part of the prayer service. I mean, for me. It was the small print in the liturgy, a morbid recitation in the interstices of the worship. But no more. Now I inhabit the interstices.

The mourner's kaddish is only one of the varieties of kaddish that are recited in the house of worship. There are the full kaddish, the half kaddish, the rabbis' kaddish. (The mourner's kaddish is a slight abridgment of the full kaddish.) They are all variants of the same utterance, of the sort that scholars describe as a "doxology," or an expression of praise. But look at the language. The kaddish is not so much the praise of God as a prayer for the praise of God. It is a messianic supplication, except that the eschatological improvement is here imputed not only to the Jews, but also to the God of the Jews. (In the Sephardic rite, the messianism of the kaddish is explicit.) This is mysterious.

In the liturgy, the kaddish plays an important formal role. It structures the worship, dividing major prayers from minor prayers, marking pauses between orders of prayer. And its spiritual role? It must be significant, judging by a famous statement in the Talmud that "the world is sustained in existence . . . by [the utterance of] 'May His great Name be blessed' at the conclusion of teaching and preaching." This passage gives a sense of the antiquity of the proclamation at the heart of the kaddish. (The origins of the congregational response about the divine name are Biblical.) The Talmudic statement also suggests the original function of the kaddish: it was an eschatological peroration to an academic discourse. After "teaching and preaching," these words were recited. And they continue to play this role in the Jewish liturgy in the form of the rabbis' kaddish, which adds a petition for the welfare of "Israel, and its teachers, and their students, and the students of their students, and everyone who is occupied with the study of Torah here and elsewhere." In a fragment of the kaddish from the eleventh century in Cairo, the names of the masters and the officials of the academy are mentioned; and Nahmanides reports that the Jews of Yemen expressed their gratitude to Maimonides for his spiritual and political assistance by adding his name to the kaddish: "In your lives and in your days and in the life of Rabbi Moses ben Maimon . . ." (It would seem that the kaddish was a kind of intermezzo to which personal entreaties and contemporary allusions could be added.) In the twelfth century in Egypt, Maimonides himself provided a succinct description of the function of the kaddish in a responsum to the community of Aleppo. Asked whether the kaddish must be said at the conclusion of a prayer that was composed "for Sabbaths, festivals, and days of joy" by Sa'adia Gaon in the tenth century, Maimonides replied: "Under no circumstances is the kaddish to be recited except at the well-known points in the mandatory prayers or after an exposition of any matter of Torah, that is, after a discussion of laws, or after commentary, or even just an explanation of a single [Scriptural] verse, when the rabbis' kaddish should be said. I do not see any reason, however, that kaddish should be recited at the conclusion of these supplications that were composed by his eminence the Gaon." A similar rule appears in a compilation of the traditions of the French communities of the eleventh and twelfth centuries known as the prayerbook of Rashi, who was the other immeasurable figure of medieval Judaism. "Whenever the congregation recites verses from Scripture or passages from Talmud, it must follow them with the recitation of kaddish." Scripture and study: these were the original occasions for the kaddish. Not a word about mourning.

Another important source for the early history of the kaddish, and this illumination I owe to the collapse of communism. "With the fall of the Iron Curtain that surrounded the eastern bloc for decades," writes the erudite editor of the trove known as Guenzberg 566 in the Russian State Library, formerly the Lenin State Library, in Moscow, "the manuscript treasures that are stored there are being brought to light, bit by bit." Guenzberg 566 includes a large collection of responsa by Abraham ben Isaac, a pioneering jurist in Provence in the twelfth century. Abraham was the head of the rabbinical court in Narbonne and the author of the first code of law produced by the Jews in Provence. One of his responsa turns out to be a brief review of the liturgical occasions of the kaddish. "As for the ritual of the kaddish about which you asked," he writes to his correspondent, "we do not possess any clear information about it from our early sages [in the Talmud]. Later sages claimed that it is founded on this verse [in Leviticus]: 'I will be sanctified among the children of Israel.' And from what our rabbis stated [in the Talmud] about this verse, that the *kedushah* may not be recited unless ten [men] are present, they concluded that anytime ten people are assembled for the fulfillment of an obligation of prayer or an obligation of study, they must sanctify the occasion [with a kaddish]." The *kedushah* is the recitation of the verse from Isaiah—"Holy, holy, holy is the Lord of hosts"—known as the trisagion, or "thrice holy": *kadosh, kadosh, kadosh.* And the word *kaddish* is itself another form of the word for "sanctity." The kaddish hallows.

Abraham then surveys the liturgy, showing that the appearance of the kaddish at various points in the service is warranted by the rule that he has provided, since each of the liturgical units demarcated by the kaddish represents the fulfillment of a specific obligation of worship or learning that the kaddish marks and sanctifies. "There must also be a kaddish," he notes, "after every psalm or every chapter [of Scripture] or every Talmudic law or every Talmudic legend that it is the custom to read in some places at the conclusion of the service." Scripture and study: the kaddish attends the Divine Word, as it was told to the Jews and as the Jews tell it.

In the Talmud, a few lines past the passage to which Abraham ben Isaac refers, it is reported that there were rabbis in Palestine who asserted that one may not interrupt one's recitation of the central prayer of the worship except to utter the response: "May His great Name be blessed!" Referring to Ezekiel's bustling vision of the celestial realities, these rabbis insist that "one may interrupt even one's study of the work of the chariot" to proclaim those words. The knowledge of the godhead must yield to the blessing of the godhead. But the rabbis in Babylonia disagreed with the rabbis in Palestine, and so "the law is not in accordance with their view."

Abraham ben Isaac concludes his ruling with a brief discussion of the kaddish at the funeral. "The [recitation of the]

Justification of the Judgment is an obligation that people are required to fulfill—as [the Talmud] states, the study of Torah is canceled for the sake of a funeral or a wedding—and so it must be sanctified [with a kaddish]." He hastens to add that kaddish is not recited at a wedding: "If you desire to know why kaddish is not said when the bride is brought to the wedding canopy—which is, of course, the fulfillment of an obligation in a quorum of ten—the answer is that this rule does not apply, because people come to a wedding only for the general purpose of honoring [the bride and the groom], and they do not utter any words at all, so what would a kaddish sanctify? After all, the kaddish is not recited where there is no required utterance or psalm of praise." At a funeral, by contrast, there is a required utterance, and it is the Justification of the Judgment, which is a selection of verses from Scripture, and so the kaddish must be recited. This, again, is not the mourner's kaddish.

Abraham also records a difference of opinion among the geonim, as the early medieval authorities in Babylonia were called. "Some geonim ruled that a kaddish is not to be said after the Justification of the Judgment until it can be said over something that is itself a ritual obligation, whereas other geonim ruled that it must be said at once, for the burial is itself a ritual obligation." All these sages seem to agree that the Justification of the Judgment itself is not a ritual obligation; but Abraham differs with them all. "And this concludes your inquiries into the reasons for the marvelous blessings," Abraham writes at the end of his responsum. "May our God open our hearts to His law and to the distinctions of those who extol His word, and may He succor us and take us under His wing, amen, amen, selah!"

I conclude that the liturgical function of the kaddish has nothing to do with its content; and that the kaddish at the funeral has nothing to do with the mourner's kaddish; and that the mourner's kaddish has nothing to do with mourning. So what exactly is this exclamation whose servant I have become?

Some friends have opened a teahouse nearby. Now my mornings will be perfect: from the shul to the teahouse, where I will sit tranquilly upstairs, in the corner by the window, and hunt for the history of the mourner's kaddish. (Teaism, the place is called. I have always found poetry in abstract nouns. And a friend remarks: from theism to teaism.)

II

Where shall I start, in my search for the mourner's kaddish? In the glittering letters of Rabbi Akiva. Sometime in the seventh or eighth century, many centuries after Rabbi Akiva, there appeared a pseudo-epigraphic work called *Otiyot De'Rabbi Akiva,* or *The Alphabet of Rabbi Akiva,* an early and extravagant production of the mystical imagination in Judaism. This short but dense work considers, letter by letter, the cosmological and eschatological properties of the Hebrew alphabet, and what it reveals about the godhead. In the consideration of the seventh letter of the alphabet, the letter *zayin,* there appears an extraordinary passage in which the kaddish is endowed with the power to save the souls of the dead from hell. The passage is a catalogue of God's keys, based upon all the Biblical verses in which God is said to open or to release something. It is the last key in the catalogue that interests me. "He has the key to Gehenna, for it is written [in Isaiah], 'Open ye the gates, that the righteous nation which keepeth the truth may enter in.'" Where is the hell in this verse? In a pun. "Which keepeth the truth," in the Hebrew, is *shomer emunim*; but the word *emunim* is a plural, and it looks very much like the plural form of *amen,* so that the verse may be read as: "Open ye the gates, that the righteous nation which keepeth the amens may enter in." That is how it is read in the Talmud, and that is how pseudo-Akiva wishes to read it. "Do not read *shomer emunim,* except in the sense that [the verse refers to an individual who] says amen. For it is for the sake of a single amen that the wicked utter in hell that they are raised from hell."

And when do the wicked rescue themselves with these salvific syllables? When they respond to the kaddish! The text tells the story: "In the future, the Holy One, Blessed Be He, will sit in the Garden of Eden, teaching and preaching. All the righteous of the world will be seated before Him. And all the celestial servants will be standing there, the sun and the planets to God's right, the moon and the stars to God's left. The Holy One, Blessed Be He, will expound before them the new Torah that He will give them in the future by the hand of the messiah. When He speaks [the nonlegal portion of his discourse that consists in] his homiletics, Zerubbabel ben Shealtiel rises and recites 'Magnified and sanctified!' [that is, he recites the kaddish]. His voice resounds to all the ends of the earth, and all the creatures of the earth respond: amen! Even in Gehenna, the wicked souls of Israel, and also the righteous souls of Israel who still tarry there [until the conclusion of their judgment], they, too, say amen. They say this from the depths of hell—as it is written, 'Open ye the gates, that the righteous nation which keepeth the amens may enter in'—until the whole world shakes with the sound. The Holy One, Blessed Be He, hears their words. He makes an inquiry. 'What is that great noise I hear?' The angels who attend Him reply: 'Lord of the Universe, those are the wicked of Israel in Gehenna, and the righteous of Israel still in Gehenna, saying amen in hell.' Immediately He is overcome with mercy. 'What can I do for them,' He says, 'that will supersede the requirements of justice? After all, their own evil inclinations brought this upon them!' And then, in that very moment, He takes the keys of hell and, in the presence of all the righteous souls that are before Him, presents them to Gabriel and Michael, instructing them: 'Go and open the gates of Gehenna, and raise them up from hell! For it is written, "Open ye the gates, that the righteous nation which keepeth the amens may enter in."' Gabriel and Michael depart at once, and they unlock forty thousand gates in Gehenna, and they lift them out of there. . . . They seize every single one of them with their own hands and raise them up, like a man who rescues his friend from a pit by pulling him up with a rope. Then Gabriel and Michael make them clean and lovely, and they heal them of all the blows that they endured in hell, and they dress them in fine and beautiful clothes, and they take them with their hands and bring them, refreshed and dignified, before the Holy One, Blessed Be He, and before the assembly of the righteous. . . . When they arrive at the gate of Eden, Gabriel and Michael enter first, to be received by God. He responds to them and says: 'Let them go, so that they may enter, and come inside, and see My glory.' And when they enter, they prostrate themselves, and they bow, and they bless the Lord, and they praise the Lord, in the company of the saints and the perfectly righteous."

The kaddish in this text is not the mourner's kaddish, obviously. It is the rabbis' kaddish, the kaddish that is recited after study—in this case, after God's study! Still, the function of the kaddish is significantly expanded here. It is promoted from an accompaniment of pedagogy into an accompaniment of eschatology. It is associated with the dead, with the redemption of the dead.

When God completed His discourse, Zerubbabel ben Shealtiel recited the kaddish, as any good student would recite it in any house of study after the discourse of any rabbi. Zerubbabel was a historical figure. A scion of the House of David, he led thousands of Jews out of Babylon and back to Jerusalem, where he served as governor of Judea under the Persian King Darius I in the sixth century B.C.E. Since his origins and his activities were tinged with redemption, Zerubbabel became the hero of one of the great apocalyptic romances in Jewish history, the anonymous *Sefer Zerubavel,* or *The Book of Zerubbabel,* which appeared in the seventh century, around the same time as *The Alphabet of Rabbi Akiva.* It is a communication to Zerubbabel by Michael, the angel known also as Metatron, which recounts the final war of the forces of God against the forces of Satan. (The work is especially striking for its vilification of the Virgin Mary.)

The rabbis were humble, but they were not modest. In this passage from *The Alphabet of Rabbi Akiva,* they celestialized their own customs! God teaches and preaches as they do. His students conclude the lesson with the kaddish, as their students do. And then God instructs His angels to open the gates of hell on the basis of the rabbis' reading of a verse in Scripture. The Lord of the Universe is persuaded by a Talmudic pun to interfere with the justice of the universe.

Angels are even more embarrassing to the idea of God than human beings.

It is more than three months since my father died. My sister surprises me when she confesses that she still cannot bring herself to listen to music. I see again that the kaddish is my good fortune. It looks after the externalities, and so it saves me from the task of improvising the rituals of my bereavement, which is a lot to ask.

The rabbi is away, and the sermon this morning was delivered by a member of the congregation, from what the shul calls the "people's pulpit." The preacher's theme was reward and punishment, and he was quoting Rabbi Tarphon's great parable—"the day is short and the work is great and the workers are lazy and the pay is plentiful and"—when abruptly he stopped, because a black bird had flown through the window into the shul. It looked like a starling and it was hurling itself furiously against the walls, disrupting the congregation with alarm and amusement. Someone suggested that the women in the upper gallery open the high windows, so that the poor frenzied creature might escape. Sunlight began to flood the chamber from above, when suddenly a woman's voice was heard: "It's dead!" A shudder went through the shul. The bird had not been flying, it had been dying. The man at the pulpit made a little joke to restore order, and to blunt the imputation of significance to the fatal flight of the starling, but he defeated himself when he completed Rabbi Tarphon's pronouncement—"and the boss is pressing."

Driving to shul this evening, I was complaining in my mind. Back and forth, back and forth, back and forth: sometimes I feel not like the tradition's heir but like the tradition's puppet. By the time the prayers started, I was in no state for praying. But my consternation dissolved at the sight of a little boy in the corner of the room, with earlocks and fringes and thick glasses, and his twin brother right next to him. Their bearded and caftaned father had sat them down before a kabbalistic edition of the prayerbook and opened it to one of its typographically preposterous pages, in which the ordinary meaning of words is sacrificed to a mysterious arrangement of the letters. The little boys puzzled over all the loose letters, large and small. The one began to yawn, the other began to giggle. Early signs of critical intelligence.

I walked from shul to Dumbarton Oaks, to the old stone bench near the bottom of the hill at the far edge of the gardens. For years I have been coming to this bench for a little loneliness. The forsythia were blazing, as they blaze at this time every year. This year I beheld the slope of yellow fire and thought: a hill in hell.

Flames in bloom.

What next, in my search for the mourner's kaddish? Three or four hundred years after *The Alphabet of Rabbi Akiva* attached the rabbis' kaddish to the redemption of the dead, a story about Rabbi Akiva introduces the mourner's kaddish and announces that its function is the redemption of the dead. The story is robustly told in *Maḥzor Vitry,* a liturgical, legal, and exegetical compendium whose primary author was Simhah ben Samuel of Vitry, or Vitry-le-Brûle, a small town in Champagne, in northeastern France. It records the practices and the opinions of the Jewish community in the age of Rashi, in the eleventh century; and it was considerably enlarged by material from subsequent centuries. In this rich book, I read: "A tale of Rabbi Akiva. He was walking in a cemetery by the side of the road and encountered there a naked man, black as coal, carrying a large burden of wood on his head. He seemed to be alive and was running under the load like a horse. Rabbi Akiva ordered him to stop. 'How comes it that a man does such hard work?' he asked. 'If you are a servant and your master is doing this to you, then I will redeem you from him. If you are poor and people are avoiding you, then I will give you money.' 'Please, sir,' the man replied. 'Do not detain me, because my superiors will be angry.' 'Who are you,' Rabbi Akiva asked, 'and what have you done?' The man said, 'The man whom you are addressing is a dead man. Every day they send me out to chop wood.' 'My son, what was your work in the world from which you came?' 'I was a tax collector, and I would favor the rich and kill the poor.' 'Have your superiors told you nothing about how you might relieve your condition?' 'Please, sir, do not detain me, for you will irritate my tormentors. For such a man [as I], there can be no relief. Though I did hear them say something—but no, it is impossible. They said that if this poor man had a son, and his son were to stand before the congregation and recite [the prayer] "Bless the Lord who is blessed!" and the congregation were to answer amen, and the son were also to say "May the Great Name be blessed!" [a sentence from the kaddish], they would release him from his punishment. But this man never had a son. He left his wife pregnant and he did not know whether the child was a boy.

And if she gave birth to a boy, who would teach the boy Torah? For this man does not have a friend in the world.' Immediately Rabbi Akiva took upon himself the task of discovering whether this man had fathered a son, so that he might teach the son Torah and install him at the head of the congregation to lead the prayers. 'What is your name?' he asked. 'Akiva,' the man answered. 'And the name of your wife?' 'Shoshnia.' 'And the name of your town?' 'Lodkiya.' Rabbi Akiva was deeply troubled by all this and went to make his inquiries. When he came to that town, he asked about the man he had met, and the townspeople replied: 'May his bones be ground to dust!' He asked about the man's wife, and he was told: 'May her memory be erased from the world!' He asked about the man's son, and he was told: 'He is a heathen—we did not even bother to circumcise him!' Rabbi Akiva promptly circumcised him and sat him down before a book. But the boy refused to receive Torah. Rabbi Akiva fasted for forty days. A heavenly voice was heard to say: 'For this you mortify yourself?' 'But Lord of the Universe,' Rabbi Akiva replied, 'it is for You that I am preparing him.' Suddenly the Holy One, Blessed Be He, opened the boy's heart. Rabbi Akiva taught him Torah and 'Hear, O Israel' and the benediction after meals. He presented the boy to the congregation and the boy recited [the prayer] 'Bless the Lord who is blessed!' and they answered, 'May the Great Name be blessed!' At that very moment the man was released from his punishment. The man immediately came to Rabbi Akiva in a dream, and said: 'May it be the will of the Lord that your soul find delight in the Garden of Eden, for you have saved me from the sentence of Gehenna.' Rabbi Akiva declared: 'Your Name, O Lord, endures forever, and the memory of You through all the generations!' For this reason, it became customary that the evening prayers on the night after the Sabbath are led by a man who does not have a father or a mother, so that he can say kaddish and 'Bless the Lord who is blessed!'"

Here is a very early record of the mourner's kaddish. I note that this kaddish is established only for Saturday nights. The text explains why. "On the Sabbath the sinners of Israel are released from Gehenna, and they find rest on the Sabbath until the Jews conclude their evening prayers [on Saturday night]. That is why the prayers are prolonged, so that those souls will not hurry back to hell."

"'What is your name?' he asked. 'Akiva,' the man answered." This is striking. The savior finds his namesake in the saved: a tale of two Akivas. What do the two Akivas have in common? Well, it was said of Rabbi Akiva that "every day he would carry a bundle of wood—half of it he would sell for his living, the other half he would use for his own purposes. His neighbors protested, saying, 'Akiva, we are choking from the smoke [of your burning wood]! Sell us the wood, and buy some oil, and study by the light of a lamp.' He replied: 'The wood fills many of my needs. I study by its light, I warm myself by its heat, and I sleep on it." But there is a deeper affinity between the two Akivas. Before he became one of the masters of his age, our hero was a humble shepherd and completely unlettered. He began his education at the age of forty, and he once confessed that in the years when he was "an ignorant boor" he had wanted to "break the bones" of scholars. And here he is, remedying the ignorance of the son of this other Akiva, saving this other Akiva from the consequences of having raised a child who is not competent in his tradition.

Lodkiya: this must be Laodicea, the port city on the coast of northern Syria. Akiva was known for his travels. He made quite a trek to establish the kaddish.

Akiva taught the condemned man's son not for intrinsic reasons, but for extrinsic reasons. Somebody else needed that the son should know these things. Somebody else was counting on it. This motive for study is often overlooked. Knowledge is not only for oneself, it is also for others; not only for the satisfaction of one's own thirsts, but also for the fulfillment of one's obligations to others, whose occasions require the interventions of tradition. The great unlettered Jewish community of America could use a couple of million encounters with Akiva. Or do they expect their children to save them? Their children, who will inherit an ignorance of Jewish tradition unprecedented in Jewish history?

A century or so after *Maḥzor Vitry,* in a work called the *Kol Bo,* an anonymous anthology of laws and customs from the French communities, the link between the kaddish and the legend of Akiva and the condemned man is clearly stated. The text tells the story and then explains: "And it was on this basis that the custom became widespread that the son of a dead man says kaddish."

In the Talmud, I come upon a story about Rabbi Judah that must have served as an inspiration for the story of Rabbi Akiva and the condemned man. It begins with a strange statement by Rabbi Hisda: "A man's soul mourns for him all seven days." An affecting notion. The soul grieves for its separation from the body! In Rabbi Hisda's view, it seems, the soul enjoys its terrestrial circumstances. Spirit may be the opposite of matter, but it is matter's loyal opposite. And the text continues: "Rabbi Judah said: If somebody has died and left no mourners to comfort [him], then ten men go and sit in the dead man's place. It happened that a man died in Rabbi Judah's neighborhood. He left no comforters, and so every day Rabbi Judah collected ten men and they sat in his place. After seven days [when the week of mourning ended], the dead man appeared to Rabbi Judah in a dream and said: 'Set your mind at rest, because you have set my mind at rest.'" The soul of the dead in need of the services of the living; the services of the living as the rituals of mourning; the dream in which the dead thanks the living for carrying out the mourner's duties, and promises a reward of measure for measure: all these elements are present in the story of Rabbi Judah and the story of Rabbi Akiva. Of course, there is an important difference. The dead man in the story of Rabbi Akiva left a son. Also, Rabbi Judah's objective is to comfort a soul, but Rabbi Akiva's objective is to rescue a soul. Where there is a son, more may be asked.

A drizzly morning. I am dwelling in Ashkenaz. Washington is less real to me than Worms. In the *Sefer Ha'Rokeaḥ*, or *The Book of the Perfumer*, by Eleazar ben Judah of Worms, the influential pietist and jurist of the late twelfth and early thirteenth centuries, the regulations for the "additional prayer" on the Sabbath (it follows the morning prayer) end with these words: "And the orphan rises and says kaddish, and everyone leaves the house of worship." (They can almost taste lunch.) And in his commentary on the prayerbook, Eleazar the Perfumer completes his discussion of the liturgy for Saturday night, for the aftermath of the Sabbath, by noting that "the orphan says kaddish," and then tells the story of Akiva and the condemned man, concluding that "a boy who says [the kaddish] saves his father from punishment." So in the late twelfth and early thirteenth centuries, the mourner's kaddish was said by a minor in shul on the Sabbath, at midday or at twilight.

In the early-thirteenth-century compendium of laws by Isaac ben Moses of Vienna called *Or Zarua*, or *Sown Light*—light is sown for the righteous, the psalmist sang—I find this: "It is our custom in the land of Canaan [Isaac's designation for Bohemia], and it is the custom of the communities of the Rhineland, that after the congregation says 'There Is No God Like Our God' [Ein Keloheinu, a popular hymn near the end of the service], the orphan rises and says the kaddish. In France I saw that they are not scrupulous about who says the kaddish, [whether] an orphan lad or a lad who has a mother and father; but our custom is the more reasonable one, owing to the story of Rabbi Akiva." His source for the story, and for the derivation of the kaddish from it? "This is what my teacher Rabbi Eleazar of Worms found."

In Isaac, a nice detail: "But in France I saw that they are not scrupulous about who says the kaddish, [whether] an orphan lad or a lad who has a mother and father, but our custom is the more reasonable one, owing to the story of Rabbi Akiva." In Ashkenaz, it seems, the additional Sabbath service was concluded by a child. But there were different reasons for this practice. In France, it was so that the child could learn. In Germany, it was so that the child could mourn. The kaddish began as mourning for minors.

At the teahouse this morning with a liturgical handbook for cantors and precentors by Nathan ben Judah, a rabbi of thirteenth-century France ("I have always acceded to the views of my friends, and they asked me to put the prayers in the proper order . . ."). It provides a confirmation of Isaac's remark about the French custom of kaddish for kids. When he comes to the sequence of the afternoon prayers on the Sabbath, Nathan lists what he calls the minor's kaddish. He explains that "all the many recitations of kaddish by minors were instituted to instruct them in the practice of the commandments." That is to say, the status of the mourner's kaddish was lowly. The purpose of the recitations by the boys was pedagogical. Those prayers were not mandatory. "For if they were mandatory prayers, how could minors acquit the congregation of its duty? For someone who is not required to perform a certain obligation cannot perform this obligation for someone else." (The latter is a Talmudic dictum.) And yet the boys were required to rise and mourn. Ah, Jewish boyhood . . .

One of the primary methods for the transmission of tradition is the premature termination of childhood.

For many centuries, children in Western art were represented as grown-ups in miniature. Childhood has a history, and it was not until the early modern centuries that boys and girls were depicted as boys and girls, and not as little men and little women. I will always have a fondness for the awkward figures of those shrunken adults in the old paintings. In their teleological understanding of childhood, in their impatience for adulthood, those pictures remind me of my own beginnings. For my parents and my teachers proceeded according to the principle that it is never too soon. (Young man, what were the precious stones in the breastplate of the high priest? In the proper order, please!) I think of my early years, and I admire those distorted images for their verisimilitude.

It appears that the custom of allowing boys to act like men was not uncontested. In the sixteenth century, Joseph Karo writes that "it is amazing that a minor is permitted to officiate before the congregation at the conclusion of the Sabbath and to lead the evening prayer. . . . Since a minor is not a bearer of responsibility, he cannot acquit the congregation [of its responsibility], for it has been taught that someone who is not required to perform a particular obligation cannot perform this obligation for someone else. And I have heard that Rabbi Joseph Abudarham challenged this custom . . . and that the great Rabbi Isaac de Leon agreed with him that the custom should be annulled." (Abudarham and De Leon were jurists in Spain in the fifteenth century.)

It is never too soon? No. It is never too late.

When I came to shul this morning, somebody was sitting in my chair. This threw me off. I have established my point of regard upon these proceedings, and I do not want it to be varied. This is entirely a matter of my own weakness; but I am relying upon the sustenance of repetition. I do not worry about monotony. I seek a year of regular movement. I must be a motor.

Who dares to suggest that the rabbis do not keep up with the times? In a Jewish newspaper, I find an advertisement by an entity called the Kaddish Foundation. "Is it difficult for you or a friend to go to shul to say kaddish? Call Toll-Free to see if we can help you." Among the services offered is the "saying of daily *personalized* kaddish." Also, and rather ominously, "future planning available." There follows a phone number, and a fax number, and this: "http://www.mnemotrix.com/kaddish." Kabbalah! (This stuff about "a friend": are they proposing gift certificates? Now there's a bar-mitzvah present.)

A controversy in Brooklyn. A cousin suggested to my mother that the fate of my father's soul is too precious to be left to his errant son, and that she ought to retain a man in shul to recite the kaddish for the duration of the year. "Hire somebody," my cousin said. I was furious. I do not deny that I live undevoutly, or that the fulfillment of this obligation will be arduous for me. But it is *my* obligation. Only I can fulfill it. Only I will fulfill it. My pious relative appears not to have grasped the character of this particular piety. It is for sons, not for strangers. I proposed to my mother that I refer my cousin to some of the sources of the custom. "But nothing too difficult," she wickedly replied. So I put forward a passage in a well-known omnibus of the practices of mourning that was composed by the head of the rabbinical court in Columbus, Ohio, and published in 1947. "The strongest and most vigorous bond that links the younger generation to its people and its Torah," the rabbi wrote, "is the kaddish. It lifts up not only the soul of the deceased, but also the soul of him who recites it. It brings him to the bosom of Israel, and in the days of his mourning he learns to recognize his people and his Father in heaven. Much to our chagrin, however, this, too, has been endangered. In our time, people treat the kaddish in a carefree manner. They hire strangers to say it for them, trouble-seekers who are ready with a kaddish for any calamity at all, reciting it for a dozen dead on the anniversary of their death and for half a dozen dead in the year after their death. And meanwhile the mourners rot lazily in their beds! They do not grasp that it was precisely for the mourner that the kaddish was established, so that he may learn a chapter in Judaism." So tell my cousin that I will not be rotting; and tell him also that there are many kinds of rot.

I don't much like the Ohioan's notion of the kaddish as a boon to Jewish identity. There is already too much kaddish Judaism in the land. But religion is not the work of guilty or sentimental children. I mean, real religion.

The summer is disappearing and I notice that I'm not noticing. This is what my Judaism used to be like. I would observe that I was not observing. —I will never be free of the framework. Never.

III

I am coming to the conclusion that the mourner's kaddish was developed by Franco-German Jewry sometime in the twelfth century, in the generations after Rashi. (The narrative of Akiva and the condemned man in *Maḥzor Vitry* must represent one of the later strata of the book.) For I have searched for the prayer in what has come to be known as the Rashi literature, the anthologies of his practices and his opinions, and I have not found it. In this literature, there is only a single conjunction of the kaddish with the dead, and it is "the kaddish of the resurrection of the dead" that is recited at funerals. It was this kaddish that I recited in my daze at my father's funeral, the kaddish about the renewal of the world and other chimeras. The text from Rashi's time differs from the text that they put before me only in that it adds an expression of longing for the messiah.

In the protocol of the eleventh-century funeral, as I read it in the Rashi literature, the funeral kaddish concludes the proceedings. And after the mourner has recited it, "every person present grabs a handful of earth or pebbles and smells it and proclaims [the verse from Psalms], 'Remember that we are dust!' And then they throw it over their shoulders behind them. They do this three times, to put a stop between themselves and the dead. And there are some who tear grass from the ground and proclaim [the verse from Psalms], 'and they of the city shall flourish like grass of the earth!' This is what they do in Germany." ("Germany" is my best guess for the weird word that appears in the text.) Words of resurrection, symbols of resurrection. I will call this the resurrection kaddish. Yet the resurrection kaddish was not an innovation of the sage of Troyes. It is mentioned already in the minor Talmudic tractate *Soferim*, or *Scribes*, which is actually a post-Talmudic text, much of it dating from the eighth century. In this early text, though, the resurrection kaddish is situated not at the graveyard but at the threshold of the house of worship, where the mourners and their families were to be found. It is nothing like the mourner's kaddish as we know it.

I tell an old friend that I am in shul every morning and every evening. "The angel of death is the best sexton," he observes.

There is another piece of the puzzle in the Rashi literature. On one occasion, the association of the kaddish with mourning seems to have been emphatically denied. "Once it happened that a person was buried during the middle days of a holiday, and those present were reluctant to utter the Justification of the Judgment and the kaddish. For the kaddish does not occur except for the sake of the verses in the Justification of the Judgment." The Justification of the Judgment, or *tsiduk ha'din,* is the heart of the funeral service. It is a short prayer, Talmudic in origin, consisting mainly of Biblical verses that affirm the truth and the rightness of God's disposition of man, notably this verse from Deuteronomy: "He is the Rock, his work is perfect: for all his ways are judgment: a God of truth and without iniquity, just and right is he." (In the version of the liturgy that I was given to recite at my father's funeral, this verse is followed by an extremely undistinguished poem based upon it, a wordy rhyming supplication.) And the kaddish in question here is not the resurrection kaddish, but the ordinary kaddish that was the traditional peroration to "Scripture and study." No verses, no kaddish. This passage shows that the kaddish had only an indirect relation to death and its business.

The reluctance of these mourners to speak the funeral verses on the holiday was owed to the fact that public mourning is suspended on Sabbaths and festivals, so that joy will be unqualified by sorrow. But Rashi, who was present at the funeral, did not agree with them. In fact, he astonished them. "Our rabbi stood up and recited the Justification of the Judgment and the kaddish, for it is neither a lament nor a dirge, but an expression of assent and an acceptance of the verdict of heaven, and so the holiday is not violated." A few lines later the text promotes Rashi's intervention into a general principle: "Our rabbi taught that it would be a fine thing if the Justification of the Judgment were to be recited on Sabbaths and holidays, for it is neither a lament nor a dirge, which are forbidden." It would be a fine thing if it were to be recited: Rashi's language suggests that he is proposing a revision of Jewish practice.

I conclude that the kaddish, in Rashi's day, played only its traditional role, in and out of the context of mourning. It was still a liturgical corollary to a pedagogical activity. Indeed, in Rashi's reading, the liturgy of mourning that the kaddish accompanied was itself not construed as an expression of mourning, even if it was expressed by mourners. "Neither a lament nor a dirge": this seems odd. In this unlachrymose interpretation of the prayer of justification, Rashi seems to have divorced language from reality. Of course these words are a lament and a dirge! Just see where they are said. In my own experience of this prayer, certainly, I could not separate the rhetoric of acceptance from the knowledge of what I accepted.

In all those centuries, the kaddish that was said with the Justification of the Judgment was not the mourner's kaddish; but it occurs to me this morning that the purpose of the mourner's kaddish is precisely the justification of the judgment. I have no way of knowing about the fate of my father's soul, but I know what the death of my father has done to my heart. I have been slapped by the nature of things. I have a choice between anger and acceptance; and I would like to be angry. But I would not like to be stupid. So I must begin the labors of acceptance. My kaddish is one of those labors; or so I will have it be. When I rise to recite the kaddish, I will justify the judgment: not the disposition of his soul, but the disposition of his life; not because I know it to be right, but because I know it to be true.

You took my father from me, magnified and sanctified may Your great Name be. . . .

Rashi's change of procedure must have seemed odd also to the compilers of the Rashi literature, since in one of the sources, *Sefer Ha'Pardes,* or *The Book of the Orchard,* Rashi's ruling that the Justification of the Judgment may be said on a day of joy is immediately followed by its very opposite. The text records Rashi's view that the prayer may be said on Sabbaths and holidays because there is nothing cheerless about it, and then continues: "Nonetheless it [the Justification of the Judgment] is not said on Sabbaths and festivals, because it causes anguish and diminishes the joy of the day, though the blessing 'Blessed is the truthful judge' is said, since it is short and quick. There are those who are especially stringent and do not recite the Justification of the Judgment after midday on the eve of the Sabbath, but he [Rashi] does not know the source for this stringency. The Jews are scholars and the sons of scholars, not prophets and the sons of prophets, and the customs that they have learned from their forefathers are like the Torah, which it is forbidden to augment or to diminish. The essence of the matter is that a blessing is commanded to be said in its time, even if its time is the Sabbath, and the Justification of the Judgment is commanded to be said during the seven days of mourning, whenever they occur. Thus it is not said [on Sabbaths and holidays] in those places where it is the custom not to say it on Sabbaths and holidays"—but in those places where it is the custom to say it, it is said.

This text is unclear to me. Rashi has been shown to contradict himself rather grossly. Either the Justification of the Judgment causes pain or it does not cause pain. Both views cannot be Rashi's view, yet they are both attributed to him. I don't get it. The passage looks to me like an interpolation that was intended to explain a contradiction between Rashi's opinion and the custom of Rashi's time. The teacher was saying one thing, the community was doing another thing. There was no way to reconcile the people's practice with the teacher's idea, except to invoke the prestige of custom. I like the drama of the teacher defying the community and the community defying the teacher. Philosophically speaking, though, the appeal to custom is a form of special pleading.

The plot thickens. A note by the modern editor of *The Book of the Orchard,* the book in which Rashi rules for and against the public acceptance of death on Sabbaths and holidays, indicates that he did indeed interpolate this perplexing passage into the text. The editor was Hayyim Judah Ehrenreich, a Hungarian scholar and the erstwhile rabbi of the town of Deva in Transylvania, and his edition was published in Budapest in 1924. He found Rashi's other opinion, he says, in two sources: *Maḥzor Vitry,* and *Shibbolei Ha'Leket,* or *Stalks from the Gleaning,* by Zedekiah the Physician, a digest of laws and customs that was compiled in Italy in the thirteenth century. "It was missing from here [*The Book of the Orchard*], and I restored it to its place," writes Ehrenreich. My confidence in him is shaken when I consult *Maḥzor Vitry* and discover that Rashi's other opinion is nowhere to be found. Indeed, Rashi's other opinion was not found in any of the works of the Rashi literature until Ehrenreich put it into one of them. "If the reader should find things that do not seem right," he writes at the end of his introduction, "I hope that he will give me the benefit of the doubt, for it was not in a palace of princes that I worked, nor at a table that was set with luxuries." I am not sure why the man's reduced circumstances should matter. His procedure looks presumptuous to me. But I will give Ehrenreich the benefit of the doubt, for it turns out that his circumstances became even more reduced. In 1942, he and his family were murdered by the Nazis.

I plow this ground some more and turn up a nugget of gold. It is further related that Rashi went from the funeral to the home of the bereaved. There he found the mourner sitting on a chair like the others, and receiving their words of comfort. Now, the ancient rabbis instructed that those who come to console the mourner must not speak until the mourner speaks. "But it was hard for our rabbi to sit silently. For what solace is there in silence?"

"What solace is there in silence?" Let this be the mourner's motto, the motto of this injured year whose end I cannot see. (And then I will seek a little silence.)

Rashi could not bear to see the man in pain, and so the enemy of silence broke the silence and offered a small sermon of consolation. "Thus he began a discourse and addressed the mourner with words of solace." Rashi's discourse was a reading of this verse from Psalms: "Also unto thee, O Lord, belongeth mercy, for thou renderest to every man according to his work." Here is what he said about it: "Is it really mercy that He renders to every man according to his work? Surely it is punishment that He renders to every man according to his work, is it not? No, [the meaning here is that] a man's just deserts will be paid to him from out of the exertions of his body and from out of his work, as when his children and those whom he has raised are taken from him, so as to redeem him; and this is the great mercy that He renders to each individual and to all His creatures." The first thing I notice about Rashi's homily is the new information: it was the burial of a child at which Rashi had assisted. He had come to comfort a grieving father. But what rough comfort, to explain to a man that his child had died for his sins! The rabbi was asking the mourner to follow him into the farthest reaches of theodicy. Is it really possible that this man was comforted? Is it really possible that he cared more for his own innocence than for the innocence of his child? Rashi's combination of mercy and justice is not anything that I can understand.

Needless to say, Rashi's sermon of consolation had a source in the tradition. He based it on a similar asperity given in the Talmud by the sage Ulla to Rabbi Samuel ben Judah, whose daughter had died. Ulla explained that God had spared the wicked peoples of Moab and Ammon because they would eventually produce the "two doves" Ruth and Naamah, and he asked the mourning man to reason *a fortiori*: "If God spared two great peoples for the sake of these two doves, would not your daughter, too, if she were worthy and deserving of goodly issue, have lived?" Then Rashi brutally spelled it out to the broken man before him: "If your daughter had deserved to have children and produce a posterity, she would still be standing in the world. So, you see, there is no point in being angry or particular about her." Take heart, sir. There was no reason for your daughter not to die!

Divine goodness is not human goodness. From the idea that God saves us, it does not follow that He considers us humanely.

So what if your dead are not essential for the salvation of the world? They are your dead.

The tale in the Talmud (as in the Rashi text) begins before Ulla's arrival at Rabbi Samuel's house. "Rabbi Samuel ben Judah's daughter died. The [Babylonian] rabbis said to Ulla: 'Let us go and console him.' Ulla replied: 'What have I to do with Babylonian consolations? They are blasphemous! For they ask what could have been done, as if they would have done something, as if something could have been done.' So he went alone to the house of the mourner . . ." What Ulla (and Rashi) preached to the man who buried his child was quietism. He wished to disarm the mourner spiritually, to preempt an attitude of revolt. "So, you see, there is no point in being angry or particular about her." These are the words of a rabbi who recognizes the threat that tragedy poses to religion. And still I cannot accept these words. A person who has buried a child has a right to raise a fist to the heavens. Anger is not apostasy. Quite the contrary. It is another way of acknowledging God's responsibility for the world.

—Nothing could have been done. There is no use beating your head against the wall.
—But I want to know why nothing could have been done. There is a use in beating my brain against the wall.

What death really says is: *think.*

The story of Rashi's day concludes: "After the holiday he [Rashi] saw him [the father of the dead girl] busy repairing his kegs while he was still in mourning, and so our rabbi refused to enter the man's house to console him, explaining that work is forbidden [to mourners] even if it is performed [for them] by others in a different house. Why should I comfort him if he is a sinner?" Mercy and justice, indeed.

When mercy seasons justice, it is the proportions that matter.

I was checking a reference in the Talmud and I found this: "Why do a man's sons or daughters die when they are young? So that he may weep and mourn over a worthy person." For the rabbinical tradition, the death of children is an excruciating problem—a knife in the heart of the doctrine of reward and punishment. Insofar as death is a punishment, children cannot die of their own account, since they are not accountable. So it is the life of the parents that must somehow explain the death of the children. This passage is such an explanation, and it is appalling. Innocence is sacrificed for goodness! (The Hebrew word for "worthy" here is *kosher,* as if to say "a kosher person." I have never liked this usage. It has an inhuman air. Objects are kosher or not kosher; not people.)

But an objection is hastily offered. "'So that he may weep': but this is a pledge taken from him!" I'm not sure I understand this. Rashi explains: "He has not yet sinned, and his guarantee is taken?!" That is, is it really possible that God would accept the death of a man's children as a kind of promissory instrument, as a way of ensuring that in the future he will do the right thing and mourn over a kosher person? No, if the children died, it must be because the father has already sinned. And so the text revises itself. "Why do a man's sons or daughters die when they are young? Because he did not weep and mourn over a kosher person, for he who weeps and mourns over a kosher person is forgiven all his sins, because of the respect that he renders." I'm not sure that this is really an improvement. In the first version, the children die for the father's sinlessness. In the second version, the children die for his sin. The whole calculus strikes me as, well, unkosher. (There is no explanation of the death of children that is acceptable.)

Goodness is the goal of moral life; but innocence is the condition of those who are disqualified from moral life, such as children. Goodness marks the end of innocence.

There is something remorseless about religion's obsession with remorse.

When I left shul this evening, I walked over to the park. The heavy summer air was filled with fireflies, hundreds of them, burning and vanishing, burning and vanishing. The park was a field of floating, passing intensities. I sat for a while and watched the little eruptions of brilliance. Wherever I looked, there was the beginning and the ending of light. No light lasted long, but there was not a moment of total darkness. This, I thought, is another ideal of illumination.

The glow passes. But the afterglow need not pass. The problem is that its survival is in our hands. Unlike the glow, the afterglow is not an experience; and we prefer an experience.

I have read of people whose lives are transfigured in an instant. I do not believe that such a transfiguration can happen to me. For what changed those people was not only the instant, but also their subsequent fidelity to the instant. This is the paradox of revelation. It disrupts the order of things and then depends upon it.

Without tradition, a revelation is merely an epiphany. It can inspire nothing more than art.

The claim of tradition is that it is a light that does not dim as it travels from its source. This is outrageous.

Mystics, too, live in the past. But they remember what happened to themselves. And personal memory can dispense with historical memory. The mystic is the believer without belatedness.

It is not possible to have an unephemeral experience of the unephemeral. It is possible to have an unephemeral memory of the unephemeral.

We do not live before the eternal. We live after it. Or the lucky ones do. For the others, there is the apparatus of eschatology, which is designed to assure them that their glimpse still awaits them. This, at least, is the spiritual advantage of the idea of revelation: it teaches that we are seeking what is already there.

Pascal's wager is so uninteresting. Like all bets, it lives in the future. It is just another presentiment, just another theology of postponement, in which the present is disowned.

I have begun to notice that my prayers are refreshing my life with language. Three times a day, Hebrew music.

The Rashi literature is rather a mess, with texts and fragments of texts appearing and disappearing in a variety of compilations, but I don't mind. It quickens the chase. In an edition of Rashi's responsa, I am not surprised to find the tale of Rashi at the funeral and after the funeral, related more or less as the other sources relate it. In the responsa, though, the story begins earlier, and the new information is rather delightful. It appears that Rashi's vexations of that day began before the funeral. "It happened once that someone died during a holiday and our rabbi was wearing a new garment, and he was concerned about his garment and did not wish to rend it for the dead." There are predicaments whose pettiness is proof of their humanity. (I must confess that as I began to foresee my father's funeral, I also gave some thought to the question of which of my own precious frocks I would submit to the rabbi's razor.)

The tale continues: "He wanted to remove it prior to the moment of [the person's] death," and rend not this outer garment but the shirt that he was wearing beneath it, but when "he looked at the collar of his shirt, he discovered that it had already been rent for somebody's death." Yet that was not the problem. The problem was that "he checked the repair that had been done, and saw that it was loose, whereas [the Talmud states that] one does not rend a garment that has been pinned together or basted, but a garment [that has been sewn] with an Alexandrian stitch, since it is good and strong." The rabbis follow you into your closet! Still, they refuse to allow death to decimate a man's wardrobe—and so, after an appropriate amount of time has passed, clothes that have been torn in mourning may be mended and rent again. (Except clothes torn in mourning for a parent, for a teacher, for a Torah scroll that has been burned, for the Temple, for evil tidings, for the sight of Jerusalem in its desolation, for a king, or for a chief of the Sanhedrin. These may be basted, but not mended.)

Yet there is a complication. There are satisfactory and unsatisfactory methods of mending. An unsatisfactorily repaired garment may not be rent. "What is a mended garment? A garment that is mended completely, for every need." According to Rabbi Hisda, a Talmudic sage of the third century, a repair with an Alexandrian stitch will suffice, because (as Rashi explains) the repaired garment "is virtually whole." But what is an Alexandrian stitch? In a brief but wide-ranging discussion of ancient and medieval sewing, Aaron of Lunel, in Provence in the fourteenth century, reports that Abraham ben David of Posquières, in Provence in the twelfth century, "commented that an Alexandrian stitch is like our own method of sewing, in which the surface is even on the outside but [the stitch obtrudes] on the inside." Sounds familiar. But this is no time for me to lose myself in the history of tailoring. Suffice it to say that Rashi's shirt could not save Rashi's jacket. The great man sacrificed his finery. "He kept his new garment on and he rent it."

The rending of the mourner: this act of violence dignifies the external truth and the internal truth of what has happened.

The ancient rabbis declared that "he who approaches the dead in a torn garment robs the dead; and it is worse to rob the dead than to rob the living, for one may pacify the living by returning what one has taken from them, but one cannot pacify the dead by returning what one has taken from them." But one of the many novelties that the Jews of America have introduced into the tradition is the practice of pinning a small piece of black crepe to their lapels, so as not to rend their garments. All those hours of shopping must not have been in vain! Ruin a suit? Not in this enlightened age.

The drollery aside, there is a philosophical point to this sartorial turmoil. It is that the outer refers to the inner. The text about Rashi also cites the Talmudic injunction that the cut must be made on the outermost garment, "even if he is wearing ten garments," so that it will mark the mourner visibly. (For this reason, too, Rashi's jacket was doomed.) A respect for the invisible requires a respect for the visible.

Upon the death of a father or a mother, however, "even if he is wearing a hundred garments, he rends them all," until he "exposes his heart." The deeper the visible, the deeper the invisible.

The rending for parents must be public. And so a woman need not expose her heart. "A woman rends only the outermost garment. Rabbi Judah said: A woman should rend the undergarment, turn it back to front, and then rend her other garments." Also, a woman may begin to mend her garment after the first seven days of mourning; and in Rabbi Judah's view, immediately. A woman's honor is not abrogated by despair.

Why did Rashi have to rend? What was his relation to the dead girl?

All this tearing and cutting. Life rips you up, so look ripped up. Flaunt your disintegration. But it must have gone too far, since it is noted in the Jerusalem Talmud that "as the mockers multiplied, they stopped rending." The mockers, too, were not wrong.

Make sorrow into a norm and you make it into a manner.

"A man in tatters does not rend." So say the rabbis, very decently. But there is another opinion. "Rabbi Judah says: He rends." In Rabbi Judah's view, a man down on his luck is not a man down on his responsibility. And there is decency also in this opinion. Here, in a few words by these ancient Jews, is the great modern debate about the meaning of poverty.

In the Maimonidean code: "He who has lost many dead at once rends once for them all. If his father and his mother were among them, he rends once for them all and once for his father and his mother." Law must anticipate disaster. Of course, there are many ways to lose a lot of loved ones at the same time; but when I read these words, only one way comes to mind.

I'm falling behind on my work, and I know the reason. It is that I am almost without patience for reflecting on anything except my mourner's texts. I thought I'd confine my study in honor of my father to the tranquil hour at the teahouse, but it isn't working out that way. When I leave the teahouse, the day's study is over, but the day's thinking has just begun.

Isaiah of Trani was a Talmudist in Italy in the thirteenth century, whose readings and rulings were highly valued by subsequent generations. Having studied in Germany and traveled in the Mediterranean, he was a link between the north and the south. In one of Isaiah's responsa, cited by his Italian contemporary Zedakiah the Physician, the story of Rashi at the funeral is adduced. (It is adduced twice, in fact. This is the source upon which poor Ehrenreich relied.) Isaiah believes that it is not a story told by Rashi's student about his teacher, but a story told by Rashi about his own teacher. This is not textually plausible; Isaiah must have been the victim of a copyist. His contribution to the discussion is, rather, his demurral from Rashi's interpretation of the liturgy of resignation. He thinks that Rashi was wrong. He does not agree that the Justification of the Judgment (and the kaddish that attends it) should be recited on Sabbaths and festivals, because he does not agree that there is nothing funereal about it. "It is not correct to say it [on Sabbaths and festivals]," he writes. "If it contained nothing except an assent and an acceptance of the verdict of heaven [as Rashi claims], it would certainly be permitted. But certain things are included in its recitation that cause anguish, so much anguish that there is no lament in the world greater than [this prayer]. It is full of pronouncements that sadden the human heart. The essence of the Justification of the Judgment is the blessing 'Blessed is the truthful judge,' as it is taught [in the Talmud], but all the verses and the images with which we fill the Justification of the Judgment are there only to break a man's heart, and to put him in mind of the day of death, and to subdue his nature. And therefore it is not proper that they be uttered on a day on which the sages forbade the uttering of lamentations." Isaiah is right. The acceptance of judgment is not an exclamation of happiness. How, in the aftermath of a death, bless its author without anguish?

Isaiah supports his position with two earlier medieval authorities who forbade the recitation of the grim prayer on days of joy, a certain Rabbi Meshullam whom I cannot identify, and Natronai Gaon, the influential and prolific head of the academy in Sura, on the southern Euphrates, in the ninth century. And Isaiah makes his own inclination clear: "We are aware of those who forbid the recitation [of these prayers], and their views are right." And among these authorities is . . . Rashi! Here is the unexpected passage that so impressed Rashi's modern editor: "And [Rashi], too, who permitted [the Justification of the Judgment on Sabbaths and holidays] in the name of his teacher, concluded his discussion [by saying] that the custom that they learned from their forefathers is not to be augmented or diminished, and therefore there is to be no casting doubt on the matter. The universal custom that is not to be said is not to be uprooted." In other words: Rashi, who said that it is permitted, said that it is forbidden. Now there is a master!

This is what must have happened: Rashi's "first" reading, his true reading, his radical reading, in which he permitted the acceptance of death on a day of joy, collided with a norm, and so the practical implication of his idea had to be resisted. He had to be turned against himself. At least Isaiah's text is alive to the contradiction. But is it credible? Is his report of Rashi's about-face any more trustworthy than his report that all this did not happen to Rashi at all?

Here was a clash between theory and practice, between the authority of a mind and the authority of a community. In the Jewish tradition, a contradiction between a theory and a practice is not like a contradiction between a theory and a theory. You can disprove a theory, but you cannot disprove a practice. A custom does not require proof. It requires understanding. And a custodial feeling: think any thoughts you want, but do not overthrow the customs that have made it all the way to you. This sounds like a mindless behaviorism, but it is not. After all, many customs have come down to you, denoting many concepts. You cannot practice all the customs and defend all the concepts. You must take your pick. Indeed, thinking critically about the customs is a way of thinking critically about the concepts. The rabbis admire the collective spontaneity that is expressed by the development of customs (they even say that "a custom overrides a law"), but they do not admire it uncritically. There are "erroneous customs" and "bad customs" for which no basis in text or reason may be found, and such customs may be nullified. The veneration of custom is not a surrender of the mind to anthropology. A ritual life is not an unexamined life.

Ritual is the conversion of essences into acts.

The evanescence of human life is the reason for human ceremony. Since things pass, things must be repeated. Only the eternal can dispense with repetition.

The ideal of epiphany, the thirst for what Americans call "peak experiences": all this is a little cowardly, an attempt to escape the consequences of living in time. Of course, the epiphany may arrive; but after the epiphany, there will arrive the moment after the epiphany. The peak experience will peak. And there will occur, in the most quotidian way, an experience of eschatological disappointment.

Epiphany is one way of attacking our temporality. Ritual is another. Epiphany is more vulnerable to time's counterattack than ritual. (But who would not exchange ritual for epiphany? Or so I used to think.)

Customs have reasons, but their reasons are not their only reason. They exist also because they have existed. Time is an essential ingredient of a custom. Every custom shows the smudge of time. That is why customs seem so opaque. Yet they owe their beauty in part to their opacity. They are like one of those Indian statues whose features have been blurred by the touch of hands over centuries. What they lose in definition, they gain in devotion.

Meir ben Baruch of Rothenburg was the supreme authority in matters of law for the Jews of Germany in the thirteenth century. He was a very prolific writer, but the only one of his extended legal works to have survived—and it was not published until 1789—was a compilation of the laws of mourning. I have found a remarkable comment in Meir's discussion of a woman's rending. Meir cites a different version of the Talmudic text that I read a week ago: "In the matter of rending, the same rule applies to men and women. Rabbi Simeon ben Eleazar disputes this, and says that a woman should rend the inner garment, turn it over, and then rend the outer garment." (In the text that I read, Rabbi Simeon's view was attributed to Rabbi Judah.) Meir notes that "the law is based on the view of the rabbis [and not on the view of Simeon ben Eleazar] that a woman does not rend any differently than a man." But how can this be? A woman cannot bare her bosom in public. "Since one is required to rend in public, before the people, this is certainly a debasement of the woman, and in the view of everyone [who has discussed this question] we must protect her against impure thoughts."

This is Meir's answer: the woman rends, and there is no need to worry about her debasement, because "the evil impulse does not rule in the hour of sorrow." As proof, Meir cites another Talmudic text that permits women to take part in a funeral procession: "Where it is the custom for women to follow the bier, they follow it; [where it is the custom] to walk ahead of it, they walk ahead of it." Meir explains that "we are not troubled that men will look at them."

"The evil impulse does not rule in a time of sorrow." What a statement! Is it true? It is too soon for me to tell. I'll find out, I'm sure. Still, I am refreshed by Meir's statement, because it goes against the grain of what I have been taught to believe about the relation of mortality to sexuality. I remember vividly the opening sentence of that book by Bataille: "Eroticism, it may be said, is assenting to life up to the point of death." One climaxes, one dies; and the most genuine sex is violent sex, because it reveals the danger, the longing for destruction, that lives at the heart of this heat. As if it were death that arouses! But this evening I do not see the power of death to arouse. Maybe the evil impulse within me is not ruling in the hour of my sorrow; but I insist that there is a fundamental difference between sex and death. Death is not a climax. It is nothing as coherent as a climax. It happens when it happens, and it will not happen again. (And it cannot be remembered with pleasure.) The interpretation of desire as a longing for death is nothing but the glorification of a particular form of desire, but desire comes in many forms. And so tonight I will entertain this proposition, against Bataille: eroticism is assenting to life in perfect indifference to death.

Still, Meir's formulation does not entirely please me. Why impute erotic experience to the evil impulse? That is precisely Bataille's tenebrous point. Meir's formulation plays right into the hands of the religion of transgression.

An acquaintance with your limits is not an acquaintance with your end. You know your end only once. For this reason, your limits are more stimulating than your end. They mark your span. They taunt your soul every day of your life.

At the end of Meir's discussion, then, are we left with Jewish women in mourning baring their breasts before their friends and their neighbors? Not exactly. Meir concludes with a practical animadversion. Finally he does not trust sorrow to quiet desire. He notes that the Talmudic injunctions about the rending of the mourners also include this: "And the *efikarsin* is not an obstacle to rending." That is, the obligation of rending may be fulfilled without rending the *efikarsin*. What is the *efikarsin*? In the Talmudic usage, the Greek word refers to an undershirt, but the medieval authorities understood it differently. Rashi writes that it is a garment "on his head, so that it is not an obstacle and there is no need to rend it." Meir describes it as "a scarf in which one is wrapped, so that it falls onto one's face and covers the rent in one's garment." Undershirt or scarf, it will certainly get in the way of lewdness. As Meir concludes, "thus she can cover her rending with her *efikarsin.*" Thus does the law preserve both the equality and the modesty of the Jewish woman in mourning. Problem solved.

Despair is no excuse for impropriety. (I wish I believed that.)

Meir observes, incidentally, that there were those who ruled according to the opinion of Simeon ben Eleazar, that a woman is not required to rend in the manner of a man. The reason, Meir suggests, is the principle enunciated by Samuel, the early-third-century sage: "In matters of mourning, the law takes the lenient view." And Meir then cites the principle that is enunciated in the Talmud immediately after Samuel's principle, that "mourning is one thing, rending is another." Since rending occurs at the moment of the sharpest pain, a stringency about rending is understandable, and it is not to be generalized into a stringency about mourning. This is why the law, finally, must reject Simeon ben Eleazar's opinion. But never mind all this. It is Samuel's principle that I must remember. In matters of mourning, the law takes the lenient view.

But what if the mourner does not take the lenient view?

At the teahouse I turn the page to find that the rabbis were under no illusions about the stubbornness of desire. Meir records the Talmudic provision for the ghastly case of a baby that died before it was a month old. Such a baby "may be carried [to burial] in one's bosom, that is to say, it does not require a bier. And it may be buried by a woman and two men—that is to say, a quorum of ten men is not necessary." But here is the qualification: the baby may be buried by a woman and two men, but not by a man and two women, "since the sorrow may not be sufficiently great and they may be brought to sin, just as we have been instructed [elsewhere in the Talmud] that a man should not be alone with two women." The rabbis are taking no chances. Still, there is a dissenting opinion. Abba Saul, a sage of the second century who once gave his occupation as a gravedigger and told a fantastic tale about chasing a deer into the thighbone of a giant corpse, ruled that the burial of a baby may be carried out even by a man and two women. For Abba Saul, the evil impulse does not rule in a time of sorrow. The rest of the rabbis are not so sure. They wish to patrol even the grieving heart.

Look at the night sky. You are not seeing only the light of the stars. You are also seeing the journey of the light of the stars toward you. Admire space and you admire time. In this way, immensity conducts you to history.

Yet that history is nothing like our history. A few years ago I read a book about the mass-extinction debates among geologists. I learned that the history of life on earth, as it is told by rocks, is marked by a series of global catastrophes. "However," one of the contributors to the volume concluded, "study of the tempo of the extinction episodes reveals that they took place over extended periods of time ranging from about 1 to 10 million years or more. The deliberate pace of the extinctions was, in fact, the antithesis of catastrophic. They took place over evolutionary, not contemporary, time." This helped me to understand the difference between natural history and human history. It was humans who devised mass-extinctions in "contemporary" time, who accelerated the pace of disaster so that it outstripped the pace of evolution, who invented catastrophes that could be experienced as catastrophes. We are the most accomplished catastrophists in the history of life.

When I consider the expanse of my tradition, I forget sometimes that it is not a thing of nature. All this, a human plenitude!

There are moments when the tradition seems so much greater than me that it cannot possibly need me. (But in shul this evening they needed me. I was the tenth man.)

In Rashi's "prayerbook," another compilation of his ritual and liturgical practices, I make a jarring discovery. In a discussion of the short reading from the Torah at morning services on Mondays and Thursdays, the text describes the concluding prayers that follow the return of the Torah to the ark, and adds: "And the boy rises to say kaddish." Is this the mourner's kaddish? It is! For the text immediately specifies that in the recitation of the kaddish the boy omits one of the sentences of the full kaddish and proceeds directly to "May a great peace from heaven. . . ." The mourner's kaddish, in Rashi's time? I am puzzled. So far my researches have pointed to a later origin. And I can't find any other mention of the boy and his kaddish in the Rashi literature, though I will keep looking. Meanwhile I will conclude that this passage refers not to Rashi (I note that it is not attributed directly to him, for it does not add that "we heard this from our master"), but to the school of Rashi, that is to say, to the customs of the twelfth century that were established by his heirs.

Many years ago, when I studied the philosophy of religion, I was marooned by the ontological proof for the existence of God. I appreciated the desire for certainty, and I recognized that this proof was designed to confer upon the existence of God the highest certainty—the certainty of a necessary truth. But that is where the proof became useless for me. The perfection of necessary truth seemed to raise it above the conditions of knowledge. A necessary truth is true whether or not it is known. It owes its sublimity to its indifference to the epistemological vicissitudes. But religion taught that God had to be known, not only in the sense that our knowledge of God was a human need, but also in the sense that our knowledge of God was a divine need. This was senseless, for me. I saw no way in which "that than which nothing greater can be conceived" is not diminished by an entanglement with that than which something greater can be conceived. When I expressed my objection to friends and rabbis, I was met with assurances about paradox and miracle and absurdity and unfathomable goodness and leaps of faith. But you are changing the rules in the middle of the game, I said. You are lowering the standards for your God. The certainty about which we were speaking was the greatest certainty, a thing of the mind. (And it is the soul's privilege to be tutored by the mind: Anselm's proof was offered in a prayer.) So make your leaps, but for me they are a disappointment. Have your absurdity, but do not speak to me about necessity.

How sincere is the profession of your own insignificance if you believe that you are being heeded by that than which nothing greater can be conceived? ("Come now, insignificant man," Anselm begins. . . .)

Abjection, I mean genuine abjection, is not a disorder, or any sort of soul-storm; and there is nothing morbid or glamorous about it. Abjection is just an inference from experience, a conclusion calmly drawn from the commonplace observation that there is a difference in scale between yourself and the universe.

I study the old texts because I hope to be infected by their dimensions, to attain the size of what I read.

Lowliness is not a feeling. Lowliness is a method.

Jews who open their books do so for one of two reasons: to make themselves more like the tradition or to make the tradition more like themselves.

In the Talmud, an anonymous passage offers another reason for the suspension of mourning on holidays. "A mourner does not comport himself as a mourner on a holiday, for it is written: 'And thou shalt rejoice in thy feast.'" This sounds like Rashi's notion, the priority of joy to grief. But this text explains the prohibition in terms of a different priority. "If his mourning began before the holiday, then a commandment that applies to the community comes and supersedes a commandment that applies to the individual; and if his mourning began on the holiday, a commandment that applies to the individual cannot come and supersede a commandment that applies to the community." The disruption of the part must not become the disruption of the whole. I must not expect the community to defer to the immediacy of my experience. Quite the reverse. The community must expect me to transform the immediate into the mediate, and thereby to avert the detonations of pain and pleasure that would damage the common order. And in those circumstances in which such mastery of the self is difficult, in which the immediacy of my experience is too strong to be subdued, I must take my place in the margins, where I am called a mourner.

The limits of suffering only make it worse. I suffer, but the world does not suffer. If the world suffered when I suffer, then my suffering would be eased, at least inasmuch as I would not experience it as a form of chosenness. Job's question would lose its force.

When my parents' universe ended, the rest of the universe did not end. This was history's insult to the Jews of Europe. They were denied the compliment of apocalypse. The catastrophe was not complete. The towns are still there. Only the Jews are gone.

So should a suffering man dream of the destruction of the world? No, no, no. It is because suffering is partial that it is not final. (When it is not final.)

Rage against the indifference of the world, and then exploit it. Since the world does not care about what happens to you, you have a chance.

In *The Book of the Perfumer*: "There was a change of custom in Worms in the time of our teacher: someone died on the New Moon, and the Justification of the Judgment and the kaddish were recited. But they did what they did out of respect for a great scholar." An exception was made because an extraordinary individual had died. Otherwise the mourner's prayers would not have been said on the New Moon, which is a day of joy. (A minor day of joy, but still a day of joy.) The third-person mention of "our teacher" refers, I expect, to the Perfumer himself; this must have been an interpolation by a student. And the report continues: "In Mainz, when somebody died on the third day of Sivan [when lamentations are not recited, because the festival of Shavuot, or Weeks, the anniversary of the day on which the Torah was given at Sinai, is a few days away], the Justification of the Judgment was recited." So there was no single custom in Ashkenaz! In Mainz, they acted in the spirit of Rashi's "first" opinion, and marred the holiday with sorrowful words. In Worms, they acted in the spirit of Rashi's "second" opinion, and the holiday was unmarred. But hold on. A few lines later, among "the customs of Rabbi Kalonymos," it is reported by the Perfumer that "in Worms, on the New Moon, the Justification of the Judgment is recited on the way to the cemetery, and the kaddish is recited at the cemetery. But in Mainz it is recited only at the funeral of a scholar." This is the opposite of what was just stated! Oh, this is exasperating.

I have a hunch that the more lugubrious custom was the custom of Worms. My hunch is based on a remark by the Perfumer elsewhere in his book, in his discussion of public fasts. There he notes that "in Worms, on the New Moon of the month of Sivan, they fast to commemorate the persecution." A fast day on the New Moon? This is bizarre. The persecution must have been severe. And it was: on Sivan 1, 4856, or May 24, 1096, the mob that traveled with the Crusaders made its second and final assault upon the Jewish community of Worms and destroyed it. The events of that day are described in a Hebrew chronicle: "On the first day of the month of Sivan, the very day that Israel arrived at Mount Sinai to receive the Torah, they terrorized the Jews who were left at the court of the bishop, and they wantonly abused them, as they had the first group [a week earlier in the first attack], and they put them to the sword. But the Jews were fortified by the example of their brethren and elected to be slain so that the Name would be sanctified before all, and they offered their necks so that their heads could be cut off for the glory of their Maker. There were also those who killed themselves, to fulfill the verse 'the mother was dashed to pieces upon her children.' Fathers fell upon sons and were slaughtered together, and they slaughtered each other, every man his wife and his children; and grooms slaughtered brides, and merciful mothers slaughtered their only children. All of them wholeheartedly accepted the judgment of heaven. As they delivered their souls to their Creator they cried, 'Hear, O Israel, the Lord is our God, the Lord is One!' The enemies stripped them and dragged them and cast them away, sparing only a small number of them, whom they forcibly baptized in their stinking waters. . . ." Is it any wonder that the Jews of Worms were not reluctant to recite the Justification of the Judgment on the New Moon? They were accustomed to regarding affliction by the light of the new moon.

Did the Jews of Worms justify the judgment and recite the kaddish at funerals on days of joy because natural death put them in mind of unnatural death? If so, then they were truly my forefathers.

Be careful. Read closely. From the report of the Perfumer, it seems that the Jews of Worms uttered these prayers not at the funeral, but on the way to the funeral. This was their liturgy for the funeral procession. Maybe it was their concession to the holiday, their way of distinguishing the liturgy at a funeral on a day of joy from the liturgy at a funeral on an ordinary day. Anyway, they said it.

I have on my shelf, from the good old days when I was poor from the purchase of arcane books, a book that might have served the Perfumer as his source. It is the book that was known as *Ma'aseh Ha'Makhiri*, or *The Work of the Makhirites*, a document of the very early history of the community in Ashkenaz. It, or the bulk of it, was not published until 1910 (and under a different title); and when it was published, its editor believed (as I did when I bought it) that he had published another part of the Rashi literature; but scholars have shown that this book preceded the Rashi literature, and served as a source for it. The Makhirites were four brothers, Nathan, Menahem, Nehemiah, and Yakar, who were the sons of Makhir, who was the son of Menahem, who was the son of Makhir, who was the brother of Gershom, the extraordinary Rabbi Gershom, the Light of the Exile, the founding rabbi, if there was one, of the culture of Ashkenaz. Though the brothers lived and worked in a variety of places, they were the scions of Mainz. Their book was produced in the last years of the eleventh century, in the darkness of the First Crusade and its aftermath. (In 1084, a dozen years before the atrocities, the Jews of Mainz were blamed for a fire that destroyed a large part of the town, including Jewish dwellings, and many of them left for Speyer.) The work is essentially a compilation of customs. Perhaps they were recorded to secure them against the turbulence of the time. In the Makhirites' book, there is a brief discussion of aspects of mourning, and it includes this: "Things were done in Worms that were never done in Mainz in the days of our teachers: on the New Moon, they read the verses of the Justification of the Judgment on the way to the cemetery, and they said the kaddish of the resurrection of the dead. In Mainz, however, the Justification of the Judgment and the kaddish are not said on the New Moon, except for a great scholar." These are the sentences that appear almost verbatim in the Perfumer a hundred years later.

There follows a responsum on the same subject that was sent by Rabbi Meshullam, or Meshullam ben Moses, the teacher of Nehemiah the Makhirite, to Nehemiah, who lived in Worms for a while. (So this is the Meshullam cited by Isaiah of Trani!) It appears that Nehemiah had been puzzled by the funeral practices that he saw in Worms, and asked his rabbi in Mainz for a clarification. Meshullam assured his student of the validity of the custom in Mainz: these prayers were not to be recited on the New Moon or on Purim or on Hanukah or during the festival week, "except when they mourn a man who is exemplary in his generation and everyone recognizes the authority of his rulings, so that his yes is yes and his no is no." And Meshullam adds: "And since they don't say the Justification, why would they say the kaddish? For the kaddish is not said except after a discourse on Torah and the reading of verses."

In the years before the Crusades, there was no mourner's kaddish. In the years after the Crusades, the mourner's kaddish makes its appearance. This cannot have been a coincidence. The Crusades provoked the first major attempt to exterminate an entire Jewry in Europe. It failed, but it left many, many mourners in its wake.

Today I saw a blind man crying. His eyes were good for that.

In his compendium of the laws of mourning, Meir of Rothenburg writes: "I have heard from Rabbi Isaac of Vienna that our teacher Rabbi Gershom, the Light of the Exile, mourned his son because he converted [to Christianity]." The Light of the Exile, the dark of the exile. Meir was writing three hundred years after Gershom, and he was anxious about the legal implications of the master's heartbreak. "He [Isaac of Vienna] also told me that we are not to derive a practice from what he [Gershom] did, for he did this only out of anguish, as his son did not have the good fortune to repent." According to Jewish law, an apostate may not be mourned, and Gershom's son chose apostasy. Yet the father's love exceeded the father's horror, and he mourned. (Isaac's account in his own work is factually and theologically more complicated.) What worries Meir is that the act of the great rabbi might become a precedent, as the acts of great rabbis often do. So never mind the pathos, he warns. The law is the law.

A few lines down, in the Makhirites: "In Speyer, a man's little daughter died on the day before the eve of Passover. They went to the cemetery and Rabbi Eliakim the Levite was with them, and he permitted them to say the Justification of the Judgment and also the kaddish. I have no idea what his reason was. This is simply what I saw."

Elsewhere in the Makhirites, in the discussion of Hanukah: "They did not justify and did not mourn on Hanukah. And they maintained that already Rabbi Leontin had mourned for a scholar [on Hanukah]." Rabbi Leontin! In the history of Ashkenazic Jewry, you cannot recede any further into the mists of time. Here is a figure of romance, for those who find romance in such things. Leontin preceded even Gershom, and was his teacher. He flourished in Mainz in the tenth century. (The community was founded sometime after 917, when the family known as the Kalonymides migrated north from Lucca.) This controversy about mourning, then, may be found in the very origins of Ashkenaz. But why was Leontin's opinion so important that the Makhirites took pains to preserve it? In truth, he was merely ratifying the opinion of Rabbi Papa, the Babylonian sage of the fourth century, who remarked in the Talmud that "when faced with [the death of] a scholar, there is no festival, to say nothing of Hanukah and Purim." (Rabbi Papa hastened to add that the joy of the day yields to the grief of the day only "in the presence" of the scholar, that is, at his funeral. Far away from the funeral, the festive spirit rules.) What was so memorable about Leontin's insistence that the death of a scholar trumps the joy of the day? The Israeli scholar Avraham Grossman has an explanation. He writes that "there is no doubt that [Leontin's ruling] had an impact beyond the legal question with which it dealt. It joined other rulings and other tales that together created, in the consciousness of the community of Ashkenaz in those days, a heightened admiration for Torah and for its bearers: for the scholars."

Well, well. The kaddish turns out to have played a role in the development of what is perhaps the most defining characteristic of Judaism in exile: the charisma of learning. When the Jews of Mainz made a distinction between scholars and other members of the community, and when they translated this communal distinction into a distinction between protocols of mourning, they were defining not a social elite but a spiritual essence. They were proclaiming the supremacy of mind.

I was driving across Memorial Bridge in the direction of Arlington Cemetery. It was a rainy afternoon, and clouds were hanging low on the green hills. The mists obscured everything. I couldn't see a single grave. And suddenly I imagined the disappearance of all the graves here, of all the graves everywhere. I saw only the mansion on the hill, and smooth slopes that concealed no dead. Then the clouds started to lift. In the distance I saw a funeral. Death's funeral! I will climb to the spot and I will say the kaddish. Not the kaddish for the dead. The kaddish for death.

When I returned from shul, I found Avraham Grossman's new study of the early sages of France in my mail, a timely gift from a friend in Jerusalem. I sat down to read the long chapter on Rashi. In a manuscript in Jerusalem, Grossman discovered a more detailed account of what happened to Rashi at that funeral: "It happened once that someone died and was buried on the holiday. There were many distinguished rabbis assembled at the funeral, and they were confused and perplexed about what to do: should the Justification of the Judgment be said, or not? Rashi stood up and said it alone, and not a single sage challenged him." This is high drama. In this account, Rashi does not suggest a course of action. He acts. He agitates for sorrow. Grossman thinks that this incident took place not long after Rashi's return to Troyes after a decade of study in Mainz and Worms, sometime around 1070, when he was thirty years old. I guess he brought the custom of Worms with him. In Mainz, on one of the days of the holiday, they would have said the Justification and the kaddish only at the funeral of a scholar; but in Worms they would have said it also at the funeral of a girl. Rashi was attending the funeral of a girl. He rose to make a public acceptance of a child's death. To disembarrass God.

From a riveting footnote in Grossman, I learn that later it all came home. Rashi is known to have been the father of three daughters, but he may have had a fourth daughter who died in his lifetime. From published sources and from manuscript sources, Grossman quotes this report: "Rabbi Solomon [Rashi] rent his garment upon the death of his daughter during the week of the festival, even though the laws of mourning are suspended during that time." So the great man's lachrymosity stood him in good stead.

And what about Rashi's sermon of consolation to the man whose daughter had died? "If your daughter had deserved to be fruitful and build something great in the world, she would still be standing in the world," the rabbi had advised the mourner. "So, you see, there is no point in being angry or particular about her." Did he think these thoughts when his own child was lowered into the ground?

Back and forth from my desk to my shelves, ten, twenty, thirty times a day. The sources swirl around me. I am drugged by books. The sweet savor rises from the pages. A delirium of study.

The prospect of clarity makes me delirious, so the joke is on me.

More, more. When Rashi claimed that the Justification of the Judgment and the kaddish were "neither a lament nor a dirge," he was drawing upon a distinction in the Talmud. "During the week of the holiday, women may wail, but they may not clap [their hands in an exclamation of grief]; Rabbi Ishmael says that the ones near the bier may clap. On the New Moon, on Hanukah, and on Purim, they may wail and they may clap, but neither on these days nor on the festivals may they [recite a] dirge. Once the dead has been buried, they neither wail nor clap. What is a wail? When all are in unison. A dirge? When one leads and the rest respond." These were specifications for the funeral. Obviously the wail and the dirge were specific liturgical forms. The dirge was the more elaborate form, so it was frowned upon for major and minor festivals, whose business was the organization of joy.

In Spain, in the thirteenth century, Nahmanides sketches the post-Talmudic career of this Talmudic passage, in a legal opinion of the early geonim. The geonim were the masters of the academies of Babylonia, in the region that we call Iraq, in the early medieval centuries. They were the founders of post-Talmudic Judaism, or Judaism after "the end of instruction" in the fifth century, when the Talmud was redacted. One of these sages, reports Nahmanides, was asked whether a mourner may recite the Justification of the Judgment on the New Moon. The gaon's reply begins by quoting the Talmudic passage about the grieving women, and observing that its stipulations are "law that is not disputed by any of the sages." Thus the Justification of the Judgment may be recited in the style of a wail, in unison, and not in the style of a dirge, as call and response. (Nahmanides does not identify the author of this responsum, but those are the same words that I read a few days ago in Isaiah of Trani, who was quoting Natronai Gaon.)

Then Nahmanides cites a responsum by Hai Gaon, the greatest of the geonim, who died in 1038. This text sheds light on the early history of the custom. Hai was asked how the Justification of the Judgment was done "on the other days that are not like the week of the festival. Is it said as a wail or as a dirge, or do you have another custom in your academy?" And Hai responds: "In the tradition of Babylonia, nothing is said that may be described as the Justification of the Judgment. That is the custom of another place, which the earlier geonim recorded when they were asked about it; but here we have no such custom." (So the Justification of the Judgment must have originated as a Palestinian custom, as one of the "customs of the land of Israel.") But Nahmanides does not want to leave the impression that his predecessor made no provision for a day of joy that has been ruined by a visit from the angel of death. Immediately he cites another opinion of Hai's (I have found it also in the recent edition of Guenzberg 566, the manuscript in Moscow, which identifies it as a responsum to the rabbis of Fez): "It is our custom to recite the kaddish for the dead on the second day of a festival and to demand the reason as on an ordinary day." (To demand the reason? I have no idea what this means. Tomorrow's task.)

Hai is referring to the funeral kaddish, the resurrection kaddish. Thus the protocol of the funeral in Hai's time and place seems to have called for the kaddish, but not for the Justification of the Judgment. This is very striking, for this reason: the prayer of justification, remember, consists largely of Scriptural verses, and it was the reading of these verses that called for the kaddish in the early Ashkenazic sources. ("For the kaddish does not occur except for the sake of the verses.") In Hai's custom, however, the kaddish stands alone. It is dissociated from its traditional function as a peroration for the encounter with Torah, and associated explicitly with mourning. This is not the mourner's kaddish. But it is certainly a kaddish more focused on the funeral.

When I say post-Talmudic Judaism, I mean only chronologically. Spiritually and historically, the expression is senseless. In the absence of the Talmud, there is no Judaism. There is only Jewishness.

Moses of Coucy was a French scholar in the early decades of the thirteenth century. His *Sefer Mitsvot Gadol,* or *The Great Book of Commandments,* was the first comprehensive codification of the law that was produced by Franco-German Jewry. Moses was an itinerant preacher who traveled to Spain and elsewhere "when there was a call from heaven to journey through all the lands to castigate the communities of Israel," and he conducted large revival meetings at which "thousands and tens of thousands" of his brethren were exhorted to repentance. In his epitome of the laws of mourning, he remarks upon the controversy about mourning and joy in Ashkenaz. "It was said about Rabbi Solomon [Rashi] that he rent his garment for a certain dead person on one of the intermediate days of the festival." This is all that Moses knows of the incident. And then he changes his frame of reference, and moves from the titan of eleventh-century Troyes to the titan of twelfth-century Cairo, and concludes with almost verbatim quotations from Maimonides: "The dead are not to be mourned publicly on Hanukah and Purim, or on the New Moons, but otherwise all the customs of mourning are to be practiced. . . . This refers to the ordinary dead; but scholars are to be mourned on a holiday, and certainly on Hanukah and Purim and New Moons." (Moses of Coucy's code of law was the first important foothold in the north for Maimonides' code of law.)

All these customs. All this legitimacy. A long schooling in pluralism.

"To demand the reason": What did Hai Gaon mean? I have sought and I have found. And what I have found is an institution of beauty. This, from a compilation of geonic material: "This was the practice in the house of the mourner and in the house of worship when mourners were present. The man who led the prayers declared: 'Gentlemen, demand the reason!' That is to say, why have those people over there wrapped their heads and covered their faces? And the entire congregation responds: 'Blessed is the judge of truth!' That is to say, we know that they have done this because someone has died." Among the ways in which mourners must manifest their sorrow, according to the Talmud, is the wrapping of their heads. (This custom is no longer practiced. I wonder when it became obsolete.) And the text continues: "And when people arrive who were not present earlier, the man who leads the prayer declares to them, too: 'Gentlemen, demand the reason!' And they, too, respond: 'Blessed is the judge of truth!' And they begin to console the mourners." This must have startled the newcomers. Suddenly they were summoned to a meeting with mortality. In a world in which we die, nobody may be allowed to live superficially.

The text also gives a practical explanation for the summoning: "Since not every mourner has the ability to say what he feels, the early sages instituted the demanding of the reason to break the silence, so that the consoling may begin."

"The demanding of the reason" was a colloquy between the leader of the congregation and the congregation. The mourners were not addressed. Their solitariness was respected. But had they been asked, had the reason for their peculiar appearance been demanded of them, I know what the mourners would have replied. We look this way, they would have said, because we are demanding the reason. . . .

Gentlemen, demand the reason. Ladies, demand the reason. Children, demand the reason. Strangers, demand the reason. Clouds and leaves and chimneys and sparrows and all that appears before my eyes through the glass behind which I sit as I demand the reason, demand the reason!

Isaac ibn Ghiyyat was an important jurist and teacher in Spain in the eleventh century. Nahmanides preserves this opinion of his: "It has been our custom, since the days of our earliest sages, not to recite the Justification of the Judgment over the dead on the New Moon and on the intermediary days of a festival and on Hanukah and on Purim." Isaac gives a number of reasons. On all those occasions, for example, the liturgy includes mandatory exclamations of joy, such as: "This is the day which the Lord hath made, we will rejoice and be glad in it!" A confrontation with death does not comport easily with such an exclamation, "and so the Justification of the Judgment is canceled." And no sooner has Nahmanides cited Isaac's opinion than he cites the contrary opinion of Isaac's great French contemporary. "And we have ascertained about Rabbi Solomon the Exegete [Rashi] that, as his pupils reported in his name, he said the Justification of the Judgment and the kaddish on the middle days of the festival, since it is not a lament and therefore not a violation of the holiday, but it is an assent and an acceptance of the verdict of heaven." Nahmanides is persuaded. He proceeds to his own ruling, which rejects the Spanish tradition to which he was heir and accepts the French tradition that Rashi created: "And so it is right that during the week of the festival the Justification of the Judgment and the kaddish are said in the normal manner, and so, too, on the second day of the festival [a day of joy greater than the middle days but lesser than the first day]. But on the first day of the festival, when the dead are not attended to, nothing is said. And this is the law." Rashi cast a very long shadow. Clearly the Spanish practice was deeply rooted; and it is a measure of Rashi's authority that a report by his students of his behavior at a funeral could overthrow it. (I wonder when the mourner's kaddish penetrated Spanish Jewry along with the other innovations from the north.)

I get to shul early this evening. There is only one thing to do when you get to shul early. You open a book. Since I have been thinking about the encounter between Ashkenazic culture and Sephardic culture in Nahmanides' time, it occurs to me to have a glance at the glosses of Asher ben Jehiel on the Talmudic texts that are pertinent to my pedantry of the last few days. Asher was a great fertilizing figure. He fled from Worms to Toledo, where he became the head of the academy in 1305. The leader of German Jewry became the leader of Spanish Jewry. And sure enough, in his glosses he touches on all the disputes that I have been following. First, the intramural dispute within Ashkenaz: "On the question of whether to say the Justification of the Judgment and the kaddish on the New Moon and Hanukah and Purim, the sages of Ashkenaz were divided. The scholars of Worms said it on the way [to the cemetery], and the scholars of Mainz did not say it, except for a great scholar." (He cites also Meshullam's responsum to Nehemiah the Makhirite.) Second, the extramural dispute between Spain and Ashkenaz: he gives Isaac ibn Ghiyyat's opinion and he gives Rashi's opinion. And that is where Asher leaves it, with a picture of ferment. Asher's son Jacob, who composed the *Arba'ah Turim*, or the *Four Columns*, the most important code of law after Maimonides, and the code whose classification of the law became canonical, also leaves the matter there. He merely reproduces his father's gloss. Asher does add this, though, referring to geonic times: "In an exchange of customs between the community in Babylonia and the community in the land of Israel, it is written that in the views of both, the Justification of the Judgment is not recited during a festival." When Rashi stood up at that funeral, then, he challenged a consensus. He destroyed an old tradition and created a new tradition.

A new tradition: what enchanting words! But sober up. If we created a new tradition, upon whom might we rely for its transmission?

What is new cannot survive except as what is old. This is the undoing of revolutionaries. Sooner or later you will cherish something so much that you will seek to preserve it. If you fail, and it is lost, you will lament its loss, and you will blame yourself, and you will probably be right.

The opposite of traditionalism is sensationalism, or living merely now.

From the account of the laws and the customs of mourning by Eliezer ben Joel Ha'Levi, an important jurist in Germany in the late twelfth and early thirteenth centuries, I get a sense of Rashi's little revolution. "Rabbi Solomon [Rashi] ruled that even in the middle days of the festival it is permitted to recite the Justification of the Judgment" at a funeral; and Eliezer adds that "in the registry of differences between the customs of the land of Israel and the customs of Babylonia, it is written that in the opinion of both communities it is forbidden to recite the Justification of the Judgment in the middle days of the festival." Thus Rashi rebelled against a universal custom. Eliezer also records that the scope of Rashi's innovation expanded to include funerals at other festive times of the year: in the entirety of the month of Nisan, the time of Passover; and in the month of Sivan, in the week before and the week after Shavuot, or Weeks (he cites the example of his great-grandfather Eliezer ben Nathan, one of the important authorities in Mainz in the eleventh century, who memorialized the horrors of the First Crusade in prose and poetry); and in the month of Tishrei, from the tenth day of the month, which is Yom Kippur, until the beginning of the month of Ḥeshvan. At these times, "the Justification of the Judgment is recited along the way [to the cemetery], and the kaddish is recited after the interment." So there were occasions when the kaddish was all that was said at the grave.

"The registry of differences between the customs of the land of Israel and the customs of Babylonia" is a geonic document. In Eliezer's report, it shows that Rashi acted against a time-honored practice. But I have a reprint of an edition of this "registry" of the early medieval customs of the Jews of the Middle East that was published in 1937, and it flies in the face of Eliezer's report. Indeed, it flies in the face of historical knowledge. Here is what it lackadaisically records: "The communities in the land of Israel mourn the dead on holidays. The communities in Babylonia do not mourn. And there are some versions that record the opposite." Of course!

What is tradition without confusion? But I don't mind such confusion. It is an existential excess, a measure of vitality.

A tradition that is completely transparent is a tradition that is completely over.

I take it back. I do mind such confusion. (I was taught to mind it.) And so I have acquired a more recent study of "the customs of the land of Israel," and I have brought it with me on a gray morning to the teahouse. I learn that the correct name for the old "registry" is "The Differences Between the People of the East and the Children of the Land of Israel," or, less tendentiously, between the Babylonian community and the Palestinian community. It is a compilation of fifty-five legal and ritual contradictions; it was probably compiled sometime between the seventh century and the tenth century; and the identity of its compiler is not known. I learn also that my guess a month ago was right: the Justification of the Judgment is a Palestinian custom. As the editor of the volume writes, "the custom has its origin in the land of Israel, like other customs pertaining to mourning which were not familiar to the geonim in Babylonia . . . and even though the geonim did not know it and did not confer their prestige upon it, this custom was accepted throughout the dispersions of Israel."

Here is how the conflict between the Jewries appears in the book: "The Justification of the Judgment and the kaddish are recited over the dead as always, but there are some who dispute this and hold that the Justification of the Judgment is not to be said on a holiday. The people of the east do not speak before the dead on a holiday, and the children of the land of Israel speak before the dead." It seems that the conflict concerns not the Justification of the judgment on days of joy, but eulogies on days of joy. In Babylonia, there was no language for the funeral, there was only moaning and wailing—another geonic fragment responds to a report of the Palestinian custom of justification by remarking that "we don't know in what it consists, whether it is a form of mourning, such as 'oh, woe, woe!,' or whether it is tears"—and so the custom was not to speak before the dead on a holiday, because such speech would have introduced a new level of lugubrious expression; but in the land of Israel, where the funeral was characterized by the discourse of justification, a eulogy seemed less innovative, less controversial.

There, that's better. A little more darkness dispelled. But as I leaf through these old Palestinian practices of mourning, I come upon a practice that astounds me. "It is the custom that the son says kaddish together with the reader who is leading the prayers, even when he is grieving [and not yet mourning]." Can this be? A kaddish required of the son, in the aftermath of the death of the parent, to be recited publicly in shul? And required even in the immediate aftermath of his parent's death, in the short, miserable period between the death and the burial, when respect for one's dead, and for one's own wretchedness, exempts one from all the requirements of the law? I don't know what to make of this. It is certainly the earliest version of the mourner's kaddish upon which I have stumbled. I note that the editor does not cite early sources to establish its provenance, he cites only late sources that purport to describe early customs. I'm baffled.

In the morning I told a terrible lie, and when I rose to say kaddish in the evening I was ashamed. This is more than I bargained for.

IV

In Spain, in the eleventh century, Isaac ibn Ghiyyat offered a more intriguing reason for the restraint of sorrow on days of joy. The Rock whose work is perfect is not invoked on the New Moon and the intermediary days of festivals and Hanukah and Purim, Isaac says, because "we do not favor the Justification of the Judgment for the death of a common man over the Justification of the Judgment for the death of Moses, and it [the Justification of the Judgment for the death of Moses] is suspended when the New Moon falls on the Sabbath." If the joy of the holiday is great enough to abolish the mourning for Moses, then surely it is great enough to abolish the mourning for his lessers, or all the Jews who ever lived.

The justification of the death of Moses? Isaac is referring to the Justification of the Judgment that is a regular part of the weekly liturgy. On the afternoon of every Sabbath, these verses from Psalms are said: "Thy justice is justice everlasting and thy law is the truth. Thy justice, O God, is also very high, who hast done great things: O God, who is like unto thee! Thy justice is like the great mountains; thy judgments are a great deep, O Lord thou preservest man and beast." And the tradition provides two particulars about the day of Moses' death: it was the seventh day of the month of Adar, and it was the Sabbath.

And so, as *Maḥzor Vitry* states, "'Thy justice is justice' is said in the afternoon prayer on the Sabbath for the purpose of justifying the judgment, so as to honor Moses, who died at that very hour on the Sabbath." The French rabbis agree with the Spanish rabbi that the memorial utterance is not said on a Sabbath that coincides with a holiday, so as "to honor the joy of the day, which is added to the contentment of the Sabbath. This Sabbath is accorded greater respect than other

Sabbaths, and so on this Sabbath the grief of the soul is not mentioned. For joy was explicitly attributed to the holiday [by Scripture], which is not the case with the Sabbath." And the text in *Maḥzor Vitry* concludes: "This was sent by Rabbi Solomon of Lyon, and it became the custom." (Who was Solomon of Lyon? I have never heard of such a figure. The text indicates that this is a later interpolation into the book.)

The memory of death is compatible with the happiness of the Sabbath and incompatible with the happiness of the holiday. Why? The answer is that Tolstoy was wrong. All happiness is not alike. The rabbinical distinction between the happiness of the Sabbath and the happiness of the holiday seems to be a distinction between happiness in action and happiness in contemplation. On the holiday, there is rejoicing, an active celebration (and so more work is permitted on the holiday than on the Sabbath). The happiness of the Sabbath, by contrast, is a meditation on reality made in a condition of rest, a satisfaction with the created world so profound as to be philosophical, and so the consciousness of mortality may be included in this wisdom. (Though mourning doesn't feel Sabbath-like to me.)

There is joy and there is contentment, there is grieving and there is mourning: the rabbis were alive to the many shades of the heart, to the lights and the darks. They made regulations out of them.

But it was not long before the myth that Moses died on the Sabbath fell out of favor. Isaac of Vienna reports in the name of Jacob ben Meir Tam, known as Our Master Tam, the fierce Talmudist of the twelfth century and Rashi's grandson, that the view that this Sabbath prayer is a commemoration of the death of Moses was a geonic view, formulated in the ninth century by the prolific Sar Shalom Gaon. (Provenance, provenance, provenance! But provenance is a thing of consequence in a culture of customs; and ideas are customs, too.) And then Isaac writes: "But I was told by my teacher Rabbi Judah the Pious that this is impossible." Judah the Pious, who died in 1217, was the founder of the Jewish pietism of the Rhineland, a severe and somewhat anti-intellectual turn toward asceticism that had a lasting impact on the development of Judaism. (One historian compared Judah the Pious to Francis of Assisi.) Isaac reports that Judah analyzed a few ancient texts—including a very early work of Jewish "historiography," a chronicle of the history of the world that was composed in the second century—to show, based on the date given by the rabbis for the fall of Jericho, that the day on which Moses died must have been a Friday, so "in this way we learn that Moses died on the eve of the Sabbath and not on the Sabbath." And to his teacher's refutation of the legend, Isaac adds a refutation of his own. He cites the ancient story that on the day of his death Moses wrote thirteen copies of the Torah, one copy for each of the twelve tribes of Israel and one copy "in case anyone attempted to distort a single thing." (Having spent the day "busy with Torah, which in its entirety is life," Moses pleaded futilely with God to spare him.) And from this "it follows that Moses did not die on the Sabbath. For if he did, how could he have written?" Writing is forbidden on the Sabbath!

Still, a problem remains. If Moses did not die on the afternoon of the Sabbath, why is the Justification of the Judgment recited on the afternoon of the Sabbath? The great pietist has an explanation. "Rabbi Judah the Pious told me," Isaac continues, "that we recite 'Thy justice is justice' in the afternoon prayer on the Sabbath because its verses speak of Torah, angels, and hell. This is what I heard him say. He did not explain his reasoning, because I did not ask him to explain." Torah, angels, and hell? Isaac is rightly perplexed. His master's words are very obscure. Isaac launches into his own interpretation of his teacher's pronouncement, to show that each of the three verses of the prayer treats one of the themes that Judah elliptically enumerated. The verse that describes God's judgments as "a great deep," he explains, "speaks of Gehenna, and we praise the Lord of the Universe that those who keep the Sabbath are not judged in Gehenna on the Sabbath, even though their other deeds are rotten."

And this returns me to the eschatological detail that served as the basis for the establishment of the mourner's kaddish at the conclusion of the Sabbath. It is that the Sabbath is a respite from purgatory, and therefore the prayers at the end of the Sabbath must be charitably prolonged. It is one of the functions of prayer at the conclusion of the Sabbath to be a prayer for the dead. And indeed, Isaac's discussion of the Justification of the Judgment is immediately followed by a recollection of his other illustrious teacher, Eleazar ben Judah of Worms, or the Perfumer, who said that the man who leads the prayer "must prolong it greatly, because the souls return to Gehenna immediately afterwards, and for as long as he extends [the prayer] they do not return; and also because it is appropriate to provide an escort for the departing Sabbath as one would provide an escort for a departing king; and also because we want the Sabbath to leave late, and so we stretch the prayer out. And I humbly do so myself. I have heard, moreover, that Rabbi Eliezer the son of our great Rabbi Meshullam was a cantor, and it was his custom to prolong the prayer with all his might. Moreover, it is written in the prayerbook of Rabbi Amram that the prayer at the close of the Sabbath must be drawn out." Rabbi Amram was a Babylonian authority in the ninth century, whose prayerbook is the earliest complete Jewish liturgy.

(Eliezer ben Meshullam was, I think, a figure in thirteenth-century Speyer.)

Is there any torture greater than sitting in shul helplessly as the cantor prolongs the prayer with all his might? Oh, the things one does for one's dead!

From the fertile imagination of the Perfumer, in his commentary on the liturgy: "The judgment [of the dead] is justified during the afternoon service on the Sabbath because on the Sabbath the dead are relieved of the judgment of hell. On that afternoon the souls are made to stand by a gleaming fountain of water that flows at the entrance to the garden, and they rinse themselves in the water to cool their bodies from the fire. And so we recite, in awe, the three verses of the Justification against the three things that they committed, their iniquity and their transgression and their sin, and we attest that He convicted rightly, He judged rightly, He acted rightly." The Perfumer notes also another custom that was derived from this fantasy: "Since the souls at that hour are standing by that fountain, the geonim and the [post-Talmudic] rabbis established the custom that we do not drink water between the afternoon service and the evening service on the Sabbath, because we would be stealing it from the dead. As for [the report in the Talmud that] the school of Rav Ashi was not punctilious about drinking water at the conclusion of the Sabbath, we may conclude that the prohibition against it was established later, or that they drank water after the evening prayer, when the Sabbath was over and the souls had returned to the netherworld."

Stealing the water of the dead? This is serious. Zedekiah the Physician provides a fuller treatment of this offense. "According to a rabbinical legend, when an individual drinks water at twilight [on the afternoon of the Sabbath], it is as if he were stealing the water from his dead. And I have found this in the responsa of the geonim: 'We have heard it said in the name of the early sages that for the duration of twilight, permission is granted to the souls of the dead to drink water. And when one drinks water at the hour when the souls of the dead are drinking water, the souls of the dead who are one's kin are not permitted to drink. For this reason, the sages said that it is as if one were stealing from one's own relatives. But this does not apply to all one's relatives, only to the relatives for whom one must mourn: one's father, one's mother, one's brother, one's sister, one's son, one's daughter, one's spouse. Also, it applies only for the twelve months of mourning. Why? Because the sages stated that for twelve months, the body endures and the soul rises and falls, but after twelve months the body is no more and the soul rises and no longer falls.'"

They give you their lives and you take their water!

One family, one well.

Water, water. I have been combing the authorities of Ashkenaz, and I have found that the expropriation of the water of the dead was a very contentious matter. I begin with Isaac of Vienna, who introduces the twelfth-century debate: "When the afternoon [of the Sabbath] comes, Maimonides wrote, it is the practice of the righteous to recite the afternoon prayer and then to eat a meal. But there have been places where this was the custom and Our Master Tam [Jacob Tam, Rashi's grandson] scolded them and said that it was forbidden, citing the tale in the Jerusalem Talmud about a man who drank water between the afternoon prayer and the evening prayer, and the angel of death came and slew him, because he drank when the dead were drinking and so was a robber of the dead." Isaac is vexed by the contradiction between the authorities. He seeks practical advice. "I asked my teacher Rabbi Simhah ben Samuel for a practical ruling, and he told me not to eat on the Sabbath between the afternoon prayer and the evening prayer, because Our Master Tam forbade it." But he does not accept his rabbi's advice. "I did not understand this. All that Our Master Tam prohibited was water. But food, and wine, and honey, and beverages? Surely they may be permitted!" Isaac considers some Talmudic passages about the difference between the afternoon prayer of the individual and the afternoon prayer of the congregation, and finally concludes: "It seems to me that he whose custom it is to eat incurs no loss."

Water, water. Zedekiah the Physician adds that the lenient places to which Isaac referred were in France, and that Jacob Tam's interlocutor was Meshullam ben Nathan of Melun. This does not surprise me, since the imperious Jacob waged a well-known war against Meshullam's rulings, which he excoriated as subversions of tradition. (His epistles to Meshullam are classics of rabbinical invective.) Zedekiah also reports that "there was once an incident in Lorraine [where it was customary to refrain from eating on Sabbath afternoons], and there was danger [because the fast of Yom Kippur was to begin at sundown], and it was only with difficulty that permission was granted to eat on the eve of Yom Kippur just before the service began. (The rabbis prescribed the confession of sins [on Yom Kippur] to be recited before the food and the drink, because they worried about lightheadedness.)" Danger? It is an obligation to precede the fast with a meal that marks a pause between ordinary life and the mortifications that are about to begin—and the prohibition against eating and drinking on the afternoon of the Sabbath endangered this ritual of differentiation. But finally it did not annul it. Zedekiah reports that the fast of the Ninth of Av was similarly threatened, but in that case, too, the reluctance to eat and drink on the afternoon of the Sabbath was "with difficulty" overcome.

Water, water. Mordecai ben Hillel, in Germany in the thirteenth century, whose massive anthology of rulings and commentaries on the Talmud preserved the opinions of many medieval rabbis, provides more details about the dispute between Jacob and Meshullam: "When Rabbi Meshullam established the practice in his town of Melun that there is a meal after the afternoon prayer on the Sabbath, Our Master Tam wrote to him inquiring after his reason. Rabbi Meshullam responded that in his text of the ancient rabbinical legend he had a different formulation. His text said that 'those who eat and drink on the afternoon of the *eve* of the Sabbath [steal from the dead],' and the reason is that [by Friday afternoon] the dead are exhausted from the judgment they have endured all week. And for this reason he was strict about not drinking on the afternoon of the eve of the Sabbath." Mordecai notes that it was Jacob Tam's father—Meir ben Samuel, or Meir the Venerable, who was married to Rashi's daughter and was one of the earliest Tosafists, or glossators on the Talmud—who reported the incident in Lorraine, which must have occurred in the eleventh century. And Mordecai notes that it was Jehiel ben Joseph of Paris—the rabbi who valiantly defended the Talmud at a public "trial" in Paris in 1240 and watched it consigned to the flames a few years later—who "heard that there is no need to be careful about drinking for more than the twelve months of mourning, because the sages stated that the body endures and the soul rises and falls for twelve months, but not for longer." And finally Mordecai adds (I can't tell whether this comment is Mordecai's or Jehiel's): "And it is the custom of the whole world to be careful [about drinking the water of the dead] even after the twelve months have passed."

Even after the twelve months have passed—in other words, always. Every afternoon of every Sabbath all the dead are guzzling the water at the gates of Eden.

I must say that Meshullam's reply to Jacob seems fair to me. Meshullam was not subverting tradition, he was honoring tradition; except that his tradition differed from Jacob's tradition. According to the text in Jacob's possession, the dead drink to prepare for the flames. According to the text in Meshullam's possession, the dead drink to recover from the flames. It is true that Meshullam seems to be the only rabbi with the Friday version of the text. Still, nobody denied the flames.

No water on Sabbath afternoons? It seems odd, impractical, silly. Isn't there enough water in this world and in the next world for the dead and the living? (Now they've got me "reasoning" this way!) And I am not the only one with this anxiety. I do not refer only to the lenient rabbis of eleventh-century Lorraine. In his glosses on Maimonides' code of law, Meir Ha'Cohen of Rothenburg, the scholar of the late thirteenth and early fourteenth centuries who sought to supplement the Maimonidean masterwork with the traditions of the French and German communities, suggests a qualification of the custom: "Even according to those who forbid [drinking water], the prohibition applies only to drinking water from a river. But drinking water in one's household is permitted." This is sensible. It is also consistent with the myth that occasioned the controversy. A river in this world may flow to or from a fountain in the next world; but not the water in the bucket by the hearth, in the goblet on the table. The dead have no claim on it. The living, too, have needs.

Why not steal from the dead? They steal from the living.

Meir Ha'Cohen also reports that "Rabbi Simhah heard Our Master Tam instruct that the third meal [of the Sabbath] is to be eaten following the afternoon prayer." But Meir is puzzled by this report. "In all the other places it is stated that Our Master Tam forbade the drinking of water between the afternoon prayer and the evening prayer." Then Meir records the view of the influential Eliezer ben Joel Ha'Levi, who was active in Bonn in the late twelfth and early thirteenth centuries: "Though his father acted stringently in this matter, Rabbi Eliezer ben Joel ruled leniently [and permitted the drinking of water on the afternoon of the Sabbath], saying that it is an insubstantial matter." And so it is! Reason is as refreshing as water.

And here is a delicious animadversion on the custom by Joel Sirkes, the legal commentator in Poland in the early decades of the seventeenth century: "Our Master Tam established that there will be no meal [on Sabbath afternoons] because it was their custom in those days to drink water with a meal [and the drinking of water was forbidden]. In our country, however, we drink wine, so there is no reason to worry about the danger." Water more dangerous than wine! And the wine drinker is tough on the water drinkers. Remarking upon the old debate between Jacob Tam and Meshullam of Melun, Sirkes advises that "since there is a danger, one should [accept both their views and] refrain from both." That is, water should not be imbibed on Friday afternoon nor on Saturday afternoon. Surely a man with wine in his glass should be kinder to a man with water in his glass.

Drink the water of the dead and stay sober.

An old man approaches me as I am about to begin the prayers. It is the anniversary of his father's death, so may he lead the worship? According to custom, he has priority; and so I yield. As I return to my corner in the back of the room, I think: one day I will be in his place. I used to find it hard to imagine my father dying. Now I find it hard to imagine my father dying long ago. But one day his death will be old, and I will stand at the head of the congregation, and I will be old. —Stepping into another person's place, or: tradition.

Magnified and sanctified . . . Magnified and sanctified . . . Magnified and sanctified . . .

The burning of the Talmud in Paris: there is a report of this atrocity in Zedekiah the Physician. He interrupts his discussion of the laws of fasts with an historical aside. "We have written this to commemorate what happened in our own time, as a consequence of our many sins, when our holy Torah was burned in the year 5004 [1244]. On the Friday of the week in which Numbers 19–21 was the portion of the Torah read on the Sabbath, some twenty-four wagonloads of volumes of Talmud and law and lore were burned in France, as we have heard. We have also heard from rabbis who were there that they made a dream-inquiry to ascertain whether this had been decreed by the Creator. They were answered: 'This is the ordinance of the Torah.' . . . From that day onward, some individuals have imposed fasts upon themselves on the Friday of that week."

"This is the ordinance of the Torah": the answer that the rabbis of France received was cruelly ironic. It was the Torah that ordained the devastation of the Torah! (In 1242, actually.) And so they must not murmur. They must accept the judgment. The response to their dream-inquiry was also a scholarly reference, a quotation of the Aramaic translation of the opening words of the Torah reading of that cursed week. And the dream-inquiry? The dream-inquiry was an esoteric avenue of last resort for rabbis in perplexity.

A dream-inquiry into the law? A scandalous idea! For the system of Jewish law is a proudly immanent system. It protects its integrity even against the intervention of God. Questions are answered by means of ratiocination, not by means of divination. "Henceforth a prophet has no authority to innovate," the ancient rabbis declared. Most famously, a dispute in the first century between Rabbi Eliezer and Rabbi Joshua about the ritual status of an oven was settled in Rabbi Joshua's favor, even though Rabbi Eliezer's position was supported by miracles. For a miracle is not a proof. "'If the law is as I say it is,' [Rabbi Eliezer said], 'let it be proved by heaven!' At that moment a Divine Voice declared: 'Why are you arguing with Rabbi Eliezer? The law is always as he says it is.' Whereupon Rabbi Joshua rose and said: 'It is not in heaven!' And Rabbi Jeremiah explained: 'Since the Torah has already been given at Mount Sinai, we pay no heed to a Divine Voice.'" (The ending of the story is extraordinary: "God smiled and said: 'My sons have defeated Me, my sons have defeated Me.'" But Rabbi Eliezer did not smile. He was excommunicated for his presumption, and he died a bitter man.)

"It is not in heaven": Rabbi Joshua was triumphantly quoting a verse from Deuteronomy. And yet there were scholars for whom it was in heaven, jurists who did pay heed to a Divine Voice. There is a small, almost subterranean tradition of rabbis looking to heaven for relief from the mind's contradictions. The dream-inquiry mentioned by Zedekiah the Physician in the thirteenth century was one of the techniques of juridical divination. And Zedekiah cites also another dream-inquiry. The inquirer was Jacob of Marvège, and the subject of his appeal to heaven was nothing other than the dispute between Jacob Tam and Meshullam of Melun about food and drink on the afternoon of the Sabbath, when the dead are returning to hell.

Jacob of Marvège was the author of *She'elot U'Teshuvot Min Ha'Shamayim*, or *Questions and Answers from the Heavens*. It is one of the most exotic works in the legal literature of the Jews, a collection of eighty-nine succinct questions and succinct answers. (Jacob gives the date of one of his inquiries as 1203.) After he has been vouchsafed the answer to a question about the ritual impurity of a man who has suffered (or enjoyed) an issue of semen, Jacob writes: "When I saw all this, I asked whether all this had really come to me from God or not. It was a Tuesday night, the nineteenth day of the month of Kislev. This was my question: 'O exalted King, great and mighty and awesome God, who keeps His covenant and His kindness with those who love Him, please keep Your covenant and Your kindness with us and order the holy angels in Your service who are tasked with the responses to dream-inquiries to answer truthfully and correctly the question that I will ask before Your throne, so that every matter is properly established, and is clearly and lucidly derived from Scripture or law. I hereby inquire about the instructions that came to me in the answer to the question that I asked regarding the ritual immersion of the man who had an issue of semen: did these words emanate from the Holy Spirit? And are they useful? And may I reveal them to my father-in-law Rabbi Joseph, and instruct him to promulgate them among the scholars of the land? Or did they come to me from a strange spirit, and are they useless, and would it be best if I concealed them and kept them to myself?" The response to the rabbi's question about the authenticity of his illumination was in the affirmative. "They replied," Jacob writes, "[that] it was truly the word of God, and also that these matters were ordained long ago by the Ancient of Days, and also that today was another day of tidings. I waited until dawn, and an hour later they responded . . ." There follows the celestial ruling about the polluted man, which is given in the form of a verse from Deuteronomy. (The method of seeking a Divine Voice in a serendipitous Biblical verse is as old as the Talmud.) And the ruling about the polluted man is followed by a verse from Genesis: "I am with thee and will keep thee in all places wither thou goest." That is what God promised Jacob's forefather Jacob.

The thirty-ninth of Jacob's "responsa from the heavens" is this: "I also asked about those who eat [and drink] between the afternoon prayer and the evening prayer [on the Sabbath]. Is it a sin, as Our Master Tam ruled, or not?" Evidently the judge in Marvège could not adjudicate between the stringency of Jacob and the leniency of Meshullam. And how did the godhead reply? With a Biblical verse and a legal precedent. A Biblical verse, because this is an oracular communication; and a legal precedent, because the right law is in the particulars. (The answer is heavenly, but the question is earthly.) "They answered: 'And ye shall eat in plenty, and be satisfied, and praise the Name of the Lord your God that hath dealt wondrously with you.' And the proof is the fast of Yom Kippur, and the fast of the Ninth of Av, and other fasts." I assume that Jacob's oracle is making the same point that was made a century earlier in Lorraine, where it was permitted "with difficulty" to eat and to drink on the afternoon of the Sabbath that preceded a fast. The godhead's brief discussion of these fasts is a little obscure, but its conclusion is as clear as Jacob wished it to be: "We deduce that it is permitted to eat [and to drink] between the afternoon prayer and the evening prayer [on the Sabbath]." The godhead ruled for Meshullam and the thirsty living, and against Jacob and the thirsty dead.

At prayer today I tried, but I failed.

Zedekiah the Physician sums up the controversy about the acceptance of God's judgment on the Sabbath: "It is the custom to recite 'Thy justice is justice' in the afternoon prayer on the Sabbath. There are those who say that we say this prayer as the equivalent of the Justification of the Judgment, because we have received a tradition from our ancestors that Moses died on the Sabbath in the afternoon, and so we are justifying the judgment of him. But Rabbi Shneiur explained that [we say the prayer because] the hour is approaching when the wicked are returned to judgment in Gehenna, and so we are justifying the judgment of them." (Shneiur lived in the first half of the thirteenth century in Normandy. He was the father of three scholars known as "the great ones of Évreux.") For the death of Moses or for the death of everybody else.

Moses did not die like everybody else, but like everybody else he died. The death of Moses dramatically confirms Judaism's seriousness about finitude. Finally the most exceptional man of all was not an exception. The ancient rabbis invented a long and moving narrative of Moses' death. Again and again the man who spoke with God "face to face, as a man speaketh unto his friend" appeals for a reprieve from mortality. Again and again his appeals are denied. "And at the moment when Moses saw that nothing could deliver him from the way of death, he said: 'He is the Rock, His work is perfect, for all His ways are judgment: a God of truth and without iniquity, just and right is He.'" He, too, justified the judgment.

When he came to explain the recitation of the Justification of the Judgment on the afternoon of the Sabbath, Mordecai ben Hillel denied that it was in commemoration of the death of Moses. No, the three verses of resignation are an expression of solicitude for the souls of the dead, who are returning to the fires. And Mordecai adds a few liturgical particulars. "When the New Moon begins on a Saturday night [after the Sabbath], the Justification of the Judgment is not said, because the dead are not returning to their judgment, as Rabbi Aftoriki stated: 'The light of hell rests on Sabbaths and on New Moons.' . . . It is also not said on a Saturday night when a festival begins [after the Sabbath], even though the dead do return to their judgment on festivals. It is out of respect for the holiday that the Justification of the Judgment is not said, so as not to publicize the fact that the dead return to their judgment on a holiday." This is not an anxiety about the reputation of the dead. It is an anxiety about the reputation of the holiday.

Rabbi Aftoriki? Never heard of him. The light of hell? I am happy to hear of it. I have always believed that hell shines a light. By the light of hell the spirit may flourish. But the light is a fire, so the spirit must not approach the light too closely.

Mordecai attributes Rabbi Aftoriki's remark to a fifth-century collection of rabbinical homilies for the holidays. I have the critical edition of this text (I knew the editor when I was a boy), and I scour it for this rabbi with the odd name. I do not find him; but I come away with trophies. About the Talmudic statement that the punishment of the wicked in Gehenna lasts twelve months, a thinker named Hezekiah had this to say: "Six months in the heat and six months in the cold. For a start, the Holy One inflicts them with an itch. Then he moves them into the heat, whereupon they say: 'Is this all there is to God's hell?' So He takes them out into the snow, whereupon they say: 'Is this all there is to God's chill?' [So He moves them into the heat.] In the beginning they say wow, and in the end they say woe."

It appears that God is also the most perfect of torturers. He permits His prisoners no repose, no coherence. They are warmed until they burn. They are cooled until they freeze. What they can bear is sadistically intensified into what they cannot bear. Worst of all, God knows about the special pain of small punishments. An itch! Hellish, indeed. (The Jews among whom I grew up always confused an annoyance with a torment.)

If hell is an itch, then heaven is a scratch. And who would not prefer this world to an itch or a scratch?

"God's hell." What an admission! But it is the truth. If there is a hell, it is God's.

Searching for Rabbi Aftoriki, I read this: "Why did the Holy One create Gehenna and the Garden of Eden? So that they may borrow from each other. And how much space is there between them? Rabbi Yohanan said: The breadth of a wall. Rabbi Hanina said: The breadth of a hand. The rabbis said: They are right next to each other." Borrow from each other? Space, I presume. Heaven and hell are like neighbors who help each other out when the one or the other gets too crowded. Heaven and hell do not compete, they collaborate. And they are the same neighborhood. The neighborhood of judgment. —The language of this passage is obscure. There is a more literal way to render it. "Why did the Holy One create Gehenna and the Garden of Eden? So that they may rescue from each other." I have long suspected that heaven, like hell, is a place from which one would wish to be rescued.

Aftoriki has turned up! He appears in the Talmud, in a discussion of oaths in the laws of torts and in a discussion of eggs in the laws of forbidden foods. Except that Aftoriki appears not as the authority who utters these opinions, but as the son of the authority who utters these opinions. About oaths, we hear from "the father of Rabbi Aftoriki." About eggs, from "Dostai, the father of Rabbi Aftoriki." The father is marked by his son and the son is marked by his father. And then, in the passage from the fifth-century text that the thirteenth-century Mordecai ben Hillel quotes, the son himself finally speaks. And what does the son suddenly say? He insists that the light of hell is mercifully dimmed, that the souls of the fathers are given a weekly reprieve. Was Aftoriki speaking after the death of Dostai? Was it the fate of Dostai's soul that moved Aftoriki to speak? Perhaps the father's death freed the son's tongue, the son's mind.

Your father dies and you are free. And what do you do with your freedom? You think, and write, and pray, about your father. Congratulations!

Even as a son, you must speak in your own name.

Your analysis of your tutelage loosens it. Understand authority and you have crippled it. This is how authority changes hands. No wonder God always wanted to exceed the grasp of the mind. (It is one of the essential attributes of power to be obsessed with how it is known.)

I am at the teahouse with Nathan ben Judah's manual for cantors. He records a clear instruction: "We say the Justification of the Judgment for the souls that are returning to their judgment after the Sabbath—and if the day after the Sabbath is the New Moon, then we do not say it, because they do not return to their judgment [on the New Moon]."

Does all this amount to another source for the introduction of the mourner's kaddish at the waning of the Sabbath? In the Rashi literature, remember, it was stated, about the kaddish at the funeral, that "the kaddish does not occur except for the sake of the verses in the Justification of the Judgment." And here, as the sun is setting on the Sabbath, we have the Justification of the Judgment. Might the mourner's kaddish have originated as the accompaniment of these verses, which came to be interpreted as fulfilling the very function that the mourner's kaddish came to fulfill, which was to spare the souls of the dead?

The "prayerbook" of Solomon ben Samson, Rashi's older colleague who was murdered in Worms in 1096, is the oldest commentary on the liturgy of Ashkenaz. (It survives in a single manuscript in Oxford. Recently it has been attributed to Eliezer ben Nathan, who lived a century later.) Solomon records that "Thy justice is justice" is recited at the conclusion of the Sabbath in memory of Moses. He also says that, for the sake of the dead, the prayers at that hour "must be prolonged. This is the custom." So there was no mourner's kaddish, as I suspected, in the eleventh century. But Rhenish pietists in the thirteenth century composed a commentary on Solomon's commentary, and it presents a somewhat different picture. It mentions the old custom described by Solomon, adding that the three verses of the prayer honor not only Moses, but also his brother Aaron and his sister Miriam, who all died at twilight on the Sabbath. And then the text revokes the custom, noting that Samuel of Évreux "found it written in Judah the Pious's hand that Moses did not die on the Sabbath."

The anonymous authors of this commentary do not mean to deny the dead the offices of the living. They propose instead that the souls are succored by a different prayer at the conclusion of the Sabbath: the collection of verses about redemption known as the *kedushah d'sidra,* the centerpiece of which is the great exclamation by Isaiah, "And one cried to another and said, Holy, holy, holy is the Lord of hosts: the whole earth is full of His glory!" This is an abbreviated version of one of the most important prayers in the Jewish liturgy. The text explains: "We say the order of the kedushah at the departure of the Sabbath because the sinners of Israel are returning to Gehenna at that hour . . . and even if a man has been sentenced to the judgment of hell, hell is cooled for him if he was careful about the kedushah service during his lifetime. Therefore we say the kedushah as the Sabbath departs to save our own souls from Gehenna, and to provide some atonement for the sinners of Israel who are in hell, who will have at least a respite until the completion of this prayer." It is interesting that in this thirteenth-century text it is the kedushah, and not the kaddish, that fulfills this obituary function. Why? After all, the mourner's kaddish already existed. How to explain this? I have an idea. The kedushah that is prescribed for the souls of the dead is known as the *kedushah d'sidra,* or the "kedushah of the lesson." It was formulated in the academies of Babylonia in the geonic period, to be said after the recitation of the verses from the Prophets that followed the conclusion of the morning study; and it was said in Aramaic as well as in Hebrew, so that it would be available to all. (That is how it is still said every morning.) Thus the *kedushah d'sidra,* or the "kedushah of the lesson," was strikingly similar to the *kaddish d'rabbanan,* or the "kaddish of the rabbis," which was the original form of the kaddish that was eventually adapted to the needs of the mourner. (Excuse me, to the needs of the dead.) So perhaps this kedushah was a variety of the mourner's kaddish. It was, you might say, the mourner's kedushah.

In the Talmud, it is Rabbi Akiva who enunciates the view that the Sabbath is a respite for the dead. It occurs in one of his extraordinary disputations with "the wicked" Tinneius Rufus, who was the Roman governor of Judea. (In 132, he set out to suppress the Bar Kokhba rebellion, which Akiva had welcomed as a messianic event.) "How is the Sabbath different from all other days?" the tyrant asked the rabbi. The rabbi rose to the provocation. "A necromancer will be my proof," he replied, "for he can raise a ghost on any day of the week, but on the Sabbath the ghost will not be raised. And if you do not believe me, go and try it with your father, may his bones be ground to dust." The Roman accepted the challenge. "He raised the ghost of his father on the first day, and on the second day, and on the third day, and on the fourth day, and on the fifth day, and on the sixth day—and on the Sabbath the ghost was not raised. His [dead] father said to him: 'My son, he who does not observe the Sabbath properly in your world is forced to keep it here.'" Rome, helpless before the Sabbath!

And the story continues: "His son asked him: 'And what work do you do on the weekdays?' He replied: 'On all the days of the week we are judged, and on the Sabbath we rest, and we rest at the conclusion of the Sabbath for as long as it takes for the order [of worship] to be completed. When the order is completed, the angel that is appointed over the spirits, whose name is Dumah, comes and seizes the spirits of these people and hurls them downward!'" (In another ancient source, I find this version: "At the beginning of the Sabbath, the angel that is appointed over the spirits proclaims: 'Sinners, leave Gehenna and rest, as the Jews are resting!' And at the end of the Sabbath, he proclaims: 'Sinners, return to Gehenna, for the Jews have completed their orders [of worship]!' for it is written [in Job], 'of the shadow of death, and without any order'—that is, when the order is complete, go to death.") Here, perhaps, is another reason that Akiva was chosen to be the hero of the medieval legend about the condemned man and the invention of the mourner's kaddish. He was associated with the reprieve at the end of the Sabbath. (Not surprisingly, the story appears in *Maḥzor Vitry* in its discussion of the concluding prayers of the Sabbath.)

I step out of shul into a torrent of rain and flee to the teahouse. A churlish wind is blowing. In my shelter I have the company of Zedekiah the Physician, who obliges me with another morsel of information. He gives Akiva's retort to the Roman, and then he gives the liturgical consequences. He reports that Aha of Shabha, a gaon of the early eighth century, believed that a reading from Psalms was added to the conclusion of the Sabbath so that the dead would not be hustled back to hell, "which is why it was the custom to recite it melodiously and in an unhurried manner."

Zedekiah also records an opinion of his older brother Benjamin. (He quotes his brother often and reverently. Benjamin was an important Talmudist and an accomplished poet. He was known especially for the elegies with which he marked the misfortunes of the Jews in thirteenth-century Italy. The family was one of the oldest Jewish families in Italy, and believed that it was descended from one of the four Jewish families that, according to legend, were deported to Rome by Titus after the destruction of Jerusalem. It is said also to have been the first Jewish family to be known by a family name: Anav, or humble.) Benjamin believed that this selection from Psalms—the concluding verse of the ninetieth chapter, "And let the beauty of the Lord our God be upon us; and establish thou the work of our hands upon us; yea, the work of our hands establish thou it," followed by the entirety of the ninety-first chapter—is read for protection against the demons. "On the Sabbath, protection is not necessary," Benjamin explained, because "the Sabbath protects itself and its protectors, and there is no reason to fear the demons. . . . But at this hour, when [the Sabbath departs and] we return to the profane time of the week, protection becomes necessary, because the agents of destruction have been granted permission." The world is suddenly a more dangerous place, and so the ninety-first Psalm ("He is my refuge and my fortress . . . his truth shall be thy shield . . . there shall be no evil befall thee . . . for he shall give his angels charge over thee, to keep thee in all thy ways . . .") is read apotropaically, for the purpose of averting evil. But it is not the demons of the living who return to work when the sun sets on the Sabbath. Permission has also been granted, Benjamin adds, "to Dumah, the angel in charge of the spirits, to return the souls of the wicked to Gehenna for judgment—and therefore it was the custom to read this psalm at the conclusion of the Sabbath, because it is a prayer for safety from the demons and the judgment of hell." And Zedekiah adds that "the kaddish, too, is said in an unhurried manner, so as to delay their entry into judgment."

Why is the keeper of the spirits called Dumah? Solomon Buber (the grandfather of Martin Buber and, more important, the scholar whose editions of ancient and medieval rabbinical lore transformed the modern study of these sources) notes that the Hebrew *dumah* may derive from the Greek *daemon.* I have a less learned and more mischievous idea. I think that the name was the result of a coarse reading of a verse from Psalm 115: "The dead praise not the Lord, neither any that go down to silence." The Hebrew for "silence" is *dumah,* as in "the silence of the grave." They who go down to silence are they who go down to the grave. But the angelological temper is not terribly refined. It preferred to read not that the dead go down to *dumah,* but that the dead go down to Dumah. Why have meanings when you can have beings? Why strain the mind when you can strain the imagination?

The mind cannot do without the imagination, but the imagination can do without the mind. Is this proof of the superiority of the imagination? Not at all. This is proof of its inferiority. It is not enough to make pictures of reality. One's pictures must be tested. Beauty must be examined for truth.

Self-sufficiency is not only a state of independence. It is also a state of constriction. Only a small soul does not need others. To subsist within oneself is a prideful and paltry subsistence.

The solipsist is always true to himself.

Thoughts begin with definitions and then they are held back by them.

There is little point in traveling on your own power if your own power will not take you far. (Emerson preached self-reliance, but he relied on nothing less than the universe.)

It occurred to me today that I might spend a whole year in shul, morning prayers, afternoon prayers, evening prayers, and never have a religious experience. A discouraging notion. Yet I must not ask for what cannot be given. Shul was not invented for a religious experience. In shul, a religious experience is an experience of religion. The rest is up to me.

A cool dawn in August. Morning dew everywhere. Praying is pleasant. When I enter the teahouse, I am greeted with the news that they have pies this morning. I am looking for the version of the story of Akiva and the condemned man in the *Zohar Ḥadash,* a seventeenth-century compilation of mystical material, following up an eighteenth-century bibliographical tip in an annotation by the Gaon of Vilna. And in my search for it I discover also a rich description of hell, culled from ancient rabbinical sources. In this conception, hell is arranged in seven levels of sinners. (Two less than you-know-who! As I say, it is a fine day.) These levels are piled one on top of another. Each has a name, and each is an orbit of fire, and each is staffed by "angels of subversion." (The heretics, the apostates, and the traitors, who make it to the fifth level, are exceeded in their doom by "those who slept with their mothers" on the sixth level, and the seventh level is so dire that its victims are not identified, except that "those who descend to that place never ascend again.") On the Sabbath, however, "judgment leaves the world, and the wicked in Gehenna have a rest and the angels of subversion do not govern them."

The Sabbath in hell must be the sweetest Sabbath in the universe.

In the famous concluding section of *The Law of Man,* Nahmanides gives a detailed account of hell and heaven, Gehenna and Eden. (He insists that hell is an actual place, which the rabbis "measured in width and in length.") He provides a general statement of this eschatology: "The punishment of Gehenna takes place immediately after death. . . . This is the rule: It is explained in the sayings of the sages, and it is upheld by those who received the Torah, that Gehenna is the location of the verdict, where the sinners are punished in their souls with suffering and anguish that have no counterpart in this world. For the pains of the material world afflict a lowly body coarse in its matter and blunt in its sensation, whereas the burden of punishment and pain falls on the soul that is fine and delicate in its substance. A man feels more than a donkey feels when he is pricked by a needle, for the donkey is coarser; and even among human beings, those who are physically finer and purer in their thoughts and their creations feel suffering and pain more than those who are physically coarse and confused in their thoughts and their feelings. . . . So, too, the pains of the soul are felt more intensely than the pains of the body."

I do not doubt that this is true. The soul is more exquisite than the body. But the rest of the scheme? The rest of the scheme is fiction. And yet I cannot disdain it—or rather, I can only disdain it if I can also disdain the distinction between the body and the soul. For this fiction is the result of that distinction. If you believe that there is a difference between the corporeal and the incorporeal, and you believe that it is a difference in kind, so that the one cannot be reduced to the other, then you must believe also that the career of the one is not the career of the other, and you are left with the question of what becomes of the soul away from the body. Only the materialist need not trouble about the afterlife.

Forget this business about the body and the soul, says the materialist. No, say I, because then I will understand even less.

The afterlife is an answer of the imagination to a question of the mind.

When I read the eschatological speculations of the rabbis, I think: they were wrong, but they were not spectacularly wrong. They repudiated materialism. But they did wild things with what they rightly concluded.

Is there a way of conceiving the soul so that it is not material and not immortal?

I have no reason to believe in the immortality of the soul. But I also have no reason to believe that the death of the soul has anything to do with the death of the body. So how does the soul die? I don't know. Perhaps we kill it. The urgent question is not whether the soul survives the death of the body. The urgent question is whether the soul survives the life of the body.

The notion that I am essentially spirit may be preposterous, but the notion that I am essentially flesh is more preposterous.

—So show me something like the soul, something that does not live like the body and does not die like the body.
—Easy. I will show you reason.

Once you concede the existence of immaterial but intelligible objects or propositions, once you recognize the existence of things that are real but not actual, you are in the realm of reason; and the realm of reason leads directly to the realm of religion, in the sense that religion, too, traffics in real but not actual entities. This is not to say that all religion is rational, or that all the statements of religion must be believed as the statements of reason are believed. Yet some of the statements of religion may compel this kind of belief. The important task is to learn to think critically about the various claims that are made for the immaterial world.

Reason opens the floodgates and reason closes them.

The immaterial world is not the same as the spirit world. And belief is not the same as credulity. Anyway, there is nothing glamorous about credulity. It is the epistemology of children and mystagogues and crowds.

For many years I have lived without religion. But I could not have lived without the possibility of religion.

However many things we invent, there are still things that we discover. And discovery is a mode of experience. (Indeed, a mode of revelation.) Also, a thought is an experience. Thoughts are not only thought, they are also lived. In this sense, reason is not the enemy of mysticism.

When Nietzsche lost his faith, he concluded that God is dead. This is not critical thinking. This is narcissism. I understand the idea that if God exists, then you must believe in Him. I do not understand the idea that if you do not believe in Him, then God must not exist.

The fact that I spend my entire life in darkness does not prove that there is no light. My experience is not the only philosophical datum that counts.

Nihilism is materialism in a bad mood.

What the nihilist fears most is objectivity. His name for objectivity is God.

At the teahouse, I am absorbed by these lines by the Perfumer: "For the first seven days of mourning, the soul wanders back and forth between the cave in which it is buried and the house in which it lived. After seven days, the body has been wormed and the soul will return to its giver. Give Him what He gave you: a pure one." In fact, the Perfumer did not write these lines at all. They are a pastiche of two ancient rabbinical statements, the former from a pseudepigraphical work of the early geonic period that purports to be the work of a first-century sage, the latter from the Talmud, though the Perfumer has abbreviated it slightly, giving it an almost archaic eloquence. (I recognize his sources!) The Perfumer's pastiche is an expression of the Perfumer's pietism. Like a man rubbing two sticks of wood together to make a spark, he rubs two texts together to make an idea. His idea is purity, purity, purity. But I learn something else from this example of the technique. I learn that superstition can sometimes be a force for stringency. Out of myths, morals.

In shul on the Sabbath I am delighted to run into somebody I haven't seen in decades. He was the smartest kid (as we used to say) in high school. He tells me that he is now head of laser research at one of the country's most important military laboratories. The Yeshiva of Flatbush brings you . . . weapons of mass destruction!

Aaron of Lunel also cites the myth of the wandering soul, but the lesson that he draws is not ethical, it is ritual. "There are those who say that it is for this reason that a candle is placed on the floor in the doorway of the house, so that the soul can see where it is going as it wends its way to its house. . . . Perhaps this was why it was the custom in certain places to put a candle behind the door."

V

Here, once more, is the story of Rabbi Akiva and the condemned man, the founding myth of the mourner's kaddish, as it is told in *Maḥzor Vitry:* "A tale of Rabbi Akiva. He was walking in a cemetery by the side of the road and encountered there a naked man, black as coal, carrying a large burden of wood on his head. He seemed to be alive and was running under the load like a horse. Rabbi Akiva ordered him to stop. 'How comes it that a man does such hard work?' he asked. 'If you are a servant and your master is doing this to you, then I will redeem you from him. If you are poor and people are avoiding you, then I will give you money.' 'Please, sir,' the man replied. 'Do not detain me, because my superiors will be angry.' 'Who are you,' Rabbi Akiva asked, 'and what have you done?' The man said, 'The man whom you are addressing is a dead man. Every day they send me out to chop wood.' 'My son, what was your work in the world from which you came?' 'I was a tax collector, and I would favor the rich and kill the poor.' 'Have your superiors told you nothing about how you might relieve your condition?' 'Please, sir, do not detain me, for you will irritate my tormentors. For such a man [as I], there can be no relief. Though I did hear them say something—but no, it is impossible. They said that if this poor man had a son, and his son were to stand before the congregation and recite [the prayer] 'Bless the Lord who is blessed!' and the congregation were to answer amen, and the son were also to say 'May the Great Name be blessed!' [a sentence from the kaddish], they would release him from his punishment. But this man never had a son. He left his wife pregnant and he did not know whether the child was a boy. And if she gave birth to a boy, who would teach the boy Torah? For this man does not have a friend in the world.' Immediately Rabbi Akiva took upon himself the task of discovering whether this man had fathered a son, so that he might teach the son Torah and install him at the head of the congregation to lead the prayers. 'What is your name?' he asked. 'Akiva,' the man answered. 'And the name of your wife?' 'Shoshnia.' 'And the name of your town?' 'Lodkiya.' Rabbi Akiva was deeply troubled by all this and went to make his inquiries. When he came to that town, he asked about the man he had met, and the townspeople replied: 'May his bones be ground to dust!' He asked about the man's wife, and he was told: 'May her memory be erased from the world!' He asked about the man's son, and he was told: 'He is a heathen—we did not even bother to circumcise him!' Rabbi Akiva promptly circumcised him and sat him down before a book. But the boy refused to receive Torah. Rabbi Akiva fasted for forty days. A heavenly voice was heard to say: 'For this you mortify yourself?' 'But Lord of the Universe,' Rabbi Akiva replied, 'it is for You that I am preparing him.' Suddenly the Holy One, Blessed Be He, opened the boy's heart. Rabbi Akiva taught him Torah and 'Hear, O Israel' and the benediction after meals. He presented the boy to the congregation and the boy recited [the prayer] 'Bless the Lord who is blessed!' and they answered, 'May the Great Name be blessed!' At that very moment the man was released from his punishment. The man immediately came to Rabbi Akiva in a dream, and said: 'May it be the will of the Lord that your soul find delight in the Garden of Eden, for you have saved me from the sentence of Gehenna.' Rabbi Akiva declared: 'Your Name, O Lord, endures forever, and the memory of You through all the generations!' For this reason, it became customary that the evening prayers on the night after the Sabbath are led by a man who does not have a father or a mother, so that he can say kaddish and 'Bless the Lord who is blessed!'"

The themes of the story? That the dead are in need of spiritual rescue; and that the agent of spiritual rescue is the son; and that the instrument of spiritual rescue is prayer, notably the kaddish.

The study of Jewish history is an invitation to travel. So far I have found the story of Rabbi Akiva and the condemned man in an obscure tenth-century work that was written as an ancient-style midrash on the Ten Commandments (in this version the son is taught only the blessings that are recited when one is called to the Torah in the house of worship, and the kaddish is not mentioned); in twelfth-century France; in thirteenth-century Provence; in thirteenth-century Spain; in thirteenth-century Germany; in thirteenth-century Austria; in fourteenth-century Spain and North Africa; in fifteenth-century Germany; in sixteenth-century Poland; in sixteenth-century Palestine; in seventeenth-century Holland; in eighteenth-century Lithuania; in twentieth-century Germany (in Berdichewski's collection of Jewish folktales); in twentieth-century Israel (in a responsum by Ovadiah Yosef and in Aaron Roth's *Shomer Emunim*, or *Keeper of the Faiths*, one of the crudest works in the history of Judaism). The durability of the story is remarkable. There are still other citations to check, but I have enough. The important bibliographical fact is that none of the sources in which I have found the story are classical sources. I have not come upon the story of Akiva in a text that is contemporary, or roughly contemporary, with Akiva. The story looks to me like a medieval invention about an ancient figure.

There are interesting variations in the story. (So many variations, in fact, that the frustrated Menasseh ben Israel, in seventeenth-century Amsterdam, exclaimed that "no one version is like the other.") In most versions the condemned man meets Rabbi Akiva, but there are versions in which he meets one Rabbi Zmira'ah or "a scholar" or "a certain rabbi" or "a man." In some versions the encounter is real, and in other versions it is a dream. In some versions it takes place in a graveyard, and in other versions in a landscape of fire that is identified as one of the stations of hell. In some versions the man's punishment is his Sisyphean labor, and in other versions he is burned in a fire set to his wood and then sent back to begin again. In some versions the liturgical obligation that results is the kaddish, and in other versions it is the call to the Torah on the Sabbath, or to the reading from the prophetic books on the Sabbath, or the leading of the evening prayer after the Sabbath, or (in the words of Bahya ben Asher in thirteenth-century Spain) "any blessing uttered publicly in the house of worship." In some versions the condemned man is guilty of oppressing the poor, and in other versions he is guilty of having sex with a betrothed maiden on Yom Kippur, or more generally of an all-purpose, all-encompassing wickedness. (Having sex with a betrothed maiden is a crime that the rabbis in the Talmud attribute only to the most extreme villains, such as Esau; but committing the abomination on the Sabbath of Sabbaths is a nice touch.) In fifteenth-century Spain, Isaac Aboab gives the lost version of the tale from *Midrash Tanḥuma,* a collection of early medieval homilies also of uncertain origins. This is the version whose loss is bemoaned by all the late medieval and early modern sources, and it is almost exactly the one in *Maḥzor Vitry,* except for this addition: the condemned man identifies himself as a crooked tax collector *and* a Yom Kippur rapist. In the *Zohar Ḥadash,* he identifies himself this way: "I am a guilty Jew, and there is not an evil or a sin in the world that I neglected to commit." I believe him.

The account of the tale in *Tanna D'Bei Eliyahu Zuta,* or *The Teaching of the School of Elijah, The Lesser Version,* a late ancient or early medieval work of obscure origins, is especially interesting. Rabbi Akiva is not the hero of this account. Its hero is Rabbi Yohanan ben Zakkai, the scholar of the first century who was smuggled out of the siege of Jerusalem and, with the permission of the Romans, established an academy by the sea, thereby severing the fate of Judaism from the fate of Judea. "Rabbi Yohanan ben Zakkai said: 'Once I was walking along the road and I encountered a man who was gathering wood. I spoke to him, but he did not reply. Then he came over to me and said: "Rabbi, I am not alive. I am dead." I said to him: "If you are dead, then what need have you of wood?" "Rabbi," he replied, "listen to what I am about to tell you. When I was alive, my friend and I busied ourselves with sin in my mansion, and when we arrived here [in Gehenna] we were sentenced to the punishment of fire. While I gather wood, they burn my friend. While he gathers wood, they burn me." I asked him: "And how long is your sentence?" He replied: "When I came here, I left behind my pregnant wife. I know that she is pregnant with a boy. I beseech you, watch over him from the day of his birth until he is five years old, and then take him to a teacher, so that he will learn to read Scripture. For the moment he says 'Bless God, who is blessed!' they will lift me out of the punishment of hell." ' " Those salvific words appear in the morning prayer and the evening prayer. They are like the words of the kaddish, but they are not the words of the kaddish. So this is not precisely the story of the invention of the kaddish. Still, the invention of filial intercession is here. What is also here is the sin of sodomy. This blackened wretch is enduring not the consequences of forbidden heterosexual lust, but the consequences of forbidden homosexual lust. "When I was alive, my friend and I were busy with sin in my mansion": the confession has a tone of aristocratic decadence. (The word for "mansion" is the Aramaic word *palterin,* which also means "palace." In a text that was found in the Cairo Genizah, it appears weirdly as *ofin pat palter,* or "baking bread in a bakery." Solomon Schechter observed that this cannot be right—

baking is not an activity that lands a Jew in hell—and he concluded that the Aramaic word is a corruption of the Greek word *pederastia.* Schechter's etymology seems far-fetched. I have another suggestion. I used to discuss the history of homosexuality with a very learned friend who died a few years ago, and I remember that he mentioned a Greek ideal known as *philetairia,* or the love of comrades. *Philetairia, palter, palterin:* I detect an iniquitous root. . . .)

A lovely morning, a heavy heart. A few months ago I worried that my mourner's life would interfere with the rest of my life. Now I worry that the rest of my life will interfere with my mourner's life. The temptation is growing to surrender to the drill and the sadness. I have a gift for being cheerful in cheerless circumstances, but my gift is failing me.

Solomon Schechter was convinced that the earliest version of the legend of Akiva and the condemned man, "the origin of all the versions in our possession," appeared in Tunisia in the eleventh century, in *Ḥibbur Yafeh Me-Ha'Yeshuah,* or *An Elegant Composition on Deliverance,* by Nissim ben Jacob, the great scholar of Kairouan. Nissim composed his book of stories for a sorrowing relative, to console him for the death of a son. In his dedicatory preface, he writes that "you have informed me that the heretics [that is, the Muslims] have a book that treats of relief after distress and adversity . . . and in your desire for the words of the Torah you have asked me to compose a work of Torah for you on this subject, compiled from the tales of our wise men and our pious men, of our rabbis, so that you will not have to consult books that are outside our tradition." So does the tale of Akiva and the condemned man have an Islamic source or an Islamic parallel? I have the Amsterdam edition of 1846. The story appears near the end, almost word for word like the version in *Maḥzor*

Vitry, with one interesting difference. In Nissim's version, the condemned man is guilty of an abuse of power, but he was more powerful than a tax collector: "I was a rich man and a judge, I was one of the notables of the community, and I would favor the rich and kill the poor." Still, Schechter was wrong. A look into the subsequent scholarship reveals that the story does not appear in the Judeo-Arabic original at all. It seems to have been introduced into Nissim's text by an editor in Europe.

A dream: I am walking in Oak Hill graveyard in Georgetown. It is night. Near the little stone chapel I meet a man in a pinstripe suit and shiny shoes. In each hand he carries a legal briefcase. His face is streaked with soot. He asks for my help. Both his briefcases are filled with wood, and he is seeking somebody to carry the rest of what he has gathered. —My interpretation of my dream: I am possessed by my texts, and I believe that lawyers are sinners.

Back to the *Zohar Ḥadash,* where the story of Akiva and the condemned man appears twice. This version ("a bizarre version!" exclaims Schechter) includes an extraordinary element. When asked for his name, the condemned man tells his interlocutor, "I do not know, because the guilty of Gehenna do not remember their names." And a few pages later, "I am a guilty Jew, and the wardens of Gehenna will not tell me my name." This wrinkle on the man's suffering is absent from the other versions of the story, where the man's name is a bit of information useful for locating his son. In this account, however, the disappearance of personal identity is a form of punishment. Namelessness is hellish.

It occurs to me also that the force of this particular punishment is owed to the style of naming in the world of the rabbis. It was, remember, a world of patronyms, in which a man's name was established by the name of his father: Reuven ben Shimon, or Reuben the son of Simeon. If you know whose son you are, you know who you are. And so the torment of anonymity has a dark beauty in this story about the origins of kaddish, this story of the son as the savior of the father.

There is more. In this account, the savior-son is given a name. He is called Nahum Ha'Pakuli, or Nahum the Pakuli. A prooftext is given for the appellation, a verse from Isaiah that says about the drunken priest and the drunken prophet, *paku pliliyah,* "they stumbled in judgment." Then the author proceeds to a pun. The Hebrew verb *paku* means "stumbled," but in Aramaic the same root has a different meaning: "released," "extracted," "took out of." So Nahum Ha'Pakuli is the one who released his father from the judgment of that world. Or as we would say, the one who sprung his father. He is Nahum the Rescuer. Yet his name, Nahum, means "comfort," "solace." So Nahum Ha'Pakuli is The Comforter-Rescuer, the one who consoled his father by setting him free. I hereby pronounce Nahum Ha'Pakuli the father of the mourner's kaddish. I will soon get on his trail.

Fictions are not all that grow from fictions.

What is the difference, for me, between studying and wallowing, between avidity and morbidity? Sometimes it is hard to tell. Obsession has many uses. Its intensity sometimes disguises the fact that it is a method of insulation.

The kaddish: language allegedly acting on cosmology.

A visit after dark to the Jefferson Memorial, to weaken the momentum of melancholy. Rabbi Akiva is nowhere to be seen; and God is represented here faintly, only by the religion of reason, which is not fastidious about the particulars of ritual. A perfectly clear sky. I can make out the last sliver of the waning moon in the Tidal Basin, where its reflection gently rides the ripples made by a small wind. The place is hushed and open. A few quiet words with a friend, a few sighs from a place far from reason, a few minutes of well-being.

I am thinking that there is a nasty quality to the legend of Rabbi Akiva and the condemned man. It is premised on the turpitude of the parent whom one is instructed to honor. My father was a pretty good man, and I don't much like consigning him to this lurid, pessimistic cosmology. Anyway, the obligation of kaddish lasts eleven months and not twelve months precisely because the rabbis chose to dissociate the deceased from the rabbinical pronouncement that the wicked receive their punishment in the twelve months after they die. (After a year of excruciation, they find release: "And after twelve months their body is no more and their soul is extinguished in flames and a wind disperses them beneath the feet of the righteous.")

It was in a sore and sullen mood that I brought my kit of texts to the teahouse this morning, but my mood was dispelled by Menasseh ben Israel. In his *Nishmat Ḥayyim,* or *The Soul of Life,* written in 1651, a neo-Platonizing work of theology designed to prove the immortality of the soul, Menasseh includes a discussion of the kaddish, and in his discussion I found that my objection to the kaddish, my feeling that it insults my father as much as it honors him, had been anticipated by none other than Isaac Luria, the mystical master of the sixteenth century. "So great is the power of the kaddish," Menasseh writes, that "Rabbi Isaac Ashkenazi [Luria] wrote that it is good to recite it even on Sabbaths and holidays and New Moons, because its purpose is not only to save [the soul of the dead] from Gehenna, but to lift it from the lower Eden higher and higher, level by level." Menasseh also quotes a work of which I have never heard, which defends the kaddish (the one recited annually, on the anniversary of the death of a parent) against the objection that it imputes wickedness to the deceased by implying that, long after the twelve months of judgment have passed, year after year, anniversary after anniversary, the deceased still languishes in hell. The kaddish is not only a recourse for the wicked, claims this author, but it also "raises the righteous from level to level . . . and every one of these ascents is described as a departure from the world from which he came."

In his analysis of the kaddish, Menasseh is an optimist. He believes in the power of persuasion. This is no surprise, I guess. He was the man who petitioned Cromwell to let the Jews back into England.

I have tracked Luria's interpretation of the mourner's kaddish to its source. It was recorded by his amanuensis Hayyim Vital, who established the more or less canonical corpus of Lurianic teachings in a vast work called *Ets Ḥayyim*, or *The Tree of Life*. This work is a series of "gates" dealing with different mystical doctrines, and Luria's comment appears in the gate that treats the art of mystical prayer, in the middle of a long analysis of the hidden "intentions" of the kaddish upon which the mind must concentrate during its recitation. These intentions, or esoteric meanings, are established by a close and intricate analysis of the letters in the prayer, of their patterns and their associations. I confess that I have always found this system of meditation tiresome. It is an overwrought and unintelligible diversion from the plain sense of the liturgy, which is quite mysterious enough. But

Hayyim interrupts this theosophical pedantry to attest to his master's practice of the mourner's kaddish: Luria "recited the kaddish according to the Spanish rite, and not according to the rite of the Arab lands, to which extraneous additions have been made," and he recited it every year—morning, afternoon, and evening—on the anniversary of his father's death. Hayyim also gives the opinion about the mourner's kaddish that Menasseh cites (Menasseh found it in Hayyim's book), but a little more fully. In Hayyim's account there is nuance that pleases me. The view that the mourner's kaddish saves the dead from hell is described by Luria as "the opinion of the masses." It is, in a word, vulgar. In the refined view of the mourner's kaddish, by contrast, the prayer raises the dead to heaven. Is it refined to believe that this prayer gets my father into heaven? I don't know. But I do know that it is vulgar to believe that it gets him out of hell.

The idea of hell is more coarsening than the idea of heaven. Heaven is not a fantasy of cruelty. One may be improved by a fantasy such as heaven.

There are differences between individuals and between societies that may be explained by the fact that some fictions are more ennobling than others.

When I arrive at shul this evening, it is surrounded by policemen. They arrested a man near here a few hours ago, and the man tossed a gun out the window of his car, and they are looking for the gun. But enough excitement, it is the hour for the service of the Lord. Just as we are about to start the prayers, two hasidim stroll in. They are from central casting: hulking black caftans, black velvet hats disclosing black velvet yarmulkes disclosing shaved heads, long and expertly curled earlocks, the works. "Cops," I say to my neighbor, chuckling. "Undercover cops." And this reminds him of a story. A friend in the New York Police Department once told him about a couple of cops who were staking out a shul in Brooklyn on the Sabbath, and disguised themselves as hasidim. It appears that they had not been briefed about the laws of the Sabbath and the length of the Sabbath prayers. One of them became impatient and lit up a cigarette, which on the day of rest one is strictly forbidden to do; and there he stood, in his hat and his beard, puffing away. My friend was told that the poor bearded cop was taken aback by the vehemence of the citizens.

I overslept this morning. It felt strange to start a day without praying and without studying. But it also felt wonderful. A little rest in a year without rest.

According to Rabbi Akiva, "five things are twelve months long": the judgment of the generation of the Flood, the judgment of Job, the judgment of the Egyptians, the judgment of Gog and Magog in the future, the judgment of the wicked in Gehenna. What do these five years of judgment have in common? Pain construed as purification. The association of pain with purification has always seemed uncontroversial to me. But I remember a conversation with a philosophy professor in college, a conversation about Nietzsche, in which he remarked that the association of truth with suffering was nonsense, that truth is indifferent to happiness and unhappiness, that truth is equally available or equally unavailable to the happy man and the unhappy man. I was shocked. The idea that pain is useless hurts.

This evening is the beginning of the metaphysically torrid month of Elul, which ends in Rosh Hashanah and the season of judgment. And the rabbi elected to preach about definitions of ownership as they are broached by the case of a Jew who lent his ox to a non-Jew for the Sabbath! Not a word about sin and atonement. Just torts, sweet torts.

In the *Kol Bo,* the bad news and the good news. The bad news: "For twelve months the soul rises and falls." The good news: "After twelve months the soul rises and does not fall."

On my desk, my books are like my peonies. I am pleased by the sight of them closed and clenched with promise, and then I am pleased by the sight of them opening, until they reveal the fullness that I expect of them.

The first day of the month of Elul. The season of introspection begins. This year the consideration of my own sins, a cheerless and irregular affair, will bring me relief from the consideration of my father's sins, which the obligation of kaddish demands that I consider. The other day, waiting for the prayers to begin, I was reading this passage in the Talmud: "According to the school of Shammai, there are three classes on the Day of Judgment: the absolutely righteous, the absolutely wicked, and the average. The absolutely righteous are written and sealed immediately for eternal life. The absolutely wicked are written and sealed immediately for Gehenna. The average descend into Gehenna and howl and ascend." (Rashi, compassionately, on the word "howl": "They scream and weep in their torment for one hour, and then they ascend.") I have read this passage many times before, associating it always with my own fate. Not this time. Now I imagine the sound of *his* howl.

About the eschatology of the average, the school of Hillel differs with the school of Shammai. The school of Hillel denies that ordinary individuals make the acquaintance of hell. Instead, "He who abounds in kindness tilts [the scales] toward kindness." This reprieve for the common lot is supported with a variety of prooftexts. I note that the discussion in the Talmud is provoked by Hillel's preference for mercy, not by Shammai's preference for justice. The preference for justice needs no explanation. It is entirely consistent with the system of rewards and punishments. But the preference for mercy seems to thwart the system. Explanations must be found for God's interference with the consequences of our actions. (Grateful explanations.)

When I couldn't sleep last night, I took advantage of my wakefulness. I sat at my desk turning pages, until I settled on an ancient comment about one of the Psalmist's most famous exclamations. "My God, my God, why has thou forsaken me?" The rabbis said that this was addressed not to God's measure of justice, but to God's measure of mercy. For "it makes no sense to ask of the measure of justice why it has forsaken you." Justice is made of objectivity and necessity; it is an unfeeling engine of entailments. To suspend justice would be to suspend the moral structure of the world. But mercy is another matter. It is an uncoaxed benevolence, and an intrusion of care into the workings of cause and effect, as one intrudes a stick into a wheel to stop it from turning. The difference between justice and mercy is the difference between logic and grace. I closed the book, I returned to bed, I slept.

We do evil, so there must be mercy. But if there is mercy, will we do good? Surely the certainty of God's goodness rigs things. It lessens the tension that is required for virtue. Remember Heine's jab, his unwitting gloss on Hillel: "God will forgive. That is his profession."

Mercy is not grace, because it preserves the traces of human accountability. In this sense, mercy is less than grace, and it is more.

Today I was ungovernable.

Reviewing the ancient teachings on heaven and hell, Menasseh ben Israel polemically observes: "Please note that there is no mention of other places [aside from the Garden of Eden and Gehenna], such as the places that the wise men of the nations mention, the ones that they call limbo and purgatorio." So there is no stalling for dead souls, no suspended destinies, in Judaism. Except that in Menasseh's account—indeed, in the whole rabbinical story of the year in the netherworld—Gehenna certainly seems to function as a purgatory. It is the first stop of the soul, where there occurs a purgation. For "the soul cannot cleanse itself from its filth except in Gehenna," writes Menasseh, and so virtually nobody is spared a visit. "There are righteous individuals who deserve to experience the fate of wicked individuals once or twice. . . . They do not tarry in hell, they pass through it speedily."

Do I really believe these stories about the souls of the dead descending and ascending, this pornography of reward and punishment? I have no evidence that any of this is true. And I have no patience with the excuse that it is emotionally true; truth is not an emotion. Yet these eschatological inventions are useful, in that they compel me to regard my father's life as a whole, the corporeal and the incorporeal; and the volatility of all these death-pictures suits these weeks and months, the disequilibrium of my situation. And behind the garishness of these rabbinical hallucinations, I can recognize their decency. They are the grotesqueries of conscience.

Can one be frightened into goodness?

Words of encouragement, from Kant: "A routine illusion does not provide one with so much material for new observations as does an illusion that is strange and ingeniously excogitated." This is what I need to hear, a lapsed man suddenly unlapsed.

In this year I will acquaint myself with the pleasures of resumption.

It was a bright morning and I went for a short walk under a white sky, to the little park at the edge of Georgetown, where I watched the dogs run. I am disconcerted by my enthusiasm for all these eschatological visions. I am not a visionary.

I prefer to think of the visions as philosophical fables. It occurs to me today, for example, that the rabbinical doctrines about death and the afterlife have the consequence of preempting any idea of predestination. In this way, they protect the friction of ethical life. In the absence of all these posthumous ordeals, reward and punishment would be utterly mechanical: goodness moves up, badness moves down, all with a monstrous inexorability. But goodness and badness are almost never unmixed, since the heart is hungry and the will is free. It is human complexity for which the myth of judgment allows.

And the trial of the soul in the twelve months after the death of the body? I will think of this judicial fairy tale as an allegory for the absence of clarity in most moral reckonings. The suspense represents the possibility of fairness. For there are two sides to every human story. Complications must be considered, and extenuations must be offered, and testimonies must be gathered.

In Agnon's compilation of rabbinical texts on the Days of Awe, he cited this from Hayyim Yosef David Azulai, one of the most colorful scholars of the eighteenth century: "There are places where it is the custom that the sexton proclaims, for the entire month of Elul, after the afternoon prayers, 'Return, wayward sons!' "

—Return, wayward sons!
—But I am here.

I am wayward, but I am here.

Modern philosophy is certain that it deposed the distinction between the body and the soul a long time ago, and replaced it with a variety of materialisms. The brain, the circumstances of power, the genes, the rules of common practice: these are the keys to the kingdom now. At Oxford years ago, when I read Ryle, I was myself thrilled by the soul's overthrow. "The ghost in the machine": Ryle's mocking description of the idealist explanation of human behavior embarrassed me. But I am not embarrassed anymore. It's not that I have myself done the philosophical work that is required for an adequate defense of the ghost. It's that my everyday experience makes it plain to me that human behavior cannot entirely explain itself, or be entirely explained by the physical or the pragmatic. There is something in human behavior that outlives the physical—not in heaven or hell, but in the understanding. I think of this as the analytical afterlife; and without the analytical afterlife I cannot account for the courage and the generosity and the despair that I have witnessed. My father sickened and died when his body failed him, but the manner of his dying—the resistance that he mounted against his illness, and then the decision that he made (I am certain that he made such a decision, a day or two before he died) to start on his way out of the world—cannot be reduced to his body and its renal realities. My father's dying was not the dying of a purely material being. When he died, we lost his ghost to his machine.

When a person chooses to end his life or to sacrifice his life for others, he is not acting merely according to the rules of life-ending and the conventions of life-sacrificing. Pragmatism is such a puny theory. What are those rules and those conventions, anyway? And it is the same with all of life's exceedings. There are so many questions for which the pragmatists have no answers. Human transformation is not a "practice." There are changes for which we have no rules and no conventions. That is why we fear them and honor them; they are accomplishments for which experience cannot have been a guide.

The belief in the distinction between spirit and matter is not a simple belief. The relations between the terms may be complicated. Matter is not uniformly dead. And not all mental processes are spiritual processes. Like the body, the soul may extend in many directions at once, or get in the way of its own movements. The dualism exfoliates.

I detest the condescension of the materialist. It is he who has the easy task. Intellectually speaking, the materialist is a man of leisure.

Can one be frightened into goodness? Absolutely, says the Jewish tradition; and so we are sounding the shofar every morning for the entirety of this month. The sound is supposed to rattle its hearers into repentance. Repenting is not what I do best; but the early morning blast certainly concentrates me.

As I was leaving for shul, the man who looks after the building found a gun in the garden.

This afternoon I had another thought about the kaddish. The son's redemption of the dead father, the dead father's protection by the son: is this not an allegory for the power of the present over the past? For the past is at the mercy of the present. The present can condemn the past to oblivion or obscurity. Whatever happens to the past will happen to it posthumously. And so the saga of the family is also the saga of the tradition. Kinship is stewardship.

It tickles me to think of history in hell. I was taught that I must revere the past. Perhaps I must also pity it.

The life of the dead: an idiotic notion. Also the secret of civilization.

Insofar as civilization is a communion with the past, and regards an absence as a presence, it is mysticism.

If the materialists were right, tradition would be impossible.

In the month of Elul, it is the custom to visit the cemetery, and so we will travel to my father's grave. And this will be the first Elul in which we have a grave to visit. I mean, historically. My grandparents and my aunts and my uncles are buried in a ravine in Galicia, along with all the other Jews who were murdered by the Germans on that obscene day in that obscene month of that obscene year. Nobody in our family was, as the rabbis in America say, laid to rest. (Except for my father's parents, who died in their own beds in the summer of 1940. Their death was their reward.) For my mother, this is a wound that has not healed. Elul reminds her that their lot was not like the lot of the Jews among whom they found refuge. With an unspoken bitterness, my parents watched their friends and their neighbors journey to the cemeteries of Long Island in the weeks leading up to Rosh Hashanah, in the natural rhythm of the generations. It is no wonder, I guess, that my mother's mourning for my father became a kind of super-mourning, an encompassing sorrow, in which she could at last perform the duties of a mourner not only for her husband, but also for her father and her mother and her brother. The great bereavement was no longer deferred. On my father's grave we will inscribe the names of his martyred brother and sister, as he requested; and my mother has requested that the same lasting kindness be done for her family, too. So here is another of the infernal inversions that await some of the children of Israel, and their children: we will greet a grave with gladness.

In Manhattan, on Friday evening, there are only a few men in shul. I am surrounded by soul-crushing banter, and I don't have the patience for it. (Sometimes the shul is Judaism's last bulwark against religion.) I say my kaddish and run. On Saturday morning, things get worse. Not wanting more of the same, I head a few blocks north, to an egalitarian congregation where I usually run into friends. I arrive early. At the appropriate point in the morning service I rise to say kaddish. Foolish me! There is no kaddish. The progressive men and women of this congregation have improved the liturgy by leaving this kaddish out. I hasten to check with a friend that the kaddish that appears later in the service has also not been expunged; he seems a little annoyed by my inquiry, but he assures me that my moment will come. A little while later a young man rises to deliver the sermon. "I want to discuss this week's Torah reading in the light of an article in this week's *Jewish Week,*" he says. "A distinction must be made," the young man observes, "between what the Torah wants and what the Republican Party wants. Now, according to *Sefer Yetsirah* . . ." And so on. I wonder whether the young man also believes that a distinction must be made between what the Torah wants and what the Democratic Party wants. But it is not the politics of the place that offends me. *Sefer Yetsirah,* or *The Book of Creation,* is an ancient work of Jewish mysticism, and one of the most opaque works in the Jewish tradition; and I am quite certain that the young man at the pulpit wouldn't be able to find his way out of it if his life depended on it. But what I really want to know is this: on what ground, precisely, was that kaddish eliminated? Surely not on the grounds of egalitarianism. I agree that Jewish women should be legally and ritually enfranchised by their religion; and it is only a matter of time, I think, before they find satisfaction. But why does tampering with the misogynistic elements of the tradition justify tampering with the other elements of the tradition? Why is egalitarianism so often accompanied by a general slackening? And why are the good women of this congregation not embarrassed by the relaxed standards by which they have gained their admission? Still, I have a kaddish to say, so I stick it out. The rest of the service is not much more than the religion of singing, a pseudo-hasidic hootenanny. I can't wait to plead for my father and leave. If I must be alienated, I prefer to be alienated from the real thing.

In the testament that the Gaon of Vilna left his family when he set out for the Holy Land—he set out sometime before

1783, and never made it, and died in Vilna in 1797—he warned them that "it is better to pray at home, because in the house of worship it is impossible . . . to avoid hearing empty words and slanders." Right. Banality is the enemy of sanctity. But what to do? The Gaon offers one of the most outrageous suggestions in the Jewish tradition: "The best guarantee is that you never, heaven forbid, cross your threshold, that you never leave your house."

I confess: after Friday night and Saturday morning, I took Saturday night off. But on Sunday morning everything in shul was fine. No time for chatter. A refreshing, businesslike efficiency. The clacking of the wooden boxes that house the phylacteries. The brisk worship of the Lord. Below us, sunk in darkness, was the grand sanctuary. A shaft of light fell across the red coverlet on the high table and onto the base of a marble column, where the fading flowers were interrupted in their tenebrous post-Sabbath decline. How I love an empty shul. It is the opposite of a ruined shul. It is a house of promise.

On a bright Monday morning, my mother, my sister, and I go to the cemetery. My father is buried in our family's plot in the far corner of a quiet cemetery in Elmont. We stand in stillness before the humbly marked grave. The din of the cicadas is everywhere. My mother and my sister softly read the traditional prayers. ("Peace be upon you, my man and my husband. You were the foundation of my house and the joy of my dwelling. You illumined my darkness. But now my sun has set and I am left alone and destitute. . . ." "In the darkness of this grave rests the body of my father. All the treasures that came to me from ancient days are buried here. . . . Woe! I have lost my most precious possession. While you were with us I did not recognize his worth, I did not love him and honor him properly. I did not want to hear his chastising words. But I sinned, and here on this hallowed ground I will confess my iniquities. . . .") It is very hard to watch my mother and my sister, whispering and sobbing in the sunlight. Then I recite the memorial prayer for my father, and almost falter. I have the powerful sensation that we are not three, we are four. We are together, though one of us is in the ground. I thought again of the raft. During my childhood, my conception of my family was governed by a single metaphor: we were four of us on a raft. The raft was never far from my young mind. The image was owed, no doubt, to what I knew of my parent's experience of adversity and flight. It satisfied my sense that we were tossed and vulnerable, but also that we were irreversibly joined, that we were separated from those around us by the rough seas of memory, that we were all we had. These notions had mixed consequences for my attachment to the world. I know now that it would be a mistake to think that the family is all there is. At my father's grave, however, I think: this is not all there is, but this is all there is of *this*. We linger a little at the spot. My mother is evidently pleased by the serenity of the place. At last she has what she always wanted, for herself and her family: rites.

In my father's shul in Brooklyn this evening. Old men led by young men mourning old men. Today the commonplaces of their conversation move me. ("You spend so much time praying to grow old when you should be praying to stay healthy. . . .") Then a walk home along Sheepshead Bay, to let the pressure out of the day. I walked this mile with my father for thirty years. The neon lights across the bay cast gaudy colors on the water. Russian houses with guard dogs, Russian men fishing, Russian lovers, Russian kids doing drugs in an old Cadillac. A family of devoutly garbed Muslims out for a stroll. The old neighborhood, new. I wonder if these people chafe beneath this horizon as I chafed beneath it. But my chafing turned out to be my neighborhood's gift to me. These were the limitations that launched me. And all along the bay this evening I saw the launches of another time. A place belongs to those who have a use for it.

I brought to the cemetery the manual of supplications called *Ma'aneh Lashon*, or *The Responses of the Tongue*. It is a curious book. Its reputation for prolixity is deserved. The "prayer to be recited on father's grave" is a torrent of words that runs on for pages. These prayers are premised on a horror of silence. They are designed to keep the grieving talking. No nothingness, certainly not at the cemetery. The title page of the edition that I have with me says that these "memorial prayers and meditations" were "translated with many original additions by Prof. G. Selikovitch." Judging by the typeface and the Yiddish table of contents, I guess that the book was produced sometime in the 1910s or 1920s. But who was this unelliptical professor who made himself so inevitable? An encyclopedia provides the answer. Getzel Selikovitch was a Lithuanian Jew who studied Egyptology in Paris, served as Kitchener's translator on the expedition to relieve Gordon at Khartoum, translated Buddhist texts into Hebrew as *Torat Buddha*, translated part of the Egyptian *Book of the Dead* into Hebrew, composed an Arabic-Yiddish textbook (a utopian volume if ever there was one), and finally became a distinguished Yiddish journalist in New York, where he died in 1926. So there I was, with Kitchener in Long Island! (There is at least this to be said for the displacements of modern Jewish history: they bred biographies.)

Back in Washington, talking with my mother on the phone about our pilgrimage to Elmont. She says that she visited my father's grave "with anger, with more and more anger" about what was done to her family and to her people in Poland. She confesses that she stayed away from cemeteries for years, and was delinquent in her duty to visit the graves of cousins in Long Island, because she did not wish to unleash this anger. "It's not that they're not alive, it's that they didn't have a proper end." I cannot tell her to accept what happened, to make peace with it, to justify the judgment. "Blessed art Thou, O Lord our God, King of the Universe, who created you justly, who nourished and sustained you justly, who brought death upon you justly, who knows justly how many you are, and who will justly return and restore you to life. Blessed art Thou, O Lord our God, who quickens the dead." This is the blessing that one says upon entering a cemetery. It addresses the dead, as if to provide them with an analysis of what has befallen them. But I do not see how such an analysis can be addressed to my mother's dead. I do not see how such a peace can be made. I do not see how such a judgment can be justified. For my mother and the others, anger is the first obligation of grief.

Suddenly, in the middle of the day, in the middle of my work, I missed my father's voice.

Another timely gift from Jerusalem. It is a copy of *The Responses of the Tongue* printed by one Pinchas Moshe Balaban in 1859 in Lvov, or Lemberg. Lemberg was the metropolis of the region in Poland in which my parents grew up, and my mother went to high school there. (She saw Josephine Baker in Lemberg.) The years have made the paper of this old Lemberg book as soft as cashmere. The title page is framed by a lovely floral woodcut, and it informs me that the work is attributed pseudepigraphically to Rabbi Eleazar ben Arakh, who lived in the latter half of the first century. Why him? (I recall from my reading that he demonstrated a special skill at condolence, when his teacher Rabbi Yohanan ben Zakkai was mourning the death of his son.) And who wrote these prayers, anyway? A quick check in a work of bibliographical reference shows that *The Responses of the Tongue* was first published in Prague in 1615, and then again in 1620, and forty times more, in Hebrew and in Yiddish, before 1800. The language in the Lemberg edition is unlovely and awkward in its appropriation of Biblical and rabbinical texts, and the tone is vaguely kabbalistic. This edition is very different from the one that I took to Elmont. Prof. G. Selikovitch took extraordinary editorial liberties; his versions are almost unrecognizable.

The professor altered the text most profoundly with a single grammatical change. In the 1859 edition, these are not prayers for the dead, or prayers about the dead, but prayers to the dead. "Peace be upon you, and greetings, my master, my father, my teacher. . . . It is my duty to honor you in your life and in your death. . . . I have not done ill only to my own soul, but against you, too, I have sinned. It was my task to vindicate you, to raise you to a higher plane, but instead I have raised the lowly and lowered what is high. . . . So you and I will plead for mercy from on high. . . . Please, please do not stop praying for me, and also bestir the angel of my [astrological] sign to pray for me, and to hurry. . . ." Selikovitch excised the second-person and replaced it with the third-person. Thus his version of the prayer to be recited at the grave of one's father includes no address to the dead. It begins (the translation is his, too): "Here, in the gloom of the grave, rests the body of my father. Here lies buried the precious treasure that was mine of yore—my beloved parent who walked in righteousness and integrity before Thee." So Selikovitch sought to refine things philosophically. He twisted the old language to a conception of the cemetery that was less superstitious. ("The angel of my sign!") In his prayer, the son above ground does not chat with the father below ground. Instead, the son reckons with his own shortcomings. The intercession of the dead for the living is replaced by the intercession of the living for themselves. Mournful reflection passes into moral reflection, and it is the role of the dead to stimulate such a passage.

In the old version, these prayers reverse the religious situation of the kaddish: in the house of worship I intercede for the soul of my father, in the graveyard I ask that his soul intercede for me. I must say that I don't take kindly to the idea. I will speak of my father, since he is dead; but I will not speak to my father, since he is dead. (In my mind, though, where he lives, I will speak to him endlessly.) I will do my duty, but I will not be made a fool.

Spirituality is surrounded by superstition. It is a permanent siege.

Is there a way to be a good son and not run afoul of reason?

A member of our shul has lost his sister, and so he will now lead the prayers for a while. I'm a little peeved. Leading the prayers is a stronger fulfillment of my duty than saying the kaddish, or so it seems to me. But I'm also a little pleased. I can return to the ranks and sit at the back of the room and think my thoughts about the words that I hear from my lips. The problem is that my attention wanders. And that is not a small danger, spiritually. What a threat ordinary consciousness poses to the soul!

To fail spiritually, you do not have to fall. It is enough that you do not rise.

In an essay on Aby Warburg, I read of his refusal to say kaddish for his father. I had forgotten this episode. The piece sends me back to my old Warburg file, where I find a translation of Warburg's letter to his brother, written on January 30, 1910, the day after his father's death, in which he explains his refusal to attend a memorial service for his father: "Now *Minḥah* [the afternoon service] will be recited. The Mourner's Kaddish is a matter for the eldest son: it signifies not only an external act, but this public memorial service demonstrates acceptance of the moral inheritance. I will not make myself guilty of such public hypocrisy. No one is entitled to demand this of me. There remains the possibility that you would say the Mourner's Kaddish and I take part only in the general one. For anyone in the know this would be an even clearer abdication on my part as the chief moral heir of my father. . . . I ask you to understand my attitude and to explain it as best as you can to Mama, whom I have begged to be so good as to excuse me. I shall simply go on a journey or be ill; then the matter would look plausible to the outside world. No one will miss me anyhow: the *kehilla* [community] and the stock exchange always regard you as the eldest." And almost a month later, a few days before the service, Warburg wrote in his diary: "To rend one's clothes, to put on carpet slippers, to say Kaddish, morning and night, regardless of whether one is oneself again attacked by demons, proves: 'I do not abandon my family in these circumstances.' The kehilla wants more: I am to take part in a mourning service requiring my active participation in the cult, thereby putting in these circumstances a clan-like seal on the moral inheritance of the members of the family. There is no style in this, especially if one respects Father. My respect for him lies in my not hushing up the absolute antithesis of Weltanschauung through an external cultic act: for I am dissident. . . . My character of Dissident must be respected just as much as the character of the Orthodox."

Years ago, when I studied Warburg and the great melodrama of fathers and sons in the Jewish world of Wilhelmine Germany, I was fascinated by this defiance. The rebellion seemed heroic, even if it was pretty conventional. Now I find Warburg's sentiments repugnant. They are so self-regarding, so adolescent in their infatuation with sedition, so absurdly confident about philosophical opinions whose origins are transparently psychological. "I do not abandon my family in these circumstances": and why should one abandon one's family in such circumstances? "My character of Dissident must be respected": this, by one of the most spoiled young men in Germany! His family not only respected him, his family indulged him. And on what grounds, exactly, was Warburg rejecting what he called "the cult"? Surely not on the grounds that it offended reason. After all, he fled from reason straight into a lifelong cult of irrationality. Perhaps he hated Judaism on the opposite grounds, for its rationality, which is what the German Jews liked to find in it; but then he didn't know too much about Judaism, and was merely preferring the unreason of others to the unreason of his own. Warburg has no tolerance for those who recite the kaddish, for they do so "regardless of whether one is oneself attacked by demons." He wants demons. (He got them.)

"Regardless of whether one is oneself attacked by demons." Fine, let us have demons. But they are waiting for you in shul. A regular commemoration of one's father is a regular invitation to one's demons. Kaddish is not for the faint of heart. The ritual memorialization of a parent does not bring only stability. It brings also instability. Warburg would have loved it.

The Sabbath departs sweetly this week. Walking to shul for the afternoon prayer, I come upon gospel practice in the church up the street. A few voices, men's and women's, rise into the fetid August air. A black man with white hair is high on a ladder with a paintbrush, touching up the front of the old brick house. He sees me pause before the church and eyes me suspiciously; then he sees my yarmulke and smiles. After the prayers, the rabbi gives an interesting class about the conditions under which a Jew is legally required to save a person in mortal danger, and also to intervene on behalf of a person's endangered property: another instance of the unlibertarian character of Jewish law, as the rabbi trenchantly presents it. After his class, we partake of the "third meal." The food is better than usual, and the room is full of high spirits. Then the evening prayers. Out with hallowed time, in with unhallowed time. This is followed by the blessing of the New Moon, when the doors of the shul open and emit a couple of dozen Jewish men onto the sidewalk, fervently keening at the moon. We are greeted by stares. I cannot restrain my laughter. The archaism of this prayer has offended many Jews for many centuries—it is an entreaty to the moon!—but until now I had not seen its comic side. I see it now, in the amazed faces of the passersby. In Georgetown, wereJews!

I have not forgotten the father of the kaddish. I have been rummaging for Nahum Ha'Pakuli, but I have been coming up empty. I ask the rabbi to avail me of the diabolical CD-ROM in his possession, the one with the Babylonian Talmud and the Jerusalem Talmud and many, many rabbinical texts, entire continents of the tradition, all of which may be unlocked by "key words." (I have no doubt that this technology will debase knowledge and reduce these materials, like all the materials that it holds, to the status of information.) The results of his search are also meager. There is not a single mention of Nahum Ha'Pakuli in ancient rabbinical literature. But there is Simon Ha'Pakuli. He is mentioned twice in the Talmud, as the man who edited, or put into some sort of official order, the Amidah prayer, or the "eighteen blessings" that are the centerpiece of the Jewish liturgy. This was an important contribution. Rashi explains that the Aramaic word *pakuli* is the equivalent, in French, of *coton,* or "cotton." Cotton, I guess, was Simon's business. So here are the two Pakulis, Nahum the Rescuer and Simon the Cottonworker. What do they have in common? The one earned his reputation with prayer, the other with the redaction of prayer. And there may be a chronological link, too. The one was put to liturgical work by Rabbi Akiva, the other was put to liturgical work by Rabbi Gamaliel; and Rabbi Akiva was the younger contemporary of Rabbi Gamaliel. Could the rescuer and the redactor have been the same man?

What is the history of the mourner's kaddish among the Sephardim? It is not mentioned in Maimonides' twelfth-century code of law. In the responsa of Isaac ben Jacob Alfasi, Maimonides' great precursor in codification, I have discovered a ruling that suggests that the Judaism of North Africa and Spain did not look favorably upon such prayer. Alfasi lived in the eleventh century, and spent most of his life in Fez, until he was forced to flee to Spain, where he became the acknowledged master, and died in 1103. The text of Alfasi's responsum is terse: "Answer: The kaddish is not recited after the burial of the dead until a verse from Scripture is read, such as 'But he, being full of compassion, will forgive their iniquity' or 'He will swallow up death in victory' or similarly pertinent verses." Was there someone who wished to transform the kaddish into a prayer for the dead, into a funeral prayer in its own right? Alfasi is forbidding it. His point is that the burial itself does not qualify as an occasion for kaddish, which requires the cover of Scripture. He is insisting that the kaddish keep its old function, as the peroration to the Divine Word, at the grave, too.

And there is another piece of evidence from Alfasi's younger contemporary Abraham bar Hiyya, a theologian and a man of science in Spain who died sometime around 1136. Abraham composed a work of popular philosophy called *Hegyon Ha'Nefesh Ha'Atsuvah*, or *Reflections of the Sad Soul*, the first work of Jewish philosophy that was written in Hebrew, and in his concluding chapter on eschatological matters he observed, moralistically: "Let it not occur to you that you may repent after you die, for if you regret in the next world a thousand regrets for the evil deeds that you did in this world, it will avail you nothing. . . . And so, too, he who thinks that he will profit from all the deeds that his children and his people do for him after his death, and all the prayers that they pray for him, is thinking foolish thoughts. In the eyes of all the sages and all the philosophers, this is a vain hope. . . . We have not found a passage in the Torah from which we may conclude that the actions of the living in this world acquit the dead, except in one case, taught by reason and attested to by the Torah, which is the case of the man who stole something and did not return it before he died: he is punished for this in the next world, but if the stolen property is returned to its owners after his death, then he deserves to be relieved of his punishment in the next world, if he regretted his deed while he was still alive. There is something in this world, though, that does bring credit to the dead, according to the sages, and that is the study of Torah, if it is taught by somebody to whom he taught it before he died, and is taught in his name."

Abraham is making a tough point. Prayer for the dead, in his view, constitutes an interference in the workings of justice. The living should not intrude upon the judgment of the dead. A man lived as he lived. No amount of posthumous eloquence should be allowed to extenuate the facts of his case. (The exception for the dead thief is made in the Talmud, though it is not much of an exception, since the return of property that was stolen by an impenitent thief does not affect his fate.) Of course, Abraham is being tough not on the dead, but on the living: he fears the relaxation of moral and religious life that may result from the certainty that those who live after you will fix things for you. From Abraham's text, I conclude that in this Jewish culture there was a time-honored opposition to kaddish-like prayer. Eventually it must have yielded to the influence of the north.

It heartens me to hear from Abraham that study may accomplish what prayer may not accomplish. This confirms one of my oldest prejudices.

The funeral kaddish appears, of course, in the Babylonian and North African and Spanish traditions. Hai Gaon's responsum to the rabbis of Fez prescribes a particular text for the funeral kaddish. And Nahmanides, in Catalonia in the thirteenth century, describes a received "order of customs" for the funeral, and for mourning in the aftermath of the funeral, which includes the funeral kaddish, in the longer version that promises the new world and the resurrection of the dead; and then he observes that "in our day these customs are obsolete, as they were not based on any strict obligation, but were merely practiced by the generations." In his own day, he testifies, there is a simpler protocol, and it retains the funeral kaddish. Nahmanides cites the minor Talmudic tractate *Soferim,* or *Scribes,* as his source (no doubt he accepted it as Talmudic text, though in fact it was composed a few hundred years later), noting that it limits the recitation of this kaddish to the mourning "for a student and an exegete." Thus, on the day of the funeral, "after the worship, in the morning and in the evening, the mourner's blessing over the wine is uttered in the presence of the worshipers, and after this blessing the kaddish is recited as it was recited after the burial of the dead, and [the passage about] the new world and so on is not said [in the kaddish] except for a student and an exegete. The reason is that the new world is not invoked for ordinary persons, but only for one whose deeds substantiate that he is worthy of the resurrection of the dead. And it is similarly the law that in the cemetery, after the burial, this [the resurrection kaddish] is not said [for ordinary persons]." But this is obnoxious! An expression of elitism is not especially appropriate to a ritual that marks the way of all flesh. All die equally, and all should be mourned equally. And so law was softened by custom. "It became the custom," Nahmanides concludes, "that it [the resurrection kaddish] is uttered for everybody, even for women, so as to avert conflict, since the generation is not all alike."

"Even for women": a grudging impulse toward fairness is still an impulse toward fairness, I suppose.

All this is not the mourner's kaddish as it developed in Ashkenaz. It is only the liturgy of the funeral, and it is not significantly different from the funeral kaddish mentioned in the Rashi literature prior to the development of the mourner's kaddish in Ashkenaz by his heirs. By the end of the thirteenth century, however, there is evidence of the mourner's kaddish in Spain. In 1291, Bahya ben Asher of Saragossa, in his commentary on the Pentateuch, mentions an obscure ancient source in his gloss on a verse in Deuteronomy and writes: "From this we learn that the devotions [*hakdashot*] that the living are accustomed to dedicating on behalf of the dead profit the dead—all the more so if the son makes such a devotion [*makdish*] on behalf of his father, for he is the father's merit, since the son partakes of the fruit of the father. Hence the regulation that the son says kaddish, or any blessing recited publicly in the house of worship, on his father's behalf, as they recounted in legend in the tale of Rabbi Akiva." That is the mourner's kaddish, no doubt about it. Abraham bar Hiyya's old aversion to prayer for the dead seems to have been overcome.

Moving along my bookshelves, I note that the mourner's kaddish does not appear in the great study on the liturgy that David ben Joseph Abudarham produced in Seville in 1340; but a half a century or so later there is more evidence that the Ashkenazic innovation has taken root in the Sephardic world. The influential jurist Isaac ben Sheshet Perfet flourished in Spain in the last decades of the fourteenth century, and in 1391, as a consequence of the anti-Jewish riots, he fled to North Africa, and died in Algiers in 1408. In one of his responsa, he tells the story of Akiva and the condemned man. This was the question to which the story was his answer: "It was the custom in Spain that a man whose father died would recite the rabbis' kaddish for the entirety of his year of mourning, based on the tale about the encounter with his father, who had met his judgment and was black as coal. I saw this story in that country, but I do not remember it. And may my master also apprise me as to its source, so that I may know the [Torah's] ways of pleasantness and its paths to peace." Clearly this question was addressed to Perfet by a fellow refugee from Spain, and the testimony of this displaced Jew could not be more plain. Perfet's reply gives his own sense of the provenance of the custom. "It is not in the Talmud that we have," he writes, "though perhaps it is in one of the midrashic works." He proceeds to quote in its entirety the entry on the mourner's kaddish in the book of customs by Aaron ben Jacob Ha'Cohen of Lunel, the Provençal scholar of the late thirteenth and early fourteenth centuries, who quotes Meir of Rothenburg's more or less contemporary ruling that "it is a commandment to say the kaddish for his father and his mother, though he is not to say kaddish for his mother during the lifetime of his father, if his father feels strictly about it." (The latter qualification is itself evidence that the mourner's kaddish was a familiar institution in Germany in the latter half of the thirteenth century, to which stipulations about its practice were already attached.) This is followed by Meir's abridged version of the tale of Akiva. In Perfet's understanding, then, the mourner's kaddish was an innovation of the community in Germany that came to the community in Spain by way of the community in Provence.

It is worth noting that Perfet was asked not about the mourner's kaddish, but about the "kaddish of the rabbis" as it came to be employed for the purposes of mourning. (The "kaddish of the rabbis," remember, is the oldest version of the kaddish, the one that was designed for the conclusion of an academic discourse, the one that calls for blessings "upon the scholars and their students and their students' students, and upon all who occupy themselves with the study of Torah, in this place and in every place.") Still, here it is recited by the mourner in Spain, precisely as Alfasi did not want it to be recited. It is also worth noting that, even though Perfet was asked for the basis of the recitation of the rabbis' kaddish by mourners, the sources that he adduced in his answer refer to the mourners' recitation of kaddish generally; and of the "concluding kaddish," the one at the end of the services; and of the public reading from the prophetic books that follows the reading from the Five Books of Moses in shul on the Sabbath; and "there are also mourners who lead the entirety of the evening service on Saturday night after the Sabbath, since that is the hour when the souls of the sinners return to Gehenna, from which they rested on the Sabbath." In citing all these practices, Perfet may have wished to expand the liturgical role of the mourner that his Spanish correspondent had described. In any event, the mourner's kaddish had arrived. Indeed, by the middle of the fifteenth century, not long before the Jews were expelled from Spain, the scholars Joseph Abudarham and Isaac de Leon were complaining about the spread of the custom of allowing boys to say kaddish for their parents at the end of the Sabbath, and doing their best to uproot this alien practice.

Today I became a Washington insider. The rabbi gave me a key to the shul. Now I can come early or stay late. I have a haven. I like being alone with my religion. And this key in my pocket feels almost like a reward: I spent years in the study of my tradition precisely so that I will never be locked out.

A small sting, in Nahmanides. His text for the funeral kaddish is pretty much the text that we use, the text that I read at my father's funeral—except that there are a few more words. Having appealed for the renewal of the world and the resurrection of the dead and the rebuilding of Jerusalem and the restoration of worship in the Temple, the mourner at the funeral portrayed by Nahmanides appeals also for another outcome: "May we and all our brethren in Israel be spared destruction and captivity and death." Finally, a version of the kaddish that mentions death! In a way, these words provide relief from the words that preceded them. For the resurrection of the dead is finally a denial of death—the most literal and dogmatic and complete denial of death that is imaginable. Perhaps that is why I was so unaffected by those words after the body of my father was lowered into the ground. At that moment, the reality of death was the only reality. To be sure, the mention of death in this version of the kaddish still refers to the hope for resurrection; but oh, to have been given the word "death" to utter then and there! From Nahmanides' discussion, it seems that this language was geonic in origin. It appears in a responsum by Hai Gaon that Nahmanides quotes elsewhere in his book. And he reports that it was still used in his day. Why in the world did it fade away?

I confess to a friend that I am tiring of this prayer for the dead that leaves out the dead. Magnified, sanctified: these flatteries of heaven are grating on me. They are starving my sorrow. Do you know Jabotinsky's explanation of the kaddish? my friend asks. Jabotinsky's explanation of the kaddish! I am startled. My friend says that Jabotinsky made a similar objection to the obsequies of the mourner, and then met the objection with a philosophical fantasy. He promises to provide me with the passage.

My father revered Jabotinsky. In 1933, Jabotinsky visited Stryj, my father's town in Poland, and my father never forgot his visit. (He liked to annoy me with his recollection of his hero, who was not my hero.) Also in 1933, I now learn, Jabotinsky began to publish, in a Russian journal in Paris, a novel about the Jews of Odessa in the early decades of the century. It appeared three years later as *The Five,* a chronicle of the Milgrom family and its five children. (Some years later it was translated into Hebrew.) Near the end of the book, in an account of the funeral of the eldest daughter, who dies in a fire, the narrator denounces the kaddish with a humanist's indignation. "We have beautiful prayers," he remarks about the liturgy of the funeral. "But there was an additional prayer that was recited, a strange prayer, a prayer that made no sense. It did not speak of the loss even once. Instead it was full of praises and exaltations of the murdering God. When I heard it, I bit my lips with rage and said to myself: I would stone you, Lord, if a stone could reach you, if you were not hiding so far away!"

There is more in this fine, free-thinking voice. A day or so later, the narrator visits the mourners. The grieving father "was sitting on the floor of the salon, in the customary way, unshaven in the manner of mourners, and reading the Book of Job, in accordance with Jewish law, from a thick Bible with a Russian translation." The old man talks about Job, and then, "after a brief silence, he began to speak about the prayer that had irritated me at the cemetery." The old man, too, censures the mourner's kaddish. He, too, is offended by its servility, by its indifference to human despondency: "This prayer called the 'kaddish,' it is the mourner's principal prayer, it is said during all the days of mourning, and according to our law it is enough, there is no need to say anything more. And what does it say? 'Magnified and sanctified may His great Name be. . . .' Only this. Nothing more. Not a word about the dead, not a hint about what has happened. Not even 'I surrender to your holy will.' Just a bunch of silly words: 'Blessed and praised and glorified' and five or so more compliments of that kind. I'm sorry, but it reminds me of what Boris Mavrikovich wrote to Anna Mikhailovna from Italy: 'Dear, Beloved, Honorable, Esteemed Anyatochka. . . .' How can God stomach it? All these bowings and scrapings should make him nauseous!"

But the old man has not concluded his analysis of the kaddish. His impiety does not have the last word. "Still, the truth is that this prayer is not at all nonsense. It was designed for a purpose. He was damning the devil.
—He? Damning the devil?
—I mean he who composed the prayer: Rabbi Akiva, if I'm not mistaken. A very shrewd man, actually. This is what he was thinking. A disaster occurs. A man stands at the open grave, rather like a ruined merchant. He has lost everything. He has no reason to live. He stands at the edge of the pit and presents his bill, his accounting for the damages, to the Lord

of the Universe. He is furious. He shakes his fists and he vilifies the heavens. And next to him, behind the tombstone nearby, Satan squats and lies in wait for this moment, when the man at the grave explodes with curses, when he declares openly, once and for all: 'Excuse me, Lord of the Universe, but you are capricious and cruel and coarse. And also stupid. Be gone! I refuse to know you!' This is what Satan has been waiting for. As soon as he hears these words, he takes them down carefully and precisely, and with his transcript of blasphemy he races to the Garden of Eden, and addresses God: 'See what you get for your goodness! And see from whom: from a Jew! From your own agent and representative on earth! So go quietly, old man. I am in charge now.' This is the devil's plan. But the businessman standing at the grave, he is no fool, he guesses Satan's game. He asks himself: 'Will I really delight the devil? Will I really allow evil to rule the world? No! It shall not be! I'll show him, damn him'—and at this point—now do you understand?—the man begins to list all those praises of God, to run through all those compliments. Without reason: but who needs reasons? It is reason enough to lay the devil low, to drive him into dust, to strike him until he is a heap of bones. To say, in other words: 'You, Satan, keep out of this! Whatever grievances I have against God—that is our business. We have been partners since ancient times. Somehow we will settle the manner between ourselves. But don't you poke your nose into this.' Now do you understand? It is the same idea as Job's: God and the Jew are partners."

So the man with the kaddish has a mission. He speaks up against darkness, against nothingness. This, too, is humanism, with or without God.

The struggle against evil is a greater struggle than the struggle against God.

The grieving, the aggrieved. They are the same, until reflection intervenes. Reflection parts the assertions of grief from the assertions of grievance, so that mourning can transcend its own narrowness. The world cannot be understood from the standpoint of a personal injury.

In the company of death, subjectivity is wild. So subjectivity must be tamed. The taming of subjectivity is the work of the kaddish. Three times daily, the inner perspective of the mourner is unmagnified, unsanctified. Psychology is belittled.

Objectivity is death's gift.

A messenger comes to the mourner's house. "Come," says the messenger, "you are needed." "I cannot come," says the mourner, "my spirit is broken." "That is why you are needed," says the messenger.

After the evening prayers I was overcome by a feeling of revulsion at myself. All this fidelity, all this reflection on fidelity: I am becoming sanctimonious. My gloomy year in shul is turning into an occasion for self-congratulation. But I have not forgotten how I have lived. The fulfillment of this duty cannot erase what I know about myself. A good student is not the same thing as a good man. A good son is not the same thing as a good man.

The man who carves the gravestone calls. He needs the verse from Psalms for my father's stone. I am finding many verses in which David thanks God for saving him, but they are all in the first-person singular; and the inscription on this stone must refer to the fate of more than a single individual. I scour Psalms for gratitude in the plural. In chapter 34, verse

18, I find it. Six Hebrew words, meaning: "They cried out and God heard them and from all their troubles he rescued them." Perfect! The words are plain, vernacular, direct. They are unusually artless for this great poet, but I am not looking for art. (And I say these words every Sabbath, in the morning prayer.) I fax the words to my sister, who likes them. She shows them to my mother. My mother approves. This is her epitaph, too.

VI

Bera mezakeh aba. The son acquits the father. Or, the son vindicates the father. Or, the son vouches for the father. Or, the son shows merit in the father. This is the principle on which the mourner's kaddish is founded. It is stated in the Talmud in a discussion of the wicked kings of Judah who are denied their portions in the world to come. The rabbis wonder why the name of Amon was not included on the list of the damned. Amon was a king of Judah in the middle of the seventh century B.C.E., and he is generally considered to have been the worst transgressor king of all the transgressor kings. In the Talmudic text before me, Amon is accused, among other things, of sleeping with his mother. (The mother: "Have you pleasure, then, from the place whence you came?" The son: "Do you think I did this for any reason except to anger my Maker?" Amon's incest was nothing personal. He was making a philosophical point.) Amon is said to have been more evil even than his evil father Menasseh—and yet the father's name appears on the list of the damned, and not the son's. Why not? The answer is: "Out of respect for Josiah." Josiah was the son of Amon, and a righteous king. He presided over a great religious revival. And so Amon is vindicated by Josiah. The father is acquitted by the son. Still, a problem remains. Why was Menasseh's name not omitted from the list "out of respect for Hezekiah"? Menasseh was a wicked king who had a righteous father, Hezekiah; but he is nonetheless denied his portion in the world to come. The rabbis' answer is: *bera mezakeh aba, aba lo mezakeh bera.* The son acquits the father, the father does not acquit the son.

I must record Rashi's amplification of the mother's angry question to the son who had violated her. "Have you pleasure, then, from the place whence you came?" Rashi explains: "A man is satiated by the place from which he came and does not desire pleasure from such a place." This is not merely an observation about the nature of incest. It is also an observation about the nature of home. There are many reasons to have a home, but the pursuit of pleasure is not one of them.

The son acquits the father, the father does not acquit the son. The rabbis drive the point home. From a verse in Deuteronomy, they deduce that "Abraham is powerless to save Ishmael, Isaac is powerless to save Esau." As patriarchs, Abraham and Isaac were the founders of a people; but as fathers, they could do nothing to save their recalcitrant sons. I have found another version of this reading, and it adds something: "The fathers do not deliver the sons, Abraham does not deliver Ishmael, nor does Isaac deliver Esau. But [from the verse in Deuteronomy] we learn only that the fathers do not deliver the sons. From what do we learn that brothers do not deliver brothers? From [the verse in Psalms] 'none of them can by any means redeem his brother.'" So I am not my brother's keeper, exactly; or at least that is not the whole story. The whole story is that my brother must also keep himself.

It is a few hours later, and I have been wondering why the rabbis insist that the father cannot vouch for the son. It is a prescription of pain for the fathers, who love their sons. I leaf through the folio volume before me, searching for a commentator who was similarly vexed. I find one. He is Samuel Edels, the commentator on Talmudic law and Talmudic legend who lived in Poland in the early seventeenth century. "There are some wicked people who do not wish their sons to be like themselves, but wish them to be righteous—and so the son acquits the father by demonstrating that the father, his wickedness notwithstanding, castigated him and pointed him toward a good path. But the father does not acquit the son, since the son had a teacher from whom he could learn, but he did not learn." This is clever. What worries Edels is the fate of the son of a wicked father. Were the father to acquit the son, because he is like the son, then the son could not be acquitted, because he is like the father! Yet it is not always the case that the wicked wishes his wickedness upon his son. Sometimes he wishes his son a good life, a better life than his own. This makes the wicked father incompletely wicked—and *that* is the merit that the son of the wicked may adduce for his father's acquittal. (What charitable casuistry!) The incompleteness of the father's wickedness also returns the son to his own resources, to his own freedom. For the son had a teacher from whom he could learn. Did he learn? That was up to him. Thus the character of the father cannot determine the fate of the son. The son is forever a moral agent. In this, he resembles the father. And what is the difference, really, between an incompletely wicked man and an ordinary man? I conclude, following Edels, that the father is guilty and not guilty, and the son is guilty and not guilty, and that is why they can depend on each other. End of today's lesson.

One of the most dreaded eventualities in a man's life has overtaken me, and what do I do? I plunge into books! I can see that this is bizarre. It is also Jewish. Anyway, it is what I know how to do.

Menasseh ben Israel, on the principle that the son acquits the father: "The son acquits the father with ten things, and they are: closing his eyes, washing his body, shrouding him, burying him, justifying the judgment, kaddish, charity, fasting, a candle, a eulogy." I came a few minutes too late to close my father's eyes, but I kissed his head, on which I felt the creeping chill. I pulled the sheet over him, and I sat with him after the loosing of his spirit. I justified the judgment, in the language of the liturgy and in my heart, at his freshly covered grave, an hour or so after I delivered his eulogy. I am saying kaddish. I am giving charity. I am not fasting. May my book be my candle.

A morning haze. Nothing is lucid. I stumble over the words of the kaddish. (Not the only time, lately.) At the teahouse the lines in my book blur and I spend most of the hour staring into the street. Another sinking spell.

In *Yesh Noḥalin,* or *The Bequest,* by Abraham Horowitz, a book-length ethical will published in Prague in 1615, I find a simpler solution for the problem that perplexed his contemporary Samuel Edels. Horowitz's interpretation is the opposite of Edels's interpretation. "It seems to me," he writes, in his discussion of the kaddish, "that the reason that the son acquits the father and the father does not acquit the son is this: the soul of the father is in the soul of the son, he is bone of his bones and flesh of his flesh. Indeed, the rabbis said that the son is 'his father's leg.' They also said that there are three elements in a man, and one of them is the father. Thus all the ritual observances and all the good deeds of the son derive directly from the father. But the worth and the piety of the father—on what basis would it reflect well on the son? This is easy to understand." His father's leg? This is a concept in the law of inheritance, according to which an heir steps into the precise position of his parent. But Horowitz is extending it beyond its legal meaning, into a general rule of generational identity: where the son walks, there the father walks. (The three elements in a man, in that Talmudic passage, are God, the father, and the mother.)

Horowitz thinks that this is easy to understand. I don't think so. Goodness is not so tidily transmitted from generation to generation. The son always interferes with his patrimony, for better or worse. Moreover, the son of a good man deserves as much praise for his accomplishments as the son of a bad man. It is not even the case that the son of a good man has an advantage over the son of a bad man: I have known the children of good people, and I have observed that it is rough to be raised in a house of virtue, too. Horowitz empties the son's kaddish of its significance, since he diminishes the autonomy of the son. In his view, kaddish is a surrogacy, and the son is a medium through which the father is acting on his own behalf. This is nonsense. I am not my father's surrogate, I am my father's son. I am my own man. And I am unlike my father. —A few pages later Horowitz suggests that "when the son, with his good deeds, causes the world to admire the father and to say: happy is he who sired such a son, happy is he who raised such a son . . . it is as if the father is not dead." But the father is dead.

My father was a troublesome man. Some years ago, I was complaining about him to a friend, and my friend advised me that sooner or later a reversal takes place, that there comes a moment when the parent becomes the child and the child becomes the parent. This was good advice. It helped me to detach myself more effectively; and without such detachment I would have been useless to my father and to my family during the hard last years of his life and during the season of his death. I think that kaddish is the perfect symbol of such a reversal. Suddenly the chain of transmission turns around. *He* needs *me.* The pathos of kaddish lies in the magnitude of the helplessness of the dead, in the magnitude of their dependence upon the living. The commentary to Abraham Horowitz's book was written, appropriately, by his son, and on his discussion of the principle that the son acquits the father, Jacob Horowitz comments: "As the parent has mercy on his children, so must the son have mercy on the forlorn soul of his father and his mother." There is the reversal.

My father was an immoderate man. About my welfare, certainly, he was immoderate: it was either the best or the worst, there was no such thing as a small danger or a small disappointment when it was his son who faced it, it was always a matter of salvation. The extremism of my father's love for me sometimes made it pointless to go to him for help. My trouble would only scare him, and I would wind up having to help *him*. But he did so much for me, he did so much for me.

This is Horowitz's explanation of the mourner's kaddish: "The father who makes the [proper] bequest to his children will enjoy the next world for this reason . . . : since the sons [who do good works] are acting on the words of the father, who commanded them to act justly and in accordance with the law, their merit will redound to the benefit of their instructing father. As our sages said, 'the son acquits the father.' That is to say, the son vindicates the father in the world to come even when he does something good of his own volition, without having been ordered to do so by his father. And the same may be seen in the legend about Rabbi Akiva." Horowitz gives the legend, and concludes: "From this we see that when the living recite the kaddish and [the prayer] 'Bless the Lord who is blessed!,' the dead will be forgiven, and the soul of the one will live by virtue of the other." —I'm late for work.

Horowitz also has some practical advice concerning the kaddish: "Not everybody is ready and able to lead all the prayers and the kaddish and 'Bless the Lord' at all times, and not everybody knows how to chant before a crowd and a congregation, and so the early sages established something that would be equally available to all: that at least this kaddish may be said at the end of the worship, for it is easy to do, and everybody, even a small boy, knows how. But of course every man who is learned, or even a little learned, will lead the afternoon, evening, and morning prayers as often as he can, for the more he leads the prayers and the more he recites the kaddish, the better it will be for the souls of the dead. Even if he does not have a good voice, he should stand before the congregation and lead the prayers and not be embarrassed. Those who lack the strength or the knowledge to lead the entire service should at least lead [the concluding prayers], for in this way one acquits his dead father more vigorously and more grandly than by merely saying the kaddish." Thus the kaddish is not highly prized by Horowitz. It is, strictly speaking, the least that a son can do. Three hundred years or so after its founding, the mourner's kaddish is still considered an expedient, a low fulfillment of duty, a concession to the ignorance or the incompetence of many mourners.

I returned from the teahouse and sleep returned to my eyes, but not in a friendly way. It came like water under the door. I slept desperately for hours.

Here is Horowitz's characterization of the mourner's kaddish: "This kaddish is not a prayer that the son prays for the father before God, that He raise him from the lower depths. It is, instead, a privilege and a good deed that accrues to the dead when his son publicly sanctifies the Name of God [by reciting the kaddish] and the congregation responds. . . . And this is all the more the case when the son fulfills any of God's commandments because his father enjoined him to fulfill it." What a fine, unmorbid view. I like the idea that the kaddish is not a prayer for the dead. And I like the recontextualization of the kaddish in Jewish life, so that it is no longer as pivotal an instrument of identity as modern Jews, in the poverty of their religious means, make it to be. Horowitz nicely restores the proportions.

At the teahouse, a scandal! In 1909, David de Sola Pool, a British Jew who went on to become one of the most important rabbis in America, published a monograph in Leipzig, called *The Old Jewish-Aramaic Prayer: The Kaddish,* an old-fashioned "literary and historical investigation" of the text of the kaddish in its many versions and variants. De Sola Pool included only a short appendix on the adaptation of the kaddish to the needs of the mourner. In these scanty pages, I read this intriguing sentence from Abraham Horowitz's book: "The father should command his sons to fulfill a specific commandment [after his death] and if they fulfill it, it is more highly regarded than the kaddish. And since this is the case, the father is not without recourse if he has a daughter." This gladdens me. I have been admiring the women whom I see insisting on their right to say kaddish, and saying it; and here is an authority whom they can use. To be sure, Horowitz has not granted a dispensation for women to recite the kaddish; but here is an egalitarian alternative to the kaddish, "more highly regarded than the kaddish," of which women may avail themselves, too. Horowitz has explicitly stated that women have the obligation, and the privilege, of participating in the memorialization of their parents. Now, the scandal: I have been using an edition of Horowitz's book that appeared in Manchester in 1993. I scour Horowitz's introduction, which includes his general discussion of filial duty, for the tolerant passage that de Sola Pool cited. And it is nowhere to be found. The editor has cut it out! In its place there is a scar that robs the text of its coherence. Incoherence is less to be feared, I guess, than a few words of encouragement for these impertinent Jewish women. I am disgusted by this bowdlerization of the text. It is cowardly. It is a sign of decadence.

May a woman say kaddish? It is a controversial question. It sounds to some like a feminist provocation. But ask the question differently. May a daughter say kaddish? Suddenly the controversy disappears, at least for me. If you deny the kaddish to a daughter, then you do not understand the kaddish. The kaddish is not an obligation of gender. It is an obligation of descent. This is not about men, this is about sons. This is not about women, this is about daughters.

I listened to some old recordings by Heifetz today, to sweeten my afternoon; and they conjured up my father. He was not a very musical man, but he loved the violin. No surprise there: it is the instrument that tugs the best.

In shul in New York, a woman comes to say kaddish. I see her every time I'm here. She enters quietly and glides swiftly into the women's section, which is behind a wall of glass. I wonder if she can hear the prayers. Her face shows awkwardness and determination. She is not unwelcome here, but her presence is a challenge, an act of contention. Still, she has not come here to make a criticism. She has come here to mourn a parent, and to pray. I admire her. I'm also afraid that she will catch me looking at her, and misunderstand me. She is here to repeal a certain kind of male regard.

"An unusual thing happened in Amsterdam, and was widely known there." So begins a short and stirring responsum by Yair ben Hayyim Bacharach, the influential Talmudist and jurist in Germany in the seventeenth century. "A man died without leaving a son, and prior to his death he requested that, for the twelve months after his death, ten men should be retained to study in his house, and at the conclusion of their studying his daughter should say the kaddish. And the scholars and officers of the congregation did nothing to stop her." What a clever man! He anticipated controversy, and gave his daughter cover: her kaddish was to be said after study; and it was to be said in the presence of ten men; and it was to be said at home, not in the house of worship. The man wanted a kaddish and he got one.

Bacharach's analysis of this woman's kaddish is extraordinary. He condemns it, but in a way that has the consequence of legitimating it. This is how he begins his opinion: "Even though there is no proof that would contradict it—for women, too, are commanded to sanctify the Name, and there was a quorum of ten Jewish men present—and even though the tale of Rabbi Akiva, which is the basis for the recitation of kaddish by mourners, speaks only of a son [whose kaddish may redeem his father], it is reasonable to assume that a daughter, too, may bring benefit and calm to the soul of the dead, for she, too, is his progeny." Splendid! But alas, there is more. "All this notwithstanding, we must be concerned that, as a consequence [of allowing the daughter to recite the kaddish], the force of the customs of Israel, which are also Torah, will be weakened, and everybody will build his own altar on the basis of his own thinking, and will treat the words of the rabbis with derision and jest, and come to scorn them." For this reason, the daughter's kaddish must be prohibited.

I am not surprised by the prohibition, but what strikes me about Bacharach's prohibition is that it is not based on a substantive objection to the kaddish that was said by the woman in Amsterdam. Quite the contrary. His responsum affirms that, from the standpoint of what may be done for the soul of the father or the soul of the mother, the daughter is the equal of the son. Instead Bacharach appeals generally to the traditionalism of Jewish life, and warns of the danger of innovation. (Amsterdam was a haven for the crypto-Jews of Spain and Portugal, who brought many confusing practices with them, and so the defense of tradition in Amsterdam was sometimes deemed especially urgent.) This is fine, but it is also weak. For innovation is not only a danger for Judaism, it is also a reality for Judaism. The history of traditional Jewish life is the history of new customs as well as old customs, of creativity as well as conservation. New rituals abound. Of course, a new ritual may be contested; but Bacharach has already conceded the grounds on which the new ritual of the daughter's kaddish may be contested.

Bacharach proceeds to an analogy. He compares the daughter's kaddish with the custom of bowing at certain points in the Eighteen Blessings, the prayer that is the centerpiece of Jewish worship. The Talmud explicitly identifies the points at which one must bow, and then notes that "if someone wishes to bow at the end of every blessing and at the beginning of every blessing, he is instructed not to bow." Here, then, is another instance of ritual initiative, of the zeal of a devout Jew who wishes to exceed his or her instructions. Bacharach cites the comment of the Tosafists on this Talmudic passage: "But why not let him bow more? What is the problem?" A good question. And the Tosafists have an answer: "The problem is that he should not uproot the words of the sages, because it must not be said that anybody may invent his own stringencies. There is no rabbinical enactment [for more bowing]. Also, there is a concern about insolence." Bacharach means to say that the daughter who insists on her kaddish is like the supplicant who insists on bowing and bowing and bowing: her enthusiasm must be restrained.

Bacharach foresees an objection to his analogy, and he meets it. "Should you suggest that the case [of bowing during prayer] was a stipulation of our early sages and appears in the Talmud [and therefore is a stricter matter than the case of the mourner's kaddish, which does not appear in the Talmud, and therefore may be permitted to women in mourning], it must be replied that all the more must this custom, which is not in the Talmud but originates nonetheless in the midrash, be strengthened, like all the customs of Israel. . . . The rabbis often provided more protection for their own enactments than for the Torah." And therefore the daughter's kaddish must be rejected. But then Bacharach cripples his own analogy! In the case of bowing, "it does not say that they prevent him from bowing, it says only that they instruct him not to bow; and it does not even say that it is undignified, which is why, in my view, it is not mentioned by Maimonides in his code." So the Talmudic precedent seems like a mild precedent. The daughter's kaddish, too, is not undignified. Is it, therefore, permitted? No, not quite. The language of the rabbis was mild, Bacharach explains, because they were describing the enthusiasm of an individual, the idiosyncracies of personal piety, "and so the others will not take a lesson from it. They will conclude only that this man [who keeps bowing] is coarse in spirit. That is why the Tosafists rightly referred to the reason for discouraging this [as an individual's insolence]." A woman saying kaddish, by contrast, would become an example. "And so, in the matter before us, since it is done in public and is widely known, [the daughter's kaddish] must be prohibited. This is my humble opinion."

And this is my humble opinion: here is the sort of stringency that is an incitement to leniency. Take heart, daughters of Israel!

Insolent, the woman who says kaddish? Hardly. She appears every morning to submit herself to a duty. She is asking for more, not for less. When she seeks a leniency, she seeks a yoke.

Was Bacharach alone in his understanding of a woman's right to the kaddish? Apparently not, or so I conclude from a decision handed down in the generation after Bacharach. In a responsum by Jacob ben Joseph Reischer of Metz, an authority in the late seventeenth and early eighteenth centuries, there is evidence of the existence of a daughter's kaddish. Reischer received an inquiry from a former student in Kreuznach, a rabbi who was himself in mourning for his mother: "A man died here, and he had only two small daughters, the oldest of them four years old. When he lay sick, he asked me to give permission for his older daughter to recite the kaddish after his death, though never in the house of worship. But now his father comes along and demands to say kaddish for his son in the house of worship in the company of the other mourners." What is to be done? Relying on a number of authorities, Reischer answers that the father may indeed recite the kaddish for his son. Even though the Talmud states that "the son acquits the father [and] the father does not acquit the son," and even though the kaddish of the son for the father owes its efficacy to the fact that it is said "by his seed, who sanctifies the Name of Heaven, and so it is not appropriate for the father" to say it for the son, still there is reason to believe that a pious father may endow the soul of his son with merit. It is right, moreover, "to pacify the dead who died without sons." Thus a compromise kaddish for the mourning father may be worked out among the mourners in the house of worship. But not in the Kreuznach case. In the Kreuznach case, Reischer explains, there is no need to call upon the dead man's father, because the dead man's daughter is doing what must be done! "In the matter before us, the dead has already been pacified by the kaddish that the daughter is saying with the prayer quorum at home (for in the house of worship she is certainly not to be allowed to say any kaddish whatever). Moreover, when it comes to his [the dead man's] father leading the prayer [in the custom of the mourner], his father is to lead the prayers only at the house, in the prayer service at which the daughter recites the kaddish; but he is not entitled to the leadership of other services and to the other recitations of the kaddish." In Reischer's opinion, the daughter's kaddish is utterly uncontroversial. Reischer remarks upon it matter-of-factly. It is as if Bacharach's reasoning has been retained and his ruling discarded. And the daughter saying kaddish in Kreuznach was four years old!

I am spending a few days looking into the subsequent career of the daughter's kaddish, or its lack of one. What I find is a discouraging pattern in the reception of Bacharach's precedent. His ruling is retained, but his reasoning is discarded. Thus Ezekiel Katzenellenbogen, in the middle of the eighteenth century, in a sprawling, encyclopedic responsum on the protocols of the mourner's kaddish ("these are the visions and the provisions that I saw in the revelation to Ezekiel, general conclusions that I have drawn from the particulars in all their implications, which I have collected, to the best of my mind's ability, from all the rulings and the responsa and the dialectics, on the subject of the recitation of all the kaddishes here in the holy congregations of Altona, Hamburg, and Wandsbeck"), reports Bacharach's ruling simply as "no female says kaddish," full stop. Katzenellenbogen implicitly disputes Bacharach's claim that, from the standpoint of the mourner's kaddish, the daughter counts as the father's progeny. In Katzenellenbogen's view, her biological status is vitiated by her legal status. What qualifies a son for the job of saving his father's soul, claims Katzenellenbogen, is the fact that he is his father's heir; but a daughter does not inherit. And this has the additional consequence of requiring a discrimination not only among the children, but also among the grandchildren. Citing the tale of Akiva and the condemned man, Katzenellenbogen writes: "The rabbis [in another Talmudic passage] were careful to specify that a man leave a 'son who is an heir,' since the son of the son counts as an heir, and inherits with the sons, and so may recite the kaddish; but if he has a daughter, she does not recite the kaddish, in accordance with [Bacharach's] opinion that no female says kaddish, and the son of his daughter likewise does not recite the kaddish. As the Jerusalem Talmud says, the sons of daughters are not like sons." Pretty harsh.

Later in his text, in a checklist of the customs of the kaddish, Katzenellenbogen summarizes his prohibition: "If a man dies and does not leave a son here or elsewhere, but his son has a son, then it is permitted to assign the kaddish to the grandson, as a compromise with the other mourners who are present [in the house of worship], but not more than one kaddish from time to time [in the course of the year]. . . . But this applies only to the son of the son. The son of the daughter—not to mention anybody else who is saying the kaddish for this deceased, even if they are his relatives, including his father—has no kaddish in the house of worship if there are other mourners present." In the old system, the mourner's kaddish was not said by all the mourners together, as it is said now. It was said by a single mourner, a designated mourner, who was chosen according to an elaborate hierarchy of sorrow. (When did the system change?) Katzenellenbogen has consigned the son of the daughter to the bottom of this hierarchy; and the daughter herself is below the bottom, in the netherworld of her gender. (I note that Katzenellenbogen's stipulations are addressed to "kaddish in the house of worship." Perhaps he means to imply that the daughter may recite the mourner's kaddish at a service at home, like the pioneering woman of Amsterdam. But why would she bother, if only the kaddish of a legal heir can do the trick?)

The nineteenth-century history of Bacharach's ruling is no more uplifting. In a manual of the laws of the mourner's kaddish written by Ephraim Margolioth, a scholar and a businessman in Galicia in the late eighteenth and early nineteenth centuries, there appears this "law": "If a man has no sons, but has a daughter, and prior to his death he orders that ten men shall be employed in study at his house, and at the conclusion of their study the daughter shall say kaddish—he is not to be obeyed, and this must be prevented from taking place." Margolioth is referring, obviously, to Bacharach's responsum; but here again is Bacharach's ruling without Bacharach's reasoning. And Margolioth continues: "All the more so it is prohibited to allow her to recite the mourner's kaddish that appears in the prayer service. Even if she is a single woman, she is forbidden to recite it; and all the more so is a married woman prohibited from making her voice heard in public, heaven forfend, in the saying of the kaddish, in the house of worship or in a prayer quorum at home." A woman's voice is the very sound of lewdness, according to Jewish law. It is emphatically not to be heard. So what is a mourning woman to do? "If she wishes to acquit her dead father, however, she should scrupulously observe all the times of prayer, in the house of worship or at a private service, and listen intently to the kaddish that is said, so that she may say a purposeful amen, which will find favor. And He who knows our thoughts will think of this as if she had said the kaddish herself and fulfilled her father's request."

Margolioth's text comes with a commentary, written in 1906, by a certain Meshullam Finkelstein of Warsaw. His commentary is not especially interesting, except that it makes matters worse. Finkelstein cites Reischer's approbation of the kaddish of the girl in Kreuznach, and observes: "It is my humble opinion that in our day, when lewdness is common, we are not to act according to this custom and allow a daughter to say the kaddish, even in a service at home and even after study. . . . For she will certainly want to sound lovely . . . and she must not do so, because the loss will be greater than the profit: instead of the others santicfying the Name of heaven by her offices, as she intended, the others will hit a stumbling-block." Finkelstein also reports that "in our time we have not seen such a thing [as a woman reciting the kaddish]." Speaking ethnographically, then, the customs varied: there were communities in which daughters said kaddish and communities in which daughters did not say kaddish. And what, in Finkelstein's opinion, should a bereaved daughter do? He repeats Margolioth's advice—she should harken to the prayers and express her sorrow with her amen—and then adds: "He who knows our thoughts knows what she is thinking: that she would be sanctifying the Name publicly if she were a man."

If she were a man! If she were a man, she might have Finkelstein's view of women, so it was good that God did not make her a man. —It is unreasonable, I know, to expect people to exceed the limitations of their tradition. Still, it is not unreasonable to expect decency. A basis for decency can be found in every tradition; but you have to want to find it.

In 1849, Margolioth's remarkable student Zvi Hirsch Chajes, an enlightened Galician rabbi and scholar who became one of the most formidable polemicists against religious reform, cited his teacher's strictures against the sound of a woman saying kaddish. Chajes was inveighing against "the custom of the community in Hamburg, and more especially now in the temple of the Reform Jews in Berlin, that men and women sit together." In this, he said, the reformers "have conspired and raised their hand against the Torah." Chajes was alarmed that the proximity of women to men will afford men "a glimpse of her flesh if she is dressed thinly." Such proximity "is especially forbidden because of the men who stand near her and hear her voice. Even if it is true that these Reform services are characterized by perfect silence, so that no one's voice is heard, still there are reports that women assist at the service by singing in choirs, and there is no greater wantonness than this. . . . These people do not acquit themselves of the obligation of prayer." (What about Deborah, the Biblical heroine who was famous for her song? On the authority of his teacher, Chajes notes that "Deborah did not herself raise her voice in song before the people, she merely provided the musical arrangement and the lyrics." She was not a great Jewish singer. She was a great Jewish composer.) Chajes then cites Bacharach's ruling, and his account of it is bizarre: "On the question of a dying man who instructed that his daughter recite the mourner's kaddish, see the responsum by Rabbi Yair Bacharach, in which he responds that it is proper and just for every righteous and God-fearing woman, married or single, that she not make her voice heard if a man is present. [Like Hannah, when she prayed in Shiloh], only her lips should move, but her voice should not be heard. Otherwise the man who hears her may be aroused to an evil thought, which is worse than a sin. The woman must be very careful that she is not responsible for the failure of the men."

But Bacharach said nothing remotely like this! His analysis of the mourner's kaddish was an egalitarian analysis—and then his egalitarianism collided with his traditionalism. Chajes's account of Bacharach is tendentious and terrible.

"The woman must be very careful that she is not responsible for the failure of the men." No. The man must be very careful that he is not responsible for his own failure. The joke on this little exercise in misogyny is that it robs men of their moral agency. They are portrayed as pathetic creatures who must be protected from women. For women have power. And since they have power, they must be made powerless.

Poor Bacharach. The reception of his responsum sank even lower. In the library of the shul in Georgetown, I come upon a short work on the laws of mourning that was published a few years ago in Chicago. It was written by a very distinguished rabbi, the scion of a great family of rabbis, who wrote it in memory of his grandson. In his pages on the mourner's kaddish, he summarizes Bacharach's opinion: "He wrote that if the deceased has no son, but has only a daughter, and the daughter is married, then her husband must recite the kaddish." This is fiction! And he continues: "And if the daughter is not married, then as a matter of legal principle she is allowed to say the kaddish, except that she should not do so, since she would cause the customs of Israel to be weakened; and since her action would be widely known, it must be prohibited." Well, that's better. Bacharach said nothing about the women's marital status, but he did say the rest of what is here attributed to him. And then the distinguished rabbi offers his own opinion. It is lenient, and practical, and hilarious. "In our time, when some men and women are for women's rights in the matter of being called up to the Torah [during the service, when men are called up to the Torah], Orthodox rabbis must not bar women from reciting the kaddish when the opportunity presents itself, because then the influence of Conservative rabbis and Reform rabbis will grow. For this reason, it is forbidden to prevent a woman from saying kaddish." So this modern authority has a use for Bacharach's large view of "legal principle." He needs it not to help women, but to hinder rabbis. The daughter's kaddish is a tactical retreat in the great denominational wars of American Judaism. Throw them the kaddish, and the upstarts will be appeased.

Today two women appeared in shul, looking like tourists. But they were not tourists, they were mourners. They rose to say the kaddish with the rest of us. Against these women, these texts are helpless. They love their religion and they love their parents. There is nothing subversive about these women. They merely will not be denied.

I tell a friend about my little researches in the sexual history of the kaddish, and I strike a nerve. She recalls the death of her mother in Brooklyn many years ago—more specifically, the night that they had trouble gathering a quorum for prayer in her house, so that the kaddish could be said. "The house was filled with women, but they looked right past us and went hunting for men. It seemed bizarre." My friend became a lawyer and a judge who worked tirelessly and successfully to put an end to gender discrimination in American law; and her strong feelings about the subject were born, she says, on the night that she failed to count for her mother's kaddish. I promise to show her Bacharach's text. And a few days later a text arrives from her in the mail. It is an excerpt from a letter by Henrietta Szold, written in 1916. When her mother died, a gentleman named Hayim Peretz, a friend of Szold's, offered to recite the kaddish for her. Szold declined: "It is impossible for me to find words in which to tell you how deeply I was touched by your offer to act as 'Kaddish' for my dear mother. I cannot even thank you—it is something that goes beyond thanks. It is beautiful, what you have offered to do—I shall never forget it." But Szold knows that she owes her friend an explanation. "You will wonder, then, that I cannot accept your offer. Perhaps it would be best for me not to try to explain to you in writing, but to wait until I see you to tell you why it is so. I know well, and appreciate what you say about, the Jewish custom; and Jewish custom is very dear and sacred to me. And yet I cannot ask you to say Kaddish after my mother. The Kaddish means to me that the survivor publicly manifests his wish and intention to assume the relation to the Jewish community which his parent had, and that the chain of tradition remains unbroken from generation to generation, each adding its own link. You can do that for the generations of your family. I must do that for the generations of my family. I believe that the elimination of women from such duties was never intended by our law and custom—women were freed from positive duties when they could not perform them, but not when they could. It was never intended . . . that their performance of them should not be considered as valuable and valid as when one of the male sex performed them. And of the Kaddish I feel sure this is particularly true." I am in agreement with Szold's general characterization of the status of women in Jewish law, though there are sticky particulars with which such an analysis must deal. Then her letter leaves her view of her tradition for her view of her family: "My mother had eight daughters and no son; and yet never did I hear a word of regret pass the lips of either my mother or my father that one of us was not a son. When my father died, my mother would not permit others to take her daughters' place in saying the Kaddish, and so I am sure I am acting in her spirit when I am moved to decline your offer. But beautiful your offer remains nonetheless, and, I repeat, I know full well that it is much more in consonance with the generally accepted Jewish tradition than is my or my family's conception. You understand me, don't you?" I wonder if the gentleman understood. I wonder also what the Szold girls did. Did they say kaddish for their father, or was no kaddish said? And did Henrietta say kaddish for her mother, or was no kaddish said? I will assume that she did her duty.

The sun was a circle of fire as it rose over the rooftops of Adams-Morgan. It was a strong sight. I was not up to it.

I stayed late in shul this evening, for a few minutes of sanctuary. I was browsing through Mordecai ben Hillel's thirteenth-century compendium on the tractate of the Talmud that treats the practices of mourning, and I made an exhilarating discovery. Mordecai includes a fragment of a responsum by his master, Meir of Rothenburg. "As for your inquiry about making mourning easier for women than for men, I do not understand it. For in the language of the rabbis [in this matter], man and woman are equal." (Indeed, Meir adds, "it would be more plausible to make mourning easier for men, for men have the duty to procreate [and in the early days of mourning this is forbidden].") Meir was not speaking about the kaddish. Still, "in the language of the rabbis [in this matter], man and woman are equal."

I have sighted Akiva among the Christians! He was spotted in Jacques Bénigne Bossuet, bishop of Meaux, the great preacher of the Counter-Reformation and defender of French Catholicism in the seventeenth century. Bossuet tells the story of Akiva and the condemned man in the middle of an apology for the prayer for the dead.

In the wake of the Reformation, the prayer for the dead divided Christendom. In the words of one historian, "Catholics asserted that prayer could liberate the dead from their purgatorial sufferings, while Protestants rejected the doctrine of purgation after death and denied that prayer had any effect at all on the condition of the dead in the next life." Calvin called the prayer for the dead "a perverse mode of prayer." The most that Luther conceded in the way of such intercession was this: "Dear God, if the departed souls be in a state in which they may yet be helped, then I pray that you would be gracious." And he added: "When you have thus prayed once or twice, then let it be sufficient and commend them unto God." Catholic scholars argued for the antiquity of the prayer and for its efficacy, while Protestant scholars rejected it as a futile and relatively recent innovation in the history of the Christian tradition.

Bossuet defended the prayer for the dead against two Protestant controversialists named Roque and Blondel, who claimed that it was unknown among the Jews until the second century, until the age of Akiva. Bossuet disputed this claim with the story of Akiva and the condemned man. The cleric had read the story in a Latin translation of the minor Talmudic tractate *Kallah*, or *Bride*, a compendium of laws relating to betrothal, marriage, and sexual relations. This tractate was in fact produced after the Talmud, in early medieval times; but Bossuet is animated by the antiquity of the source. Indeed, he seeks to show that Akiva was not the author of the prayer for the dead, that it was much older. It may be found, he says, in *Second Maccabees*. More, "it was in continuous use, from time immemorial, in all the synagogues."

Bossuet's telling of the tale is accurate, except for two embellishments. The first embellishment is the appearance of purgatory. It is the place to which the unredeemed man bears his burden of wood. In Akiva's dream, according to Bossuet, the redeemed man "tells him that by his intercession he was delivered from purgatory and is now in the Garden of Eden, that is to say, in the terrestrial paradise to which the Jews believe that the souls of the righteous go." Bossuet has intruded Christian eschatology upon Jewish eschatology. The second of Bossuet's embellishments is his description of the kaddish. "Rabbi Akiva set out to find the son of the dead man, and taught him the prayer that begins with the word *kaddish,* that is, *holy,* which is found in the rituals of the Jews." This is a mistake. There is such a prayer to be found in the ritual of the Jews, but it is not the kaddish, and it does not begin with the word "kaddish." It is the kedushah, a responsive prayer that is recited in the recapitulation of the Eighteen Blessings and features prominently the verse "Holy, holy, holy is the Lord of hosts," the so-called trisagion from Isaiah that entered the Christian liturgy in the West as the *Sanctus.*

The Christian ignorance of Judaism is one of the great tragicomedies of history. —But how many Jews, like the Catholic cleric, have read the Akiva story as the story of a prayer for the dead?

I have been led to Bossuet by an old essay by Salomon Reinach, the Jewish archaeologist of Gallic civilization and the historian of ancient religion, whose Voltairean contempt for the rabbis did not prevent him from becoming a leader of the Jewish community in France in the early decades of this century. In 1900, he published a paper on the origins of the Christian prayer for the dead, specifically on its Egyptian origins. Reinach refuted Bossuet's views, arguing that the Christians adopted the prayer in the time of Tertullian, around the turn of the third century; and that there is no evidence that it figured in the Jewish liturgy in Akiva's day; and that it can be traced to the Orphic cult in Egypt, and to "certain Jewish communities, particularly those in Egypt," in the Hellenistic period. Early in his essay, Reinach makes a striking statement: "The pagans prayed to the dead, the Christians prayed for the dead." And the Jews? They do not pray to the dead. Do they pray for the dead?

A prayer for the dead is only slightly less ludicrous than a prayer to the dead.

Actually, Bossuet's attribution of purgatory to the Jewish eschatological tradition is not so far-fetched. The rabbinical conception of the twelve months after death may certainly be described as purgatorial. (Though the Christian purgatory was distinguished from the *regio gehennalis.*) And there may even be a historical coincidence. It has been argued that the idea of purgatory was a creation of the twelfth century, of the militant feudal world of the Crusades. One historian has dated the appearance of the term "purgatory" to the decade between 1170 and 1180. I have no way of knowing whether this is correct, but it does not escape my attention that the birth of purgatory may have occurred at the same time as the birth of the kaddish. Yet this is, as I say, a coincidence. I do not believe for a minute that the one was the cause of the other. Judaism was diversified by influence, but it was developed by its own force.

Tonight, for the first time since I became dependent on a quorum of ten men, we failed to muster a quorum of ten men. The gracious, restless, devout young lawyer who does the mustering worked the phones. "Aryeh? Get up! Get out of bed! What? Yes, it's the shul! Come on, get into your shoes!" Then he put the phone down and triumphantly announced: "OK, that's five." And so it went. Our musterer didn't count us in the customary way, with the traditional verse of ten words. His mnemonic device was the ten plagues. The sun was setting—and we were only up to boils! Then hail arrived, and then locusts, and then darkness and the plague of the firstborn straggled in, and we were ready. I was moved by the alacrity with which these people had dropped what they were doing and rushed to Georgetown, so that other people might be spared a dereliction of their duty.

There will come an evening next spring, after my kaddish is completed, when my phone will ring in the twilight hour. I will not have forgotten today's twilight hour, I hope.

The terrible twenty-eighth chapter of Deuteronomy was read in shul this morning, the chapter known as "The Chastisement," in which God enumerates, in excruciating detail, the punishments that await the people for betraying the covenant. It is the most sadistic, dystopian passage in Scripture, and in shul it is read in a hushed tone and quickly. I was asked to read the portion from the prophets that follows it, the sixtieth chapter of Isaiah, a chapter of extravagant consolation. The mourner stood before the congregation to console it! Near the end of the reading, a verse lay in wait for me: "And the days of thy mourning shall be ended." All of a sudden public meanings were usurped by private meanings. I stifled a sob.

A lean, unworldly man sat in the back of the shul, a man with worn, bony features and a long gray beard, in thick glasses perched distantly on his nose, in a caftan that bound him tight. He prayed at his own pace. He had about him the perfume of asceticism. I liked him nearby. When I left the shul, I saw the pietist pause in the light of the high sun that was drenching him. Whatever he was thinking, I'm sure that it was not about the light. I was witnessing a collision between two orders of beauty. The light was beautiful, the indifference to the light was beautiful.

It is Labor Day. Washington is a ghost town, but these days I keep company with ghosts. In the stillness of Georgetown in the evening the light is soft, a lowered radiance in which the structures of the brick houses disappear into their surfaces, which are ripe with patterns and textures. I see only small things. When I lead the prayers, I can't control my mind. It roams. Small things, small things. My thoughts and my words have nothing to do with each other. But the words keep coming, unimpeded by my abandonment of them. The triumph of rote.

Later in the Talmud, thousands of pages away from the statement that the son acquits the father but the father does not acquit the son, a complication is considered. It is David's lament for Absalom. "And the king was much moved, and went to the upper room above the gateway and he wept, and as he went he said, O my son Absalom, my son, my son Absalom! would God I had died for thee, O Absalom, my son, my son! . . . The king covered his face, and the king cried in a loud voice, O my son Absalom, O Absalom, my son, my son!" The rabbis have a query about these verses: "Why [did David say] 'my son' eight times? Seven times, for the seven levels of Gehenna from which David raised him; and as for the eighth, there are those who say that it was to restore Absalom's head to his body, and there are those who say that it was to bring him to the world to come." What David uttered, then, was not a lament, it was a prayer; and it had the consequence of saving the soul of his son from hell and inducting it into heaven. So the father acquitted the son! This contradiction was pounced upon by the Tosafists, the Talmudic masterminds of Franco-German Jewry in the high Middle Ages, and they resolved it this way: "Since Absalom met with his deserts in this world, when he died a peculiar death, the prayer of his father profited him. . . . Also Absalom was never an idolator [unlike the evil kings in the other Talmudic text, who were beyond help]. And so we may conclude that the statement that the father does not acquit the son means that respect for the [good] father does not prevent the [evil] son from being counted among the wicked for whom there is no prayer, but still there is profit in prayer, which is why David prayed for Absalom." These are all extensions of mercy. For souls whom the world treated with rare cruelty, and for souls who were not guilty of the worst betrayal, there is hope. The father still does not acquit the son, but the father's prayer will be heard.

Over dinner I describe all my comings and goings to shul to a friend, and she says to me, almost in protest: "But I believe in God and you don't!" If she means that I do not believe in the way that she believes, then she is right. Still, I'm not praying and studying entirely for filial reasons. I am not *only* a son.

A soul is never only a son. Quite the contrary. Either a soul or a son, sometimes.

Samuel Edels makes an interesting comment on the matter of Absalom. He recalls the prophet's curse upon David in the wake of his iniquity with Bathsheba: "Behold, I will raise up evil against thee out of thine own house." This, according to Edels, was a premonition of Absalom's tragedy. Edels writes: "Since his son was punished as a consequence of his actions, it is fitting that he raise his son from Gehenna. And so David said, 'would God I had died for thee!,' [because] 'it was my sin that caused this to happen to you.'" This is the same commentator who insisted earlier on the autonomy of the son. Is Edels contradicting himself? I don't think so. In this passage, he is being realistic about autonomy. Autonomy is unconditional, but it occurs in conditions. The son is free, but the son is also influenced. This is not a contradiction. It is the raw material of moral life. Who would deny the influence of the father? In his first discussion, Edels established the responsibility of the son. In his second discussion, he establishes the responsibility of the father. Nobody gets away.

It is one of the pleasures of the Talmudic tradition that the discussion is endless but not aimless. The screw keeps turning.

Sometimes tradition is solid and sometimes tradition is liquid.

In all this wrestling with memory, family, identity, morality, history, and divinity, there is a subject with which I am not wrestling, and it is death. But it turns out that mourning in the Jewish tradition is not really about death. The Jews are not interested in extinction, except to oppose it. Still, I am interested in extinction, since I expect it. The Jews will not die; but Jews will die, and I am one of them.

I cannot say that the death of my father was an evil. I wish that it had not happened, but I knew that it would happen. It wounds me, but it does not darken my picture of the world. Against an evil, by contrast, I may protest, intellectually and practically. We may restrain ourselves from sinning. We may not restrain ourselves from dying.

Perhaps love is not philosophically significant. A refreshing thought. (And an easement for love.)

In the Wisdom of Ben Sira: "The man who teaches his son will make his enemy jealous and exult over him before his friends. When his father dies, it is as though he were not dead, for he leaves behind him one like himself." And I have found the same thought in the rabbinical canon: "Rabbi Simeon bar Yohai said: He who has a son toiling in the Torah, it is as if he did not die." Here the erasure of the distinction between the father and the son is taken very far. I understand that the purpose of Simeon's statement is to praise continuity over discontinuity. And I understand that the transmission of tradition demands a significant similarity between the father and the son. But the statement is too extreme for my taste, and not only for its denial of the finality of death. The finality of the difference between the father and the son must also not be denied. There is truth also in the opposite proposition: He who lives exactly as his father lived, it is as if he did not live.

I've been leading the prayers all week and I'm getting tired of my own voice. I don't belong at the forefront of this action.

It is September and I am waking at the same ungodly (no, godly) hour, and now the hour is dark. I had come to depend on the sun to startle me into motion, to compensate me for my chore with what it would show me. The morning light was the bait. Now I open my eyes to the morning darkness. Oh well, I'm sure it's good for me. (The story of this year: one thing that is bad for me followed by eleven months of things that are good for me.)

I brought *Sefer Ḥasidim,* or *The Book of the Pious,* to the teahouse this morning. It is the strangest production of medieval Judaism. It records the values and the fantasies and the practices and the experiences and the interpretations of the pietists of Ashkenaz in the twelfth and thirteenth centuries. Attributed to Judah the Pious, it is really a commonplace book of a spiritual sensibility, in which rarefied notions of theology and ethics mingle with demons and witches. I have always loved this book and dreaded it. Its authors were still stunned by the Crusades, and its pages are shot through with death and the consequences of death. I have identified a number of texts in the book that are pertinent to my mourner's themes, and it is time to start through them. As soon as I open the book, however, I am struck in the face by a blast of unreason. No, no, no. Not this morning. I don't wish to travel to that planet this morning. I close the book. I sip my tea and let the hour slip away.

In New York, a friend's fiftieth birthday party. I can't stay long: it is the Sabbath before Rosh Hashanah and penitential prayers are to be said around midnight, inaugurating the days of low fear and high gravity. A short visit to Gramercy Park, hugs, kisses, gossip, a few drinks, and I'm back in a cab, hurtling up Madison Avenue. A hurricane has narrowly missed the city, but it has made the city torrid, and the people in the streets look like they are searching for trouble. I am tempted to join them, to tell the cabbie to turn around and thereby stop me from surrendering the rest of my night to my religion. But I tell him nothing. In no time at all he puts me down at the shul. Hundreds of young men and young women are pouring in. I feel a little disoriented. Tonight I am not proud of living doubly. Tonight the transit between the worlds was too swift. I scattered myself. The prayers fly by, I cannot put my mind anywhere. Finally my dispersal is halted by the curt Aramaic supplication near the end of the service, the one attributed to Sa'adia Gaon, that pleads for release for "the broken of heart" and "the crushed of spirit." It humbles me truly. For my heart is not broken, my spirit is not crushed. I am the victim only of satiety. —There isn't a kaddish in this service, but it was not for a kaddish that I came. I came because I am a member of the congregation.

Back in Washington, which the hurricane missed not so narrowly. The river is riled and muddy and breaking its boundaries. It is carrying all sorts of broken things. In shul, they have replaced the wine-colored curtains and coverlets with curtains and coverlets of white, which is the color of the aspiration to purity. In the hall of study, near the naked flame-shaped bulbs in the candelabrum that stands in the middle of all this whiteness, the glare of the chasteness hurts my eyes, like the first snow of winter. I feel reprimanded by it. When I was a boy, my father liked to show me that the cantor had exchanged his black robes for white robes. I knew that a climax was imminent. I remember the cantor weeping beneath his white miter.

In an obscure passage in *The Book of the Pious*, there is a report of a particular kaddish by a particular son for a particular father. It tells of a dying man's requests concerning his wife and his son. His request concerning his wife, in the matter of the disposition of property, is hard to make out. The text here is corrupt, or maybe I just don't understand it. But this, I think, is what the rest of the passage relates: "A man who was dying asked a certain Jew to teach his son the kaddish. It happened that the son of a pietist was saying kaddish at the same time. When it proved difficult to teach the kaddish to the son, [the teacher suggested] that the pietist's son recite the kaddish [for the man whose son was failing to learn it]. But he was reminded that it was his duty to teach the kaddish to the son, and that it was the son's duty to recite the kaddish for his father." The passage seems to be an advertisement for the pietists, whose sons had no trouble with the task. (Shul politics, as they say in Brooklyn.) This might be the earliest anecdotal evidence of the mourner's kaddish.

Pietism is a form of elitism. And humility is snobbery's most devious disguise.

"If one be found slain . . .": thus begins a curious chapter in Deuteronomy that instructs the Israelites in the procedure of expiation for a murder when the identity of the murderer is not known. The procedure is this: a heifer that has never felt a yoke is to be beheaded in a parched riverbed, and the elders of the city that is nearest to the spot where the body was found are to wash their hands over the heifer and say, "Our hands have not shed this blood, neither have our eyes seen it. Be merciful, O Lord, unto thy people Israel whom thou hast redeemed, and lay not innocent blood unto thy people's charge." In the Talmud, the rabbis are struck by the language of this supplication. It seems a little redundant. Why add "whom thou hast redeemed" to "thy people Israel"? They explain that the verse refers to a specific redemption: the verse is implying that "this atonement deserves to cover also all those who came out of Egypt." But all those who came out of Egypt died in the desert, which means that this is a ritual of atonement for the dead. And this provokes the pietists of the Rhineland. "How can a deed atone for an individual who did not perform it in his lifetime?" An excellent question. The text in *The Book of the Pious* supports the question with an analogy: "Is it not the case [in the Talmud] that a guilt-offering whose donor has died may no longer be brought [to the Temple]? For there is no atonement after death. Indeed, it is the agonies of dying that atone for a man's sins." What did the rabbis have in mind, then, when they suggested that the living may absolve the dead? They had in mind the relationship of the father and the son. "What they meant was that the son acquits the father. If a man sins, and he arranges for his son to study Torah and to do good deeds, then the son brings merit to the father, because the father brought merit to the son."

This is quite a claim for the spiritual power of the son's mourning. The son is the exception to the rule that there is no expiation for others, no expiation after death. There are no moral proxies, except one. The passage continues: "And if the fathers instruct the sons to do certain things after the fathers die—when the sons do them, it is as if the fathers did them." The identification between the father and the son is total. In this instance, there may be atonement after death because there is no essential difference between the living and the dead.

"Be merciful, O Lord, unto thy people Israel whom thou hast redeemed": the pietists derive a practice from these words. "It was on this basis that the custom was established to give charity for the dead, with the aim of improving their lot." And another institution of assistance is also established. This is the institution of prayer for the dead, about which *The Book of the Pious* has much to say. (The kaddish is not mentioned in these passages.) "We have learned that the dead pray for their children," the text continues, citing an ancient interpretation of a Biblical verse. "Similarly, it profits the dead that the living pray for them, or that they give charity for them. . . . For what need have I of prayer? What need have I of charity?" No, it is the dead who are the needy.

The intercession of the dead for the living does not perplex the pietists. The intercession of the living for the dead perplexes them greatly. And so they immediately establish a limit. Prayer for the dead "will work only for an individual who has merit but has sinned. If the individual has no merit, it will not work." If nothing good can be said about a man, then there is no point in praying for him. This is a drastic and exquisite qualification. It secures the idea of justice against the idea of mercy. An individual cannot escape his or her just deserts. The system of reward and punishment will not be subverted. Of course, there are not many individuals about whom nothing good can be said. Most people are morally complicated. They have merit and they have sinned. Thus the pietists may have limited the prayer for the dead philosophically, but they have not limited it practically.

So forget an eschatological fix. The son cannot come between the father and the consequences of the father's life. There is no mourner *ex machina.* Morality is love's boundary. Sounds rational, no? Well, almost. Consider what follows: "In this world, he may profit the soul of the dead. But if he kept his mouth shut in this world and did not make his request, then he should also not make his request in the future," that is, in the world to come. A stipulation! And immediately an objection to the stipulation: what about Elisha ben Avuyah? Elisha was the most tragic figure in classical Judaism. He lived in the second century. He was a great sage who became a great renegade, and came to be called Aher, or the Other. Both Rabbi Meir and Rabbi Yohanan promised to save his soul after they died. "When I die I shall cause smoke to rise from his grave," Rabbi Meir vowed. The smoke would show that the poor man had been punished; and "when Rabbi Meir died, smoke rose from Aher's grave." "When I die, I will extinguish the smoke from Elisha's grave," Rabbi Yohanan vowed. The absence of smoke would show that the poor man had been forgiven; and "when Rabbi Yohanan died, the smoke disappeared from Aher's grave." (And when Rabbi Yohanan died, it was said at his funeral that "even the gatekeeper of Gehenna could not stand up to you!") Why could they not have saved him when they were alive, as the medieval pietists insist? "Because the sins of Aher were too great," the medieval pietists explain. "When they were alive, their beseeching would not have been enough. They had to use force in the next world," whatever that means.

I am glad to be reminded that the rational and the irrational run into each other, that sense may be discovered in nonsense and nonsense in sense. And I am also glad to know that the appeal of a disembodied soul accomplishes nothing. A soul without a body lacks the authority of a soul with a body. We mourn on earth.

The author of this passage is worried that his animadversions may dissuade the living from praying for the dead. For this reason, he concludes firmly that "prayer in this world nevertheless improves the lot of the dead." Elsewhere in *The Book of the Pious,* however, the restrictions on the prayer for the dead are noted again and again. One of the early entries in the book is a collection of three folktales on the subject. The first tells of "a pietist whose custom it was to pledge charity for the souls of the dead—for the souls of his family, and then for the souls of all the dead. When he was asked why he did so, he replied: 'Because I may be the beneficiary of one of those meritorious souls, and I do not wish to be ungrateful. And also so that they, too, will not be ungrateful, and for their sake I will be rewarded.' The text then wonders how this is possible. Is not a guilt-offering void unless it is brought by the guilty man himself? The answer given is that "charity is like the beheaded heifer," which established that retroactive expiation is possible. And then there is this story: "A man was walking and was lost in a wood. At night, by the light of the moon, somebody saw him, and recognized him, and realized that he was dead. He was about to flee, when the [dead] man said to him: 'Don't run from me. I will not harm you. I am so-and-so [that is, he gave his name].' The frightened man exclaimed: 'But you have been dead for years!' 'That's right,' he replied, 'but I have no rest, owing to the field that I stole [when I was alive]. They tire and torment me in the forest as a consequence of the property I stole.'" And then there is this story: "A gentile died, and a few days later his servant came upon him during the night. 'Don't run from me,' he told him, 'I will not harm you.' 'But you are dead!' the servant replied. 'That is true,' the man said. 'But they tire and torment me because I took so-and-so's property by force. Now, please tell my wife to return it.' The servant said: 'But they won't believe me!' 'Tell them to appear at a certain place tomorrow,' the dead man said, 'and they will see me there.' The servant returned to town and told everybody. 'This is what I was told by the man who has been dead for days,' he announced. [They were skeptical.] 'Did he give you proof?' they asked. 'Tomorrow you will see him in a certain tree,' the servant replied, 'and then you will believe me.' They went to the spot and saw him in the tree; and when they looked for him in his grave, he was not there. 'Now return the stolen property to its owner,' the servant declared, 'and the man will find rest.' "

For their tellers, these tales demonstrate that the living may affect the condition of the dead. "But hold on," the text objects. "This story is about a gentile! Is it true or false?" But "it doesn't matter. There are similar stories about Jews." Superstition is universal. All God's children are haunted. And another objection: "How could the actions of the living in this world benefit the dead in the next world? After all, the [dead] man did not do this good deed when he was alive." This is the protest of morality against superstition. The answer is: "His sons are the ones acting on his behalf." The intercession of the living for the dead is possible only in one instance. The intercession must be filial.

And yet the pietists do not accept the filial suspension of the ethical. Not even a man's son has the power to interfere with his just deserts. "Moreover," the text continues, "there is a distinction. If a man has no merit of his own, all the charities and the kindnesses in the world will profit him nothing. Yet if he has merit of his own, but also sin of his own, and it is owing to his transgressions that he is banished from the Garden of Eden, or judged in Gehenna, or wearied by thorns, or toyed with by demons—or if he is a righteous man who deserves to join the company of the righteous, but is barred from their company as a consequence of a sin—then it profits him that the living pray for him and give charity for his sake, and that the property that he stole is returned. . . . Though the living can do nothing that will help an individual who is not found to be meritorious after his death."

But there is a loophole. Nothing can be done by the living for the dead "unless he instructed that [a certain deed] be done after his death, and it was done." One may prepare an avenue of posthumous rescue. The text gives the example of Moses, who instructed that the bones of Joseph were to be carried from Egypt to the Promised Land. It was Joshua and the Israelites who accomplished the deed—and yet Scripture credited Moses for it.

"Unless he instructed that [a certain deed] be done after his death, and it was done." Such as instructing your daughter to say kaddish for you?

The inflammation of their imaginations notwithstanding, the pietists of Ashkenaz are really quite indignant at the idea of an interference in the system of reward and punishment. Finally they champion morality against magic. I read on: "If gifts are given on behalf of the dead in this world and in the future—riches profit not in the day of wrath for the sinner, and for one who causes others to sin. If the dead man prevented others from giving charity and doing good deeds; or if he failed to study Torah and to do good deeds, so that he did not himself earn the merit of fulfilling the commandments and acting kindly; or if he did not faithfully provide for charity to be given after his death—it will profit him nothing if others give even a houseful of gold for the sake of the dead. One man has the virtue and another man has the reward? No, this will not work. For what, then, do the wicked lose? They would enjoy themselves in this world, and then gain Eden through the toil of others!"

The pietists of Ashkenaz had a mania for penitence. They developed the most extreme and elaborate penitential protocols in medieval Judaism. And they availed themselves often of the methods of mortification. They were ascetics. So what follows is not surprising: "If he [the dead man] had both virtues and vices, then the living may fast on his behalf, and pray that the punishment of the dead be lessened in proportion to the mortifications, and the obligation of charity, that the living takes upon himself." Yet asceticism, too, cannot release a man from the consequences of his life: "This will benefit the dead only if he did good and ill, but if he did no good, it will not benefit him." The text proceeds to some ancient examples of the lengths to which the living will go for the sake of the dead. It cites the posthumous efforts of Rabbi Meir and Rabbi Yohanan for the soul of Aher, the heretic whom they loved. And then it cites this legend about Rabbi Simeon bar Yohai, the charismatic scholar of the second century who escaped the Romans and for twelve years hid in a cave with his son. (The revelations that he received in the cave made him into the hero of Jewish mysticism.) Embellishing a passage in the Talmud, the pietistic text relates that "Rabbi Simeon bar Yohai wished to acquit the entire world from judgment. 'I have seen the ranks of those who will be shown the Divine Presence, and they are few. Indeed, if they are only two, then they are myself and my son.' And he also said: 'In the cave I acquired so much merit, and I accepted so much pain and suffering, but not for myself. No, I accepted torments that were not my just deserts, because I measured them against the torments that the wicked are destined to endure for their sins, and in this way I could acquit them from the day of judgment.' "

I did not know this legend of Simeon bar Yohai, and it is astounding. For the purpose that is here attributed to Simeon can only be described as a Jesus-like purpose. Except that this is not the end of Simeon's soliloquy. His desire to save the world with his own suffering is constrained by the moral reality of the world. "If the wicked have some merit, still they will not be harmed by what I have done. If they have no merit, still they will not be admitted, as a consequence of what I have done, into the Garden of Eden. For it makes no sense that a man will be given the world to come without having striven for it."

Nobody dies for anybody else's sins. There is mercy, but there is not a release from responsibility. Morally speaking, there are no miracles.

A few pages earlier in *The Book of the Pious,* the fundamentals are stated soberly. "No being and no demon has the power to deny the righteous any of their right rewards in the world to come. They will gain what they truly and perfectly deserve, for it is impossible that their deserts will not come to them in full. Similarly, if an evil man dies, there is no way to pray for him so that he will be vindicated with the just. Such a prayer will accomplish nothing. For the reward that awaits the just is for nothing other than the toil and the trouble that they endured in the performance of the commandments. But he who followed his appetites into the delights of sin, how is it possible that he will inherit a good portion? Such a notion is obviously nonsensical and remote from reason."

And the rest of this is not remote from reason? No, not all of it.

The Perfumer was one of the great pietists of Ashkenaz. He was the pupil of Judah the Pious, who founded this turgid, sublime sect. His discussion of mourning concludes with a passage "from the notebook of Rabbi Judah the Pious (and in his *Book of Glory* you will find the proof of what he says)." It is this: "The spirits of the dead roam the world, to harken to what has been decreed for the world. Sometimes they invite the living to go along with them; but if a man or his progeny accepts the invitation, they will die. No, he must say to the spirits of the dead: 'In the name of God, I do not wish to join you, or any other dead.' On the morrow he should go to the graveyard and remove his shoes and prostrate himself on their graves and say: 'For the sake of God, who desires that man shall live, do not come after me anymore. It is God's will, and it is my will, that I refuse to join you, and to join any dead. Do not stalk me or my loved ones, not you and not your agents. Because I want to live in this world, not in that world!' "

The struggle of religion with itself. More evidence of the inalienability of thought.

This week the morning prayers are preceded by penitential prayers, and I must rise even earlier, a few minutes after six o'clock. This is taking a toll. I was useless at the office. All day long I couldn't tell whether I was tired or sad. What's the difference? Tired or sad, my powers are not available to me.

Whenever I read Kafka, I wonder: what sort of dejection is this, that leaves one the strength to write, and write, and write? If you can write about the wreckage, the wreckage is not complete. You are intact. Here is a rule: the despairing writer is never the most despairing person in the world.

I rise in the dark—"in the early morning watch," in the words of the liturgy. There are heavy rains. A few minutes late to shul, I arrive in the middle of one of the medieval poems about penitence. The obscurity and the preciosity of some of these compositions is impossible to exaggerate. It is hard for me to get past the high style, to see these pages as anything but literature. Yet the fervor in the room is real. I am in a gathering of genuinely religious people. All the other explanations for what they are doing here are moot. Their faith is an irreducible quantum. They are here because they believe, and I am here because they believe.

Last night I went to bed in a fury. My nights are ruined by my mornings. My mornings are nights. I want to do nothing but what I am doing. Black bile.

I recall the Talmudic promise that "in matters of mourning, the law takes the lenient view," and I think: not in the experience of this Jew.

The most ancient of the special supplications of the morning appears at the conclusion of the service: "He who answered our father Abraham on Mount Moriah, He will answer us. He who answered his son Isaac when he was bound on the altar, He will answer us. He who answered Jacob in Bethel, He will answer us." And so on through Joseph, Moses, Aaron, Phineas, Joshua, Samuel, David, Elijah, Elisha, Jonah, Hezekiah, Hananiah, Mishael, Azariah, Daniel, Mordecai, Esther, and Ezra. The liturgy is riddled with appeals to what the tradition calls "the merit of the fathers." Adducing ancestors is a Jewish habitude. Ancestors are Judaism's saints.

This morning I am struck by the pertinence of this liturgy to my present obsessions. Here we are, beseeching God that the merit of our fathers stand us in good stead. So the fathers do acquit the sons! Indeed, this is one of the axioms of Jewish prayer. And the opposite view, the view that prefers the agency of the sons to the influence of the fathers, the view that excited me in recent months, is the minority view. From Ephraim Urbach's study of the ancient sages I learn of the antiquity of the debate. There is extensive speculation, in the midrashic commentary on the splitting of the Red Sea, as to whose merits were responsible for the miracle, and a disagreement between two of the earliest authorities in the Talmud. Shemaiah imagined God's reasoning this way: "The faith that their father Abraham had in Me suffices that I should split the sea for them." And Avtalyon, this way: "The faith that they have in Me suffices that I should split the sea for them." The fathers or the sons. The attainments of the past or the attainments of the present. The generations are declining or the generations are progressing.

Urbach: "Avtalyon and the long line of sages who attributed the miracles and the redemptions to the merit of the deeds of the people of Israel, and not to the merit of the fathers, were concerned about an excessive reliance on that latter merit, and certainly about a weakening of the feeling of responsibility." In other words, life is lived in the present. But the party of the present lost out to the party of the past. Urbach concludes that "the inveighing of the sages against the dependence on the merit of the fathers did not meet with great success."

And so the distinction between piety and filial piety became blurred. Here are the foundations for Freud's mistake. Religion is most certainly not merely the worship of the father. God is not the father, and the father is not God. And yet (this is the kernel of truth in the Freudian husk) the entanglement of God and the father is tight and deep. For spiritual reasons, therefore, a disentanglement is necessary. Spiritually, the war of the generations is a necessary war.

The sins of the father, God told Moses, will not be visited on the sons. That is a promise of fairness. But neither should the saintliness of the fathers be visited on the sons. Fair is fair.

I spoke to my mother, then to my sister. They are dreading the holidays that begin tomorrow night. The Days of Awe, these holidays are called; but this year the awe is all at my father's absence. I am dreading their dread. But we'll get through it, a flinch at a time. Anyway, the only way to deal with those who cannot be of assistance to you is to be of assistance to them.

This evening I was jealous of the strollers in Dupont Circle, the ones who were moving purposelessly.

VII

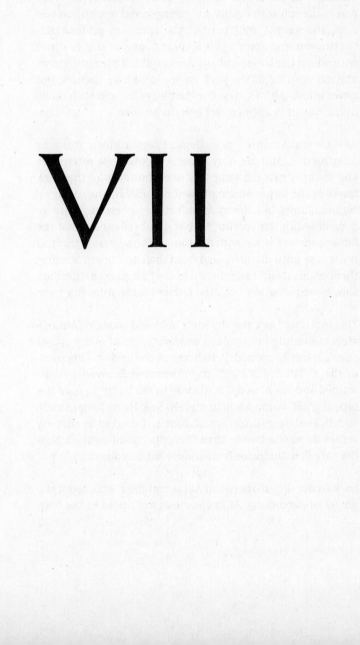

A few minutes with a page of Talmud in shul. The page is rich for my researches. It gives Rabbi Akiva's view of the influence of the father upon the son. "He said: The father merits the son with beauty and strength and wealth and wisdom and years." By "merits," the tradition understands "bestows merit upon": this is a catalogue of the qualities with which the father endows the son. (It is a plainly ungrammatical reading of the verb *zokheh* in Akiva's dictum, but never mind.) Akiva's view does not leave the son with much in the way of qualities to achieve on his own.

Akiva is expounding a genealogical determinism. It is very unattractive. And not only to me: I follow a few references and discover that the same lack of enthusiasm for the hegemony of the father was expressed not only by the medieval commentators, but also by Akiva's contemporaries. A dispute is recorded in the Tosefta: "Rabbi Akiva taught . . . that the father endows the son with five things. The sages said that this is the case until maturity, and from then on the son acquires them on his own." I am pleased to see that Akiva's determinism, his explanation from the fathers, is the minority view.

This morning I saw the shy early light and thought immediately of binding my arm and wrapping myself in my prayer shawl. It has happened. I am living in the grid of obligation, in the straitened state of cognition that Soloveitchik described and I deplored. On my way to shul, I try to fight it. I repeat small commands to myself: See. Hear. Taste. Smell. Touch. See. Hear. Taste. Smell. Touch. It used to be that my senses demanded more than their due, and I obliged. Now they are demanding only their due. But it is due them.

Back to the dispute between Akiva and the rabbis about the power of patrimony. After the views are stated in the text, there is an interesting exchange. Akiva denies that beauty, strength, wealth, wisdom, and years have anything to do with maturity or immaturity. He asks: "Do we know of someone who was lame until the age of maturity, and at the age of maturity suddenly recovered his power to walk? Do we know of someone who was deaf until the age of maturity, and at the age of maturity his ears suddenly opened? Do we know of someone who was blind until the age of maturity, and at the age of maturity his eyes suddenly opened?" The answer, Akiva implies, is no, we do not know of personal transformations of such consequence. The child is father to the man; and so, therefore, is the child's father. If you wish to know the son, study the father. Akiva is making a radical claim. It is that the attainments of the individual are not acquired, they are inherited. About some of these attainments—strength, beauty, wealth—this is plausible, even trivial. But wisdom? To include wisdom is to reduce the moral to the natural. (My Darwinist acquaintances would be delighted. Akiva's superstition, they would gloat, was a premature scientism.)

But the rabbis are ready with a retort. "They said to Akiva: Don't we know of someone who could walk until the age of maturity, and at the age of maturity suddenly went lame? And don't we know of someone who could hear until the age of maturity, and at the age of maturity suddenly went deaf? And who could see until the age of maturity, and at the age of maturity suddenly went blind? We must conclude, therefore, that the father is responsible for the endowments of the son only until that time." In the view of the rabbis, there is individual development, individual agency. The man is father to the man. If you wish to know the son, study the son. Patrimony explains something, but it does not explain everything.

The evening of Rosh Hashanah in Brooklyn. A twilight of falling, drifting leaves. My father is everywhere. I come to shul, his grandiose shul, and slip into his seat. Tremors, instantly. He was in this place, now I am in this place. It was his place, now it is my place. I have a physical sensation of inheritance. I am my father's leg. And the men around me, with whom he prayed for thirty years, have noticed what has taken place. A few of them come over and taciturnly shake my hand. They are offering more than condolences. They are offering also congratulations. They have watched the position pass from father to son. It is such a passage of which they dream.

The prayers end and the congregation files out. In the corridor a gentleman approaches me and says: "Have a good year, Mr. Wieseltier." I am a little discomfited. I am not Mr. Wieseltier. He was Mr. Wieseltier. In a way, this marks the end of shul as I have known it. All my life I went to shul with my father, that is, I went to shul as a son. It was because I found it almost impossible to stop going to shul as a son that I stopped going to shul. I came to conflate religion with childhood. But childhood is over. And so Mr. Wieseltier returns the greeting: "And a good year to you, too."

I'm not quite ready to join my mother and my sister for dinner. I need to settle down. I walk over to the bay and sit on one of the old wooden benches, just opposite a small ruined pier. The water is calming. Two men appear. One of them is carrying a large flashlight, the other a long pole with a net affixed to the end. They are fishing for crabs. The one shines a light onto the water, the other bends low toward the water and strains hard to bring up what the light has exposed. Pretty soon their little pail is filled with food. Sometimes you have to strain hard to get just below the surface, but if you have made it below the surface, you have made it to the deep.

Melancholy can make everything into metaphor. On my walk to my sister's house, I remark on flickering lights and steady beams, on passing clouds, on the sturdy stumps of felled trees. All are the emblems of my inner states. I assault what is outside me with what is inside me. I am reminded of the "objective correlatives" that I was taught to revere, and I think: objective correlatives are acts of vanity. It is a greater task to find subjective correlatives, to train the soul to try on the forms that are outside it.

The opposite of metaphor is transformation.

I have brought to Brooklyn the great treatise on repentance by Menahem ben Solomon Ha'Meiri, the commentator and the historian of ideas in Provence at the turn of the fourteenth century. The extremely discursive Ha'Meiri combined the rationalism of Maimonides with the Talmudism of the French and German rabbis, and wrote in a supple and encyclopedic style. This vast book on repentance was a work of his youth, and it concludes with philosophical reflections on mourning. "I have seen fit to add the laws of mourning to [the discussion of repentance], because when the Torah and the sages remarked upon the individual grieving and mourning, and being wracked by the absence of those whom he loved and to whom he cleaved, they intended to enjoin this individual to make an accounting of his own deeds, so that he will know and understand that it was owing to him that this came to pass, that this whirlwind was his doing." My doing? It was his doing!

He died, but I am guilty? —I am not protesting my innocence. I know who I am. I am protesting only my innocence of his death.

Death makes me small, but it does not make me guilty. Even if I were stainless, I would be mortal; and mortality is not a stain. I am guilty of doing. I am not guilty of being. (Heidegger's conflation of finitude and guilt was an expedient way of transposing guilt from the realm of ethics to the realm of ontology, so as to make ordinary conscience seem trivial.)

If I am originally and essentially guilty, if my guilt precedes what I do, then I may do as I please. What a license such guilt is! Ontological guilt is an immoralist's dream.

One is not accountable for being. That is precisely the problem.

But Ha'Meiri does not let up. He insists that mourning is a rebuke, and therefore useful. In connection with the verse from Ecclesiastes, "It is better to go to the house of mourning than to the house of feasting, for that is the end of all men, and the living will lay it to his heart," he writes: "When the living lays it to his heart, that is, when he remarks upon the day of death, and comprehends his own end, then it will lead to the breaking of his heart. . . . And every individual, in the sudden absence of his loved ones, will be stirred to repent his sins in the midst of this evil that has befallen his people, and in the loss of its homeland. Now you understand why I have added these laws and matters [of mourning], for they unfold in the direction of repentance, since these things are the causes of the surrender of the heart and the shattering of pride, and thereby they bring about an improvement in one's deeds and a commitment to the ways of righteousness." Ha'Meiri entitles his chapter on the laws of mourning "The Shattering of Pride." In his account, the objective of mourning is the submission of the mourner. The mourner must be bettered by the death that he bemoans. Death is a communication to the living, who tend to live wantonly because they forget that they, too, will die. This is how Ha'Meiri explains the rending of the mourner's garment: "When the garments are rent, the hearts will be rent. In this way, your rending will have a particular intention and your mourning will have the aspects of righteousness and melancholy. For this reason, the rabbis ordered [the mourner] to do things that hurt."

My little niece is learning to walk and to talk. After dinner, she stumbles around the room in a circle and whispers: "Grow up, grow up, grow up." Then she pauses, remembering some other words that she has heard, and concludes her thought: "Carefully, carefully, carefully."

The Talmud records that "the early pietists always went to a house of mourning before a house of feasting," as Ecclesiastes recommended, and then asks: "What is the lesson of [the Biblical words] 'and the living will lay it to his heart'? That he who walks behind the bier must say, 'I follow this one.'" Ha'Meiri quotes this macabre passage, but in a more chilling version: "Everyone who walks behind the bier must say, 'I die next.'"

"We would like to give you your father's honor," the usher says to me in shul in the morning. I gasp. I reply that I will be honored to accept my father's honor, though I know that it will undo me, and my mother, and my sister. My father's honor was to open the ark during the additional service, at the beginning of the awesome prayer that is attributed by

Isaac of Vienna, in the name of Ephraim of Bonn, who wrote the great excruciating chronicle of the Second Crusade, to a martyr named Rabbi Amnon in Mainz in the twelfth century, and to stand before the ark for the duration of the prayer, and then to close it. When the moment comes, I ascend the few steps to the ark and I pull the string that parts the curtains. The Torah scrolls are revealed, the congregation rises, the hour of perfect sorrow has arrived. The cantor is chanting the medieval words directly behind me—"As a shepherd seeks out his flock, making his sheep pass under his rod, so will You make the souls of all the living pass before You, to count their number and take their measure and fix their endings"—and I am quietly convulsed. I lean into the ark, into the white light that is pouring from it. A single tear hangs in my eye and it will not fall. I see everything through this tear. The tear is trapping the light, it is becoming a medium of radiance. I am bereft inside a diamond, a grief-gem. From the corner of my penetrated eye I can see my mother's face buried in her prayerbook. She is weeping. I am trembling. The light isn't holding me. I grab the smooth wood of the ark and hang on. "Who by fire and who by water . . . who by hunger and who by thirst . . . who will find rest and who will find no rest . . . who will be solaced and who will be tormented . . ." The tear has fallen. I am crying uncontrollably. But for what, exactly? For my father, of course. But for what about my father, exactly? I expected him to die. I am crying for the end of his enjoyments, from his grandchildren to his quarrels. No, more. I am crying for his first meeting with death, the one from which he escaped. No, more. I am crying for the victory of his pains over his pleasures. He was an unhappy man. No, more. I am crying because being is final. I know what I mean. I fear nothing more than finality. "Man comes from dust and ends in dust. He brings his bread with his life. He is like the potsherd that shatters, the grass that withers, the flower that fades, the shadow that passes, the cloud that disappears, the wind that blows, the dust that hangs in the air, the dream that flies away." Finally the prayer is over. I close the ark. The light passes. His honor is now my honor. My deepest wound has been opened. I have extracted philosophy from my father's death; and with philosophy, terror. I slump in my seat. I hope my mother and my sister have recovered from what the usher, and the structure of creation, did to us this afternoon.

The time comes to stand up and say kaddish. I see my sister standing up and saying kaddish, too. No, not her! I have never been so completely defeated in my desire to come between my sister and what injures her. But in a few moments the feeling of failure becomes a feeling of gladness. It is right that my sister should say the kaddish. She is honoring our father exactly as I am honoring him. My disquiet at the sight of her hardship gives way to a sensation of solidarity. Meanwhile everybody else waits impatiently for us to finish so that the services can adjourn.

A man who wishes that he had not been born is mourning the dead. How can such a man mourn? He should covet the release! But he has been captured by the world. He didn't want to come and he doesn't want to go. And so he mourns.

I am reminded of my favorite dispute in the Talmud. It is one of the disagreements between the school of Hillel and the school of Shammai, the patriarchs of Jewish law in the first century. "For two and a half years, the school of Shammai and the school of Hillel were divided. The former held that it would have been better for man not to have been born than to have been born. The latter held that it is better for man to have been born than not to have been born. They took a vote and came to a conclusion: it would have been better for man not to have been born, but now that he has been born, he had better examine the deeds that he has done. And some said: he had better examine the deeds that he will do." This was the compromise between the schools: pessimism that is not nihilism.

No, it was not a compromise at all. The school of Shammai won.

The ideal of a good life based on the image of a dark life. Ethics without cheer.

It is an unvirtuous world that needs virtue. Look at the world. Do you see suffering? Then you will not wish to add to it. In this sense, lucidity is a condition of morality.

To aspire to goodness is to aspire to clarity.

"They took a vote and came to a conclusion"! The consensus of the schools was that disillusion is not to be denied, it is to be contained. These sages were not sentimental about truth. They understood that it rattles and sunders.

Pessimism in theory, but not pessimism in practice. Is this possible? A worldview is a view of the world, of the whole world. How can you not act on it?

Duty, or the art of unhappiness.

In this desolation, a small deliverance comes through the mailbox. It is a Rosh Hashanah card, sent to my mother from friends. "Dear Stella: We are thinking of you and wish you a happy New Year. We, as many others, will be missing Jack in the synagogue this year." It is sweet that they will miss

Jack. There is only one problem. My father's name was not Jack. I collapse into laughter, my mother collapses into laughter, my sister collapses into laughter. The grip of grief is broken.

In the afternoon, in my mother's house, I return to Ha'Meiri's text. From his reading of a passage in Ezekiel, I see why he insisted upon the surrender of the heart. The passage is the one in which God tells the prophet that his wife will be taken from him, but he is not to mourn her, because his seeming indifference will make the Israelites aware of their own indifference. "So I spake unto the people in the morning; and at even my wife died; and I did in the morning as I was commanded." When the people demand to know why Ezekiel is not comporting himself like a mourner, this is what he tells them: "The word of the Lord came unto me, saying: Speak unto the house of Israel, Thus saith the Lord God: Behold, I will profane my sanctuary, the excellency of your strength, the desire of your eyes, and that which your soul pitieth; and your sons and your daughters whom ye have left shall fall by the sword. And ye shall do as I have done: ye shall not cover your lips [in the manner of the mourner], not eat the bread of men. And your tires shall be upon your heads, and your shoes upon your feet: ye shall not mourn nor weep, but ye shall pine away, for your iniquities, and comfort one the other." (A "tire" is an archaic English term for a headdress.) It was from this passage in the Bible that the rabbis in the Talmud deduced many of the practices of mourning. Yet Ha'Meiri is not exercised by the legal and ritual implications of the text. He is interested instead in the spiritual obstruction of the Israelites in adversity. Their troubles made them stubborn! "When the prophet chastised them, they got stiff-necked about their troubles. The more the punishment for their sins caught up with them, the more they sinned. And so God showed him in a prophetic vision the death of his beloved and his failure to respond with the practices of mourning—a prophetic parable for the purpose of showing them that they refuse to bow to the troubles and disasters that befall them. For if they were to bow to them, they would return to God and not be swept up in their sin. . . . He announced in a prophecy that even though a very terrible thing had befallen him, in his conduct he did not display a defeated heart. Instead he stubbornly conducted himself as if he were not affected, exactly as they stiffened their necks. From this our rabbis inferred a general rule that one must mourn for the kin that have been taken from one by behaving in ways that humble the heart and mortify the soul, until the mourner's behavior rouses and awakens him to a true understanding, for then his uncircumcised heart will surrender, and he will know and recognize that his sins have caused his punishment."

In the face of death, one becomes obdurate about life; but in Ha'Meiri's homily I hear a warning that such obduracy may be a mistake, a complacency, a preening of the will. There are circumstances that must shatter you; and if you are not shattered, then you have not understood your circumstances. In such circumstances, it is a failure for your heart *not* to break. And it is pointless to put up a fight, for a fight will blind you to the opportunity that has been presented by your misfortune. Do you wish to persevere pridefully in the old life? Of course you do: the old life was a good life. But it is no longer available to you. It has been carried away, irreversibly. So there is only one thing to be done. Transformation must be met with transformation. Where there was the old life, let there be the new life. Do not persevere. Dignify the shock. Sink, so as to rise.

The stiff-necked mourner who says kaddish to unstiffen his neck.

Broken, broken, broken. Because you have understood.

Back in Washington, in shul and out of shul, dawn and dusk, day after day after day. Spirituality is declining into schedules, and they are oppressing me. I am worn and resentful. After this season of introspection is ended, and I have pondered the deepest themes, and I have rinsed my soul with my tears, and I have acquitted my father and my father has acquitted me, I will be ready for . . . a nap.

"In the day of prosperity be joyful, but in the day of adversity consider: God also hath set the one over against the other." Ha'Meiri's final homily on mourning is a reading of this verse from Ecclesiastes. He records the allegorical interpretation of the philosophers, that the verse refers to "the affairs of the world of generation and corruption," to the structure of creation: "Ecclesiastes says, consider and grasp that He consigned all this lowly matter to pass away, so how can you expect great things from matter, and seek perfection and eternity there? Do not seek there! For who can alter the order of creation, and make straight what is crooked, when its crookedness is the will of the Creator? And so Ecclesiastes said, 'in the day of prosperity be joyful,' that is, since it is not within your power to change the structure of the world and to bring forth a thing of value from corruption, or something lasting out of abject matter, then there is no rightness in man save to accept the vicissitudes of time as they occur. . . . The good and the bad, the straight and the crooked, the coming-into-being and the passing-away: to all of these the Creator gave a time and a season. . . . The cause of the bad is the cause of the good, and let us not trouble ourselves with what appears to the vulgar eye as a dearth of order and providence." But Ha'Meiri is not agreeable to such a metaphysical reading of the verse. "It is more to my liking," he writes, "to explain it according to its plain meaning." For Ha'Meiri, the verse proposes not an understanding of the universe, but an understanding of the human experience of the universe—a counsel of spiritual stability amid temporal instability. This, in his view, is its teaching: "In the day of prosperity be joyful, but even in the day of prosperity contemplate the adversity that is to come, and do not despair of retribution; since God made the one against the other, sometimes He will bring the good and sometimes the bad. In his lucid way, Ecclesiastes declared that the good and the bad are two points on a line, the one opposite the other, and the bad is as possible as the good. . . . When a man finds himself happy, in any of the varieties of happiness, it is not fitting that he should settle himself in his happiness. No, he must recall the times of trouble. It was for this reason that the rabbis [in the Talmud] ruled that on a holiday the private practices of mourning must be maintained, even though the public ones are suspended. . . . It is appropriate that one tremble instead, and not sink oneself in the happiness of the holiday with abandon [so that] one forgets all hardship and stiffens one's neck to what is in store for one. Instead the wise thing is to walk uprightly, that is, to moderate one's ways and take the middle course, and to accept everything in its time and its season, for happiness is in its time and its opposite is in its time."

Ha'Meiri is worried about the impact of the world's mutability upon the soul. One is never happy once and for all and never unhappy once and for all. As long as one lives, there is no fixity. We know no definitive days. Melancholy has no more than a partial basis in reality, and the same is true of joy. The laws of mourning, according to Ha'Meiri, were contrived to take account of this diversification of experience.

I have been warned by Ha'Meiri about the temptation of totality. Is there a more totalizing emotion than the emotion of sorrow? It sees nothing but its object and the universe that stole its object away. It regards the world from the standpoint of its wound, and thereby simplifies it. And here is Ha'Meiri, with a word of caution. Mourner! Do not mistake a season for a law.

The variability of things pleases, the variability of things displeases.

Ha'Meiri reminds the happy man not to sink into his happiness. He does not remind the unhappy man not to sink into his unhappiness. But that is his implication, and I will take it. Old rabbi, vary me!

When one considers the discontinuities of the mind and the discontinuities of the world, it is amazing that anything true has been established at all.

Having explained the complications of experience upon which the laws of mourning are premised, Ha'Meiri comments on a few details. One of them concerns the Justification of the Judgment. "In the matter of the Justification of the Judgment," he writes, "our teacher Rabbi Moses wrote that it is permitted to recite it in unison on a holiday and on the New Moon and on Hanukah and on Purim, since it is [not] like a dirge. Even though some of the geonim forbade its recitation, our custom is like the one prescribed by Rabbi Moses Gaon, according to which it [the Justification of the

Judgment] consists in nothing more than an acknowledgment of God and an acceptance of the judgment of heaven, and contains no expression of mourning that would violate the festive day; and we are not to avoid saying it. Indeed, our custom has become so popular that we even say it throughout the months of Tishrei [when the holidays of Rosh Hashanah and Yom Kippur and Tabernacles occur] and Nisan [when the holiday of Passover occurs], despite the fact that it is not a law, and despite the authority of the geonim [who preferred to] honor the festivals that fall in those months [by not reciting it]." Who is Rabbi Moses Gaon? Ha'Meiri is notorious for giving his own epithets to the authorities he cites. Could it be Maimonides? But the view that he imputes to this Moses is Rashi's. I'm puzzled. Anyway, Ha'Meiri's passage is historically interesting. It is more evidence of Rashi's reach. His legitimation of this liturgy for a funeral on a day of joy was accepted in the south of France, too.

And then there appears a mysterious sentence. "It is also our custom not to say it on the Sabbath at all, until darkness; and I am not sure whether we say it on the holidays or not." Ha'Meiri is obviously not referring to the Justification of the Judgment. So what is this prayer that is not said except on Sabbaths at nightfall? It must be the mourner's kaddish! Here it is, in the eastern Pyrenees in the late thirteenth century, for the orphaned lads of Perpignan.

"Don't you hate this?" a friend asked me in shul this evening, complaining of fatigue. I do hate it; but I must be precise. I do not hate the obligation. I hate what is becoming of the obligation. The requirements for its fulfillment are dulling the will for its fulfillment. I feel like a robot; and where does it say that the laws of Moses fall also upon a robot? But I won't stop. I will not abandon my duty in the name of my duty. That is one of the classical excuses of modern Judaism, I mean in its cheaper forms.

My absence from shul would not be more honorable than my alienation from it.

Pride is not the only appropriate response to the consciousness of origins. There must also be modesty. A boast about one's ancestors is not really a boast about oneself.

Pride is a kind of relaxation. Be proud of what the fathers were, so as not to be ashamed of what the sons are. This is one of the uglier aspects of group feeling.

In Brooklyn, again. The morning of the Sabbath, the day before Yom Kippur. I'm in shul early. I can't really concentrate on the prayers and I recite the kaddish emptily. But I am snatched from my stupor by the reading from the Torah. We are nearing the end of Deuteronomy, the end of the epic of Moses, and in the great valedictory poem in chapter 32 there appears the verse that has featured in my mourner's researches: "See now that I, even I, am he, and there is no god with me; I kill and I make alive; I wound, and I heal; neither is there any that can deliver out of my hand." I am following the reading this morning with an edition of the Scripture that was compiled by Baruch Ha'Levi Epstein, a Russian Jewish scholar who died in 1942, and the son of one of the great Jewish jurists of the modern age. (He was also a bank teller.) Epstein annotated the verses of Scripture with ancient rabbinical commentaries, and wrote a commentary of his own. Thus the Talmudic statement that the father does not acquit the son appears in connection with the verse above, as I expected. But Epstein's gloss on the text and the prooftext is better than expected. "But the son acquits the father," he writes. "It is not at first apparent from the verse why the son acquits the father. The reason is this. In most cases, the education of the son depends on the father, and so, if the son becomes worthy and attains a level of merit, the father certainly was the cause of this, and therefore he deserves to derive benefit from his son's merit. According to such an account, moreover, it would seem that the mother is also responsible for the son's merit, for it is also the calling of the woman to teach the sons, and so she, too, has a part in his qualities and in the abilities of his soul." At last, the mother! I wondered if I would ever stumble upon her in all these sources.

But this is not where Epstein's comment ends. The rest of it turns out to be one of the most sensible treatments of the subject that I have so far encountered. "Know generally that the statement that the father does not acquit the son refers only to the vindication that results from the study of Torah and the performance of the commandments, that is, to the vindication in the world to come, because the precious and exalted attainments of the world to come must be obtained by every individual with the acquisition of each one of them by himself. For the benefits of this world, however, which are lesser than the benefits of the world to come, the father obviously makes the son worthy, and the proof of this is in our prayers, which beseech that the merit of the fathers protect us. For this reason the rabbis said that a wicked man who prospers must be a wicked man who is the son of a righteous man, for his father's merits support him." Epstein's distinction between this world and the next world is a distinction between the reality of our dependence and the reality of our independence. And just as there is no contradiction between this world and the world to come, there is no contradiction between our dependence and our independence. They go together, as the conditions of our responsibility.

I expected that Yom Kippur without my father would be troublesome, that I would be commemorating him hour after hour, from sundown until sundown, in the setting of his life. The rabbi has a thought for the worshipers in the afternoon. He wants them to consider the manner in which an eleventh-century thinker understood the distinction between the wicked, the righteous, and the souls who are neither wicked nor righteous, the middling ones. The men around me try to puzzle this out. Not me. I have been trying to puzzle it out for almost half a year. Maybe that is why Yom Kippur is a bit of a fizzle this year. This year, every day has a touch of this day.

Downstairs in the shul, there is a Yom Kippur service for Russian immigrants. About three hundred of them are gathered in a large hall beneath a garish chandelier. They are hearing a sermon in Russian punctuated by Hebrew and Yiddish. I stand in the back and study my brethren. They are a hard and homely lot. And it is their homeliness that is beautiful. With the exception of a few young men and women who are showing off their prosperity, the people in this room seem not to care about appearances; they did not come to America for its surfaces. The faces are stony and happy. Despite all that has happened to them, they do not look tired. Quite the contrary. There is an air of newness about them. In this assembly of the unbreakable, I think of my parents. On these shores, almost fifty years ago, they were the unbreakables. They came not as immigrants but as refugees, when it was too late for everybody but them. They were not received warmly by the community; and I have no doubt that the warmth with which the Russian Jews are now received is partly the result of American Jewish regret about the 1930s and 1940s.

Immigrants, refugees: the differences notwithstanding, they share a quality. They are all strangers to decadence.

I am in Los Angeles. A small shul on Santa Monica Boulevard has been recommended to me. It is a converted office, a long windowless room. The modesty of the place appeals to me. But the service is a little too jolly for my taste. High spirits do not belong in the precincts of faith. I don't know a more incomprehensible remark about religion than Haydn's remark that the thought of God made him cheerful.

At my swanky hotel, I return to my texts. This is the sort of irony that used to excite me. Now it bores me. Philosophy does not have a right address or a wrong one. God, or godlessness, is everywhere or nowhere; with everything or nothing. For this reason, religion makes one a citizen of the world. Monotheism is the original universalism.

At my swanky hotel, Maimonides has some animadversions on Akiva's statement about the imprint of the fathers: "These things obtain in the majority of cases, as indeed most things that are natural obtain in the majority of cases." What he means to say is that there are exceptions. There are sons who do not inherit their fathers' qualities. Maimonides wishes to punch a hole in Akiva's determinism. Thus he records that the rabbis took issue with Akiva's opinion, and he sides with the rabbis. The son is the reflection of the father, Maimonides writes, only until "the season of responsibility." Once the son reaches maturity, "if he is righteous, his merit is his own, and if he is not righteous, his father's merit will not acquit him."

From Los Angeles to the desert, which is God's great text. It teaches that man is puny. Also, that deprivation is not death. The desert is not where living things die; it is where living things live with less. I like the idea of a kaddish in the desert. I wake before six. Over the mountains to the east, the light is arriving. The sky is yellow and the peaks are purple. The shul is in the center of the town. It is a small orange ranch house. I am greeted by a garrulous hasid with a handsome face and a long beard. "The rebbe sent me here sixteen years ago," he says. "Ten of my eleven children were born here." He warns me that he may not be able to "accommodate me" with a quorum, since the winter hordes have not yet descended on the place. I tell him not to worry. I will have honored my father by turning up; and anyway I usually experience the others as an interference.

A half an hour later, near the end of the prayers, he demonstrates for me, without knowing it, the opposite of the temperament that I have described to him. It is Sukkot, or the Feast of Tabernacles. The liturgy is distinguished by a procession of hosannas, in which the worshipers carry palm and myrtle and willow branches and a citrus fruit, which are the symbols of the holiday. (The fragrance of this fruit was one of my earliest aesthetic experiences.) This morning my host is the only one in possession of these instruments, and so he is the only one to march in the procession. I watch as he forms a procession of one. He is alone, but he is not alone. The others are missing only physically. Spiritually, he is thronged. I am forced to concede the loveliness of his lack of interest in solitariness.

At the desert shul I open a glossy magazine and find a meditation on the afterlife. "On the night of July 17, TWA Flight 800 blew up and fell into the ocean, taking 230 people to their deaths. Where are those people now? . . . I continue to be amazed at the reluctance of many people to acknowledge the consequences of their lack of belief in an afterlife." Living on in the memory of others, you see, is not enough. "People who don't believe in an afterlife must recognize that being remembered is no substitute for the afterlife. . . . What about those Jews who were murdered in the Holocaust along with every single person who loved or knew them? With no memories of them, and no afterlife, what has become of them?" What has become of them? I'll tell you what has become of them, you pious fool. Nothing has become of them. Or more precisely, they have become nothingness. That is why courage is required for the confrontation with their death, with all death. "The consequences of their lack of belief"! What do the consequences of belief, or the lack of it, have to do with the truth of belief, or the lack of it? Reality does not answer to need. I need to believe that my father is not gone, but I cannot believe it. And if I could believe it, the intensity of my need to believe it would make my belief suspect, at least in my eyes. Consolations are more frequently false than true. The universe does not owe me edification.

In the Jerusalem Talmud, there is an anecdote that sheds light on Akiva's obsession with descent. It tells of his frustration that he was not elected head of the rabbinical court. He was passed over in favor of the exceedingly young Eleazar ben Azariah. "Rabbi Akiva sat pained and said: 'It is not that he is a greater scholar, it is that he is the son of more distinguished men. Happy is the man whose fathers have given him merit. Happy is the man who has a stake with which to secure himself.'" It was a bitter moment for Akiva, this preferment of lineage to learning. And this reminds me that the discussion of fathers and sons cannot be altogether extracted from social history and the history of the family.

Akiva's reduction of the son to the father offends my modern mind, but he lived in a time and a place in which such a reduction was a social commonplace. His sweeping statement about the impact of the father upon the son was made in a world in which status was generally inherited.

And yet the social explanation does not explain enough. For Akiva was himself proof that, even in a world in which status is inherited, status can also be acquired. He rose from humble origins to the pinnacle of his society, and by his own powers. The shepherd boy who could not read until he was forty became one of the authorities of the age. Thus, in the Talmudic commentary on the tractate in the Mishnah called *Avot*, or *Fathers*, there appears this: "In the future Rabbi Akiva will indict all the poor, for if the poor are asked, 'Why did you not study?' and the poor reply, 'Because we were poor,' then they will be told: 'But Rabbi Akiva himself was very poor and destitute!'" The text goes on to note that Akiva became not only a sage, but also a rich man. The great determinist was himself a tribune of opportunity, of the free and undetermined will. When Akiva includes wisdom in the list of the qualities with which the father endows the son, he is not only contradicting the meritocratic mentality, he is also contradicting his own experience.

Akiva's resentment at the preferment of an aristocrat is not hard to understand. But there are no aristocrats of the mind and no aristocrats of the soul. Or rather, these aristocrats are not born, they are made. As this learned and wealthy son of an unlearned and unwealthy father demonstrated.

Akiva's obsession with descent: I am beginning to understand why the medieval authors of the story about the origins of the kaddish chose Akiva for their hero.

Driving through the badlands of the Colorado desert, I think: fire and water created this place, but fire and water did not have the last word. The testimony of crusts.

Back in Washington, still in the company of Akiva. On the flight back home I recalled that he was the author of one of the great paradoxical statements in the tradition. It appears in the third chapter of *Fathers*: "Everything is foreseen, and freedom is granted, and the world will be judged for good, and according to the majority of [one's] actions." We committed that sentence to memory as children. Its first two clauses are the canonical juxtaposition of the belief in God and the belief in free will. I remember our teachers insisting that the paradox was not a contradiction. This was our introduction to the problem of God's foreknowledge, and to the philosophical discomfiture that it produced. But our teachers were not discomfited: they cheerfully denied the existence of necessity in the realm of morality, and I cheerfully accepted their denial. Many years later I studied the arguments of the medieval philosophers who reasoned devastatingly against necessity; but finally logic was less persuasive than experience, which showed me in the most banal ways that the natural world explains almost nothing about the moral world. The evidence is everywhere, in any ordinary day of any ordinary life, that ethical traits are not inherited traits. There are human beings who lie and human beings who do not lie; human beings who steal and human beings who do not steal; human beings who kill and human beings who do not kill; but under the descriptions of science these human beings are all the same, they are all the members of a single species, the species that may lie or not lie, steal or not steal, kill or not kill. So the generalities of science do not reach to the particulars of behavior. Moral choices are not the objects of scientific understanding. (It is true that I inherit the power to choose, but the power to choose does not explain any particular choice.)

It is obvious that we are not completely unconditioned, but it is also obvious that we are not completely conditioned. We are just unconditioned enough to make ethics possible. (The evolutionary psychologists think that they have the answer to my objection in the Darwinian theory of variations. Darwinism, they say, does not predict that all people will act similarly. But then why *do* people act differently? The variations are not the answer, they are the question.)

Biology is to morality what sex is to love. No, biology is less than that. Sex can be an expression of spirit. Biology cannot be an expression of spirit. (The insistence that sex returns us to our animality is just another way of arousing ourselves.)

Truth is just as primordial as instinct.

Maimonides, on Akiva's dictum in *Fathers*: "This saying holds very great things, and it is right that this saying should have been said by Rabbi Akiva." Why? Is Maimonides referring only to Akiva's stature? Or is he suggesting that the subject of freedom and determinism is Akiva's subject, as I am finding it to be?

Everything is foreseen and freedom is granted. You are determined by those who preceded you and you are at liberty to escape their determinations. You are known and you are not known. You come at the end and you come at the beginning. —The legacies of Akiva.

This is the seventh day of the festival of Sukkot, or Tabernacles. It is the day of the grand hosannas. And the day of the verdict: according to tradition, the judgment that was rendered on Yom Kippur is delivered on this day. The time comes for the great procession around the shul that accompanies the chanting of the hosannas. In this procession, the verdant symbols of the holiday are carried; but I have been traveling and did not acquire them, and so I am asked to hold the Torah in the middle of the leafy parade. I hold the Torah and they march around me. The Torah and I, we are surrounded. I hold it, then I hug it, then I wrap my arms all around it, tighter and tighter and tighter. I sway with it. A few friends ask if I would like to be relieved of my burden and join the procession, and they offer their branches and fruits for me to carry. To their surprise, I decline. I am pleased to be the center of the circle. I do not wish to relinquish my geometrical privilege. I tell them that I am lucky to have the Torah in my arms for so long. I lean my head against it. I can hear the parchment crackling beneath its white velvet sheath. All I can think is that I love it. It is the physical embodiment of the sanctity of words, which is the sanctity that I have honored, religiously and irreligiously, all my life. The prayer ends. Before I restore the Torah to its place in the ark, I kiss it. I am grateful for the time we had together.

Back in shul at dusk. We have a few minutes to kill between the afternoon prayer and the evening prayer, and the rabbi asks for questions from the crowd. Somebody inquires about the extra day that is added to the holidays in the exile. The rabbi's notion is that the extra day was a way of making life in the exile more burdensome, and therefore a subtle rabbinical incitement to leave for Zion. One of the congregants is offended by the suggestion that there is anything burdensome about the multiplication of rituals and duties. I could hit him. Somehow the rabbi gets around to the Jewish community of Kobe. It seems that Kobe is in a region of Japan that is, from the standpoint of Jewish law, ambiguous as to the dateline. The Jews of Kobe, therefore, needed to know the precise date of Yom Kippur. In 1941, they dispatched queries to two authorities—"a fatal mistake," the rabbi laconically adds—and they received two different answers, that is, two different dates for Yom Kippur. The one rabbi said that the fast was on Wednesday, the other rabbi said that the fast was on Thursday. And so the dim and God-fearing Jews of Kobe fasted for two days! "They didn't stay in Kobe long," the rabbi concludes. Then a congregant has a question. He wants to know what to do on a fast day if he finds himself in Alaska, or in any place where the sun does not set. I am almost in stitches. It never occurred to me that there are places in which ritual time is interminable. From now on I will count my blessings. Where I live, the sun sets.

Today we read Ecclesiastes in shul. I always look forward a little wickedly to this occasion. It astounds me that such disillusion should be proclaimed in these surroundings, that the shul should be a haven for Epicureanism. Owing to the way I live, I always feel a little complicit in this infiltration, as if I am the one who rose at night and unlocked the door and let these ideas in. Anyway, when the reading was concluded, the rabbi called for the kaddish. With the other mourners, I rose and recited it. This is the kaddish in its oldest role, "after Scripture and study." Still, for the rest of the service I pondered this practice. On my walk home, it occurred to me that the mourner is the proper respondent to the preacher. I mean, the preacher in Ecclesiastes. For it is with the reality of death that the preacher clinches his argument for living in the present. The life that the preacher recommends—not the life of a voluptuary, but the life of a contemplative man drawing austere conclusions from the experience of his senses—is founded on the certainty that death has the last word. "For the living know that they shall die; but the dead know not any thing; neither have they any more a reward; for the memory of them is forgotten. Also their love, and their hatred, and their envy is now perished; neither have they any more a portion for ever in any thing that is done under the sun." Who better to challenge this than the mourner? His kaddish is premised on the presentness of the past. It is a proof of posterity and a wrestle with immortality. When the mourner rises to say the kaddish after Ecclesiastes, then, he is giving the answer. For the preacher, death is oblivion. For the mourner, death is not oblivion. And the mourner needs no lessons from the preacher on the reality of death. Perhaps that is why he is the congregation's representative in this disputation.

The creed of the mourner: vanity of vanities, all is not vanity.

But what about the mourner who has a secret sympathy for the preacher, the mourner for whom death is oblivion? I am such a mourner. The kaddish often seems preposterous to me. The only effect of death of which I can be sure is non-being. Immortality? The distinction between form and matter, between the soul and the body, is not yet a proof of immortality; and the flamboyant manner in which immortality is construed in the tradition does not make it easier to endorse. And yet I have evidence from the proprieties of my bereavement, from this year in shul, that oblivion is not so handily accomplished. A man dies with the death of his body, but his death is almost never complete. He survives himself in many ways, he leaves many traces of himself behind, in his works and in the people he loved. Whether or not the soul has immortality, then, the soul has posterity. The preacher erred in overlooking this distinction. I cannot be sure that my kaddish for my father is proof of his immortality. I can be sure that it is proof of his posterity.

Posterity is the version of immortality that reason can accept, that tradition can count on.

Those verses in Ecclesiastes nag at me, so I consult the commentaries. Almost all of them agree that the theme of the verses is oblivion. Abraham ibn Ezra, in Spain in the twelfth century, writes that "the living, even if they are fools, know that they will die, and the dead, even if they are wise, know absolutely nothing, and they have nothing to hope for, since they and the memory of them have been forgotten." And Yosef ibn Yahya, in Italy in the sixteenth century, comments that "it is as if [the dead] were never born." Yosef even speaks of "that yonder world of oblivion." Strong words; words that conform to the plain meaning of the text. And words that defy the ethical and eschatological traditions. Enter Rashi, who appears to have anticipated the threat that these verses pose to the faith. Rashi will have none of this existentialism. "*For the living know that they shall die.* And so perhaps they will take the day of death to heart and return from their waywardness, but when they die they have no reward for any action taken from death onward. He who toiled on the eve of the Sabbath will eat on the Sabbath. . . . *Neither have they any more a portion of any thing that is done under the sun.* The merit of their son or their daughter will profit them nothing, these wicked individuals who worshiped idols and so have no atonement after death." The despair of the preacher, according to Rashi, is not a universal despair. It is merely the despair of the wicked. Rashi has forced death back into the moral universe; the world of the nihilist back into the world of the kaddish. There is something beautiful about this intellectual coercion. It is itself an expression of panic about the end.

At last the holidays are over! Now I may return to an ordinary onerousness. Driving to shul this morning, I was smiling at the ease of an unsacralized world. Then I came to a halt in the middle of the road, where a crow was feasting on the remains of a rat.

This morning I brought to the teahouse a volume of the Jerusalem Talmud, where Akiva's statement about the father's formation of the son also appears. In the Jerusalem Talmud, however, it appears anonymously, and with a corollary: "And just as the father made the son meritorious in five things, so the son is obligated to the father in five things: he must assist him in eating, in drinking, in dressing, in putting on his shoes, in helping him get around." A nice touch, this reminder of reciprocity. (Though a modern commentator, concerned that filial obligations not rest on determinist foundations, observes that even if the father is not responsible for the merit of the son, the son's obligations to the father remain, since they are derived from the commandment to honor thy father and thy mother.) Then the text darkens. It turns to David's curse on Joab, in the aftermath of Joab's murder of Abner: "And let there not fail from the house of Joab one that hath an issue, or that is a leper, or that leaneth on a staff, or that falleth on the sword, or that lacketh bread." Against Akiva's five transmitted blessings, here are David's five transmitted curses. (The text explains that they are measure for measure.) In the case of the House of Joab, then, the father determined the character of the sons—for ill.

The failings of the fathers: this is where the illusion of determinism gets dangerous.

Before he died, David instructed Solomon not to allow the murderous Joab "to go down to the grave in peace." The

Talmudic text then tells a strange story about the execution of Joab by Solomon. "When Solomon came to kill Joab, Joab said to him: 'Your father decreed five evil decrees against me. You take them on yourself and I will meet my death.' Solomon accepted the curses, and they were all fulfilled in the House of David." Then we are shown how each of David's curses was realized in his heirs on the throne. And then the whole subject is abruptly dropped. I'm not surprised. These readings stray far from the Jewish universe. They repudiate the Biblical principle that the sins of the fathers will not be visited upon the sons. The tragedy suggested by these readings of Biblical narrative is a tragedy of destiny, not a tragedy of morality. And when the House of David begins to resemble the House of Atreus, a line has been crossed. In the Jewish view, fate is not a cosmic force. It is a reward or a punishment.

Today I was an editor as I have never been an editor before. I proofread the drawings for my father's gravestone. They are ready to go. All in a day's work.

The first portion of Genesis was read in shul this morning, and near the end of the reading, in the sixth chapter, in the passage that describes God's disillusionment with man, there appears this verse: "And it repented the Lord that he had made man on the earth, and it grieved him at his heart." I found this ancient rabbinical comment in Rashi's commentary: "A heretic asked a question of Rabbi Joshua ben Karkha. He said: 'Don't the Jews agree that God foresees what will happen?' He said: 'Yes.' He said: 'But it is written, "it grieved him at his heart."' He said: 'Have you ever had a son?' He said: 'Yes.' He said: 'And what did you do, when you had a son?' He said: 'I rejoiced, and I gave others a reason to rejoice.' He said: 'But didn't you know that your son was mortal and would die?' He said: 'In the hour of joy, joy; in the hour of mourning, mourning.' He said: 'And so it is with the Holy One, Blessed Be He.'"

The heretic may have erred about the nature of Divine omniscience, but in his error he was wise. The impermanence in the knower was owed to the impermanence in the known. How else know a temporal being, a being in time? The heretic preferred not to know the end in the beginning. He preferred to know the beginning in the beginning and the end in the end. A cheer, then, for the heretic. In the hour of joy, joy; in the hour of mourning, mourning.

Today we usher in the new month. When I walked into shul this morning, the white curtains and coverlets were gone and the burgundy curtains and coverlets were back. It was like finding shade.

Leading the worship this morning, I made a mistake. My attention had wandered. And it took everybody a minute or two to correct my mistake. Their attention had wandered, too! What skepticism cannot accomplish, distraction can.

Beware distraction. Nothing serious can be accomplished unless something is excluded from one's vision.

Promiscuity must not be allowed to hide behind complexity.

Distraction, or the corruption of complexity.

Yet distraction has its advantages. Since I have never been in one place, I have never been lost.

I bring a friend from shul to the teahouse. We are gossiping happily, when abruptly he asks: how long can you say those words and not mean them? He means the words of the prayers. I am ready with a lot of old answers, but I suppress them. His question is a good question. There is no point in taking shelter in the multiplicities of meaning. For among the many meanings of those words is their literal meaning. What to do about the plain sense of the prayers? Whatever else it is, the prayer for the restoration of the throne of David in Jerusalem is a prayer for the restoration of the throne of David in Jerusalem. There are lots of reasons for praying, but one of the reasons must be an interest in what it is that you are praying for. Sooner or later, the utterance that is purely mechanical or purely metaphorical demeans these words, and the utterer of them. When I pray alone, I don't really say all the words audibly, in the manner of speech that one is fully prepared to defend. That is why I like to lead the prayers: my chore crowds out my doubt. As for heaven, I am unclear about it and increasingly indifferent, like heaven.

Literal meanings can live without unliteral meanings. The opposite is harder to imagine.

Does prayer "work"? I know the answer, since I have just concluded an experiment. My father sickened. There were prayers for my father. My father died. So I have a result. Whatever prayer does, it does not "work."

As we left shul this morning, a friend said to me: I never rose at the crack of dawn to see my father, but now I rise at the crack of dawn to say kaddish for him. I said to him: our fathers did not have the authority to ask this of us, but our religion does.

A god is not a parent and a parent is not a god.

The eve of the Sabbath. Wind and rain. The leaves are the color of blood, as they blow across the brick walks. Oddly, this evening is the first time that I am the only person in the room saying kaddish. My words echo bleakly in the shul. It is my father's birthday, and when the congregation responds to the words of my kaddish, I think: this is his birthday present.

Menahem Azariah of Fano was a rabbi in sixteenth-century Italy, a prolific writer and an important figure in the diffusion of Lurianic mysticism among European Jewry. A tiny note at the back of a tractate of the Talmud informs me that Menahem Azariah glossed Rabbi Akiva's pronouncement about the father's influence on the son, in a work called *Ma'amar Ḥikur Ha'Din*, or *An Essay Inquiring into Judgment.* I call the Biegeleisen brothers, my erudite and resourceful booksellers in Brooklyn. For months now, books have been flying from Borough Park to Dupont Circle. Sometimes I call Biegeleisen not to buy a book but to ask about one, and none of my bibliographical queries go unanswered. The shop used to be on the Lower East Side in Manhattan, a few blocks from the Jewish bookstore where I worked as a stockboy during college. (I did not have money for the books that I wanted, so I worked for them. I trusted the proprietor to arrive at a fair rate of exchange between the money that I was owed and the books that I was given as my wages; and when I had the rudiments of a Jewish library, I quit.) I remember walking into Biegeleisen's shop on a Sunday afternoon with my father. I was excited to see the English version of Gershom Scholem's life of Shabbetai Tsvi among the new arrivals. My father wanted to know the reason for my excitement. I pointed to the book. It cost $35, which was a lot of money. "Is it really an important book?" Yes, I said. "Do you really want it?" Yes, I said. "Will you really read it?" Yes, I said. And immediately it was mine, and we were off to Gus's Pickles. It was not my father's generosity that struck me: he was always generous with me. What struck me was the joy in his face as he put the volume into my hands. —Biegeleisen says that he'll see what he can do about Menahem Azariah. He warns me that this one might be tough. Yet a few days later there arrives a handsome book printed not too long ago in Jerusalem, a hefty work of kabbalistic exegesis, *Sefer Asarah Ma'amarot,* or *The Book of Ten Essays* by Menahem Azariah of Fano, based on a Frankfurt-on-Main edition of 1898. Only the first four essays have been published, but the essay on judgment is among them.

"Gentlemen, we've got to figure out who says kaddish for Ben next month." That was the announcement after services this morning. I was puzzled. Who is Ben, and why is he preparing to die? It turns out that Ben died last winter, and his wife died a few weeks after he did, and they left nobody to say kaddish, and so his friends are sharing the responsibility. For the year in which poor Ben's soul is rising and falling, they have got it covered.

Akiva: "The father merits the son with beauty and strength and wealth and wisdom and years." Menahem Azariah interprets Akiva's account of paternity in three ways. His first interpretation is kabbalistic. He is struck by a numerical correspondence. There are five qualities in Akiva's description of the father's bequest, and in kabbalistic psychology there are five names for the soul. Each of the names of the soul refers to the soul's relationship to one of the attributes or powers of the godhead as it was structured by the Zohar. "The five good qualities [listed by Rabbi Akiva] correspond to the five names of the father's soul," writes Menahem Azariah, "so that the father bequeaths to his son after him a kind of model of what is above." What an exalted notion of patrimony! In an unmystical sense, though, Menahem Azariah's theosophical speculation is true: the child inherits a conception of the universe. We are all heirs to philosophical assumptions. There are no thinkers from nothing. (But there are many thinkers to nothing.)

"Kaddish is not said for the dead," the rabbi said to me tonight. "It is said for the living." But the living have needed to believe that it is said for the dead; and so the plot thickens. Also, I am not here for therapy.

After my father died, I was given some books about the Jewish way of mourning. I was told that the books are very popular, that they have helped many people make sense of their sorrow. But I disliked the books, because they were psychology tricked out as religion. These books were written in the 1960s, when psychology was at the height of its prestige in America; and the authors of these volumes could not imagine any higher praise of the rabbis than to say that they anticipated the categories of modern therapeutic culture. "The profound psychological insights implicit in the highly structured Jewish mourning observances," says one, "speak eloquently of Judaism's concern for the psychological integrity of the human personality." "Grief requires understanding in a psychological framework," says another. "It is important also to apply this understanding to the Jewish sources to see if Judaism accounts for the psychological meaning of grief." And what if it doesn't? What if Judaism were psychologically useless? I am still bound by love and by duty to follow its forms.

A man has fallen into a pit. Do not speak to him of the good life. Throw him a rope. But when he has climbed out of the pit, and you discover that he is not happy, speak to him of the good life.

The real lacks the power to heal. For therapy to be effective, it must be impractical. It must refer to the ideal.

Driving back from shul, a chill on P Street. Halloween is a few days away, and the shop on the corner has chosen to dress its mannequins in the costumes of clowns and to hang the big smiling puppets by their necks on a rope outside the shop. There the happy corpses hang, keening in the wind above the walk, effigies of dead cheer. I almost looked away.

Akiva: "The father merits the son with beauty and strength and wealth and wisdom and years." Menahem Azariah's second interpretation of Akiva's dictum seeks to resolve the grammatical ambiguity that bothered me, too. He concludes—and his reasoning is rather obscure—that the verb "merits" is peculiarly conjugated so as to establish the accountability of the son. And he, too, dislikes Akiva's determinism. "The father does not merit the son," he writes, "until the son can attain perfection on his own." Menahem Azariah's point is that the agency of the father does not preempt the agency of the son. A fine point, and by now a familiar one. His interpretation falls into what I now recognize as the mainstream of interpretation on this matter. The more I trace the tradition on the subject of fathers and sons, the more clearly I ascertain its philosophical program: to lay necessity low and to raise freedom high.

Sons, sons, sons. What about daughters? In fact, this problem, and this solution, exists for daughters, too. The passage in the Jerusalem Talmud that includes Akiva's statement appears in the discussion of the general rule of filial obligation: "All the commandments that the son is required to perform for the father fall equally upon men and women." This statement makes it plain that "father" and "son" mean "parent" and "child." And the analysis in the Babylonian Talmud comes to the same conclusion. (There it is not so plain. A little dialectic is required.) The gender of the rabbis' language obscures the universality of the rabbis' ruling. Sons, sons, sons: as a man, I can read myself smoothly into these texts, and as a translator I must record them accurately, as they were recorded; but they are not as exclusive as they sound. The daughters are not spared the Fifth Commandment. They, too, must honor their fathers and their mothers.

Not so fast. I read on, and the subsequent discussion in both texts, in the Jerusalem Talmud and in the Babylonian Talmud, qualifies the egalitarianism of the Fifth Commandment. The reason for the qualification is that the services that must be rendered by a child to a parent require financial expenditures, and this leads directly to the social and economic realities of the ancient (and not only the ancient) world. The Jerusalem Talmud: "The same rule applies to man and woman, except that the man has the means and the woman does not have the means, since she is under the authority of others." The Babylonian Talmud: "The man has the means to fulfill the duty, and the woman does not have the means to fulfill the duty, since she is under the authority of others." The status of the woman as daughter is undercut by the status of the woman as wife. The egalitarianism of this commandment stops at marriage.

But look, it starts again with the end of marriage. The Jerusalem Talmud: "If she is widowed or divorced, she is considered as someone who has the means to fulfill the duty." The Babylonian Talmud: "Rabbi Idi bar Avin said in the name of Rav: if she is divorced, they [the man and the woman] are equal." So there is a restoration of equality with respect to this law, but only as a consequence of misfortune. This is how the matter is authoritatively codified by Joseph Karo in the sixteenth century: "The same rule applies to the man and the woman, they are equal in the honoring and the revering of the father and the mother, except that the woman lacks the means to fulfill the duty, since she is subjugated to her husband, and therefore she is exempt from [the commandment to] honor the father and the mother while she is married. But if she is divorced or widowed, she is obligated." Yet there is more to this tortuous story of equality and inequality. Shabbetai ben Meir Ha'Cohen, the commentator on (and the critic of) Karo's code, and the author of *Megillat Efah*, or *Scroll of Darkness*, a harrowing little memoir of the pogroms in the Ukraine in the seventeenth century, cannot quite accept the exemption of a daughter from her duties to her parents. "It would appear," he writes, "that if her husband is not scrupulous [about the performance of this duty], she is obligated to do whatever is possible, exactly as a man is obligated." In his view, then, marital realities should not interfere with filial realities. If a married woman is not satisfied that her parents are receiving their due, she must act in defiance of her station as a wife. So the picture is not altogether awful, from the standpoint of equality. The law seems to make room for the daughter as well as the son. (Unfortunately, it is not always the law by which people abide. Jewish women must also contend with the power of custom and cliché.)

The days are getting shorter, the clocks have not yet been moved, and I wake long before the light. I abhor these black mornings. The darkness within is hard enough. The day should not collaborate with the night.

In the hallway at the office I run into an old friend. She tells me that she is thinking of adopting a child, and suddenly I deliver an oration in praise of adoption. I tell her that we are wrong to believe that the highest form of love is the love of a mother for a child. The highest form of love, I insist, is the love of a mother for a child to whom she has not given birth. I cannot imagine a love more unconditional. For such a love can dispense with the crutch of biology. The intensity with which I deliver these opinions surprises me. A few hours later it hits me that my ardor about adoption was another way of accomplishing what I wish to accomplish in my study of the kaddish, which is to diminish the prestige of blood, to lessen the role of heredity in the articulation of identity.

At dinner I tell a friend about my outburst on adoption. She tells me that a schoolmate recently discovered that he was adopted. He didn't like his adoptive parents, and he was setting out in search of his real parents. "Don't do it," my friend told him. "The ones you don't like—they're the real ones."

In literature, the changeling is such a fearful figure because it exposes the truth about parentage, which is that parentage is not primarily an animal relationship. One's spiritual parents may not be one's biological parents. In Jewish law, the obligation to honor one's teacher takes precedence over the obligation to honor one's father and mother.

If tomorrow I discover that the man for whom I am saying kaddish was not my father, I will continue to say kaddish for him. I am his son for a deeper reason than that I carry his genes.

"I am my father's son." If this statement is biological, it is true, but it is banal. If this statement is intellectual or moral or spiritual, it is true or it is false, but it is not banal. Or conversely: "I am not my father's son." This statement is biologically false, but it may be intellectually or morally or spiritually true. This distinction is illustrated by the children of the wicked. When the son or the daughter of an evil person renounces his or her genealogy, we understand that such a renunciation is impossible, but we also understand what he or she is doing. And we admire it, as in the case, say, of Stalin's daughter. The difficulty, of course, is that not every generational rebellion is so plainly warranted. Stalin was very distinguished in the field of evil. There are not many children who have the burden, and the clarity, of his daughter. And so the complete rejection of the elders is almost never justified.

There are emphases and exaggerations about a father or a mother that only a son or a daughter would make. In families, there is no justice. Families wound with impunity; and we call that impunity love. The iron law of families: good parents hurt good children, good children hurt good parents.

This morning there was not a single word of the prayers that held my attention. Not a single word. I left in disgust with myself. I should have done the whole thing over. Then, at the teahouse, the Perfumer helped me out. I found this, in the intense introduction to his book: "When you pray, stand in fear and reflect on whom you stand before and to whom you are speaking. If there is a worry in your heart, erase it from your mind at the hour of prayer, for when you stand before a great king it is not proper to think of your worry, it is proper to think only of the fear and the love of the king. For it is the case that many people sin to their souls in their houses of worship, when they sit like mourners and their mouths are sealed and they fail to exalt the Lord of Hosts." When the Perfumer wishes to describe the predicament of the individual whose prayer is disrupted by anxiety, he remembers the mourner. The mourner is the dispersed one, the one who cannot promise his undivided attention. The cleft man.

My cares intrude upon my prayers. But my cares are responsible for my prayers.

Finally the clocks have been moved. There is light in the morning! But the early hour of the setting sun means that the afternoon prayer and the evening prayer can no longer be said contiguously, since people will still be working at dusk and it will be hard to get a quorum. Thus the afternoon prayer will be said in the afternoon and the evening prayer will be said in the evening. (Farewell, Washington lunches!) I will find myself in shul three times a day.

It is the morning after Halloween. There are broken wine glasses strewn among the leaves outside the shul, one of them with the purple print of a woman's lips. The ruins of an excitement. I leave the shul unsatisfied, I'm not sure why. At the teahouse I open my book, but it's no use. I can't concentrate. I don't want my tradition this morning. I close my book, and give myself over to my surroundings. A woman is artfully making scones. Across the street a few men are raising a ladder against the front of a sturdy old house. A truck below my window is unloading a delivery of strawberries. Slowly I am rallied by the common order in which I find myself. I am a small, nameless, honorable figure in a genre scene. I could be mistaken for contented. And I must play my part, so I open my book.

Akiva: "The father merits the son with beauty and strength and wealth and wisdom and years." Now to Menahem Azariah's third interpretation of the ancient rabbi's dictum. It is an interpretation that stirs me. It begins with a linguistic and legalistic distinction between two Biblical terms for a bequest, and it ends with a distinction between two types of patrimony. The two terms are *naḥalah* and *yerushah.* They are introduced in the Bible to describe the inheritance of land. The former is derived from the root for "stream," and Menahem Azariah says that such an inheritance "is drawn directly, like streaming water, according to the families and the father's house, and the first one [who comes into possession] endows it for the generations and is called a *mitnaḥel* [bequeather], since he makes himself into a flowing stream for the benefit of his descendants to bequeath to their children in a straight line." Such an inheritance is natural and inalienable. From the standpoint of such an inheritance, it is not possible to differentiate between the generations. They are all brought under the same description. They are one. But this is not the case with *yerushah.* It "comes from a different place, as when the son inherits from his mother and the husband inherits from his wife." Menahem Azariah immediately notes that it is this latter term, the one that refers to a bequest that is alienable, that Scripture employs in one of its most famous injunctions: "Justice, justice shalt thou pursue, that thou mayest live and inherit the land which the Lord God giveth thee." Menahem Azariah detects an admonition in the language of this verse. He comments: "The Scripture came to warn us not to trust in the merit of the fathers so as to receive it in the manner of something natural and privileged, but instead 'justice, justice shalt thou pursue, that thou mayest live and inherit the land,' that is, so that the land will come under our jurisdiction by virtue of our own merits, as if it comes from somewhere else." As if it comes from somewhere else.

Menahem Azariah does not stop there. He notes that the term for the inheritance "from somewhere else" appears not only in the context of geographical patrimony, but also in the context of intellectual patrimony. It may be found in a famous verse in Deuteronomy (it was the first Biblical verse that I learned as a little boy): "Moses commanded us the Torah, the inheritance of the congregation of Jacob." The word for "inheritance" is *morashah*, a variation of *yerushah.* As with the land, then, "so with the Torah, about which it is written 'the inheritance of the congregation of Jacob.' For the learned do not bequeath their crowns of learning to their sons." This is a warning: tradition is an interruptible thing.

In glossing Akiva's statement, then, Menahem Azariah has driven a wedge of responsibility between four of the qualities with which the father endows the son and the fifth. Beauty, strength, wealth, years: these can be called hereditary. They come naturally. They come from the same place. But not wisdom. Intellectual, moral, and spiritual attainments are not hereditary. They do not come naturally. They come from somewhere else.

Not everything that one inherits is an instance of heredity.

"From somewhere else": Menahem Azariah's words point the understanding of tradition in the right direction, toward the unorganic, the unnostalgic, the unexpected, the heterogeneous, the multifarious, the parts that are not a whole, the various community, the autonomous individual, the diversified soul.

"I have no faith!" With these words a friend barrels into shul this evening. I am amazed. He is a religious man, or so I thought. Then he rushes to the phone and calls some of our brethren, to make sure that those who had promised to come to services are on their way. Oh, I see. My friend's faith in God is intact. It is his faith in his fellow man that is shaky. I am a little disappointed. I was hoping for a theological crisis.

"From somewhere else": Menahem Azariah's profound intuition puts me in mind of an even blunter statement of the same idea. Rabbi Yose, an older contemporary of Rabbi Akiva, declares: "Ready yourself for the study of Torah, because it is not your inheritance." I have pondered this statement for years. It is the most counterintuitive observation about tradition that I have found in the tradition. What an estrangement it proposes: the Torah not my inheritance! How can this be? If I was taught anything, it is that the Torah is my inheritance. Yet Rabbi Yose's language is not altogether perverse. He is cautioning against facility. For facility is the most likely hazard in a universe of ritual and dogma, a universe in which the most high and the most difficult is experienced with ease, regularly and familiarly, as social practice, as second nature. A world of Torah will be glib about Torah, unless it is careful. Rabbi Yose is demanding that it be careful, demanding the expulsion of ease from the religious life.

Rabbi Yose is a realist about continuity. He cautions that in the transmission of tradition there is a moment between the giving and the receiving, a moment when it is no longer the possession of the father and not yet the possession of the son, a moment of jeopardy, like the pause in a beating heart, a moment of discontinuity, a beat skipped, when what has stopped has still to start, and what has been transmitted can slip away or run out. This is the moment for which you must "ready yourself." Rabbi Yose is restoring the suspense to the story of tradition.

I was so busy this evening that I almost missed shul. As it turned out, I was the tenth man. The privilege of the one who comes last.

Tradition is never acquired, it is always being acquired. (Or it is always not being acquired: the world is full of Jews who are not Jewish, Christians who are not Christian, Muslims who are not Muslim.)

Rabbi Yose is propounding a theory of tradition. He is suggesting that it is not inherited as other things are inherited. Other things may be acquired externally, but tradition must be acquired internally. In the light of my mourner's obsessions, however, I see another basis for Rabbi Yose's statement: not in the special properties of the inheritance, but in the special properties of the heir. The reason that continuity cannot be taken for granted is also that the generations do not reproduce themselves precisely, that the fathers and the sons are never sufficiently alike for this purpose. And the differences between the father and the son represent a threat to tradition. The son may refuse what the father has given. The son may make himself into the end of the line. (Spiritually if not historically, it is within the power of every Jew to be the last Jew.) The sameness of the fathers and the sons is the necessary fiction of a tradition, but it is a fiction. And it is against this fiction that Rabbi Yose seems to be inveighing.

And this is how some of the commentators read him. Rashi: "*It is not your inheritance.* Do not say: since my father was a great sage I will be just like him, without any effort." And Jonah ben Abraham Gerondi, of Spain in the thirteenth century, one of the great moralists in the history of Judaism: "*It is not your inheritance.* You will not reach it if you do not toil for it, since it is not like an inheritance from the father that the son attains without effort; and also, since your fathers were sages and scholars for generations, do not get any ideas and say that the Torah always returns to its quarters, without work. . . . Wisdom was given only to your fathers and you will not inherit it. If you want wisdom, acquire it for yourself, with the labor of your own hands, and if you do so, you will have felicity and good fortune." For the sons, no congratulations. Only strenuous love.

"If you want wisdom": that is quite a condition. Jonah grasps that there are those who do not want wisdom. That is, he recognizes that the will exists independently of the mind, that the will is not compelled by the mind. At this point reason can only sputter.

"The Torah always returns to its quarters": Jonah is quoting a statement by Rabbi Jeremiah in the Talmud, and challenging it. Similarly, it is reported in the Talmud that Rabbi Yohanan declared that "he who is a scholar, and whose son is a scholar, and whose son's son is a scholar—the Torah will never depart from his seed." This is the other view of tradition, the biological view, the deterministic view. The view that I despise.

"The Torah is not your inheritance." This is another way of saying that the attainments of the mind are not accidents. Beauty, strength, wealth, and years: these attributes, like all the attributes of heredity, are accidents. But wisdom must not be an accident. It must be a necessity.

Tradition is the opposite of identity. Identity is an accident. There is no need to ready yourself for your identity, because it is your inheritance. And that is its scandal.

A chilly Sunday morning. The hum of praying around me was like a low flame, warming me.

The Torah is not your inheritance. But take care, for the Torah may be your disinheritance. If something happens to the tradition in your time, on your watch, if the tradition is corrupted or lost, it is still your fault. The terms of this bargain are severe.

You did not inherit it, but you disinherited it.

If you do not accept the legacy, the ones who come after you cannot resent it, tinker with it, reject it. By what right do you rob them of the pleasures that you enjoyed?

Identity dreams of the identical. It is one of the cheap thrills of traditional life that it allows one to say: I am like my father.

I was lying on the floor of my large white room and listening to the battle with melancholy in the string quartet that Fauré wrote a few months before his death. I closed my eyes. Suddenly I felt a shadow pass over me. I opened my eyes. Nothing around me had moved. I closed my eyes. I felt a shadow pass over me again.

VIII

"The Torah is not your inheritance." Maimonides' gloss on Rabbi Yose's statement refers the reader to the eighth chapter of the *Shemonah Perakim*, or *Eight Chapters*, his philosophical introduction to the anthology of ancient wisdom known as *Avot*, or *Fathers*. The subject of Maimonides' eighth chapter is the nature of freedom. I adore this chapter. It is one of the great protests against determinism, against the reduction of the moral to the natural. What moves Maimonides to his defense of freedom, he writes, is "so that you not give credence to the absurdities of the mendacious astrologers, who falsely assert that the circumstances of one's birth determine whether one will be a person of moral distinction or one lacking in it, and that the individual is compelled, by such necessity, to do the deeds that he does. On the contrary, I know that what is agreed upon in our Torah and in the Greek philosophers, and demonstrated by truthful arguments, is that a man's actions are in his own hands, that there is nothing that can constrain him that is external to himself."

Maimonides' warning against the explanatory power of astrology holds also for the explanatory power of science. For it is scientism, a particular type of explanation for moral life, that Maimonides is repudiating. The point about astrological explanation or phrenological explanation is not only that the science is bad, but also that the explanation is bad. Even when the science is good, the explanation is bad. A biological explanation is as unwarranted an extension of necessity as an astrological explanation. In both, the causes do not fit the effects that they are supposed to explain.

Maimonides' thinking was premonitory. He lived early in the history of scientism. We are living late in its history; but it shows no sign of abating. Indeed, historians will record that in America at the end of this century scientism enjoyed a revival, as Americans became so uncertain of themselves that they required for the formulation of their identities nothing less than the certainty of science or the certainty of religion. They would like to be absolved of responsibility by inevitability. The scientism of this season is the explanation of history by means of birth-order—birth-order!—as in this sentence by a professor at Harvard: "The question of why some people rebel, including why a few particularly far-sighted individuals initiate radical revolutions, is synonymous with the question of why siblings are so different." Synonymous! Scientism is never content for science to be one of the things you need to know. It demands that science be the only thing you need to know. Why isn't it obvious that such a reduction is the work of a crank? —I'm late to shul.

The place of science in life cannot be scientifically established.

Back to Maimonides. His idealism was not at all naive. He was perfectly aware that in reality there are many natural constraints upon the individual. Maimonides was, after all, a doctor. This is how he begins his chapter: "It is impossible for man to be born endowed by nature from his very beginning with either virtue or vice, just as it is impossible that he should be born endowed by nature with a particular skill." And then immediately, the complication: "Yet it is possible for him to be born inclined in his nature toward a virtue or a vice, so that one sort of activity may be closer to him than any other." Maimonides gives examples, based on the medieval theory of the temperaments, or humors. A man "whose natural constitution inclines toward dryness" is more likely, and a phlegmatic man is less likely, to excel intellectually. Still, "if an individual who is inclined in his constitution toward a certain excellence is left without instruction, and if his faculties are not stimulated, he will certainly remain ignorant." And just as the ignorant may be made wise, the cowardly may be made brave. What determines the course of a person's life, then, is not "natural constitution." What determines it is "great exertion." (Am I making the medieval divine into a modern liberal? I don't think so. The repudiation of determinism is right there on the page.)

The faith in freedom is not the same thing as optimism. For the uses of freedom are many. Maimonides insists on the reality of freedom not least in order to establish the possibility of guilt. Yet he is under no illusions about what we can control and what we cannot control. There are "things in nature that are not influenced by the will of man," he continues, such as "whether a person is tall or short, or whether it is rainy or dry, or whether the air is pure or impure, and all the other things that happen in the world, except for the motion of man and his rest." Obviously there is a realm of necessity. Who would deny the truths of science? But the matter does not end there. What is the scope of the realm of necessity? What is the reach of the truths of science? In Maimonides' opinion there are demarcations upon that scope and that reach. Finally the "moral animal" escapes the animal for the moral. We do not completely compel nature and nature does not completely compel us. There is a break in the chain of causality, a lucky crack in creation, which is where we intrude, bringing evils and goods.

All day long I walked around with a powerful feeling of the sweetness of life. This sets me back.

My sister calls. It is time to set a date for the "unveiling" of his grave. She prefers a late date. She does not yet wish to suffer the conclusion. A late date is fine with me. We'll do it in the spring. But I'm a little discomfited by the notion that we may consult our feelings about the ceremonies of our bereavement. It disturbs the soldier's mentality upon which I have come to rely.

A little farther along in his text, Maimonides touches on the problem of Divine foreknowledge—there are verses in the Bible in which God appears to decree how an individual will behave, thereby robbing the individual of his or her freedom—and in this passage he anticipates the theory of variations to which the sociobiologists and the evolutionary psychologists repair whenever the going gets philosophically rough. "The answer," Maimonides writes, "is that [the necessity posited by those verses] is as if God had ordained that those who are born in the future will include a rebel and a slave and a saint and a villain. Now, this may be the case, but it is not for this reason that one individual becomes a villain and another individual becomes a righteous person. Rather, anyone who wishes to become a villain will become one by his choice; and if he had wished to be righteous, nothing would have prevented it; and similarly nothing would have prevented any righteous person from being wicked, for the things that God said were not said about any known individual." Or: from the fact that we are a species with variations, we learn nothing about the distribution of the variations. What all of us are potentially cannot explain what some of us are actually. There will be liars among us. Why am I one of the liars? Because we are various or because I am iniquitous? (If the answer is the former, then I am absolved.)

Science grants absolution more easily than religion.

The issue is not whether biology is true. An alibi may be true, but it is still an alibi.

A biological analysis of a deed is like a chemical analysis of a painting. It is not false, but it does not account for what makes the paints into a painting. It stops before the essential part of the story starts.

The scientific explanation is always an extrinsic explanation. A lot of the world can be explained extrinsically; but not intellectual life, or moral life, or spiritual life. They are lived intrinsically. Science cannot follow them across the border. Science can only watch them disappear into the distance, and after they have disappeared it may deny that they ever existed.

Two people look at an object and fail to see it. The one says: I cannot see it, so it must not be there. The other says: I cannot see it, so I must be blind.

Pity the man who can explain everything. The materialist laughs at the difficulties with which the others are beset, but it is his own lack of difficulties that is comic.

Moving along in Maimonides. His eighth chapter also makes a pragmatic point: that morality, and personal responsibility, and social justice, and religious obligation, and reward and punishment, would all be meaningless in a world of necessity. "If man's actions are compelled, then the commands and the prohibitions of the law would be annulled, and it would all be a big lie, since man would have no freedom of choice in what he did. . . . Suppose that, under such conditions, Simeon murdered Reuben. Why should Simeon be punished, seeing that he was constrained to do the killing, and Reuben was destined to be slain? How could God, who is just and righteous, punish Simeon for a deed which it was impossible for him not to commit, and which, though he tried with all his might, he would be unable to avoid?" Even for the godless, Maimonides' question is a good one.

It is necessary, if you will pardon the expression, that we be free. Otherwise our ethical arrangements with ourselves and with others are impossible. This is what nobody ever notices about idealism: it is practical.

This morning the prayers came out weirdly wrong. I stumbled over words that I have known for years. And I kept on stumbling. I must have sounded like a person with a speech impediment. In a way, I was such a person.

The reproduction of tradition is not like the reproduction of genes. Strictly speaking, tradition is not replicated, since it is never transmitted exactly as it was received. More important, the spiritual legacy and the biological legacy differ in their reasons for survival. The former promises more than itself: the true, the good, the beautiful. The latter promises only itself. Genes survive so that genes will survive. In this respect, they are profoundly inhuman, even if they are the physical history of humanity.

In a nineteenth-century anthology of material related to *Fathers*, in the amplifications of Rabbi Yose's statement that the Torah "is not your inheritance," I am struck by this ancient passage: "Why is it unusual for scholars to have scholars among their descendants? Rabbi Yosef said: So that they will not say that the Torah is their inheritance." (Rabbi Yosef? Surely this is Rabbi Yose: the language is the same, the idea is the same.) Here the relationship of tradition with freedom is not a matter of theory. It is a conclusion drawn from reality. Socially, empirically, we see that learning is not transmitted in the way that other traits are transmitted. The same passage appears in the Babylonian Talmud, in a different tractate, and there I find a gloss by Asher ben Jehiel, the Talmudic giant of the late thirteenth and early fourteenth centuries. Asher suggests two readings of Rabbi Yosef's observation. It was made, he writes, "so that others will not say: it [Torah] is an inheritance to the children of scholars, and so we will surely fail if we approach it to study it. Or, read differently, so that the children of scholars will not say: we do not need to study Torah since it is our inheritance." Asher wishes to preempt the complacency of those who are descended from men of learning and the despair of those who are not descended from men of learning. Intellectually, descent confers no advantage and no disadvantage. It does not matter who or what your father was. The life of the mind, according to these traditions, is meritocratic.

Today I led the worship all three times. At the end of the day, one or two fellows congratulated me for it, as if it were some sort of perfect score. But there was nobody else saying kaddish in shul today, so of course I did the job. Not a big deal. But how on earth did this fine little congregation become dependent on me?

At the teahouse, further perusal of that Talmudic passage on scholars and the children of scholars. It gets better. "Why is it unusual for scholars to have scholars among their descendants?" Rabbi Yosef's answer is followed by other answers. Rabbi Shesha the son of Rabbi Idi said: "So that they will not be haughty toward the community." Mar Zutra said: "Because they lorded it over the community." Rav Ashi said: "Because they called the people asses." These late sages, from the fourth and early fifth centuries (Rav Ashi began the redaction of the Babylonian Talmud), all point to the same danger, which is the danger of elitism: in Jewish society, learning conferred status, and the inheritance of this status would have amounted to the creation of an aristocracy. In a society in which scholarship was a supreme value, scholars could assume (and did assume) an attitude of arrogance. They needed to be humbled; and what would humble them, in the opinion of these authorities, was a reminder that their status was not inherited but acquired, that wisdom will come to anybody who works to be worthy of it.

Hanging around in shul a few minutes after the evening service, I browse through the glosses on the Talmud of Bezalel Ashkenazi, a colorful Talmudist in Egypt in the sixteenth century, whose encyclopedic work preserved the opinions of many medieval authorities. He sees a subtle distinction between the comment of Rav Shesha on the one hand and the comments of Mar Zutra and Rav Ashi on the other. Why is it unusual for scholars to have scholars among their descendants? Ashkenazi is struck by the different tenses of the reasons given for this frustration. "So that they will not be haughty toward the community": Rav Shesha's reason refers to the future, to the elitism that the community must avert; but so far, according to his view, the intellectuals are blameless. The reasons given by Mar Zutra and Rav Ashi—"because they lorded it over the community," "because they called the people asses"—are given in the past tense, and thus they amount to an indictment of the intellectuals. In the opinion of these latter two sages, writes Ashkenazi, the failure of the learned to transmit their learning to their sons is "a punishment for their autocratic conduct toward the community." Rav Shesha is a moralist, but Mar Zutra and Rav Ashi are social critics. The one fears the corrupting effects of inherited status, the others attest to them.

The rabbis were determined to raise the life of the mind above the coils of social stratification. Their observation that intellectual distinction is not transmitted by birth is preceded by another observation: "Beware of the children of the poor, for Torah will come from them." The meritocratic temper could not be clearer. There will be no class analysis of wisdom. Origins may be eclipsed by brains.

Rashi reads this injunction practically: beware of the children of the poor, or "do not think them too insignificant to be taught the Torah." Nissim ben Reuben Gerondi, in Spain in the fourteenth century, points to two attributes of the poor that qualify them for the study of Torah: "They have nothing else to do, and they have a low opinion of themselves." So poverty has its uses: humble circumstances make humble people. Still, these are unsentimental descriptions of the poor. The poor are owed not admiration, but opportunity. The objective of these texts is fairness.

This morning there is a reedy, bearded man praying in the corner. After the service, he identifies himself as a Jew from Lemberg (or Lvov, as the rest of the world calls it) who is occupying himself with the protection and the restoration of Jewish graves in what is now Ukraine. I perk up. My mother's family is from the area around Lemberg, from the town of Drohobycz. I tell the man that I am from Drohobycz, once (and forever) removed. He says that he has been to Drohobycz recently, because some righteous Jews are buried there. I perk up more. Buried there? It was my understanding that there are no surviving Jewish graves in Drohobycz. (There are circumstances in which the survival of graves is the survival for which one must settle.) He hastens to assure me that my impression is correct, that he did not mean to hold out the hope of material remnants. I almost exclaim: But there is a grave in Elmont. . . .

I spilled my tea on my book as I made another serendipitous discovery in the commentators, this time in Solomon Edels's interpretation of Rav Ashi's report that the scholars haughtily called the unlearned "asses." Why asses, exactly? Edels is not satisfied that this was just a random crudity. The learned compared the unlearned to asses, he writes, because they wished to communicate their view that "it is in the nature of creation that they are not fit for learning, just as it is in the nature of the ass that it is not fit [for breeding], and therefore there are no scholars among their children; for it is the view [of the rabbis who observed that scholars do not have scholars among their descendants], and it is in the order of nature, that like gives birth to like." "Asses" was Rav Ashi's metaphor for a difference so deep that it amounts to a difference in species, to a biological difference. The snobbery that Rav Ashi reported, in Edels's reading, was really an appeal to nature, to heredity. It was an early, exclusionary expression of scientism. (Scientism is always exclusionary.) And it was Rav Ashi's aim to offer resistance to such scientism, to insist that intellectual and spiritual reproduction is not like natural or biological reproduction.

After the prayers, this morning and every morning, a few minutes of friendly banter. I have been thoroughly absorbed into the fellowship of these excellent people. I am no longer a stranger in my community. (There is even one of them whom I can't stand.) This makes me a little uneasy. I have no doubt that my observations will suffer for this familiarity. It is a boon to consciousness to be a stranger to one's own.

My reading at the teahouse rings a bell, and I rummage through an old box of scholarly papers, and finally I find what I'm looking for. It is a paper by Avraham Grossman, called "From Father to Son: The Inheritance of the Spiritual Leadership of the Jewish Communities in the Early Middle Ages," and it sheds a great deal of light on the history of the tension between intellectualism and elitism, between spirituality and heredity, in the formative centuries of Judaism in exile. In the Talmudic period, Grossman observes, the sons of scholars were honored, but "by no means did they possess the right of the inheritance of offices from their fathers. Indeed, we possess accounts of scholars who acquired intellectual authority, and even rose to the leadership of the academies, entirely on their own merit, despite the fact that they came from the poorest classes of the people." So it appears that Akiva exaggerated when he attributed the election of Eleazar ben Azariah to his lineage. Akiva was himself one of these examples of meritocracy. Still, Grossman continues, "a great change took place in the spiritual and social universe of Jewry in the early Middle Ages: the recognition, in theory and in practice, of the right of the sons to inherit the positions of the fathers in the spiritual leadership of the community. This was so even when there were other scholars who deserved, by dint of their talents, to serve in those positions." The creation of such an aristocracy occurred first in the academies of Palestine, sometime in the sixth century, and later in the academies of Babylonia, sometime in the eighth century. Grossman's discussion of this development is complicated—the disposition of spiritual offices was entangled with the disposition of political offices, and with the emergence of the academies as institutions of social and political authority—and he provides a great deal of evidence for his view. He shows that the acceptance of intellectual and spiritual heredity subsequently determined the structure of leadership in the early Middle Ages in Italy, France, and Germany. But he notes that the communities of Spain and North Africa remained immune to this development, and "allowed the decisive factor [in the awarding of authority] to be the talents of the individual."

What strikes me most is Grossman's discussion of the consequences of the dynastic style on Jewish intellectual life. The consequences, as he describes them, were "extremely negative." The academies were "transformed into professionalized structures that provided profits for their members, and this led to the weakening of the academies in Babylonia, to the lessening of their influence and to their eventual decline." And this was also the case elsewhere. The institutions of learning became formal, political, conservative, socially and intellectually shut in on themselves. It was not until the late eleventh century, in the wake of the First Crusade, that these dynastic practices were criticized and revised. In Grossman's history, then, I find my prejudices confirmed. Spiritually, intellectually, culturally, there are no dynasties. Or more precisely, dynasties are a mark of decadence. Authority belongs not to the most distinguished son, but to the most distinguished mind.

For the past few days I have been off the rails. My appetites are atrophied. My concentration is gone. Large things escape me and small things overwhelm me. I scurry from realm to realm, but it feels like an interminable crawl. On the way to shul today I drive right into the car in front of me. In shul I am especially edgy. We are commanded to serve the Lord with all our heart and all our soul and all our might, with everything we have. I am serving the Lord with all my nerves.

The downward movement of the soul. "You are lucky," somebody said to me a few months ago, in a mildly envious tone. "You have an anchor." But an anchor is also a weight; and when it doesn't fix you, it pulls you down; and its destination is always the very bottom.

In one of his novellae on the legends of the Talmud, Rabbi Judah Loew ben Bezalel, the sage of Prague in the sixteenth century, and one of the most original and sprawling and recondite figures in the tradition, explains why the Torah is not an inheritance. He attributes the limits of heredity to the most fundamental dichotomy of medieval philosophy. "The notion of inheritance does not pertain to the wisdom of the intellect that is distinct from man, for a man can bequeath to his sons only something material. Insofar as he is made of matter, he has a relation and an affinity with his son from the material standpoint. . . . But the Torah is intellectual, and it is not made of anything material that can be transmitted to his descendants. Thus a man can bequeath to his son qualities such as height and beauty and other things that are material or related to matter, but a thing that is absolutely different from matter, such as the Torah, cannot be an inheritance from one's father. For this reason, there is no reason that the son of a scholar should be a scholar." Mind and matter are different orders of being; and man exists at the intersection of mind and matter; and he must not regard mind in the same way that he regards matter. The mind of the father will not determine the mind of the son, because the mind is not in this way determined.

But hold on. I seem to be finding only what I am looking for. I am stumbling upon champions of freedom everywhere! Looking further in Loew's discussion, I see that I am reading my own disgust with determinism into him. There are passages in Loew's writings in which he defends intellectual liberty with an ardor that makes him Milton's early contemporary among the Jews; but this, I fear, is not one of those passages. Instead the text moves directly to a fantasy of the most extreme elitism. "And [Rabbi Shesha's] statement 'so that they will not be haughty toward the community' must be understood in this way: that the distinction of a scholar who is the son of a scholar is a distinction so lofty that it is not appropriate to this world. . . . It is not right that the bearer of such a distinction should be separated from the community, he should be included in the community, but if his learning were his by inheritance, then he would be separated from the community, owing to the magnitude of his distinction." Loew is awed by the idea of scholars reproducing themselves: it is the perfect perpetuation of mind.

Still, he worries about the consequences of such perfection, for the intellectual and for the community. He explains: "Know, as I have already explained, that the scholar among the people is like the mind in the human body. Even though the mind is divine, it is not completely separated from the body, but instead it is attached to it. But were a scholar to issue [biologically, by way of inheritance] from a scholar, it would be like mind issuing from mind, and it would be completely isolated from the community, insofar as it was mind originated from mind. But surely the mind is not isolated from the human being, it is joined to the human being, and so a scholar cannot issue from a scholar." There is a utopian wistfulness in these sentences. Loew lingers over the possibility of purity—mind giving birth to mind, mind owing nothing to anything except mind—and then he tears himself away. Out of a sense of responsibility toward the scholar and the community, the elitist turns his back on elitism. Loew is insisting that the isolation of the intellectual is not splendid. Mind and matter must run together. Knowledge must not refine itself out of all pertinence to life. —The hour is late and I have an appointment. I would prefer not to interrupt my work. At such moments I am tempted to swear off all engagements and to hole up with my books. But haven't I just been cautioned about the isolation of the intellectual? So in the name of Rabbi Loew, to Dupont Circle!

I bored my friend in Dupont Circle, since I went on and on about Rabbi Loew. (He asked.) There are times when the isolation of the intellectual would be a kindness to others.

Back to the book. About Rav Ashi's comment that scholars called the people "asses," Loew makes a philosophical pun, noting that the Aramaic word for "asses" is the same as the word for "material," or "made of matter." Since "the separate is the antithesis of the material," he writes, the scholars cruelly denounced the ordinary folk. (In the vocabulary of medieval Jewish philosophy, "separate" means "immaterial," "incorporeal," "spiritual.") Here, again, is the elitist struggling with himself. In Loew's account, the intellectual's sense of superiority is both right and wrong. It has a fine metaphysical foundation, and yet the intellectual is punished for it. The same complication occurs in Loew's commentary on Mar Zutra's statement that scholars should not lord it over the community. "It is impossible that the scholar not lord it over the community to some degree, and in this regard he is separated from the community." But the realistic view of the disengagement of the scholar is followed by this: "And therefore they do not deserve that there issue from their seed a scholar who includes within himself the Encompassing [or General] Intellect that emanates from the highest encompassing level, and when they lord it over the community their descendants do not come from that level. Understand this." Understand this? I'm trying, I'm trying.

What is the Encompassing Intellect? Clearly it is a cosmological term, referring to the medieval picture of the world according to which it is comprised of spheres set into motion by Intelligences or Intellects, with which the human intellect in one way or another communes. I remember trying to master the details of this cosmology in graduate school; but I don't remember an Encompassing, or General, Intellect. I head for the shelf on which the precious tomes of Klatzkin and Wolfson sit, and learn that the Encompassing Intellect is the idiosyncratic name given for the Active Intellect, the most exalted of the celestial spheres in the Aristotelian cosmology, by the fiercely anti-Aristotelian Judah Ha'Levi, the romantic philosopher and poet of twelfth-century Spain. The Encompassing Intellect is an emanation from the Divine, a spiritual substance from which the human intellect, in its highest achievement, directly acquires truths that cannot be acquired empirically. Thus the scholar who is the son of a scholar, mind determined by mind, is a figure of preternatural elevation, a supernal figure. And from such a height he stoops to slander his people! For this, says Loew, he is punished: he is forbidden to pass his elevation on to his children. —I think that this is what Loew means, but I'm not sure. I never close any of Loew's books with the feeling that I have adequately understood it.

But I come away from Loew's text with the general principle that intellectual activity is a variety of spiritual activity. It is a practice of individuation. One thinks within the confines of one mind, one vibrates within the confines of one soul. In such confinement, freedom.

I cannot think for you, I cannot save you, even if you are my child. I cannot think for you, I cannot save you, even if you are my father.

I cannot save you, even if you are my father. But doesn't the kaddish claim that I can save you because you are my father?

When you were alive, I could not save you; but now I can save you. Or so the kaddish claims. Myself, I do not believe that I can save you. But I am your son and I will persevere.

My sister calls. She says that things are falling out of her hands. In the morning she dropped an egg. In the evening she grabbed a pan in the oven and burned her hand. I tell her that I, too, am experiencing little failures, a loosened grip. What is this obscure development of sorrow that happens within her and within me at the same time?

The independence of the son from the father is proclaimed in one of the most exciting texts in medieval Jewish history. I refer to *Milhamot Ha'Shem*, or *The Wars of the Lord*, Nahmanides' account of the disputation in Barcelona. On July 20, 1263, at the royal palace in Barcelona, in the presence of James the Conqueror, king of Aragon, and many ecclesiastical and political officials, Nahmanides defended Judaism against a Dominican friar named Pablo Christiani. (He was a Jew named Saul who had studied with important rabbis and then converted to Christianity. A Saul became a Paul. More trouble.) The debate was four days long, and the final encounter took place in the house of worship, where the king made an address. The subject of the debate was the Dominican's claim that the messianism of Jesus is proved by Jewish sources, though Nahmanides brazenly promoted the discussion into an exchange about first principles. (Or so it seems from his report of the encounter. There is a Latin report, too, but I am not familiar with it.) On the second day of the discussion, Nahmanides addresses a question to his interlocutor: "Do you agree with my assertion that the sin of Adam will be annulled in the time of the messiah?" The Jew has broached the subject of original sin. And Friar Paul and King James both reply: "Yes. But not in the way you think.

What really happens is that everyone goes to Gehenna as a consequence of that punishment [for the sin in the Garden of Eden], and in the days of the messiah the punishment is annulled, because he has rescued them from there." Or, he died for our sins. Nahmanides offers a remarkable retort: "As they say in our land, if you intend to lie, get rid of the witnesses. After all, many punishments of Adam and Eve were recorded. About Adam, it was said: 'cursed is the ground for thy sake,' and 'thorns and thistles shall it bring forth to thee,' and 'in the sweat of thy brow shalt thou eat bread,' and 'for dust thou art and unto dust thou shalt return.' And about Eve, also this: 'in sorrow shalt thou bring forth children.' But all these things are still the case today! So from what we can see and what we can feel, these punishments were not annulled by the advent of your messiah. Instead you describe the annulment of a hell that is not attested to anywhere, so that nobody will be able to contradict you. Send one of your company to scout out this hell. Let us have his report!" The rabbi was not a coward. (He was almost seventy years old when he faced down the powers.) Then Nahmanides gets to the part of his argument that exercises me: "Moreover, the righteous are not punished with Gehenna as a consequence of the sin of their first father, God forbid. For my soul is as closely and equally related to the soul of my father as to the soul of Pharaoh. Surely my soul will not go to Gehenna for Pharaoh's sin! The punishments [listed in Scripture for the sin of Adam and Eve] were corporeal, punishments of the body, because my body is indeed derived from my father and my mother; and so, when it was decreed that they be mortal, their descendants became forever in their natures mortal." The body is inherited. The soul is not inherited. Nahmanides could not be clearer.

"For my soul is as closely related to the soul of my father as to the soul of Pharaoh": it is an amazing statement.

Nahmanides did not wish to be misunderstood. The Christian notion of original sin was a genealogical determinism; and against determinism, he championed freedom. But to compare his father to Pharaoh! These are strong words for a Jewish son. (In Hebrew, Nahmanides is known more fully as Moses ben Nahman; and Moses' comment in Barcelona makes me wonder what Nahman was like. If Nahman was like Pharaoh, then Moses was like Moses!)

Nahmanides had been assured that he could speak freely in Barcelona, but two years after the disputation he was arraigned for slander against Christianity. The king banished the rabbi from his realm for two years and condemned to the stake his account of the disputation (which Nahmanides had made public at the prompting of the bishop of Gerona). In the immediate aftermath of the confrontation in Barcelona, moreover, the king issued a number of anti-Jewish decrees. A virulent censorship of Jewish books was begun in Aragon. Jews were required to attend the sermons of Christian missionaries. A portion of Maimonides' code of law was burned. And all this did not satisfy the Dominican enemies of Nahmanides. They appealed to the pope, who wrote to the king that the rabbi who had written "that book full of lies" should be more severely punished. (He also promulgated the papal bull that eventually became the basis for the mandate of the Inquisition in Spain, Italy, and southern France.) And so Nahmanides prudently fled Spain. Eventually he made it to Jerusalem. The victor, on the run! But the only victories that were available to the Jews in exile were moral victories.

I have been hearing the moaning of wood. It is not like a human moan. It is not a moan of pain, it is a moan of adjustment—the whisper produced by a shift in pressure, by a strain that is ending, by an accommodation with the forces that are pushing and pulling. One day I would like to moan like wood.

Who on earth was Abraham of Minsk? I'll be damned if I know. But here is his commentary, among the "later ones" at the back of the Talmudic tractate; and here, in his gloss on the passage about the untransmittability of tradition from father to son, he sends me to a giant of the eighteenth century, or rather to his son. The giant was Ezekiel Landau of Prague, one of the most influential jurists in the history of Jewish law and a charismatic (and rather complicated) adversary of the new forces of enlightenment. He died in 1793. The son was Samuel Landau, also an interesting figure in the modernization wars, who published the second part of his father's collected responsa, *Noda Be'Yehudah,* or *Renowned in Judah.* The son's introduction to the responsa of the father is the text that Abraham of Minsk is urging on me. But there is a hitch. In the edition of Ezekiel Landau's responsa that I have on my shelf, the son's introduction is missing. I call Brooklyn for help. Not to worry, my bookseller says. There is a new edition in the works, and the early volumes are already in the store, and the son's introduction is included. I'll have it in a few days. (But who was Abraham of Minsk? Samuel Landau's edition of his father's responsa appeared in 1811. The great Vilna edition of the Talmud, in which I make the acquaintance of Abraham of Minsk, appeared between 1880 and 1886. I conclude that Abraham of Minsk was an authority in Russia around the middle of the nineteenth century. The name of one of his books is given above his commentary, but it means nothing to me.)

I was leading the worship this morning, and as usual my head was crowded with thoughts that came between me and the prayers. But then the clatter suddenly stopped, my head emptied out, until all that remained were the words, and I saw them, and I heard them, and I joined them, and to my surprise I provided the congregation with a few minutes of real prayer. I don't know how this happened. But I will attribute it to the spiritual utility of emptiness. It is not easy to become empty, but one must make the attempt. Emptying is a form of refining. There are sweets to which one must come starving.

At the teahouse with the Landaus. The new edition has arrived. It is handsome and full of interesting historical materials. I follow the son's lively narrative of his activities as his father's editor, and then I find what Abraham of Minsk wanted me to find. Samuel has remarked upon precisely the contradiction that I have been pondering all these weeks. He asks that "the merit of my father—my father, the chariot of Israel—stand me in good stead," and he adduces Rabbi Akiva's dictum: "The father merits the son with beauty and strength and wealth and wisdom and years." And immediately he, too, is vexed by the suggestion that wisdom can be biologically acquired. "This seems perplexing. Granted, it is reasonable to make such a claim about beauty and strength, which are caused naturally and are characteristics of the body, since (as the commentators [on Rabbi Akiva's statement] observed) the nature of the son tends to be like the nature of the father. As for wisdom, however, by what means can the son inherit his father's wisdom? After all, the rabbis have said: 'Why is it unusual for scholars to have scholars among their descendants? So that they will not say that the Torah is their inheritance.' . . . The statement that the father merits the son with wisdom flatly contradicts the statement that the Torah is not an inheritance." The one certainly does contradict the other. And this contradiction stings, because wisdom is plainly not a production of nature. Bring young Landau a pot of tea!

On Sunday morning I come to shul and find the window ledges lined with beer bottles. Suddenly I feel proprietary about the place. I spend a few minutes cleaning up.

How does Samuel Landau propose to reconcile the contradiction between the two rabbinical texts, between the belief in heredity and the belief in freedom? He looks closely at Akiva's language and sees that his statement speaks of wisdom generally. He has a suggestion. "The sage's intention was not to refer to the wisdom of the Torah [but to wisdom generally]. After all, there are other matters, too, in which one must have knowledge and judgment in everything that one does." And one of those "other matters" is science—in this instance, chemistry. "Wisdom is the supreme faculty of the body, as is known to the scholars of nature, who stood on this point when they analyzed the body into its parts according to the science of chemistry, which teaches that man's body is a compound of water, oil, lime, and salt. They found in their demonstrations that a man who, in his lifetime, was sharp and intellectual was distinguished by a preponderance of salt." According to such an analysis, Samuel writes, "the mind and wisdom are caused by the composition of the body and its parts, and it may therefore be said about it that the nature of the father is likely to be the nature of the son." According to a scientific interpretation of the mind, intellectual inheritance is possible; and the son may be profoundly, essentially, completely like the father. The noose of determinism is tightening. But Samuel wants to slip free of it. No sooner has he considered the physicalist analysis of mind than he rejects it. "But this is a forced way of interpreting the sage [Rabbi Akiva], for the word 'wisdom' was not used to refer to wisdom generally, but only to the wisdom of the Torah, and it is not an inheritance. More, the sages also said 'beware of the children of the poor, for Torah will come from them.'" The mind is not the brain.

Still, Samuel's rejection of the materialist explanation of Torah seems content to leave all other intellectual activities materially explained. And his rejection of scientism does not seem to be based on anything philosophical. Its grounds seems to be purely textual. Again, I must be wary not to paint the tradition in the image of my anti-scientistic desire. Yet what can it mean when somebody such as Samuel Landau rules out a scientific explanation of Torah, if not that the most exalted attainment of mind cannot be explained scientifically? It is not the low that defines the human difference, it is the high. And it is the high that science cannot explain.

To be sure, the hunt for truth is not all that occupies our minds. There are mental operations that do not require thought, and I do not doubt that we are influenced in many of those mental operations by things outside our minds and inside our bodies. But thought is not, for that reason, just a fancy physical activity.

Our commonality with the natural world is vast and wondrous, but it is not our deepest distinction, our deepest stimulation. It is not why we are ontologically exciting.

So how does Samuel Landau resolve the contradiction between the rabbis? Trivially, I'm afraid. "The son of a learned man who toils in Torah and becomes learned enjoys the merit of his father's reputation in order to make his own learning widely known, so that when he pronounces on Torah matters the people will incline to listen to him. This is the point of the saying that 'the father merits the son with wisdom': not that the father affects the son so as to endow him with wisdom, but that the son, if he acquires wisdom, may be merited by his father to spread his own wisdom far and wide, and his words will be heeded by virtue of his father. For there are many individuals who work hard at the study of Torah, who have the privilege of learning but not the privilege of teaching, and even if they send their teaching forth in treatises and books, nobody pays attention and they have bad luck. But this is not the case if his father was a well-known scholar." With this wooden point, Samuel drains his discussion of philosophical interest. For him, the issue is not determinism at all. It is nepotism. Descent is just a lucky or an unlucky break. In a world of competition, it helps to be the child of a luminary; and Samuel writes callowly, like the child of a luminary. "I, too, on this day, am trusting that the merit of my father will stand me in good stead." And so it did: in his edition of Ezekiel Landau's responsa, Samuel Landau took the liberty of including some of his own responsa! He took advantage of his genealogy, and in his introduction to his edition he sought to justify himself.

Perhaps I am harsh. Perhaps Samuel Landau was simply following in Ezekiel Landau's footsteps. For Ezekiel Landau, in the first edition of his book, had inscribed his own debt to his own father. Indeed, his belief that his father's merit was reflected in his work accounts for the title of his book. *Renowned in Judah,* he explains in a short rhymed preface, really means *Renowned for Judah,* and Judah was his father. "My name is known not owing to wisdom and knowledge, but owing to Judah, whose merit stands me in good stead." Just as the son Ezekiel wished to be honored for the father Judah, so the son Samuel wished to be honored for the father Ezekiel. Yet there is a difference. The name of Ezekiel Landau is remembered not for his father, but for his wisdom and his knowledge. The name of Samuel Landau is remembered not for his wisdom and his knowledge, but for his father. What matters is what you do, not who you are.

Genealogy is an interference in the natural democracy of thought.

Abraham of Minsk, who led me to the family romance of the Landaus of Prague, has his own solution to Samuel Landau's dilemma. It is a wonderful solution. In his gloss on the Talmudic statement that it is unusual for scholars to have scholars among their descendants, Abraham writes: "In the introduction to the second edition of *Renowned in Judah,* the son was perplexed, since this passage contradicts the statement that 'the father merits the son' and so on. But he was unaware of what is found in the Jerusalem Talmud . . . where the statement that the father merits the son with wisdom is read as the explication of the verse [in Deuteronomy] 'and ye shall teach them to your children,' which means that wisdom is what the father is obligated to teach his son. And so this has no relevance at all to this statement [that scholars do not have scholars among their descendants]." Abraham has retired a contradiction between two passages by means of a third passage. It is a classical Talmudic procedure. I remember that third passage—"and ye shall teach them to your children"—from a few months ago, but I saw in it only a prooftext. Abraham saw more. He saw that the prooftext alters the intellectual situation. The Scriptural words that were chosen to support heredity have the opposite effect. They undermine heredity. The verse implies, as Abraham rightly observes, that the father merits the son with wisdom not genetically, but pedagogically. He has a duty to teach his son. Thus wisdom is rescued from the realm of the biologically normative and installed in the realm of the ethically normative.

Abraham's challenge to determinism is made not in the name of the son's freedom, but in the name of the father's freedom. In all the worry about the agency of the son,

Abraham prefers to worry about the agency of the father. He distributes the responsibility for the tradition equitably across the generations. The son may choose to possess or not to possess the tradition. The father may choose to transmit or not to transmit the tradition. But the father, too, has been enjoined. Even things that cannot be inherited must be passed on.

This morning a rainstorm destroyed the composure of Georgetown. A mean wind pillaged the trees and made dirty mounds of the leaves. By the time it was over, the trees stood like skeletons.

So who was Abraham of Minsk? I ask around. In Brooklyn, my family's rabbi gives me a lead. He recalls that many decades ago he studied with a student who claimed to be a descendant of this scholar. I poke around a little more, and finally the prize is mine. Our hero's full name was Abraham ben Judah Leib Maskileison. The remarkable thing about his family name is that it is the title of his first work, his first collection of glosses on the Talmud. "Eison," or "Eitan," from which we have the English name "Ethan," appears in the titles of all Abraham's works, as a clue to the author's name; for the word, which connotes a mixture of steadfastness and antiquity, is the tradition's honorific for Abraham, the patriarch Abraham. Our Abraham was born in 1788 and he died in 1848. (I guessed well.) He appears to have been an indefatigable composer of commentaries, many of which (including the commentary from which I have profited) were published posthumously. He did not come to Minsk until late in his life. He was a poor man all his life.

In Brooklyn, browsing in Biegeleisen's bookshop. I find, bound in gaudy green, a new edition of the commentary on

Fathers by Menahem Ha'Meiri, the prodigy of medieval Perpignan. This edition is based on a manuscript in St. Petersburg ("formerly Leningrad," the title page triumphantly proclaims) that was transcribed a few years ago. I turn immediately to Rabbi Yose's statement that the Torah is not an inheritance, to see what thoughts it inspires in Ha'Meiri. Here is his gloss: "Even though your fathers were scholars, do not say that the matter is obviously innate in me and I may make do with little study, since it is not your inheritance. How many rivers have dried up, how many stones have brought forth water!" Ha'Meiri never disappoints. He was notable among the Talmudists of his time for his interest in the sciences, and I have no doubt that his term "innate," or "inscribed by nature," is an allusion to biological causation, which he rejects. "How many rivers have dried up, how many stones have brought forth water": I rejoice to see biology expelled by poetry.

Give me no gold. Give me no silver. Give me paper. (A prayer.)

A perplexity is reported in a responsum by Solomon ben Abraham Adret, the supreme legal authority in Spain at the turn of the fourteenth century: "You inquired about the meaning of the rabbis' statement that the son acquits the father but the father does not acquit the son, which appears to contradict their statement that he who prepares on the eve of the Sabbath will eat on the Sabbath, whereas he who does not prepare on the eve of the Sabbath will not eat on the Sabbath. Moreover, if the father does not acquit the son, then why do we always invoke the merit of the fathers?" Adret was a student of Nahmanides. Like his teacher, he defended Judaism in disputations with other faiths; and like his teacher, he had an unusually versatile and complicated mind. His responsa treat philosophy as well as law. The responsum before me is one of Adret's philosophical ones. Why should the sons affect the fortunes of the fathers and the fathers affect the fortunes of the sons? Surely every individual must provide for his own fate; and every generation, too. If the fathers did not prepare for the Sabbath, then why should they eat on the Sabbath?

Adret replies with a short composition on the nature and the limits of the influence of parents on children. "Know that, in the matter of the rewards and punishments of human beings, the rewards of the material world are material and the rewards of the spiritual world are spiritual. Now, the father begets the son; and the son is a part of the father in the flesh of his body and his sinews and his bones. The mother endows the son with the redness in him. But the son's soul is a part of his portion from the Father, and it is not transmitted from parents to children. As the rabbis in the Talmud stated, the father contributes the semen of the white substance that forms the bones, the sinews, the nails, the brain, and the white in the eye; and the mother contributes the semen of the red substance that forms the skin, the flesh, the hair, the blood, and the black of the eye; and the Holy One, Blessed Be He, contributes the soul. When people die, the Holy One takes back His share and leaves the share of his father and the share of his mother with them. As it is written [in Ecclesiastes], 'then shall the dust return to the earth as it was, and the spirit shall return unto God who gave it.' Thus the rewards of this world are physical, and they may pass from father to son. This is what we mean when we say [in the daily prayers] that 'He remembers the good deeds of the fathers.' That the merit of the fathers may accrue to the benefit of the sons in the material world: there is nothing vexing about this." But the spiritual world is another story. In the spiritual world, the individual is essentially autonomous. The soul "is not transmitted from parents to children." —It is almost dark. I must hurry autonomously to shul.

Magnified and sanctified . . . Magnified and sanctified . . . Magnified and sanctified . . .

Back to Adret. I rejoice in his separation of the realms, in his expulsion of physicalism and determinism from the analysis of the spirit. But a problem remains. If souls are free, and therefore accountable for their actions, so that they have their just deserts, then why can the son alter the fate of the father's soul? The assumptions of mythology seem to interfere with the assumptions of morality. Adret has an explanation. "The assertion that the son acquits the father but the father does not acquit the son refers [not to the material world, but] to the spiritual world. It works this way. Even though the son is a part of his father in his body and not in his soul, still he is caused by his father. For this reason, the son is commanded to honor his father and to respect him, while the father is not commanded in this way regarding his son. For what is caused must always honor its cause, even though the causation was entailed and not voluntary." I pause here, in the middle of Adret's explanation. In the Aristotelian jargon, I see a big idea. It is that the freedom of the soul does not insulate it from the contingency of its circumstances. Spirit is never absolved from a relationship with matter. We are islands of freedom in seas of necessity.

A free man is still a created man. There is nothing god-like about freedom.

Honor thy father and thy mother. In Adret's reading, this means: honor thy origin even though it is not thy source.

My origin is not my source. My origin is only an empirical fact. But an empirical fact may have spiritual significance.

"Even though the son is a part of his father in his body and not in his soul, still he is caused by his father." And Adret continues: "Thus, when a man produces a righteous son who serves the Lord, it seems as if he serves the Lord as the effect of his cause. And this is the secret of the Torah's view of fate, which is the antithesis of the astrological view." We do not live by the influence of the stars. We live by the influence of our origins—and by our immunity to any influence at all. And now Adret proceeds to explain the legitimacy of my intervention in the destiny of my father's soul. "The highest reward to which a man may aspire is that he leave something of himself in the physical world that serves the Lord. If he does so, he feels as if he himself still serves the Lord, as if he is not dead but still alive, since he begat a servant of the Lord. And so it is right that the merit of the son should benefit the father. But why should the father vindicate the soul of the son? For the father is not a part of the son. His son is not the cause of his body or his soul. So how can the merit of the father benefit the son? (Still, it profits the dead that people do good works or pray for their sake, as in David's prayer for Absalom. And this is why it became the custom in Israel to give charity for the repose of the soul.)"

So this is how I may understand the kaddish in Adret's terms: The soul of the son is not the soul of the father. His soul is his soul, my soul is my soul. The effect is not the cause. ("It seems *as if* he serves the Lord as the effect of his cause.") Yet the effect reveals the cause. The cause may be acknowledged and admired in the effect. I can change the fate of my father's soul because my father's soul lives in me, as the cause lives in the effect. No more, no less.

The effect of a cause, or life after death.

Causes do not die until their effects die. Parents do not die until their children die. But children become parents, and effects become causes. . . .

The future is a succession of antecedents.

Adret is not done. There remains the Talmudical statement that he who toiled on the eve of the Sabbath will eat on the Sabbath. Adret ratifies its stern doctrine of personal responsibility. "This refers to what every individual must provide for himself," he concludes. "This world is given to every individual to act in, and the next world is for his reward; and there is nothing that the soul can do in the next world to affect its reward, to augment it or to diminish it." About the accountability of the individual, the rabbi is stringent. He will not allow morality to be disconcerted by family. There is no extenuation by kinship.

Where there is love, there must also be justice.

Do you believe in the soul? Then you are an individualist.

When you are asked to account for yourself, do not begin with the story of your father and your mother.

—Who are you?
—I am the child of . . .
—That is not what I asked.

"He who toiled on the eve of the Sabbath will eat on the Sabbath." I will make myself ready for the Sabbath. But make me ready, Lord, for the eve of the Sabbath.

This evening there were only five of us in shul at the appointed hour, and an enterprising young man began to work the phone. He called five others and told each one of them that he must come to shul because he will be the tenth. He sounded like a lawyer in transports of leveraging, but in a sense he was telling the truth. Every man among us is the tenth man. When I said this to the fellow next to me, he said: "You're right. But I was here first."

The seat of tradition is the soul. A radical thought, because it kicks away all the externalities. (Tradition must be transmitted to the soul, which cannot be transmitted.)

Tradition is not reproduced. It is thrown and it is caught. It lives a long time in the air.

IX

The most extensive work on death in rabbinical literature must be *Ma'avar Yabbok,* or *Crossing the Jabbok* by Aaron Berachiah ben Moses of Modena, an Italian kabbalist of the late sixteenth and early seventeenth centuries. Aaron was a disciple of Menahem Azariah of Fano, and was embroiled in the great mystical controversy of the Italian community, in which the systematic theosophy of Moses Cordovero was challenged and eventually usurped (though not in Aaron's mind) by the ravishing theurgy of Isaac Luria. Aaron was also an innovator of ritual, not least in his masterpiece about the end of life. *Crossing the Jabbok* was published in Venice in 1626, and it went through many editions; a number of shorter versions were produced to serve as handbooks for rabbis and burial societies and mourners. It is a truly baroque book, crowded with customs and prayers and mysteries and homilies, in a turgid style that occasionally breaks into utterances of great simplicity and beauty. Aaron is drenched in the discourse of the mystics ("I have not deviated to the right or to the left after the opinions of the philosophers, from whose ways my soul has kept its distance"). I must admit that the high kabbalah of the sixteenth and seventeenth centuries leaves me cold. I have never found a place for myself in the extravagant edifice. I think that it is artificial and airless, an almost Tantric decadence of symbols and allegories, in which occult entities are arbitrarily hypostatized and then enormous effort is expended in the mapping of relationships between them, in the utterly unsubstantiated belief that the structure of the godhead is being revealed. The whole system has always struck me as a holy game. Sometimes the mania for symbolism is almost amusing—as, for example, in Aaron's theosophical analysis of wine. Wine, he writes, "was created to comfort the mourner." I have no objection to that. Then Aaron explains that "the secret of wine is [the divine emanation, or *sefirah,* of] Power." If he says so. And then he explains that "the wine will be white if [the emanation] inclines toward Love, and it will be red if it inclines toward Justice." I cannot follow Aaron into this silliness. And then Aaron ruins the wine! "The wine will be called good if it is mixed with water from the side of Love, where Goodness is."

Symbols are sometimes degraded by their details. There are some things that are too small to stand for anything but themselves. They deserve to escape the frenzy of interpretation.

The special integrity of small things.

The Jabbok was the brook that Jacob's family forded in the middle of night, in the flight from Esau; the brook at which Jacob found himself at dawn, when he wrestled with the angel and prevailed. "I have collected these many interpretations and homilies that together provide counsels of purity and holiness," Aaron writes, "and I have buttressed them with humility and shame, and I have called them *Crossing the Jabbok*, and with love and awe I offer them up like a burnt offering and its incense to the sacred congregation, so that with music and drums they may cross the rickety bridge from this world of punishment and extinction that has twisted the heavens, and join themselves to the delights of oneness and benevolence and holiness. . . . And so we shall all cross the Jabbok to wrestle with God until the breaking of the day, which is the resurrection." Crossing the Jabbok is not like crossing the Styx. It is a voyage up, not a voyage down.

The adept of mystery gives an account of himself that is itself mysterious. Explaining elsewhere that a man's troubles make it hard for him to devote himself to the tranquil study of divine wisdom, Aaron writes that "my father and my mother abandoned me, and I was estranged from them, through no fault of my own. I never enjoyed a meal at my father's table." He was raised by his grandmother, whom he portrays as a saintly woman who studied Scripture and law "and especially Maimonides, and she was even acquainted with the Zohar, to the best of her ability. . . . Foremost among her many good works was her generosity in retaining esteemed individuals to instruct me in the Torah and in the fear of heaven. . . . I came to be with her, and to depend on her support, from the day I was born, and the burden of my needs fell upon her and upon no one else." When she was seventy-five, Aaron's grandmother left Italy for the Holy Land, and died in Safed, the world capital of Jewish mysticism. "I was left here, alone in the years of my childhood," he recalls, "an ignorant boy without any education and knowledge, since I did not have the opportunity to attend a scholar, except briefly, and I was not acquainted even with the talk of rabbis. And so tranquillity gave way to anxiety, because I had nobody to support me, nobody to sustain me. My family was gone. My friends had forgotten me. All this, aside from the terrors that were turned upon me by a treacherous fate. So thus am I to be found, pondering my guilt and angry at what I might have done to bring this upon myself, and justifying the judgment of heaven in visiting upon me this continuing commotion, this decay that came unaccountably from my own flesh and blood, and from the accusations of another." The accusations of another? Aaron says nothing more about what was done to him. It appears that he was abandoned by his parents when he was born, and then denied again by his family and his friends after the departure of his saintly grandmother, and then slandered. This is all that he is prepared to reveal about his calamities. Still, his bitterness is plain. —An unidealized account of a Jewish childhood. This is refreshing.

In the introduction to *Crossing the Jabbok,* Aaron identifies himself as "the grandson of the glory of our house, my esteemed and wise grandmother Favorita, also known as Bathsheba. . . . It was she and nobody else who raised me like a son from the day I was born, and I owe her all the honor and respect that parents are owed." The cherished Favorita was the widow of the rabbi Solomon Jacob Raphael, who was the son of the rabbi and physician Mordecai of Modena, who was descended "from the first families who were expelled from France." Aaron wants it known that he was born into the aristocracy of adversity. Not that he has a very high opinion of himself. "My sins have turned me into trash," he confesses. And his authorial anxiety is spectacular, even by the conventions of this literature, in which everybody protests that he is nobody. "Woe is me if I write, and woe is me if I do not write." But finally he decides to take the plunge, "because everything that is done for the sake of heaven is permitted and valid." During a short visit to Mantua, "one of the great communities of Italy," he is impressed by the community's philanthropic institutions. "Even though there were many among them who did not study the Talmud and the law, with an eager heart they busied themselves in the performance of good deeds." In Mantua he hears the call. "While I was there I learned incidentally that for a long time they had fervently wished that someone in the community would come and arrange for them the protocols for prayer at the time of death." This Aaron did, so that "these readings and homilies will become familiar to all the members of all the charitable confraternities in every town and in every city . . . so that in this way they will provide a proper end and a good hope to the souls of the dying and the dead."

"Just as the son must honor his father in life," Aaron maintains, "so in his death he must take the judgment of his father upon himself." The duty of the son survives the death of the father. "And the son must do so because he is capable of unburdening his father of it, with the power of the commandments that he performs and the good deeds that he does for the purpose of blocking that judgment." There are a variety of means available to the son who wishes to intervene in the heavenly tribunal. Aaron mentions some of the practices of mourning, furnishing them with kabbalistic explanations. (The reason that a mourner must not wear pressed clothes for the first thirty days of mourning is that "the soul of the departed does not wear beautiful raiments in which to appear before the holies of heaven until after thirty days." And so on.) The mourner can also give charity in his parent's memory. And the mourner can say kaddish. "Mourners should be very strict, in the matter of the meaning of their fathers' souls, to rise early to say the kaddish." In this way, they will "unify the quality of night with the quality of day." What a lovely notion! Here the compulsiveness of the symbolist mind gives way before the sensitivity of the symbolist mind.

And there are other expedients. "Aside from the mourner's kaddish, it is good that regularly, throughout the year, the mourner should publicly recite sacred words, such as prophetic readings [on Sabbaths] and psalms and the like, for they all provide a respite for the soul of his father. And there was somebody who wrote that it is good to recite the kaddish even on Sabbaths and festivals and New Moons, because the reason [for the mourner's kaddish] is not only to rescue the dead from Gehenna, but also to raise him from the lower level of the Garden of Eden to the higher level, level by level; and so there would be a benefit even on the Sabbath." The dead may not be in hell on the Sabbath, but neither are they in heaven. And why not wish them to be in heaven? This reading of the mourner's kaddish makes it more ambitious.

It is interesting that, so many centuries after its invention, the mourner's kaddish does not appear to have been said on Sabbaths and festivals, at least in Aaron's world, and so permission by "somebody" had to be given. It is also interesting that the identity of this "somebody" is not known to the Safed-watcher from Modena. A few months ago I read the very same passage, and it was attributed to Isaac Luria by Hayyim Vital, who heard it from the charismatic divine.

This morning there were mists blowing through the streets. Georgetown had the fresh, sturdy look of a village by the sea. The familiar houses and lanes presented an unfamiliar aspect, as if the fog were clarifying the scene. The fog was a kind of light.

If a fog can be a light, then I am ready to return to my kabbalist. At the teahouse I read Aaron's discussion of the procedure of the funeral, particularly the Justification of the Judgment. And here he goes again: "In the matter of the Justification of the Judgment, it seems to this puny author that the rabbis required us to justify the judgment of heaven twenty times to symbolize the two tears that are the measure of hard judgment and the measure of soft judgment." I don't know what he is talking about. He praises the silence of the mourner, "for when a man muzzles himself, and becomes like a man without a mouth, he causes exteriority [that is, the evil element] to also be without a mouth, and so to be unable to draw sustenance from the force of the judgment." And he proposes a typically Lurianic explanation for the mourner's words of acceptance: "It is certain that he will receive a reward for his silence, and all the more so for his whole-hearted blessing of the bad along with the good, and for his rejoicing in his suffering for the sake of mending the Divine Presence [*shekhinah*]. And it is certain that he who sanctifies the Exalted is cleansed by the judgment that emanates from above, and makes himself into an altar of atonement for the mending of heaven. . . . This is also the case when an individual accepts the entirety of the Divine decree, especially when the kin of the deceased mend the flaw on high . . . [when they pray, in the Justification of the Judgment, that] 'You have acted in truth and mended in truth, and nothing evil emanates from above—no, it is we who have acted wickedly, in cleaving to the exteriorities.' . . . In reciting the Justification of the Judgment, the mourner should concentrate on sweetening the sacred judgment and absorbing it back into its source, where it will be perfumed and sweetened." In this view, there is a cosmic power to the mourner's words. It is not the fate of his father that requires mending, it is the fate of his God. The mourner's liturgy is absorbed into the great Lurianic myth, according to which the godhead itself has been shattered and must be mended.

But what about the dead man for whom I came to this shul? The mystic has not completely forgotten the mundane. He is getting around to it slowly. "Then the mourner is encouraged to make a reckoning with his own deeds," Aaron writes, "for he, too, is destined to appear in judgment." And then Aaron introduces a rather remarkable element into the funeral service. "At this point they recall the spilled blood of God's servants in the years 4856 [1096] and 5136 [1376], because there is no greater substantiation of the judgment than this." In 1096, the First Crusade slaughtered and shook the Jews of France and Germany. And in 1376? Perhaps Aaron is referring to one of the many misfortunes that befell his ancestors in France in the terrible fourteenth century. It is affecting, this custom of associating the grief of the family with the grief of the people, and providing the historical particulars. I have not seen this custom elsewhere prescribed for Jewish funerals. Yet it is precisely what we prescribed for my father's funeral. As Aaron might have said, we recalled the spilled blood of God's servants between 1939 and 1945, because there is no greater substantiation of the judgment than this.

Having addressed the wounds of God and the wounds of history, Aaron turns to the wounds of the mourners. After the collective commemoration, the individual commemoration. "Next they pray for mercy for the deceased," in an intricate kabbalistic fashion. And then, "after the Justification of the Judgment, they recite the kaddish, whose special virtue in every instance is to break the iron locks at the beginning [of a prayer] and to keep the heavens and its gates open at the end [of a prayer], and to protect the prayer or the reading from Scripture and all similar things from the denouncers and the deniers, so that they will have no strength to denounce and to deny." The purpose of the kaddish is to disarm the celestial opposition. Aaron then observes that the kaddish is "like the dew that falls from God to add life and bounty to all His emanations and to the innumerable dead who lie in the ground, and the growth of the light in the direction of redemption by the Almighty, and the flowing from that heavenly source of our messiah." The dead are like the shards of the godhead: they await salvation, which the kaddish hastens. And finally Aaron cites the traditional understanding of the kaddish. "It is already widely known that the kaddish has the power to extinguish the fire of Gehenna and to subdue the strange and hostile forces. With the power of the kaddish, the son rescues his father from the grip of the exteriorities and gets him into Eden." And then Aaron makes an amazing remark: "And with every kaddish he freezes hell for an hour and a half."

Every kaddish freezes hell for an hour and a half! This must be the most delicious observation ever uttered on the subject. Why an hour and a half? And how does Aaron know? Fifty pages later, he gives his source for his information. "The kaddish freezes the fire of hell for an hour and a half, as the *Zohar* explains in a number of places; and my teacher, the sage of Fano, may the memory of a righteous man be a blessing, includes some ancient comments on this in his composition on the secret of the kaddish, as is known to all who consult it." So I cannot stick Aaron with this nonsense! (He is referring to Menahem Azariah of Fano; but I am not eager to get ahold of Menahem's composition on the secret of the kaddish, Aaron's recommendation notwithstanding. My mental life is florid enough.)

The promise of salvation is always a specific promise. A general promise is never enough. The eschatological mind insists upon precision.

The precision of the eschatological mind is a measure of its misery. The more you suffer, the more vividly you imagine the end of your suffering. But there is another reason for all these ultimate details. It is that there is no more evidence for a general promise than for a particular promise. The notion that the kaddish freezes hell for an hour and a half is not more ridiculous than the notion that the kaddish freezes hell for an hour, or the notion that there is a hell and the kaddish will affect it. These are all undisciplined ideas. So why not picture happiness in its particulars?

When the precision of the eschatological mind is not droll, it is dangerous.

Aaron returns to the mourner's kaddish in his discussion of the early portion of the morning service that consists in a recapitulation of the order of the daily sacrifices in the Temple, a long series of readings from the Talmud that describe the elaborate preparation of the offerings, and then the bloodletting. The account of the incense is especially beautiful. I have always admired this passage: "Rabbi Nathan said: As he [the priest] was grinding the incense, he would say: 'Pound it well, pound it well,' because the sound is good for the spices." Aaron notes that the mourner's kaddish appears twice after the account of the incense. "The purpose of the incense is to placate the attribute of Justice. . . . It was not for nothing that those who established the order of the prayers placed the account of the incense [where they did], because from that point on the kaddish appears twice. The first one is recited for all the dead of the world, to freeze hell generally. The second one, after the Alenu prayer, is known as the mourner's kaddish, and it is recited by the son for his father or his mother. Thus it was their design to place the kaddish for all the dead of the world after the recitation of the order of the incense, which perfumes the judgments of hell with its magnificent power, and then they designed the power of the [mourner's] kaddish to come after it, for it freezes hell for an hour and a half." (The Alenu is one of the most ancient prayers in the Jewish liturgy. It proclaims the universal sovereignty of the one God, and since the fourteenth century it has served as the closing prayer in all the services.)

Words as spices, words as perfumes.

The mourner's kaddish, in Aaron's construction of it, is an instrument for improving the condition of the Jewish God, the condition of the Jewish consciousness of the past, the condition of the Jewish dead, and the condition of the Jewish living. It is an urgent affair. But Aaron's sense of urgency gets the better of him, I'm afraid. From the heights of mystical imagination he sinks to the depths of paternal intimidation. He issues a warning: "When, after the death of the father, the sons do not walk the straight path, the angels of judgment beat the father, saying: 'Look at what he sired! Look at what he raised!'" Guiltiness is next to godliness.

"Look at what he sired! Look at what he raised!" Historians, do not forget Aaron of Modena, when you come to write the history of aggravation.

This gives Aaron pause. Having discussed the mourner's kaddish, and the principle that the son acquits the father, he is suddenly worried about his own death, his own acquittal. And so he puts aside his homiletical work and composes an ethical will to his children, which he inserts here as a chapter of his book. It is a fine document of religious earnestness and bourgeois decency. It begins: "Let all this be a great awakening for you, my sons, so that you will act benevolently toward me, and will strive wisely and with all your energy to vindicate your poor and abject father, who certainly has need of mercy, that is, of the many mercies of heaven." Ruefully, perhaps, in light of his own childhood, Aaron reminds his sons of their good fortune: "From your childhood, God has treated you with kindness. In His greatness He placed you in school, where you regularly studied Torah. And from your childhood to this day, I have never asked anything of you. . . ." The discourse is completely familiar to me. *Alles fur di kinder,* as my father used to say. Everything for the children. Having never asked anything of his children, of course, Aaron has something to ask of them now. But it is a selfless request: "Still, there is one thing that I desire of you, that I seek after, and it is that you keep the ways of the Lord, and act justly and fairly, and do all your deeds for the sake of heaven. . . . Every morning make yourselves into day laborers, and say: Today I will be a faithful servant of the Lord of the Universe. Throughout the day, guard yourselves against anger and falsehood and hatred and contention and envy. Do not look at women. Forgive all who cause you pain. For half an hour or so, pray for mercy in the house of worship, and for God's help in repentance, and do so again the next day; or at the very least arrange to do this one day a week. And if you fast on that day, more power to you. Do not let the Torah or the Talmud slip away from you—no, study day and night, according to your abilities." Aaron then launches into an exhortation on the ethics of business: "Your dealings must always be pleasant. Be very careful to do business in good faith . . . so that everything will take place in the realm of the holy and will not quit it for the realm of mendacity and exteriority. For the profit that you earn in good faith is the bounty of holiness, but the profit that you earn in bad faith is the bounty of a strange god, heaven forfend. . . . Do not oppress anybody, for the money that comes to a man dishonestly comes to him from the influences of Satan." Then he instructs his sons on the usefulness of fasts: "I do not wish to burden you with mortification. These days everybody is repenting, and busy with mortification and the mending of their ways and whatever, but my advice to you is that every Monday and Thursday . . . it would be good for your souls, and also good for your health, if you made it your habit to eat only a bit of bread and to drink only a small measure of water at breakfast, while you concentrate on the mending of the Divine Presence and the atonement of your souls with all the souls of Israel." Mortification in moderation: the instruction of a mystic who loves his children.

And finally Aaron arrives at his priceless conclusion: "And if, heaven forfend, you throw off the yoke of Torah, you may be certain that I will be angry, in this world and in the world to come! But if you harken to all this, and you do all that I have commanded you to do, I will be so proud of you, and you will cause God to be praised in this world and in the world to come, with all of Israel, amen!" The Jewish father, under the aspect of eternity.

My father, angry in heaven? For my father, anger *was* heaven.

The first frost settled on the golden leaves this morning. Fire and ice. Little dogs playing in fire and ice. Shul was tedious.

The knowledge of death leads the mind in antithetical directions, toward certainty and toward doubt. Since death is certain, it establishes that there is certainty. (The lived, unmathematical kind.) And the certainty of death leaves the mind demanding ever more certainty, which is what the extravagant productions of the eschatological imagination attempt to provide. And yet who, thinking of death, does not also burn with doubt? The certainty of death presses hard against what we would like to believe about the immortality of the soul and the imperishability of meaning. From the standpoint of faith, then, the knowledge of death is inconclusive. I believe because I know that I will die, I do not believe because I know that I will die: both propositions have sense, have dignity. —Thoughts in a downpour on Sunday evening, on the way to shul.

On Monday morning, an uncanny echo of Sunday evening's thoughts. In shul we read the beginning of this week's portion of Genesis, in which Esau sells Jacob his birthright for a pot of lentils. Esau returns from the field. He is exhausted. He sees that Jacob has been cooking lentils and asks to be fed. Jacob sees an opportunity. "Sell me this day thy birthright," he says to Esau. And Esau makes the deal, reasoning: "I am going to die, so what use to me is the birthright?" Esau was a hunter, for whom death was a familiar risk. In exclaiming upon his own mortality, and preferring the food to the birthright, he may have been only a brute seizing the day. I have always taken Esau's question to be an expression of his brutishness. The tradition is very harsh toward him. When Esau is described in the verse as "tired," Rashi explains: "From murdering." And when Esau reflects that he will die, Rashi explains that his death will be punishment for all his violations of his birthright, which is why he wishes to be rid of it. But today I see in Esau's question a legitimate question, a philosophical question, a sober observation that mortality has the power to steal meaning from life. Today Esau looks to me not like a thug, but like a skeptic. And the sly Jacob looks to me like the opposite of a skeptic. He wants the birthright for the same reason that Esau does not want the birthright: because he knows that he will die; and the birthright—Judaism—must not die with him. "And Esau despised the birthright": this is the concluding comment of the narrative. It is Scripture's explanation of the event. If Jacob had permitted Esau to retain the birthright, the patriarchal line would have ended with his father Isaac, and the faith that was founded by his grandfather Abraham would have been scuttled. Jacob schemed in the interests of the tradition; and for the tradition, it was a choice between primogeniture and perpetuity. Thus the brothers represent a philosophical disputation. They are the twinned personifications of the twinned conclusions that may be derived from the reality of death: I believe because I know that I will die, I do not believe because I know that I will die.

My days have become pathologically busy. I am worn down by tasks and worries. And so I have taken to coming to shul early in the afternoon and the evening. I unlock the door, I sit alone, I breathe. The others will not arrive for twenty minutes or so. I have escaped the brilliant world.

Awaiting the arrival of the others, I track down a few references to Esau in the Talmudic literature, and find support for my little allegory of the brothers. On Esau's words, "I am going to die," the third-century sage Resh Lakish comments, "Esau began to vilify and to blaspheme," and he proceeds to show, by means of a linguistic analogy, that in his outburst Esau was denying God. According to Rabbi Levi, also of the third century, Esau's question to Jacob was itself a heresy, a denial of the resurrection of the dead. By "I am going to die," Esau meant that he would be dead forever. (Then count me, too, among the heretics.) And Rabbi Yohanan, also of the third century, deduces from a series of exegeses of the relevant verses that "five sins were committed by that wicked man on that day: he violated a betrothed woman, he murdered someone, he denied God, he denied the resurrection of the dead, and he rejected the birthright." For these rabbis, then, Jacob's brother was not only a barbarian. He was also an unbeliever. He was full of concepts.

My eye catches the word "mourning" a few lines above Rabbi Yohanan's indictment of Esau. I take a look, and am in Talmud heaven. Here is what the rabbis have to say about the day that Esau exchanged the birthright for a pot of lentils: "That was the day on which Abraham died and Jacob cooked lentils to comfort his father Isaac." This is consistent with the rabbinical legend that Abraham was spared the spectacle of Esau's spurning of the tradition. So Jacob was preparing the "meal of healing" that one must prepare for a mourner. And now the rabbis start, well, to cook. "Why lentils?" they ask. There must be some property of the lentil that confers upon it the power to console. Here comes an answer. "In the West they say, in the name of Rabbah bar Mari, that the lentil is like mourning: just as the lentil has no mouth, so mourning has no mouth." The meaning of this animadversion is not immediately apparent to me, but I am helped by Rashi's commentary. Unlike other legumes, which have a crack or a cleft, the lentil has no crack or cleft; and the mourner, too, has no crack or cleft, insofar as his lips remain closed and he sits in stunned silence and says nothing. It has been seven months since my father died, and I have only just discovered that I am like a lentil! And here comes another answer. "Just as the lentil is round, so mourning comes round to all the inhabitants of the world." I shall never again gaze upon a bean and not brood upon the way of all flesh.

But wait, the text seems to be growing impatient with itself. "What difference does it make?" An excellent question! But it is not a rhetorical question. It is a practical question. From the analogies between lentils and sorrows, it is seeking a lesson for human conduct. And it finds one: "The difference that it makes is whether it is possible to console with eggs." An excellent answer! For the egg has a smooth, unmarred surface, but it is not perfectly round. So the egg is philosophically disqualified. It is a poor emblem of finitude.

The wheel of fortune? No, the wheel of finitude.

"I returned, and saw under the sun, that the race is not to the swift, nor the battle to the strong, neither yet bread to the wise, nor yet riches to men of understanding, nor yet favor to men of skill; but time and chance happeneth to them all." In *Kad Ha'Kemaḥ*, or *The Pitcher of Flour*, a short but remarkable encyclopedia of the central concepts of Judaism written by Bahya ben Asher of Saragossa in the late thirteenth century, the entry on "mourning" broaches the problem of Ecclesiastes. Can the world-weariness of the Preacher be accommodated to the requirements of faith? "Owing to the profundity of its language," Bahya writes, "those who study it will think that it is the opposite of faith, but in fact it is faith itself." Bahya was right to worry about the effect of Ecclesiastes on a mourner. And this is his interpretation of the famous verse about the disappointments that await the swift and the strong and the wise, and more generally those who are relying upon their own natures: "This is instruction about the inferiority of the world, which does not persist in any particular quality but undergoes transformations. Therefore even the great ones of the world do not escape the net that is spread out to trap them, the net that is a circle that comes round in the world. For this reason, it was the custom to eat lentils in the house of the mourner. About the mourning for Abraham it is written [that Jacob prepared] 'a pottage of lentils': just as the lentil comes round, the world comes round. Some sing and some cry, some are happy and some are sad. And therefore it is not fitting for anybody with the fear of heaven to strive in anything other than the service of the Lord."

Yet there arose defenders of the egg! And of other foods, too. Already in the Talmud, the mourner's menu was more various: "Everyone may bring cakes, meat, and fish to the house of the mourner; and if a local official is present, beans and fish. Rabbi Simeon ben Gamaliel said: Where it is the custom, a hearty cooked meal." In France, Isaac ben Dorbelo, who lived in the middle of the twelfth century, and edited and expanded the text of *Maḥzor Vitry,* reports that "it is the custom to feed the mourner eggs first, because it is a thing without a mouth, to teach that we have recourse only to silence with which to accept the judgment of heaven; and because it is round, like the turning wheel of the world. Afterwards he may eat meat and whatever those who are present wish to eat." In Germany, at the turn of the thirteenth century, Eliezer ben Joel rehearses the story of Jacob's lentils and man's fate, and notes: "In these times it is the custom to eat cakes and eggs for the [mourner's] first meal." And in France, in the thirteenth century, a sinister piece of evidence: in the dossier against the Talmud that was compiled by the ecclesiastical authorities in Paris and led to the "conviction" and the burning of the Talmud in 1242, an anonymous Catholic pursuer cites the Talmudic passage about the dish of lentils that Jacob prepared for his mourning father, and remarks: "Exactly as the Jews do to this day with eggs after a funeral." In Spain, in the thirteenth century, Nahmanides cites his predecessor Isaac ibn Ghiyyat, who cites the Talmudic permission for cakes, meat, and fish ("a hearty cooked meal," according to ibn Ghiyyat, is "meat and wine"), and concludes: "It is all according to custom." Nahmanides himself cites a text in the Jerusalem Talmud that establishes the precedent of meat and wine, and the legitimacy of local custom; and he concludes that "in a community in which it is the custom not to bring the mourner any food except a stew of lentils and the vessels that were prescribed for them, no other foods are brought. In a community in which it is the custom to eat larger meals, meats and other delicacies, so is it done." The mourner needs nourishment. And in Provence in the early fourteenth century, I have found a symbolist defense of eggs, a gruesome opinion about their geometrical (and therefore their homiletical) perfection. Aaron of Lunel records that the preparation of the corpse for burial included the custom of "grinding eggs with spotted shells against his head." This, he writes, is "an ancient practice." Its reason is that "they used to transport the body outside the city limits for burial, and they marked the body in this manner so that the gravediggers would recognize that this was a Jew." Medieval graveyards must have been awful places. But why eggs? "Because they are round, and this comes round."

Isaac ben Dorbelo: what sort of name is Dorbelo? It doesn't sound Jewish and it doesn't sound French. I know whom to call; and a few days later I am the grateful recipient of a paper on the son of Dorbelo that was recently published by the Academy of Sciences of the Czech Republic. It advises me that Dorbelo may refer to a place of origin, such as d'Orville or d'Orval—but then it suggests a really enchanting explanation. Dorbelo doesn't sound Jewish because it is not Jewish; and it also is not French. Dorbelo is a messy Hebrew transliteration of the Latin appellation *Durabilis.* It turns out that there are two recorded instances of Jews who bore this name in France, in the tenth and eleventh centuries. And here is a third. Isaac ben Dorbelo was Isaac ben Durabilis, or Isaac the son of Durable. A Jew called Durable!

There came a moment in the history of the Jews when the egg was the equal of the lentil. Or so I conclude from Aaron of Lunel. He writes straightforwardly of the meal of healing that "it is the custom to feed him eggs or lentils, because they are both round, which is to say, in this world this comes round." He records the comment of Isaac ibn Ghiyyat in the eleventh century that the mourner was served eggs and lentils as his main course or as his first course. Aaron also warns that "the mourner must never peel the egg himself, because he will look like a glutton and be derided by the others. No, the comforters peel the egg for him, and he eats." Aaron also adds a sumptuary scruple about the meal: "When the meal of healing is served in the house of the mourner, it is not to be served on trays of silver or bamboo or the like, but rather on rough-planed wooden trays of willow-bark and the like, so as not to embarrass the poor." It is never an inappropriate time for a thought about justice.

Aaron's funereal fairness is owed to this wonderful passage in the Talmud: "The rich used to bring food to the house of the mourner in baskets of silver and gold, and the poor in baskets of peeled willow twigs, but the poor were ashamed, and so the rabbis instituted that everyone should bring their food in baskets of peeled willow twigs, out of respect for the poor. The rich used to serve drinks in the house of the mourner in vessels of white glass, and the poor in vessels of colored glass, but the poor were ashamed, and so the rabbis instituted that everyone should serve drinks in vessels of colored glass, out of respect to the poor. The rich [in mourning] used to uncover their faces, and the poor [in mourning] used to cover their faces, since their faces were blackened by the years of [working in] drafts, but the poor were ashamed, and so the rabbis instituted that everyone should cover their faces, out of respect to the poor. The rich used to be carried to burial on a grand bed, and the poor in a box, but the poor were ashamed, and so the rabbis instituted that everyone should be carried to burial in a box."

Aaron of Lunel then cites his predecessor Asher ben Saul, a rabbi of Lunel in the late twelfth and early thirteenth centuries, who was one of the pioneers of the customs literature. In a passage that does not appear in the portion of Asher's book of customs that has survived (I have it with me at the teahouse), he declares that the mourner must also be given bread. Asher infers this from a Biblical verse and explains: "Nobody has a right to uproot this custom, because it is a good and worthy custom. For the mourner is sunk in care and sighs for his dead and cannot be mindful about eating and cooking, because he wishes that he, too, would die." In an instant, the charm of these culinary reflections is gone. I did not expect the subject of eggs and lentils to shake the foundations.

Does the mourner want to die? I did not want to die when my father died. Death does not make you want to die, unless you already want to die. Does life, then, make you want to die? Some kinds of life, perhaps. But I have often reflected on the fact that my parents never wanted to die, their lives notwithstanding. No, the desire to die is a spiritual disposition of its own. It cannot be proved or disproved by experience. There are people who wish that they had not been born, who cannot stand the circumstances. I have known such people. They are not angry. They do not desire to do away with anything but themselves. They do not have the appetite even for stoicism. They just want to cease. Last winter, when I was attending my father at the hospital, I learned that a friend of mine had shot herself in the head. I was not surprised. She had tried it before, and she was sincerely sorry that she had failed. The world gave her no pleasure, no standpoint from which to resist pain. Finally she got out. I cannot pretend that I did not understand her. I have a guilty admiration for the desire to be unhooked from the world. Philosophically, I see the attraction of nullity. (Unphilosophically, however, the world and I are hooked.)

She found peace, a friend of hers told me. No, I said, she found death. The peace of the grave is not peace.

Is peace an appropriate ambition for the soul? Peace can be a means or an end, a condition of activity or a condition of stillness. If peace is a means, then it is desirable so that the soul can work freely, without interference, and expend its energies only on what is significant to itself; but then the soul is not peaceful, the soul bustles and strains. Such peace is an external peace. But dare one aspire also to an internal peace, to peace as an end, to a peaceful soul? Or is the end of activity also the end of meaning?

The paradise of intrinsicness.

When the philosophers called for the perfection of the intellect, they meant what they said.

The soul does not owe all its failures to its attachment to the world. The soul brings its errors and its enemies with it. This is what the spirituality of withdrawal does not grasp.

It is not paganism that makes the most radical challenge to Judaism. It is Buddhism. How I wish that history had thrown them together. Oh, the disputations!

Go ahead, deny the reality of the world. You will still lie awake at night.

I cannot any longer run to Georgetown three times a day. It is making me crazy. The afternoon service is available to me only a few blocks away, at the offices of the ultra-Orthodox lobby in town. I decided today that I will say my lunchtime kaddish there. "Can I help you?" said the receptionist, when I walked through the door. "I'm a mourner," I said. "Have a seat," she said.

The afternoon prayer in the lobbyist's offices. We worship in a small conference room on the fifth floor of a faceless building. The bookshelves are crammed with binders and tomes, the *United States Code, Annotated* in the one corner and the codes of Jewish law in the other corner. The unfamiliarity of the surroundings refreshes the performance of my duty. I prefer to pray in places not designed for prayer. The anomaly of the setting has a quickening effect. Still, I am glad that there are places designed for prayer, and not only for reasons of convenience. If there is a shul, then there is a world outside the shul, a world that is not the shul; and I may leave the concentration for the expanse.

A fascinating and moving book has appeared, a study of the customs of the crypto-Jews in Spain, and in the empire of Spain, from the fifteenth century through the seventeenth century. After the forced baptisms in 1391 and then after the expulsion in 1492, the *conversos* took the religion of their ancestors underground, and as "New Christians" they continued to perform "Judaizing" rituals. And this was true also of their practices of mourning. Thus I read that "among Iberian Jews and *conversos* lentils were rare, while most documented funeral meals included eggs. Sometimes these were cooked in ways that de-emphasized their symbolic roundness. For example, in Toledo in the late fifteenth century relatives sent a mourning family 'an omelet and two pears and two loaves of bread and grapes and a pitcher of water . . . in a basket covered with some white cloths.' But most eggs were probably hard-boiled. Among the alleged Judaizing customs of Marina Gonzalez [Ciudad Real, 1484] was that she ate eggs at her mother-in-law's *çogeurc* [funeral meal]. In Yepes in 1643 mourners ate eggs and salad. . . . Rafael Enriquez testified that these eggs were called *aveluz*. Likewise Blanca Enriquez [Mexico, 1648] said that after the funeral 'blood relations of the deceased had to eat a cold hard-boiled egg without salt (called the *aveluz*), as a sign of the pain they were feeling, and whoever brought it to the house was esteemed by the God of Israel.' When her father died, after she had eaten one *aveluz* she and his sister and another Judaizing woman 'went into an empty room and rushed around it several times, leaving the *aveluz* there for the first Catholic man or woman who should come in, so that the misfortune and bad luck should fall on them, for by that ceremony they believed that they themselves were free of it.'" This information comes from the files of the Spanish Inquisition. It took courage for these mourners to eat their eggs. In their food was their faith. When they tasted their eggs, they tasted their metaphysics.

Eggs, lentils, the philosophical stimulus of unphilosophical things.

In the same book I read also that "the documents contain numerous references to the funeral *Kaddish* and sporadic references to other prayers recited at or after crypto-Jewish funerals. . . . Prior to the Expulsion crypto-Jews might even contract with openly practicing Jews to recite the *Kaddish* in their stead for their departed relatives or for themselves. For example, Blanca Fernandez, shortly before she died in 1475, 'sent two bushels of wheat to the Jewish rabbi of Huete to say some prayers for her soul.' Similarly the *converso* Joan Lopez Coscolla [Calatayud, 1489] gave the Jew Asser Advendavit money to go to his mother's grave to 'say a prayer in Hebrew.' It is often difficult to tell whether these *conversos* were electing a way to fulfill their obligation with minimal risk, or whether they had decided that it was more proper for a Jew than for a convert to say *Kaddish* for relatives who had died as Jews. But occasionally the issue was broached directly. The *converso* Pedro de Guadalajara accepted the obligation to recite *Kaddish* and continue to pray for his parents who had died as Jews, and in 1505 he answered the Inquisitors' objections to this practice by saying, 'What is done well is never lost and may do some good.'" I am stirred by Pedro's bold little speech. It is a fine foundation for the kaddish. For a free man's kaddish, too.

In the shul in the evening, and in the lobbyist's office in the afternoon, there is a man who comes to pray. He works in a government agency. He speaks softly and he smiles kindly and his eyes bashfully sparkle. He closes his eyes when he prays, and stands in perfect stillness, except when he suddenly raises his hands high, all the way to heaven, to implore the power before whom he stands. Then his hands fall back, almost lifelessly, and he is calm again. Sometimes his face is seized by a quick agony and he drops his head in his hands. He prays in his own time, intently whispering every word, and often he is still in the middle of his worship as the rest of us are leaving. I know that he has finished praying when he opens his eyes. Here is a man of true devotion. I feel lifted by his gentleness and by his fervor. This evening, as we were concluding the service, I turned to a friend and said: "Do you see that man over there? He has faith." "Something in which we are sorely lacking," said my friend. And then, without irony: "See you in the morning."

Up at dawn. With no faith, to the house of faith. My friend is right. We do not return to shul as that man returns to it, and still we return. I keep thinking of Pedro's defense of his kaddish before the Inquisition. "What is done well is never lost and may do some good."

With no faith? No, with my faith.

The rabbis famously say that those who cannot pray for the sake of praying should pray anyway, because it will bring them to pray for praying's sake. I never liked this statement. It is behaviorism or it is opportunism, since it finds a religious utility for faithlessness, and thereby steals the thunder from belief and unbelief. Anyway, it is obvious that many people who pray do not pray for prayer's sake, and do not bring to prayer the philosophical propositions on which it must be premised. Are there times, then, when philosophy does not matter? Of course. The world would not work if it waited on philosophical understanding. It is a good thing that people act in the absence of reasons, or of clear reasons. Thoughtlessness is a lubricant of life. And yet it will not do to say that we are muddling through and that is the end of it. It is always possible to muddle through less complacently. Even though one may act without reasons, one should search for reasons. Even though one may pray without meaning it, one should mean it.

What is the most beautiful word in the language? A friend asked me that question many years ago. I answered without hesitation. The most beautiful word in the language is "philosophy."

Am I confusing philosophy with religion? No, I am associating philosophy with religion. If you care about interiority, they are both your allies. Many of religion's answers are to philosophy's questions. A shul is not only a house of religion, it is also a house of philosophy, because within its walls first principles, and an interest in first principles, are demanded. As long as there are shuls and churches and mosques, the feeling for philosophy will not be lost. The same cannot be said about universities.

The art of the question.

When I arrive in shul this evening, there are only five of us. "We're half-full," a jolly, scraggly fellow says. "No," comes the reply, "we're half-empty." Ten is ten. Not even nine is ten. Ten is ten. And so the sober fellow starts to phone around. He wishes to raise another five, but I notice that he has also another purpose. He is calling people who almost certainly will not come, so as to afflict them with a moment of embarrassment. He puts the phone down with a wicked grin.

Magnified and sanctified . . . Magnified and sanctified . . . Magnified and sanctified . . .

In a new book about Leibniz, I find an observation from one of his letters: "The just man, the man who loves everyone, strives to aid all men, even when he is unable, just as necessarily as the rock tends to fall, even when it is hanging. . . . All obligation is vindicated in the highest striving." So you do not have to fall in order to fall. And you do not have to rise in order to rise. You have only to be serious about a direction, to incline yourself toward a goal with force, to be pointed. (I have a soft spot for Leibniz. He was the last innocent philosopher. He caught the final glimpse of reason before epistemology and psychology and history and economics began to despoil it.)

Is obligation really vindicated by striving? It better be. I cannot help but notice that "vindicated" is precisely the word that the rabbis use to describe what the son accomplishes for the father with the kaddish. If obligation is vindicated by striving, then this year my obligation, and my father, and myself, will be vindicated.

A man who stopped saying kaddish for his mother a few months ago came to shul this morning. When we rose for kaddish, he rose with us. He didn't recite it, he merely stood motionless and closed his eyes, and his prayerbook fell from his hands. Did he miss his mother or his kaddish?

If I could be sure that I have grasped only the reality of a corner of a room . . .

A few days ago I thought of another way to investigate the relation of biology to morality in the Jewish tradition. What are the obligations of a child toward an evil parent? If biology trumps morality, then the character of a parent will not affect the obligations of the child. If morality trumps biology, then the character of a parent will affect the obligations of the child. And so I have been consulting the codes of Jewish law on the laws of filial duty. I am finding an interesting division of opinion among the authorities. I begin with Maimonides (who confirms the opinion of Isaac Alfasi of Fez in the eleventh century): "An illegitimate son is obligated to honor and to fear his father, though he is exempted from the prohibitions against striking and cursing his father until such time as his father repents." Here "honoring" and "fearing" are terms of law, based upon the two verbs with which Scripture enjoins filial duty, and they cover the range of services and attitudes that a child owes a parent. Basing himself on a passage in the Talmud, Maimonides insists that the sleaziness of a father who sires children out of wedlock does not abrogate his parental relation to those children. The children must overcome their judgment of their father and render to him the prescribed services and attitudes, though they are distinguished from legitimate children in that the Biblically ordained sentence of death for striking or cursing a parent does not apply to them. (They are entitled to an expression of anger, I guess.) Then Maimonides states his view generally: "Even if one's father is evil and a man of iniquities, one must honor and fear him."

Maimonides' view is not hard to understand. One does not choose one's father or one's mother. The facticity of the family is one of its essential characteristics. (It accounts for the tragic dimension of family life.) What family, or society, could long endure, if the generations based their relations to each other on admiration for each other? The Maimonidean view is the realistic view. He hopes for the contrition of the father, but he makes his ruling in the absence of the father's contrition. He makes his ruling for a world of sinners. And yet there is something a little repugnant about Maimonides' view. He has allowed the evil father to escape the consequences of his evil within his own family. The father is left unaccountable to his children. Facts triumph over ideals. Biology trumps morality.

I am not alone in my distaste for the Maimonidean leniency toward the tormenting father. In Spain in the fourteenth century, Jacob ben Asher produced the *Arba'ah Turim*, or *The Four Columns*, the code whose classification of the law became canonical. Jacob's boldness as a jurist was expressed not least in his willingness to defy Maimonides, and his ruling about the duty to an evil parent is an instance of this defiance. He cites Maimonides and tersely remarks: "In my opinion, since he [the father] is evil, he [the son] is not obligated to honor him." Jacob adduces a discussion in the Talmud which seems to suggest that the children of a thief or a usurer must return to the victims the illicit gains that they have inherited out of respect for their father, but in fact concludes that this is not the case, that such a father is not worthy of respect; and then Jacob adds, again tersely: "So long as he does not repent, they are not obligated to honor him." Morality trumps biology.

I am trying to understand a Talmudic text on levirate marriage, the one that served Maimonides as a basis for his ruling, but the text is too difficult for me. There are many passages of legal deliberation in the Talmud that I cannot master, and this is one of them. The situation can be easily remedied by a question to the rabbi, and I will ask him. Still, I am ashamed of my incompetence. I have never devoted myself to the study of the Talmud to an extent that is commensurate with my understanding of its place in Judaism. What one really knows is a sign of what one really cares to know.

The disagreement between Maimonides and Jacob ben Asher is repeated in the sixteenth century. Joseph Karo takes the Maimonidean view, Moses Isserles takes the Jacobean view. The language is the same. And a historical pattern begins to emerge. Maimonides flourished in Egypt, and Karo flourished in Palestine. Jacob flourished in Spain, but as a scion of the Rhineland, from which he had emigrated with his father, and Isserles flourished in Poland. I appear to be tracking a difference between the culture of the Sephardim and the culture of the Ashkenazim. For the authorities of the Sephardim, biology precedes morality, and the family may not be disrupted by ethical judgment. For the authorities of the Ashkenazim, morality precedes biology, and the family may be disrupted by ethical judgment. How did the family in sixteenth-century Safed differ from the family in sixteenth-century Cracow? I expect that historians of the family may shed some light on this.

Karo's reiteration of the Maimonidean view is stated more emphatically a few pages later. "If his father and his mother are absolutely evil and regular transgressors, even if they have been sentenced to death and are being led to execution, he is forbidden to strike them and to curse them." Nothing ambiguous about that. But he continues: "And if he does strike them or curse them, he is not liable; but if they have repented, he is liable and deserves to be executed for it." I am struck by Karo's attempt to circumscribe his own stringency toward the children. One's parents are one's parents—but who cannot understand that a child may strike or curse such a parent? And then there is the great qualification of the parent's repentance, which would restore the family to a morally normative condition. This hope for the father's reform appears in both schools of thought. It seems especially urgent in the opinions of Jacob ben Asher and Moses Isserles, who cast off the evil parent from the tender mercies of the child. Similarly, in his gloss on Isserles' statement that "he is not obligated to honor his wicked father," Shabbetai Ha'Cohen comments that "even though he is not obligated to honor him, he is forbidden to cause him pain." This is another attempt to circumscribe the stringency toward the parents.

Both schools of thought, then, worry about the consequences of their opinions. The rabbis for whom paternity is preferred to morality do not want to see morality abused. The rabbis for whom morality is preferred to paternity do not want to see paternity abused. All the rabbis want as many parents honored and feared by as many children as possible.

The obligation to one's parents has nothing to do with the admiration for one's parents. But who has parents in whom there is nothing to admire?

I was walking in the park, along the creek. The light was silver. A goldfinch hovered above my path a few yards ahead. The pages of a broken book drifted along the surface of the water. I was pierced—by what, I cannot say. I would like to say, but I cannot say. And I do not mind that I am lacking in words. The unsayable is precious to me. I do not wish to be only a creature of language, one of those "articulate" people to whom the world is always transparent, who can always tell you what is really going on. Sometimes I do not know what is really going on, and the clumsiness of my expression must vouch for the exertion of my mind. Anyway, I cannot conceive of the transparency of the world.

This morning I journeyed to Belorussia at the turn of the twentieth century, to Jehiel Mikhel Epstein's code of Jewish law. Briefly surveying the literature on the question of obligations to evil parents, Epstein does not see merely a disagreement; he sees a majority view and a minority view. The majority view is Jacob ben Asher's, that morality trumps biology. (This is Epstein's view, too.) The minority view is Maimonides', that biology trumps morality. It delights me that biology is the loser. But Epstein, a follower of Maimonides in his codificatory practice, is troubled by the exclusion of Maimonides from the mainstream of legal opinion. How to explain the Maimonidean position? Perhaps Maimonides meant only to suggest that an evil parent must not be treated scornfully? No, the master's language is plain. He believes that an evil parent must be honored and feared—the works. So Epstein has another idea. It is that there are gradations of evil, and the evil from which Maimonides instructed the children to avert their gaze is not the most heinous evil. In the case of the most heinous evil, Maimonides, too, would rule against the claims of biology. "Even according to the opinion of Maimonides," he writes, "it seems that [the parent must be honored and feared] only in the case of a villain of appetite, but in the case of one with an intention to outrage, such as a heretic or an apostate, it is plain that it is forbidden to honor him, as it is plain that no one is called evil unless he sins regularly, but one who commits a sin only occasionally is not called evil, and according to all the authorities one is obligated to honor and to fear him."

Epstein is speaking for another sort of realism. There is ordinary evil and there is extraordinary evil. About the latter, there is no dispute: it must be repudiated, even in one's parents. As Epstein asks, "How can the enemies of God be honored?" About the former, reasonable people may differ. It would be indecent, after all, to treat ordinary evil like extraordinary evil. A sin for pleasure is not like a sin for principle.

"A villain of appetite": this may also be translated as "a villain for one's own benefit." The villainy in question is a mixture of convenience and concupiscence, of profit and pleasure.

"A villain of appetite": I like this category of villainy, which is Talmudic in origin, because it makes a discrimination between blasphemy and pleasure, between the radical and the man who is too much at home in the world. The enjoyment of the world is not always an antinomian affair.

"One who is present at the moment of death of a Jewish man or woman is required to rend, even if the deceased sometimes committed a sin out of appetite or failed to fulfill a commandment because it was too much trouble." Thus Joseph Karo, compassionately, in his code of law. A weak or sloppy life is not to be confused with an evil life. But how often can one sin and still be only "sometimes" a sinner? This is Moses Isserles' comment on the statute: "Yet if he sins regularly, there is no mourning for him, and all the more so if he is a renegade who is an idolator." Isserles worries that Karo's compassion may be exploited. He will not permit a philosophical failing to disguise itself as a human failing.

It is an underestimation of pleasure to regard it as heterodoxy. This is what the romance of "holy sinning"—the Sabbatean and Frankist traditions of "the commandment that is fulfilled by being violated," or more generally what Auden described, in his preface to Baudelaire's journals, as "Lucifer, the rebel, the defiant one who asserts his freedom by disobeying *all* commands, whether given by God, society, or by his own nature"—does not apprehend. There is hedonism that is nihilism, and there is hedonism that is not nihilism. The former seems larger and more dangerous, but really it is smaller, because it has never really freed itself from the framework. It accepts the moralization of the senses, and simply inverts it. Yet there is another kind of pleasure that is its own framework. It is positive and sufficient unto itself. It seeks no harm. It does not defy, it enjoys. And it does not express itself in excess. Quite the contrary. Its affinity for form, in nature or in art, confers upon it a decorum, a sagacity. It cannot imagine a sin.

If you deny the authority of heaven, then why are you shaking your fist at it?

The voluptuary contemplative. A spiritual figure.

—I enjoy it because it is forbidden.
—Then you do not enjoy it.

Sin is the ruin of pleasure.

Do you wish to remain a child? Then spend your life at war with a parent. (The womb of negation.)

"He who separates himself from the ways of the community—nothing is done for him at his death. The siblings and the relatives of such an individual should wear white and wrap themselves in white, and should eat and drink, and should be happy, because the enemies of the Lord have perished, as it is said [in Psalms]: 'Do I not hate them, O Lord, that hate thee? and am I not grieved with those that rise up against thee? I hate them with perfect hatred; I count them mine enemies.'" Thus the Talmudic instruction about the death of the wicked. It is a drastic instruction, in which the love of God defeats the love of family. But who, exactly, is the individual who separates himself from the ways of the community? The nonconformist or the heretic? The sinner or the traitor? Language that is so pitiless should not be so imprecise.

And I am not the only one to think so. Mordecai ben Hillel, who lived in Nuremberg in the second half of the thirteenth century, composed a massive compendium of laws and commentaries that preserved the work of many medieval rabbis and exerted an enormous influence upon the legal development of German Jewry. (In 1298, the prodigious Mordecai was murdered, together with his wife and his children and seven hundred Jews who had gathered in a castle in Nuremberg to defend themselves against one of the mobs that had been incited by the notorious Rindfleisch, a German knight who went from town to town hallucinating about the Desecration of the Host.) At the end of Mordecai's discussion of the laws of mourning, there appears a responsum "in the matter of Reuben's wife, who was childless, and took an oath according to the Torah, placing her hand on the Ten Commandments [in an open Torah scroll], swearing, by the authority of God and the authority of the sages, on pain of a curse and a ban and an excommunication, that she would leave her worldly possessions solely to her husband. But then she forgot her covenant with her God, and forsook the prince of her youth, and as she was dying she willed her possessions to her sister's son. And then she died while she was under a ban." The question is: "Are the rites of mourning to be performed for her, or not?" The answer is, they are not. Mordecai cites a variety of sources and authorities, ancient and medieval. From the rabbis of the Talmud, he adduces the statement that "a person who dies while under a ban should be stoned—not that a heap of stones should be raised above him . . . but a messenger of the court takes a stone and places it on his coffin, so that the law of stoning is carried out"; and also the statement that "for those executed by the court there are not rites of mourning"; and also the statement that "he who separates himself from the ways of the community—nothing is done for him at his death." Mordecai also observes that, as a rule, "whoever violates an oath is called a wicked person, even if he is not under a ban." And so the verdict is pronounced: "This cursed woman knew the law and knew that the Torah rules that a husband is the heir of his wife, and she voluntarily accepted the severity of an oath and the risk of a ban—indeed, she was advised of the ban by sages of Israel, such as Rabbi Mattathias and Rabbi Baruch, the pillars of the world, and also the old and distinguished Rabbi Abraham and Rabbi Joseph the Pious of Ashkenaz. . . . How grievously she harmed her soul with such a sin, in transgressing against the law of Moses and the ban of the rabbis and her own oath! . . . Also the women must be warned. Such a thing is not to be done in Israel. . . . She was wicked toward heaven and wicked toward her fellow creatures in that she separated herself from the decrees of the community. . . . Indeed, she would deserve such a verdict even if she had not sworn or taken an oath, for if the sages have established and supported the husband's right of inheritance, then it is our duty to secure that practice as best we can, and the women must be warned. And may the denial of mourning atone for her. . . . Signed, Eliezer the Lawmaker."

So this is not Mordecai's own ruling. But who on earth was Eliezer the Lawmaker? Perhaps he was Eliezer of Touques, Meir's esteemed contemporary in France, who studied, like him, with Isaac of Vienna. It would help if I could identify Rabbi Mattathias and Rabbi Baruch, or the "old and distinguished" Rabbi Abraham. —The office calls. I am needed. Eliezer, whoever he was, must excuse me.

"And the women must be warned." This is a quotation from Ezekiel. Why was it necessary for Eliezer to employ it twice? After all, men were not exactly innocent of the iniquities that disqualified one from the rites of mourning.

The responsum that appears in Mordecai's text contains an important disquisition by Meir of Rothenburg on the definition of the deviant, or "he who separates himself from the ways of the community," which is what I want to know. In the Talmud it is stated that "whoever is present when a person dies must rend his garment." Meir of Rothenburg, in the name of Rabbi Moses and Rabbi Nahman, in the name of Rabbi Jonah (pedantry is my patrimony!), proposes a qualification. "This is the case when the dead is not a wicked individual. But when a wicked and suspicious individual dies, there is to be no rending. Indeed, there is to be rejoicing." A few lines down it is recorded that Meir bore down on Jonah's rather general characterization of the "wicked individual." Meir "added that a wicked individual is one who commits a sin with an intention to outrage, and he is called 'one who separates himself from the ways of the community,' such as an idolator or one who eats unslaughtered meat so as to outrage." The deviant, then, is not the common sinner. He (or she) who separates himself (or herself) from the ways of the community is a rebel, in mind or in will. And for such a fiend, there is no mourning. But Meir takes pity on the common miscreant. "Yet if a man commits a sin occasionally out of appetite, or occasionally fails to fulfill a commandment because it is too arduous, it is required to rend one's garments for him, because he did not intend to outrage. In this way, we have read that David mourned for Absalom, because Absalom's intention was to rule, not to outrage." (For this reason, too, the woman who violated her oath and changed her will is treated after her death as a wicked individual, for "this woman did not do so merely for profit [like Absalom], for she was about to die.") Meir is making a distinction between sins that are declarations of principle and sins that are not declarations of principle. The hedonist, the slacker, the seeker after gain: they are not wicked, they are weak, and they must be regarded humanely. But the rebel, the blasphemer: they are not weak, they are wicked. The objective of their sin is subversion.

"Rabbi Jonah" is surely Jonah ben Abraham Gerondi, the jurist and moralist of thirteenth-century Catalonia. He studied in France and was familiar with the customs of the French community. But who are Rabbi Moses and Rabbi Nahman? I have a look at Meir's treatise on mourning. I see immediately that it served as Mordecai's source. Meir writes that "I was told [this] by Rabbi Moses the son of Rabbi Meir, who heard it from the holy Rabbi Jonah of Provence." There is no mention of a Rabbi Nahman. I find a clue in the section immediately preceding this one, in which Meir refers to "Rabbi Meir of England, who wrote in his compendium on the law of mourning . . ." I consult a few books, and I have a hypothesis. "Rabbi Moses the son of Rabbi Meir" is mentioned in an English collection of medieval commentaries on the Talmud, and in all likelihood he was the son of the English glossator known as Rabbi Meir of England, and also as Rabbi Meir of London, who studied with the great Rabbi Samson of Sens. One scholar notes that "until recently Meir was known only as the author of a compendium of the laws of mourning. . . . He may have composed these rulings when he was still in France, and everything that is cited in his name in the works of the sages of Ashkenaz comes from this work, and they cite also his own behavior when he was himself a mourner." His son Moses would have been an older contemporary of Meir of Rothenburg, whose contribution to the same genre I am studying. It all coheres, it all coheres.

Mordecai continues: "Rabbi Meir nicely distinguished the occasional sinner out of appetite, because a sinner who sins regularly falls into the category of 'one who separates himself from the ways of the community.'" In Meir's discussion, the gravity of sin is measured in two ways, in terms of frequency and in terms of motive. If one does not sin all the time, and if one does not sin in a spirit of treason, then one has not betrayed the community. But what about the man who has no intention to outrage, yet always sins? In the case of such a man, Mordecai is suggesting that the difference between motive and frequency, between the man who repudiates the law and the man who never observes the law, between the man who does evil and the man who does not do good, is of no consequence. It does not matter that rebellion is not on his mind. Objectively, he rebelled. An undiabolical rebel is still a rebel. His depravity is not less real for its lack of grandeur.

Truth is not offended by falsehood. It is offended by relaxation.

Mordecai proceeds to one of the most important eschatological myths in the Talmud. "The sinners who sin with their bodies among the Jews, and the sinners who sin with their bodies among the nations of the world, descend [after death] to Gehenna and are judged there for twelve months. After twelve months their bodies are destroyed, and their souls are consumed in the fire, and the wind scatters their dust beneath the feet of the righteous." This is the fate of ordinary sinners: punishment and release. But the fate of extraordinary sinners is punishment and no release, an eternity in hell. And who are the irredeemably damned? "Slanderers and traitors and sectarians and apostates and Epicureans and those who deny the Torah and the resurrection of the dead and those who separated themselves from the ways of the community." It follows that these are the villains to whom the rites of mourning are not to be granted. Mordecai notes a textual confusion: Rashi suggested that the deviant, or the "one who separates himself from the ways of the community," should not appear on the list of the doomed as a category of his own, that it is really a characterization of all the other categories, a general description of treason, and he reports that he saw a version of the text in which it does not appear; but Mordecai is reluctant to accept Rashi's emendation. "I have checked all the books," he writes, and the individual who separates himself from the ways of the community appears in every version of the list that he has seen, "and it seems forced to erase what is in all the books." Anyway, he impatiently concludes, "the proper explanation is as I have given it: one who separates himself from the ways of the community is one who separates himself from the laws of Israel. That is the correct interpretation."

"The ways of the community," "the ways of Israel": they are the same. Jewish communities are never merely local. They are the instantiations of a people.

In the medieval world, Luciferean revolutionaries were rare among the Jews, as were lives lived in perfect indifference to the law. Mordecai's understanding of the exceptions to the mercies of Jewish mourning would not have excluded many people. But I cringe when I attach these standards to the Jews of the modern world—or rather, I see why they cannot be attached to them. Judaism needs the Jews as much as the Jews need Judaism.

The power of the Jews over Judaism is as enormous as the power of Judaism over the Jews. But the Jews have not used their power over Judaism wisely.

"The sinners who sin with their bodies." What sort of transgression is this? A libertine life? No, nothing so lurid. The Talmud explains, in the name of Rav, that this refers to "the skull that fails to wear the phylacteries." For this, hell! A thousand years after Rav, this bit of rabbinical terror was amplified by Jacob Tam, who was Rashi's grandson: "This obtains only if he has contempt for the commandment and loathes the straps of the phylacteries that are wound on his head. Yet if he is reluctant to wear his phylacteries because he fears that his body is not as perfectly clean as Elisha the man of wings, and worries constantly that he will be unable to keep his body in a condition of purity and sanctity—certainly he is not judged like the Jewish sinners who sin with their bodies." Splendid! There is the man who considers himself too good for his phylacteries, and there is the man who considers himself not good enough for his phylacteries—and then there are the rest of us, who do not waken in purity but bind ourselves nonetheless in these grim black straps, so that we may permit ourselves to think, for at least as long as we are bound, that we are good.

My skull is bound, like my mind.

Elisha the man of wings? He was a pious man of the second century who defied a Roman decree that all who wore their phylacteries would be executed on the spot by being stabbed in the head. A Roman officer saw Elisha in the marketplace in his phylacteries and chased him. When he caught him, Elisha had already hidden his phylacteries in his hand. "What do you have in your hand?" the Roman asked. "The wings of a dove," Elisha answered. And the Talmudic tale concludes: "He opened his hand and there were the wings of a dove."

Oh, yes. And what is the sin of "the sinners with their bodies among the nations of the world," who do not wear phylacteries? Rav describes it with one word: "Sex."

At the bottom of the page on which Mordecai's commentary appears, there is a gloss in letters so small that I can hardly read them. This gloss gives a different definition of the deviant who may be denied the rites of mourning. It reports that Nissim ben Reuven Gerondi, the great Talmudist in Barcelona in the fourteenth century, ruled that "these are individuals who do not share with the community in the burden of taxes and tributes, and who do not share in the pain of the community." By "taxes," Nissim refers to revenues paid to the community by its members; by "tributes," to revenues paid by the community to the powers by whose sufferance the Jews live. The difference between the definitions is interesting. In the Ashkenazic orbit, it is theological deviance that will be punished posthumously. In the Sephardic orbit, it is political deviance that will be punished posthumously. The former worries about philosophical treason, the latter worries about social treason. Were the Jews of Ashkenaz, then, less insecure politically and more insecure theologically? Not at all. This is just more evidence of the sublime indifference to their fate in which the Jews developed their religion. There is no more fundamental misunderstanding of Jewish history than its reduction to Jewish adversity.

Here is Maimonides' characterization of "those who have separated themselves from the ways of the community" in his codification of the laws of mourning: "They are people who have cast off the yoke of the commandments from upon themselves, and are no longer included in the generality of Israel with respect to keeping the commandments and respecting the holidays and attending the houses of worship and the houses of study, as if they were free for themselves." These are the deviants for whom there is no mourning. The last phrase is striking: "as if they were free for themselves." Maimonides is not denouncing freedom. He is denouncing some of its uses. His implication is that we are not to be free for ourselves, we are to be free for our duties and our God. Thus the freedom of the rebel is an inferior freedom—a form of compulsion, really. I cannot altogether accept this, since I am the grateful child of many rebellions. But who will deny that the rebel is in some respects an unfree man, ruled by angers and aspirations that he cannot control?

And here is Maimonides' characterization of "those who have separated themselves from the ways of the community" in his codification of the laws of repentance: "He who separates himself from the ways of the community, even if he did not violate any commandments, but simply holds himself apart from the congregation of Israel—who does not fulfill any commandments along with them, and does not join them in their troubles, and does not fast with them in their fasts, but goes his own way as if he were one of the gentiles of the earth and not one of them—he has no portion in the world to come." In this passage Maimonides is more severe. And the defecting Jew described in this passage is a strangely familiar figure. He is not the rebel, or the heretic, or the traitor. He is the one who wants to slip away, who never asked to be a Jew, who is captivated by the rest of the world. He does not wish to violate the commandments. He merely wishes not to fulfill them.

In Dupont Circle, window-cleaners were sliding up and down ropes, or dangling in the air. Rising and falling, or hanging precariously. Eschatology!

Isaac of Vienna writes about "a man who is known to be a sinner." He says, "Not only is there no question but that there is no obligation to provide him with a proper funeral, but in fact there is a prohibition against providing him with a proper funeral." Isaac cites a story from the Jerusalem Talmud. "There was a butcher in Sepphoris who provided Jews with meat that was either not [ritually] slaughtered or improperly slaughtered. It happened that he drank wine on the eve of the Sabbath and went up to his roof and fell over and died. The dogs were lapping up his blood. People came to Rabbi Hanina and asked if they should take the body and provide it with the proper rites. He replied: 'It is written, "neither shall ye eat any flesh that is torn of beasts in the field; ye shall cast it to the dogs"—and this man used to steal [the unclean meat] from the dogs and feed it to Israel! Leave the dogs alone, for they are eating what is rightfully theirs.'" Nasty. And then Isaac cites the pronouncement from the Babylonian Talmud that "he who separates himself from the ways of the community—nothing is done for him at his death." And he concludes: "Therefore I, Isaac the author, know in my heart that it is forbidden to take part in the burial of a man who was known to be wicked and did not repent. But an ordinary man, who was known not to be wicked—it is a duty to take part in his burial." In Isaac's reading, he who separates himself from the ways of the community is he who is "known" to separate himself from the community. The denial of the rites of mourning is an expression of social opprobrium. —Fine, but the community had better be sure. Maybe the butcher of Sepphoris had it coming, but public opinion is treacherous, and the dead cannot defend themselves.

In shul in Manhattan on a frosty morning. I am early. I wait patiently in my phylacteries and my prayer shawl in the company of three old men. All of a sudden the sighing starts, first from one corner, then from another corner, individually and then responsively, until I find myself in the middle of a symphony of sighs, of vocalized and unvocalized ejaculations of woe. "Oy." "Oy vay." "Oy." "Gevalt, gevalt." "Oy vay." "Oy, oy, oy." "Vay, vay, vay." "Oy gevalt." "Oy, oy, oy." And then "Gotinyu," the diminutive for God. "Gotinyu, Gotinyu." I begin to classify the renditions in musical terms. For the hale white-haired man, *molto sostenuto.* For the round-bellied man with the rasping voice, *adagio lamentoso.* For the little man with the soft eyes in the tattered coat, *andante tranquillo.* The complaints are real, but they are generalized. They seem to refer to no affliction in particular. This is moaning practice. I am tempted to compete, to show off my own sigh. I had a good teacher: my father was a master sigher. But I keep my peace. There is nothing generalized, for me, about this year's sighs.

After the prayers the rabbi teaches a short class in Talmud. I'm in no rush, so I sit in. "Rabbi Judah said: Three kinds of people need protection, and they are the sick, the groom, and the bride. And it is taught: the sick, the woman who has given birth, the groom, and the bride. And there are those who say: the mourner, too." Why the mourner? I know why: he is the one without a skin. But Rashi has a darker, more obscure reason: "He has fallen under a bad sign, and so the demon taunts him." In this respect, Rashi says, the mourner is like the sick. The mourner's demon: I find the superstition helpful. Meanwhile the rabbi keeps reading and explaining. He comes to this: "Rabbi Yohanan said: He who lengthens his prayer and studies it closely will end up heartsick." We are referred to Rashi, who describes this petitioner doomed to disappointment: "He is the one who says in his heart that his request will be granted because he prayed with the proper intention." His fervor in prayer fills him with a boastful confidence. Rashi is right: piety produces its forms of vanity. Still, Rashi is flying in the face of the literal meaning of the passage. Rabbi Yohanan really is worrying that prayer will not withstand too much scrutiny, too much expectation. His subject is, plainly, the efficacy of prayer. He is proposing that a little distance will prevent a lot of heartsickness. I am in agreement.

In a Jewish bookshop on Broadway, "the eighth volume" has appeared. That is, the long-awaited eighth volume of the responsa of Rabbi Moses Feinstein. When I was a boy, I never heard a name spoken with more reverence. I remember a wedding in our family at which he officiated. The waters parted when he walked into the room. And I remember sometimes catching a glimpse of him, a small huddled man with a scraggly white beard in a long outsized coat, on a small street on the Lower East Side—Rivington Street, I think. He was the greatest Jewish jurist of his age. (He died in 1986, when he was ninety-one.) His responsa are legends. They are way over my head, but a few years ago I acquired them for my library anyway. The reading of only a few of Feinstein's pages leaves me with a quiver of continuity that I get from no other source. In his writings, the line really is unbroken. These erudite rulings are the record of decades of believing Jews, in Russia and then in America, coming to this sophisticated and compassionate and indefatigable rabbi with their problems, and of him solving them. Like all responsa, they are documents of their time, and yet when I read Feinstein's rulings time is erased: the melodrama of modernity is nowhere to be found, and there is a glimpse of Judaism living and working as it lived and worked, without interruption. (Sometimes nostalgia is a sign of historical understanding.) I read in Feinstein and I think: whether or not I am lost, everything is not lost. So I pick up the posthumous volume in the bookshop to have a look, and I discover a long responsum, in twenty-one parts, from 1981, about mourning and the mourner's kaddish. And one of the sections of this responsum answers the question "whether one should say kaddish for a year for a father who violated the Sabbath and whether to say kaddish at all for a father who was a heretic." The angel of bibliography is guiding my way! I buy the book eagerly. I can't wait to crack its spine at the teahouse.

Back in Washington. Working late at the office, I call my sister. She is putting the children to bed and she wants me to hear what her little boy has learned in school. She gives him the phone and I hear a tiny, eager voice reciting, syllable by syllable, the prayer before bedtime. These are my nephew's first Hebrew words. "What do you think?" my sister asks. "I think that Hitler lost," I reply.

At the teahouse with Feinstein. "It is certainly preferable," he writes, "that kaddish be said all twelve months," but the authorities have wisely limited the obligation to eleven months, so as not to impute wickedness to one's father or mother. (The wicked, remember, are punished in hell for twelve months.) "But plainly this pertains to ordinary individuals who are known to observe the commandments," he continues. "When the son knows that they did not observe the commandments, that they were violators of the Sabbath—even if it was for the sake of their livelihood and not for any other end—he should say kaddish for the full twelve months. And all the more should he say kaddish for the full twelve months if they were violators of the Sabbath for other reasons, even just for the sake of appetite." By Feinstein's stringent standard, many mourners, myself included, should stay the course for a year. I do not wish to impute wickedness to my father, but I take Feinstein's point.

Yet there are sinners for whom not even a year of kaddish will do any good. "As for somebody who violated the Sabbath on principle, a heretic for whom mourning is not prescribed, it is not appropriate to require the son to say kaddish for him if he died in his bed." (If he was killed, however, kaddish is said.) In this ruling, paternity is abrogated by philosophy. But wait. Feinstein is not quite so hard. He continues: "Yet if he wishes to say kaddish for his father, it is permitted, for a son who is righteous may benefit even a father who is absolutely evil." Feinstein adduces the Talmudic text that I studied months ago, according to which the evil kings Ahaz and Amon were saved from perdition by the righteous kings Hezekiah and Josiah, their sons. "And even though it is not appropriate to compare oneself to them, it is still the case that, having been taught that the piety of sons benefits even fathers who were apostates and violators of the prohibition against idolatry and all the other prohibitions, it is obvious that the good deeds of sons who fear God and observe the commandments in our own time will also bring benefit in the saying of kaddish. And of course the son should desire to take his father out of Gehenna so that he may have a share in the world to come, even if the situation can be rectified only in the course of time." In Feinstein's ruling, then, morality trumps biology, and then yields to love.

All these casuistic turns, all these figments of the eschatological imagination, they are all expedients of love.

At the teahouse, a pause in study. I stare across the road, where a lamp burns on a wooden table in a second-story window. My mind empties out. All that remains is a sensation of quiddity. How final is this language, this Jewish language, in which I am living! I apprehend this more clearly at this moment than I have ever apprehended it. In this language I was born, in this language I will die. In me this language was not born, in me this language will not die. I am a vessel. I am *this* vessel. I am this vessel for *this*. I am swooning before my facts. For a moment, I will not contest the power of my facts over me.

I ponder Feinstein's comment that there is no need to say kaddish for a heretic who died in his bed. He refers me to Moses Isserles, the sixteenth-century master of law in Poland, who states at the end of his discussion of kaddish that "there are those who hold that the sons must say kaddish for a heretic who was killed by idolators." Why? The idolators merely killed another idolator. But the purpose of this ruling is to establish that this is precisely not the case. The idolators killed the heretic because he once was (or, in their opinion, he still was) a Jew. A heretic may still be martyred. As a heretic, he may not be mourned. As a martyr, he may be mourned. His children must reach past his heresy to his martyrdom, and they must honor it. The poor, difficult man may have lived as a Christian, but he died as a Jew. The world remained unmoved by his change of conviction. It is one of the lessons of Jewish history that the community of Jewish fate is larger than the community of Jewish belief. And so kaddish must be recited also for the rebel who was defeated in his rebellion.

In Feinstein's account, mourning is a mobilization. The fate of your parents hangs in the balance. Get cracking and do what you can. "Every mourner on each day should do whatever he can do for the good of his parent, and a day must not pass without him doing something for the good of his father and his mother. And even if he is saying kaddish, it is best that each day he do whatever more is possible." This is why the service should be considered in sections, so that many mourners will have the chance to lead it. Feinstein's sense of the kaddish as spiritual action in a spiritual emergency is apparent also in his discussion of those who say kaddish for people who were not their parents. "If one is saying kaddish out of friendship for the dead, kaddish should be said for twelve months." A child must not impute wickedness to his dead father or mother, and therefore must say kaddish for no more than eleven months; but a friend is under no such inhibition. A friend may permit himself to imagine the worst.

After the evening prayer, I give one of our company a lift home. He lives nearby, a few blocks from the Watergate, and I have been driving him home for months. Tonight, as he was getting into the car, he had a question. "Why do you always get such good parking spots?" And he had an answer: "Maybe you do good deeds that nobody knows about." Oh, I see. The good deeds that people know about are not sufficient to account for my good parking spots. I have been chastised!

Back to Feinstein. "One who says kaddish because he was hired by the son to do so, on the grounds that there will be days when the son is not able to say kaddish: his obligation depends on the language with which the son hired him. If he asked him to say kaddish in his stead, the kaddish is said only for eleven months. And if he told him that he was hiring him to say kaddish for its benefit to his dead father, then kaddish must be said for twelve months. For there is no distinction, in the latter instance, between the eleventh month and the twelfth month, and he knows that the twelfth month may not benefit the father as much as the eleventh month if the father was a wicked man; but it is for the benefit of the father that he has agreed to say it." I like this distinction between the needs of the sons and the needs of the fathers. The sons need to honor the fathers. The fathers need to be saved from hell. The sons cannot exceed the conventions of filial politeness, even in the rescue of the fathers;

but the sons should be under no illusions. The fathers were sinners. I get the impression that Feinstein, the famous realist, wishes that just about everybody would say kaddish for twelve months. —And Feinstein's distinction begs a question. If twelve months of kaddish benefits the dead more than eleven months of kaddish, then why not confer the duty upon someone who can say kaddish for twelve months? Why not prefer the prayer of a stranger to the prayer of a son? But the question answers itself. For what is the prayer of a stranger compared to the prayer of a son? Kaddish was not enjoined upon all the community for all the community. It was enjoined upon children for parents, and so on. Reward and punishment are universal, but we cannot care about everyone equally. The ranking of our duties must take into account the ranking of our sentiments.

Feinstein's responsum turns to the subject of the son who hires somebody to say his kaddish for the duration of his mourning. And he compares such a son to the harlot daughter of a priest! More precisely, he deduces the consequences of the son's shirking of his duty from a Talmudic discussion of the harlot daughter of a priest. It is said in Leviticus about such a daughter that "she profaneth her father," and Rabbi Meir enlarges upon this statement: "If he [her father] was treated as holy, he is now treated as profane. If he was treated with respect, he is now treated with contempt. People say of him: 'Cursed be he who begot her, cursed be he who raised her, cursed be he from whose loins she sprung.'" Rav Ashi adds that there are cases when "a man is called the son of a wicked man even if he is the son of a righteous man," and that the priest's wanton daughter is one of those cases. According to Feinstein, the shirker of the kaddish is another one of those cases. The son's refusal to carry out his obligation disgraces his father. Such a son is nothing less than "a wicked man." And what sort of father produces this sort of son? It is the usual deduction of the character of the dead from the character of the living: "We must consider him [the father] a wicked man." "And this is to his good," Feinstein adds, a little startlingly, since kaddish may then be said for him for twelve months—by the son, should he be persuaded to return to his senses (persuaded by others, of course, since "his repentance is not owed to the influence of the father"), or by those whom the son has hired. Feinstein's strictness in this matter was owed to the fact that he was combating a practice that was widespread. (It is still widespread.) But his strictures about the indolent son are also made in a practical spirit. A time of expiation is not a time of optimism. The more kaddish, the better.

The more, the better: Feinstein also writes that in the twelfth month, when the kaddish is over but mourning is not over, "it is a good thing [for the mourner] to lead the prayers, because it counts for the father that the son stands at the head of the congregation, like all the good deeds that the son does throughout the son's life." You never stop showing where you came from. ("But after the year is over, it is not appropriate to make this effort [to lead the prayers in honor of one's dead parents], because there are many people [in the house of worship] whose parents have died, and there will be conflict.")

By the mourning of their children you shall know them. By their mourning, at the very least.

From Feinstein's somber rulings I take away the suggestion that the season of mourning is a season of disabuse. The fate of your father's soul hangs on your ability to think unsentimentally about him. If you could not see the truth about him before he died, you must see the truth about him after he died. —In the entrails of superstition, a demand for clarity.

I have always hated happy funerals: we are here to celebrate a life, and so on. No, we are not here to celebrate anything. We are here to bury an imperfect man or an imperfect woman, to regard his or her frailty and therefore to be frail.

A motto: *Tristesse oblige.*

When I tell the rabbi that I have been studying this volume of Feinstein's decisions, he asks me if I have come across Feinstein's remarkable comment on women and kaddish. I have not, and he opens the book to the page. In 1982, Feinstein was asked about "matters that require the separation of men and women, and those that do not." In the second section of his responsum, he treats the question of whether there must be a partition in the house of worship if only one or two women are present, and his discussion includes this historical observation: "After all, in all the generations it was common that a poor woman would sometimes come into the house of study to receive alms, or a mourning woman would come to recite the kaddish." The casual nature of Feinstein's reference to the woman's kaddish tells me what I need (and what I want) to know. In his account of Jewish practice, the woman's kaddish is uncontroversial. In the matter of the kaddish, women are separate but equal. I understand that this is an imperfect kind of egalitarianism, but still I am pleasantly surprised. I expected to find only separate. I am delighted to find also equal.

At twilight on Friday, immediately prior to the prayers that welcome the Sabbath, we sing a song, a sixteenth-century mystical poem of eager desire. "Hurry and love, the time has come!" The singing of this song has become the still point of my week. And the pure melody with which the song concludes, the disappearance of words from the song, is a wonderful thing. The Jewish liturgy is so replete with doctrines and memories and arguments and dreams, it provides so many particulars about the past and the present and the future, its powers of description and prescription are so inexhaustible, that there remains little or no space in which the soul can just vibrate. But here, in this melody, is such a space. In the tradition, a shelter from the tradition.

My bookseller has sent along a small handbook of Sephardic customs, particularly the customs of the old community in Jerusalem, regarding death and mourning. It was written a few years ago by a rabbi in Jerusalem who was frustrated by the absence of such a handbook when he was himself a mourner. In his entry about the mourner's kaddish, I find a notable difference between the Sephardic custom and the Ashkenazic custom: "Kaddish is recited for a year for a father or a mother. It is recited also in the twelfth month, until the last week. Today the custom is to stop saying the kaddish in the first week of the twelfth month, and then to resume saying it from the second week of the twelfth month, until the year is complete." This is a different way of protecting one's parent from the aspersion on his or her character that twelve months of kaddish would imply: in this Sephardic practice, the kaddish is interrupted at the beginning of the twelfth month, but it is not terminated until the year is over. Not eleven months, as we have it; but twelve months short a week. The Sephardic way is more in keeping with the spirit of this service, I think, than the Ashkenazic way. (And this rabbi's regulation puts me in mind of Feinstein's interest in a full year of kaddish.)

A hostile winter morning. It is the month of Tevet, a month of minor fast days, all of them commemorations of disasters. My favorite has always been the eighth day of the month, which was declared a day of fasting because it was on this day that the oldest translation of the Bible into Greek was completed in the third century B.C.E. (This fast day has not been observed for many centuries, which is too bad, because American Jews deserve to mortify themselves for their linguistic treason.) Today is the tenth day of the month, on which Nebuchadnezzar laid siege to Jerusalem. Shul starts early, and it falls to me to lead the worship. I am not really familiar with the penitential compositions for this day. I don't want to err, or to cause the others to err; but things go smoothly, not least because the poem of lamentation that is at the center of the service turns out to be the work of my old friend Ephraim ben Isaac of Regensburg, the twelfth-century poet whose strong verses about the Second Crusade would have figured prominently in the dissertation that I never wrote. "My days of mourning have run on, and my heart still sighs," Ephraim writes. "Pay me for my days of mourning, bring me my reward!" As I say these words, I note gladly that they more or less retain their original meaning for me: I do not inject my grief into Ephraim's grief. It has been almost nine months now, and time is correcting sorrow's perspective. My sorrow is no longer the only sorrow that I can see.

Pausing at an intersection, I notice a woman in the car next to mine. She is gazing calmly at the red light. When the light turns green, she buries her face in her hands and weeps.

The afternoon service on the day of the fast. "Go ahead," says the rabbi, motioning to me to lead the service, as he might have motioned to any of the other mourners in the room. And then he adds: "Today we're all mourners." My father perished in New York in 1996 and the Temple perished in Jerusalem in 586 B.C.E., but we are all similarly bereaved. This is one of the great paradoxes of Jewish existence. The consciousness of history becomes so intense that it abolishes the consciousness of time.

In shul on the Sabbath, we read the story of Joseph and his brothers. I fell into a happy absorption. All around me there was the din of piety and gossip; but this noise acted as a sort of shield for my solitude, as I sank deeper and deeper into the commentators, until I could not hear the voices rising from the room and I could hear the voices rising from the book. The Torah reader pressed on, but I lingered behind, stuck on a comment. When Jacob learns that Joseph is alive, the verse reports that "Jacob's spirit revived," and my book referred me to an ancient commentary on *Fathers* in which it is said that Jacob's spirit revived because "the holy spirit that had left him was restored to him at that moment," and then I am referred to Maimonides' *Eight Chapters,* in which Maimonides writes that one of the obstacles to prophecy is sadness. As long as Jacob mourned, in other words, he was without inspiration. The condition of inspiration is happiness. What an unromantic notion! Is it really so? Can a sad man not see more? Surely the prophets themselves personified the alliance of inspiration with unhappiness. How, then, understand the upbeat Maimonides? I have an idea. It is that the relation between inspiration and happiness is tautological. Inspiration is attended by happiness because inspiration *is* happiness.

The rabbi's sermon is a reading of God's promises to Jacob a few verses later. "I will go down with thee to Egypt, and also I will surely bring thee up again, and Joseph shall put his hand upon thine eyes." Why this last promise? The rabbi proposes an answer. Jacob must have worried that he had lost his son to Egypt, that his son had been integrated into the infidel culture that he ruled—"he was worried," the rabbi said, "that in his favorite son he would not have a kaddish." And so God reassures Jacob that when the time comes Joseph will fulfill his duties as a Jewish son. I am reminded of Menasseh ben Israel's list of the ten things by which the son acquits the father: closing the father's eyes is the first on Menasseh's list. And I am reminded of my father's eyes, and how my hand immediately reached to touch them, without reflection, a dead moment of death, in which my body knew my duty before my mind. . . .

Jacob was not worried only about his son's Jewishness. In his sermon, the rabbi speculates that he was worried also about his son's character. For Jacob must have remembered that Joseph was vain, arrogant, scheming, worldly. And so God reassures Jacob that Joseph will rise from the depths of his worldliness to the love and the loyalty of a son for a father. It is precisely the complexity of Joseph from which Jacob may draw comfort. Since Joseph is many things, he will be this thing, too. He doesn't add up, but he doesn't disappoint. He carries all his worlds into all his worlds.

The hero of many-mindedness, my forefather Joseph.

When I return home, I check in Menasseh's book to see if I remembered the passage rightly. I did. What I did not remember was his prooftext for the son's obligation to close his father's eyes. It is: "And Joseph shall put his hand upon thine eyes." "And this Joseph did," Menasseh writes, "as the verse [in a later chapter] attests: 'And Joseph fell upon his father's face,' which he did to put his hand on his eyes." All those years there were so many things about myself that I did not want my father to see. I tried so hard to close his eyes, but he saw more than I believed he saw. (There were times when he chose to avert his gaze, but one looks away only from what one has already seen.)

My library looked like a graveyard tonight, and every book looked like a grave. But one must open these graves and enter them. Inside these graves, there is life.

Paper is stronger than stone. The Jews knew this.

In the *Zohar,* the central text of the Jewish mystical tradition, composed in Spain at the end of the thirteenth century but attributed to Simeon bar Yohai, the charismatic rabbi of the second century, I find an extraordinary exegesis of the promise to Jacob that "Joseph shall put his hand upon thine eyes." The exegesis takes the form of a conversation among some of Simeon's contemporaries. It begins with a simple comment: "What was the purpose of this promise that he would put his hands on his eyes? Rabbi Yose said that it was a sign of respect for Jacob, and also to inform him that Joseph was alive and would attend him at his death." But the commentary is not satisfied with such a plain reading. It seeks to soar. "Rabbi Hezekiah said: 'I have learned something [about this passage], but I am afraid to reveal it. What I have learned shows that wisdom may be discovered in the common practices of the world.' Rabbi Abba gave him a push and said: 'Say what you know, and arm yourself with it! In the days of Rabbi Simeon, things may be revealed!'" Rabbi Hezekiah is emboldened to disclose his esoteric knowledge, and launches into his interpretation of Joseph's closing of his father's eyes. "I have learned from a chapter of Rabbi Jesse the Elder about the customs of the world, that if a man has been endowed with a son, then his son must spread dust on his eyes when he is buried, to honor him, and to demonstrate that the world is now sealed from him and his son inherits the world in his place. For the image of the world may be seen in the human eye. The outer sphere of white stands for the great sea of Oceanus that surrounds the world. The next sphere of color is the land, which is surrounded by water and stands in the water. The third color is in the center of the eye, and it is Jerusalem, which is the center of the world. The fourth color is the pupil of the eye, which reflects the countenance of the beholder, and is the most esteemed of all. It is Zion, which is the central point of everything, in which the image of the whole world may be seen. There the Divine Spirit dwells, which is the beauty and the cynosure of all of creation. Thus it is the eye that inherits the world, and for this reason the father gives it up and the son takes it up and inherits it." What Rabbi Hezekiah has described is something more fundamental than the transmission of a perspective. It is the transmission of the capacity for a perspective. In closing the father's eyes, the son adopts the father's eyes. He receives the cognitive requirements of tradition.

Rabbi Abba likes Rabbi Hezekiah's reading, but he has something more arcane to propose. "He said to him: 'You have spoken well, but there is a meaning even more hidden, to which people do not pay sufficient heed.'" The discussion among these divines is a tournament of esotericism. Rabbi Abba offers his reading of Joseph's parting gesture to Jacob: "When a man departs the world, his soul is still attached to him, and until his soul leaves him his eyes see things in death that they did not see in life, as in the verse 'for no man shall see and live,' and his eyes are opened by the sight of what they see. For this reason, those who attend him must place their hands on his eyes and close them. Thus we learn the secret of the custom that at the moment of a man's death, if his eyes have remained open owing to the exalted sight that they have seen, and if he has been endowed with a son, his son must hasten to place his hand on his eyes and close them, as it is written: 'and Joseph shall put his hand upon thine eyes.' The reason for the closing of his eyes is that an unholy appearance may present itself to them, and the eye that has beheld a vision of the holy must not now gaze upon an unholy sight. Also, his soul is still attached to him, it is still in its house, and if his eye remains open and an unholy image imposes itself upon it, then everything that it regards will be cursed. And it demeans the eye, and the family of the deceased, and the deceased, that it should see something improper and unworthy. For this reason, it is covered with dust. Our colleagues have already explained the judgment of the dead in the grave. The respectful thing is that his eyes be shut to everything by the son whom he leaves in the world."

Who does not wish to believe that the last moment will be the most privileged moment, that finally one will see what one has yearned to see, that in the end will be the proof? Death as an epistemological breakthrough: the literature about near-death experiences—some years ago I devoured it in a funk—supports the notion. It is enough to make death seem like luck. But I am loath to believe it. I am afraid that I will be disappointed, then as now.

All the dying are mystics. (Nonsense.) All the mystics are dying. (Nonsense.)

Rabbi Abba's disquisition on the vision of the dying reminds me of an obscure medieval text that I read a few months after my father died. It was late in the morning. I had returned from the teahouse in a state of dejection. I opened one of Adolf Jellinek's collections of early mystical texts—I was searching for a version of the story of Rabbi Akiva and the condemned man—and found something called *Masekhet Ḥibut Ha'Kever*, or *The Tractate of the Torments of the Grave*. I began to read. "How does a man die? Angels appear before him—one of the angels that serve the Lord, and one of the angels of death, and a scribe, and an angel appointed to the scribe. They say to him: 'Arise, your end has come!' The scribe sits and reckons the number of the man's days and years. He says to them: 'No, my end has not yet come!' Suddenly he opens his eyes and sees an angel as vast as the world from its beginning to its end. From its head to its toes, the angel is made of eyes. It is dressed in fire, wrapped in fire, all fire, and there is a knife in its hands. A drop of bitterness hangs from it, and from this the man dies, from this he rots, from this his face is emptied. And he does not die until he has seen God Himself, as it is written: 'for no man shall see me and live.' In life, they do not see. In death, they see."

—In life, they do not see. In death, they see.
—No, that's not right.
—In life, they see. In death, they do not see.
—No, that's not right.
—In life, they do not see. In death, they do not see.
—That's right.

What did my father see?

If the soul leaves the body in death, and if the soul leaves the body in the apprehension of truth, then death and the apprehension of truth take the same form. Death is merely the most perfect suppression of the corporeal impediment to incorporeal knowledge.

For the materialist, of course, this is nonsense. For the materialist, truth is not spiritual. The materialist thinks with his body. This is reflected in the quality of his thinking.

Still, there is something repugnant about such a conclusion. Surely the thirst for knowledge must not lead to the thirst for death. Why must the body be destroyed? It should be enough that the body be mastered. (The view that we are only spirit can be as inhumane as the view that we are only matter.)

The mind is more like the soul than like the body.

Rationalists are more like mystics than like materialists.

A friend is studying the Diabelli Variations and remarks that they conclude abruptly, with no flourish of farewell. "You know what's missing?" she says. "A kaddish. A good-bye." I suggest to her that a good-bye has no place in a set of variations, because they are the representation in music of a world without finality. Variations are reincarnations. In variations, a theme never dies. It leads many lives. But I am not saying kaddish for one of my father's lives. I am saying kaddish for my father's one life. One does not mourn the end of a version. One mourns the end of an essence.

Does it matter that the farewell is said after he has gone? Perhaps it is more important that a good-bye be spoken than that it be heard. Something spoken that may not be heard: is this not also a description of prayer?

The sky over the river was sullen this morning. The light was stolen by large clouds of silver streaked with black. On the way to shul I felt the sting of nature's regularity. Another morning, another morning, another morning, another morning. How could the ancient philosophers have referred to nature as mind? Mind is lawless, partial, shifting; and fights for its constancies. If nature were mind, there would be days when the sun did not rise or did not set, because nature was moved or distracted or playful or hurt. But nature is constant, because it does not care.

Ecclesiastes had it backwards. There is much that is new under the sun. What is not new is the sun.

X

When I turned into Sheridan Circle this morning, the eastern sky was a hot, rippling pink. The bronze general on his bronze horse seemed to be galloping right into the radiance. I galloped on to shul. My year of prayer has made me into a student of light, a connoisseur of the heavens.

An elderly gentleman with a fine mustache was called up to the Torah. He uttered the blessings in a thick Galicianer accent. It was exactly my father's accent. These accents have a kind of talismanic effect upon me: they whisk me to another time and place, they mark my distance. These accents are a shorthand for displacement and destruction, for resilience and a multiplicity of resources, for the span of the Jewish journey. I cannot imagine Jewish life without the music of these accents. But soon they will be gone. Soon we will be entirely on our own. Then we will see.

What sort of days are these? Every afternoon I interrupt my work and walk a few blocks to put my head in my hands and whisper that "I am weary with my groaning; all the night make I my bed to swim; I water my couch with my tears. Mine eye is consumed because of grief." And a few minutes later I'm back at my desk. My bed may not swim, but my brain swims.

"A query from a convert": this is how Ovadiah Yosef, the former Sephardic chief rabbi of Israel and a man of encyclopedic learning, begins a responsum. The convert's query is this: "Is it permissible for him to pray for his non-Jewish father who languishes in his sickbed, that God may send His word and heal him, and after his death may he say kaddish for the elevation of his soul?" This launches Yosef into a legal opinion that must rank as one of the great statements of tolerance in modern Judaism. It begins sourly, with a citation from Joseph Karo, that "it is forbidden to save idolators from death, and to treat them medically even for a fee, except in a place where there is hostility [and inaction might serve as a pretext to harm the Jewish community]." But Yosef immediately adduces another authority against Karo's apparent heartlessness. Was not Maimonides himself a physician, and did he himself not treat Muslims in Egypt? If Maimonides could practice his medical arts on non-Jewish patients, then they cannot have been idolators. So Yosef writes: "Thus it is clear that if the convert's parents are Muslims, and they are ill, it is permitted to pray for their full recovery, since they are not idolators." Yosef served as the head of the rabbinical court in Cairo in the late 1940s (and displayed great courage in a place where there was hostility). Perhaps this opinion was written in those years. But his discussion moves immediately from Muslims to Christians, to establish that they, too, are not idolators, and the compassion of Jews may not be denied them. He arrives at a statement by Rashi that "in this age gentiles are not idolators," a periodization of history that has the exhilarating effect of banishing Jewish intolerance to the past. And he cites Karo's view that the non-Jews among whom we live "are not idolators, they merely cling to the custom of their fathers." Or more precisely, "the custom of their fathers is in their hands." They are not blaspheming, they are merely honoring their own traditions. Jewish law has great respect for traditionalists in the Jewish world; and in Karo's comment, in the Ottoman Empire of the sixteenth century, this respect is extended to traditionalists in the non-Jewish world. Yosef also adduces the opinion of Isaac Attia, a scholar in Aleppo in the early nineteenth century, that we are not only permitted to pray for non-Jews, "it may also be a positive obligation to pray for them, so as to practice the ways of peace. And if there should be an hour of grace and [the non-Jew] is cured, then God's Name will have been sanctified." (Yosef cites another Sephardic authority's more blunt reason for such ecumenical prayer: "We are now in exile and have need of gentiles.")

Now, what about the convert's kaddish? "After God has apprised us of all of the above," Yosef writes, "it appears that after the death of a convert's father, and similarly after the death of his mother, it is proper that he say kaddish for the elevation of their souls. . . . Even though the convert is no longer related to his father—for a person that has converted is like a child that has been born—it is nonetheless proper, since his father sired him and brought him into this world and thereby caused him to arrive at the recognition of the truth and to come to abide in the inheritance of the Lord, that he pray for him and save him from the netherworld and win him entry into the world to come." The convert may be born again, but his second birth does not annul his first birth. A man who travels far from his father still loves him. And Yosef points out that the tradition "did not deprive the stranger, who is no relation to the deceased, from bringing about the benefit to the soul of the deceased that redounds from the kaddish." Thus, insofar as he is not a stranger to his parents, the convert may say kaddish for them; and insofar as he is a stranger to his parents, he may say kaddish for them. Under any description, the son may pray for the father. (Morality dignifies biology.)

The problem of the children of evil parents is not the same as the problem of the children of non-Jewish parents. This is significant. From Moses Feinstein, I learn that the son of a man who was a heretic may nevertheless say kaddish for him. From Ovadiah Yosef, I learn that the son of a man who was not a Jew may nevertheless say kaddish for him. The ethos of Jewish law is not a tribal ethos.

This Sabbath we came to the end of Genesis. As he lay dying, Jacob requested of Joseph "a kindness and a truth." This is the kindness that one extends to the dead—"the kindness that is true," as the rabbis called it, since there is no expectation of recompense. As children we were taught that this is the highest sort of kindness. After all, the dead cannot thank you. (If they were really grateful, though, they would leave you alone.)

After Jacob dies, Joseph mourns for his father: "And he made a mourning for his father seven days." A text in the Jerusalem Talmud suggests that this is the Biblical basis for the *shivah*, the seven days after the death of a loved one in which the family does not leave the house and mourns in shock and stringency. A text in the Babylonian Talmud pits the verse in Genesis against a verse in Job and concludes enigmatically that "an individual's soul mourns for him for all the seven days." This launches Baruch Ha'Levi Epstein, whose edition of Scripture I use in shul, into a rather special animadversion on the seven days after death. Epstein shows that the Talmud makes a distinction between the first three days and the last four days. During the first three days, the body of the deceased remains recognizable, and so the corpse may be identified reliably. On the fourth day, however, the blood begins to dry, and the disfigurement begins. And suddenly Epstein has a brainstorm! He recalls that there is a law about which "the jurists wrote that there is no basis or source." The law is that "after three days without salting, the blood in meat dries up and salting will no longer remove it, and so such meat cannot be eaten boiled but must be eaten roasted." But here, in the distinction between the early days of mourning and the later days of mourning, Epstein has found the basis and discovered the source for the ruling about meat. Rotting flesh is rotting flesh, I guess. There are times when the rabbinical sensibility is not very fine.

What is the spiritual status of a broken heart? This is the question that is posed by another responsum by Moses Feinstein, also from 1981. The subject of the ruling is the mourner's fitness to lead the worship. Feinstein presents a dispute between the great authorities of the sixteenth century. According to Joseph Karo, "if there is nobody there [who is qualified] to acquit the congregation in the fulfillment of their duty, the mourner may lead the prayer." The mourner, in short, is not really suitable for this task; he is the congregation's last resort. According to Moses Isserles, by contrast, "whoever knows how to lead the prayer should lead the prayer, and this is more effective [for the mourner's purposes] than the mourner's kaddish, which was established for minors." Isserles shares none of Karo's misgivings about the mourner's qualifications. He urges the mourner to seize the opportunity to bring credit to his parent. Next Feinstein adduces a text by Joel Sirkes, an authority in Poland in the seventeenth century, who is best known for his commentary on Jacob ben Asher's code of law. In the passage cited by Feinstein, Sirkes reports Jacob's view that the mourner is not fit for liturgical leadership. Against this view he cites the view of Solomon Luria, one of the great Talmudists of Poland a hundred years earlier. Luria's formulation is unforgettable. The mourner must lead the worship, he declares, "because the King of Kings prefers broken vessels."

How does Luria know that the King of Kings prefers broken vessels? He has a prooftext, from Psalms: "A broken and a contrite heart, O God, thou wilt not despise."

In Jewish law, the person who leads the prayers is called "the congregation's emissary." He makes the community's representations before God. Can a broken man do the job? No, say those who believe that the mourner is too sunk in sorrow to be an adequate representative. (In Feinstein's paraphrase, "the congregation must send whatever will do the most honor.") Yes, say those who believe that the mourner's sorrow is precisely what qualifies him to make the address. The opinion of the former is that sorrow depletes a man. The opinion of the latter is that sorrow deepens a man. A great disputation, then, between the party of high spirits and the party of low spirits.

The issue is not the preferability of happiness to unhappiness. Who wishes to grieve? But sooner or later we all grieve; and the interesting question is whether or not grief is spiritually and intellectually clarifying. Does suffering bring light or darkness? Does an unhappy man know more than a happy man? Is a broken vessel truer than a vessel that is whole? It is a splendid controversy. Yet rabbis are not poets. They must come to a decision about the practical consequences of melancholy. And they decide for the party of low spirits. "Mourners lead the prayers," Feinstein rules, "because of their broken hearts."

Bliss is stupid.

The analytical advantages of melancholy.

I have brought Sirkes' stirring text to the teahouse. He, too, sides with the party of low spirits, and he records many pungent formulations from the centuries that preceded him. This is my favorite: "I have seen it written in the name of Rabbi Meir [of Rothenburg] that in the twelve months of mourning for his father and his mother he may be the congregation's emissary [and lead the prayer]. For what joy is there in prayer?" What joy, indeed? I will cherish that sentence always. (It must be one of the great anti-hasidic pronouncements in the tradition.)

Still, as Sirkes shows, there are limits. There are occasions when a mourner may not lead the prayers (and on those occasions I do not lead the prayers). A mourner may not represent the congregation on days of joy, on the Sabbath and on holidays. For the purpose of celebration, certainly, the mourner is useless. As Sirkes writes, "on holidays, when the leader [of the prayers] chants joyfully and makes others joyful, everyone agrees that the mourner is not permitted to serve as the congregation's emissary." And yet, "on the Days of Awe [Rosh Hashanah and Yom Kippur], if he is worthier than others in the congregation, and someone as good as him cannot be found, he takes precedence [and leads the prayers]." On days of mortification, there is nothing like a broken vessel. In the company of the cheerless, the mourner is first among equals.

But those times are rare. In the regular run of days, sorrow lives on the periphery. One does not say kaddish in a world of kaddish. Indeed, one fulfills one's obligation by excusing oneself from the quotidian, by resisting the well-being that is all around. Sirkes records a lovely statement by the Perfumer. The Perfumer recorded, as one of "the customs of Rabbi Kalonymos," that the psalms of praise that are recited on the first day of the new month, the special hallelujahs, are not to be recited in the house of mourning, "since the souls are grieving there. Thus it is not permitted to chant 'the dead praise not the Lord,' for this would be like taunting the poor." In sorrow, one always feels a little taunted by the absence of sorrow. Never mind. It will not be long before I take my place among the taunters.

I don't know what triggered it. Walking in Dupont Circle I thought: I am a man without a father. And then I thought: I am not a man without a father. I will never be a man without a father. He will not die until I die. And then I sat down on a bench and cried.

In Brooklyn, in shul. There are just ten of us: myself, the rabbi, eight old men. In the interval between the afternoon prayer and the evening prayer, the rabbi teaches a short class. His subject for this sunset is the history of a certain feature of the Sabbath liturgy, but he is defeated in his pedagogy by his pupils. They are unable or unwilling to keep up with him. They are men of faith, but most of them know very little about the prayers that they have been pronouncing for decades. The rabbi discovers that he must begin at the beginning, and so he starts over; but the activity of teaching has been robbed of any intellectual satisfaction that it might have provided him. On his gentle but frustrated face, I see the ordeal of the pastoral life. It cannot be easy, representing the extraordinary to the ordinary. The tradition must be brought down to these people (it was created, and developed, and preserved for these people, and without them it will perish); but then they, too, bring it down. The rabbi has ideas that he wishes to develop, but he must be simple, concrete, helpful. Finally it is nightfall. We can get on with the worship, and he can return to the solitary gratifications of his mind.

On the floor of a dance studio, a piece of paper on which these words are written: "Life After Death. Dance After Technique." And then: "Damnation of Gravitation." Is somebody saying kaddish around here? I watch the dancers in class, and it strikes me that I can learn something about the shul from the studio. What these men and women are doing is not rote; it is practice, and there is nothing stultifying about practice. The purpose of practice is to repeat the elements of movement over and over until they are absorbed into the body, until they are made to precede reflection, so that they may be combined and recombined, as the result of reflection, into the dance. The formal and spiritual breakthroughs of the dance are these combinations and recombinations. Might this also be the case with study and prayer? Day after day, week after week, month after month, year after year, the same words, the same symbols, the same themes. It is often objected, against the view that creation cannot take place without tradition, that tradition frequently usurps creation, and so the diligent soul fails to fly. In the studio, however, I observe the diligent movements of these turning dancers, and yet they fly. I see that tradition must be an absorption, a second nature, for creation to occur. This is what the traditionalists do not understand. They keep tradition in the forefront of consciousness, so that it becomes not their second nature but their first nature, so that one can think almost of nothing else. But thinking of tradition is not the same as doing something with tradition. The highest object of study is not study. The highest object of movement is not movement. The highest object of Judaism is not Judaism.

Sirkes refers me to Benjamin Zev ben Mattathias, the controversial rabbi of Arta, in Epirus, in northwestern Greece. I have never read any of his responsa, which were published in Venice in 1539. It takes a few days for them to arrive from Brooklyn. I find no less than five responsa that treat the mourner's kaddish, and they are all very rich. But one of them is especially riveting. In this text, the kaddish is transformed into the scene of one of the great dramas in the annals of the Jews. Here is the question that was posed to Benjamin Zev: "Reuben and Simeon lived in the region of Apulia [in southern Italy] and had converted out of their faith. They had sons and daughters. In the course of time,

Reuben, who traveled from town to town, was ambushed by robbers and murdered, while Simeon died in his bed and the gentiles buried him according to all their customs. After Simeon's death, his sons and their wives left their place and returned to the Lord their God to worship Him together. Now, Reuben's son rose and stepped to the pulpit to say kaddish for his murdered father, for his atonement, arguing that it had always been his father's intention to repent and to return; and when the son of Simeon, who died in his bed, saw this, he also rose and stepped to the pulpit to say kaddish for his father, for the atonement of his soul. But the son of Reuben claimed before the judge that there was no basis in the law for the son of Simeon to rob him [of the public recitation of kaddish], arguing that the latter's father had the opportunity, as he lay dying, to repent in the presence of the Jewish *anusim* [marranos] who attended him, and to confess his sins to them, but he did not do so, and so we may infer his beginning from his end and conclude that he did not choose to repent; whereas his own father had intended to repent. And so it is fitting, said Reuben's son, that he say the kaddish to sanctify the name of heaven and by means of the kaddish obtain atonement [for his father]." These are the circumstances of the case. "I was asked," Benjamin Zev writes, "whether the son of Simeon may say kaddish, and whether it will help the one son as much as the other son, or not."

The son of Reuben disputed the son of Simeon's right to the privilege of the public recitation of the kaddish before the congregation. But he was contesting more than a liturgical custom. He was posing to Benjamin Zev the great question of his time: is there any sense in which Jews who were forced to convert to Christianity may still be considered Jews?

The expulsions from Spain and Portugal took place in Benjamin Zev's day. Many Jewish exiles from the Iberian peninsula arrived in Apulia, and Reuben and Simeon must have been among them. (A brutal conversion of the Jews of Apulia had occurred at the end of the thirteenth century. The crypto-Jews of southern Italy were known as *neofiti.*) In Apulia, however, the refugees found little peace. A short period of security was succeeded by persecutions and expulsions, first by the conquering French and then by the conquering Spanish, who once and for all banished Jews and crypto-Jews from the region in 1540. It is against this background of anti-Jewish hatred and anti-Jewish violence that the murder of Reuben the Jewish traveler on the roads of Apulia, and the reluctance of Simeon to return openly to Judaism, must be considered. In the question that was addressed to Benjamin Zev, then, private pathos was joined to public pathos. The sons were mourning, the people were mourning. The sons had lost their fathers, the people had lost their fathers. The sons wanted their fathers to return and to find rest, the people wanted their fathers to return and to find rest.

So how did Benjamin Zev decide? He prefaces his decision with the Talmudic discussion of the individual who "consecrated [an animal for] a sacrifice, and then became an apostate, and then returned" and wished to offer his sacrifice. Such a sacrifice, said the rabbis, is not accepted: "Since it was spurned, it shall be spurned." This does not bode well for the son of Simeon. And indeed, Benjamin Zev rules unkindly. His opinion is that the son of Reuben may recite the kaddish, but the son of Simeon may not recite the kaddish. For "Reuben, who was murdered, is not at all like Simeon, who died in his bed," in a number of respects. "Reuben may have been contemplating heaven [that is, intending to repent], but at the moment when he was killed there was nobody before whom he could repent, even if he had not thought of repentance earlier." Moreover, "since he was murdered by gentiles, he is considered to have been martyred by the king, and therefore he finds forgiveness." Benjamin Zev cites Talmudic support for this leniency for political victims. And so he decides that "since the son of Reuben exemplifies the attributes of his father, it is fitting that he be given priority in kaddish and in prayer over the son of Simeon, who had no desire to repent, as on the day that he died he did not mend his ways, if only before the people in his household. About such a man it was decreed that he not be mourned and not be buried [among Jews], but he will be as refuse on the earth." After all, "even at death's door he did not repent." Nor may he appeal to the ancient tradition that the act of burial itself is an avenue of atonement for the dead. This applies only "if he is buried by Jews in a state of contrition, but to be buried by gentiles and without contrition: no."

The kaddish of Simeon's son, moreover, will not do Simeon any good. Benjamin Zev cites the legend of Rabbi Akiva and the condemned man, and points out that the kaddish brought relief to that poor soul because his wickedness was not the ultimate wickedness. "He did not deny the entirety of the Torah, he was merely taken down by a particular sin; and in any case he died in his Jewishness, and he confessed his sins, and he was buried by our brethren." Benjamin Zev is unforgiving. His notion of Jewish honor is very inflamed. This is not difficult to understand. For a Jew of his time, the duty of children toward apostate parents, toward evil parents, was not only a theological problem, it was also an existential problem. The damage was everywhere.

I slogged my way to shul this morning, through snow and ice, whipped by winds. That is how it should be. And when the prayers were over, and I left the shul, the sun was shining. That, too, is how it should be. It was not the worship that brought out the sun; but this was one of those days when you can pretend that luck has nothing to do with it, one of those lucky days.

Back to Benjamin Zev, whose anger is not easily appeased. He is not finished with the apostate Jew in Apulia, or with his son. It is not enough that such a son may not honor such a father. Such a son must actually dishonor such a father. "He is not to mourn him," Benjamin Zev writes. "Quite the contrary, it is appropriate that he scorn him." We learn this stringency, he says, from the example of Hezekiah. The good king Hezekiah was the son of the evil king Menasseh. The Talmud reports that the good son buried his evil father in an awful manner: "he dragged his father's bones in a bed of ropes." Rashi explains the significance of this filial insult: Hezekiah dragged his father's bones so as to deny his father a proper burial "on a bed of silver and gold," burying him instead "in a humiliating way, because his father was an evil man; and he humiliated him publicly so as to provide others with a cautionary example; and he did not trouble about his own honor; and he did not trouble about [his duty to] honor his parents." The injunction to honor one's father and mother was superseded by the injunction to uphold righteousness.

This is the lesson also of Benjamin Zev's next responsum, which ordains that the sons of apostates not be allowed to use their father's names in the house of worship. "There are some of our brethren who wish to find honor and to hide the disgrace of their evil fathers, who remain in their apostasy in that kingdom and do not seize the opportunity to repent, or who died in their gentileness. The sons of these people wish to be called to the Torah in the house of worship in the manner of all other Jews, as in 'Let Shemaryah the son of

Abraham come forward' or 'Let David the son of Solomon come forward.'" But the sons should not identify themselves by the names of their evil fathers. In the opinion of Benjamin Zev, their genealogy is morally void. "How can a son claim lineage from a father who was a denier of the Torah in its entirety? Go and learn from Hezekiah, the king of Israel, who scorned his father when he died and did not trouble about his own honor. Now, will such an individual be permitted to disguise his father's shame by calling himself by his father's Jewish name when he is not a Jew? For this reason such persons are forbidden to be called to the Torah in the name of their fathers, and they are forbidden to sign their names in the name of their fathers. . . . It is not fitting that such sons shall be known by such fathers."

Here, in the wrath of this rabbi, history is inscribed in the family.

How strange that the rabbis admire Hezekiah for scorning his dead father! Was it not Hezekiah whom they admired for the antithetical reason that, by virtue of, well, his virtue, he saved his dead father from the company of those who have no share in the world to come? It was precisely this filial accomplishment of Hezekiah's that led the rabbis to formulate the principle that "the son acquits the father." So which is it? Did the good son save the evil father or did he scorn him? Or did he save him by scorning him? (I am learning to think rabbinically.) I have located the legend about Hezekiah and the bones of his father in four places in the Talmud, and I spend the morning at the teahouse pondering these texts. In one of these passages Rashi explains that the son dragged his father's bones to a shameful grave not only "to sanctify God's Name by repudiating his wickedness and warning the wicked," but also "as a form of atonement." So he saved him by scorning him! It reflected well on an evil father, I guess, that he produced a son who repudiated him. The father was evil, so his son dragged his bones. But how evil could the father have been, if his son dragged his bones? Oh, the casuistry of love.

At the conclusion of his responsum about kaddish and apostasy, Benjamin Zev delivers a general opinion about the *conversos* of his time. Citing the authority of an unnamed student of Nissim ben Reuben Gerondi, the great scholar and jurist of Barcelona in the fourteenth century, he writes stonily: "It is necessary that we inquire about those who tarry among the authors of our destruction and do not leave their midst to save their souls. It is true that they initially converted under duress, but ever since they threw off the yoke of heaven and the bonds of Torah were broken, they have willingly followed the laws of the gentiles and transgress all the commandments of the Torah. More, they themselves pursue the unfortunate Jews in their midst and inform upon them and entrap them, so that the name of Israel will be forgotten. More, they betray to the state those *anusim* [marranos] whose hearts look to heaven and who attempt to serve God in secret. These people are absolutely evil. They may not give testimony [in a Jewish court]. They are lower than the gentiles, and they are to be brought low and never raised up. Even though they began as the victims of coercion, they have no portion in the God of Israel because they tarry and do not leave; and all the more so if they died in their gentileness and did not repent." This is the judicial equivalent of an epic curse.

Saying kaddish, and thinking about saying kaddish, and thinking about not saying kaddish: today the whole business was heavy.

I do not like Benjamin Zev's ruling. It defies the tendency of the authorities of the sixteenth century (who followed the authorities in the twelfth and thirteenth centuries, in the wake of the forced conversions of the Crusades) to interpret the law compassionately, so that Jews who survived Christian violence by becoming Christians might be welcomed back as Jews. For not all the rabbis met the harshness of history harshly. Quite the contrary. Leniency abounded. The law was also an instrument for mitigating the consequences of desperation, for picking up the pieces. I went looking on my shelves for an alternative to the pitiless Benjamin Zev, and I found it in his contemporary Meir ben Isaac Katzenellenbogen of Padua. His responsa do not discuss the kaddish, but there is this: "An inquiry was made of me and I was properly asked about the case of two brothers, Abraham and Ephraim, from the community of Ofen [Budapest], the sons of a man formerly known among the Jews as Ettel Shneiur. He became an apostate, and from the day of his apostasy his sons were ashamed to be called to the Torah in the house of worship, for their shame would be known every time they were called, since they used to be called by the name of their father, and now things have changed for the worse. I was asked if there is any basis on which they may be permitted to be called by their father's name as before." From this description of the circumstances, it appears that the community of Ofen concurred in the brothers' shame, and did not insist upon the public recognition of their patrimony. But Katzenellenbogen begins his ruling ringingly: "I hereby grant absolute permission." Bravo!

Katzenellenbogen gives four grounds for his decency. First, there is the Talmudic principle of "the honor of God's creatures." The sons of the apostate do not deserve to be dishonored in the community. As the rabbis taught, "it is better that a man throw himself into a fiery furnace than humiliate another man publicly." Second, there is Biblical precedent. Katzenellenbogen cites examples of a wicked son who was called by his wicked father's name (Jeroboam, Ahab) and a righteous son who was called by his wicked father's name (Hezekiah). Third, there is a pragmatic consideration: "the ways of peace." It happened that the renegade Jew was also a distinguished Christian, "a powerful man" and "an official." It would be impolitic to suppress the mention of his name. Katzenellenbogen writes that it is, after all, "the custom in these lands that the cantor, as he holds the Torah scroll, makes a blessing for the king or the minister of the state, for him and for all his officials, and even though the Torah scroll is in [the cantor's] hands we are not reluctant to mention him in the house of worship." Indeed, the Talmud recounts that the same was done for Alexander the Great. "And things greater than this were permitted so as to prevent hostility." Fourth, there is simply the benefit of the doubt.

And yet the facts of the case before Katzenellenbogen were conducive to compassion. For it happened that the renegade Jew, the father of Abraham and Ephraim, the powerful Christian who was once known as Ettel Shneiur, was distinguished not only politically, but also morally. "According to what we hear, the father of these brothers, even though he is mixed among the gentiles, still seeks the betterment of his people, and does good for those near and far, and for those who are worthy, with his person and his possessions." This apostate was not a scourge of the Jewish community. Katzenellenbogen seems satisfied that the man's Jewish heart was still intact. He was loyal, in his disloyal way. Indeed, Katzenellenbogen uses words from the Book of Esther to describe this former Jew who came to the assistance of Jews as a Christian: we have here a Renaissance counterpart of the crypto-Jewish queen of Persia who saved the Jews. Katzenellenbogen continues: "And if all this is so, then his thoughts may be recognized from his deeds, that he is regretful and fears God. This is what I have heard reliable witnesses say about him. And therefore it is right that in the house of worship we draw him closer and not alienate him, for it is clear that he is not an idolator." For all these reasons, then, the sons are not to be denied the name of their father, they are to be known as Abraham ben Ettel Shneiur and Ephraim ben Ettel Shneiur; and I presume that the right to say kaddish for their father after his death was also not denied them. Tolerance was easy in the case of a good apostate, who may even have been a secret Jew. Still, Katzenellenbogen's leniency is based on more than the facts of the case. Generally, he wants mercy for the sons and mercy for the father. He wants them all close.

Yet Katzenellenbogen has a problem. There is a precedent that contradicts his ruling. Israel Isserlein, the great authority in Germany in the fifteenth century, produced a different opinion. But the later authority is not daunted. "The awe of the great sage Rabbi Isserlein, who instructed that the son of an apostate is to be called [not by the name of his father, but] by the name of his father's father, and cited a precedent in *The Book of the Pious,*will not deter me. For in truth he did not really deal with the same situation. And so I will not differ with him, indeed I will concede his opinion in situations resembling the one about which he ruled." That is how this inextinguishable system works: distinctions are multiplied so as to preserve authorities. The acuity of the earlier rabbi is assumed by the later rabbi, who will try to maintain the integrity of both their opinions.

So what was Isserlein's opinion? I have his responsa, and I am struck by their concision. "Question: How is the son of an apostate called to the Torah, when the apostate persists in his wickedness or died in his wickedness? Answer: It seems that he should be called by the name of his father's father, as in 'Abiasaph the son of Yizhar' [Abiasaph was not the son of Yizhar, he was the grandson of Yizhar, but he was the son of Korah, whose name is omitted because he rebelled against Moses]. I later found this written in *The Book of the Pious.* Also, a great rabbi told me that his rabbi, who was one of the great authorities, decided that such a man should be called by his own name only. But this is not acceptable, for summoning him so differently from the others would be experienced by him as a disgrace. Anyway, it is better to say 'Abiasaph ben Yizhar,' since [there is a Scriptural precedent for referring to the grandfather instead of the father, as] it is written, 'Know ye Laban the son of Nahor' and 'And Mephibosheth the son of Saul came down.'" Isserlein concludes his ruling with the standard formulation of false modesty: "I have written what seems correct to my poor mind."

Isserlein takes an unforgiving view of the father, and wishes to make the son known by his grandfather. He would erase a generation so as to spare a man shame. And Katzenellenbogen does not take issue with Isserlein's reasoning. Indeed, he cites Talmudic passages about the lengths to which one must go to spare a man shame. But he also notes that there are Scriptural examples to support both opinions, including cases in which righteous sons are named with their wicked fathers "as a general designation." He suggests that Isserlein's severity is not wrong, it is merely "a late custom and an expression of a greater measure of piety." And finally he splits the hair: his predecessor, he writes, "was referring to the son of an apostate who was a child and a boy when his father abandoned the God of his fathers. Since he had never been called by his father's name and his full name was not known in public, [it would cause him no shame if he were] to be called by his grandfather's name. In the case of a grown man, however, who is accustomed to being called the son of his father—if his name were to be changed, the words would humiliate him, and this would be [as the Talmud says] like spilling the blood of an innocent man." And so the truth of his lineage must be acknowledged. In other words, the views of Isserlein and Katzenellenbogen are both right. The one applies to a boy, the other applies to a man.

"A great rabbi told me that his rabbi, who was one of the great authorities, responded that such a man should be called by his own name only. But this is not acceptable." Of course it is not acceptable, and not only for the reason that Isserlein gives. No man comes from nowhere. No man begins with himself. No one is first and no one is last. There is something more objectionable than a compromising lineage, and it is the illusion of no lineage at all.

People who think that they have created themselves are dangerous people, because they have an exaggerated sense of the malleability of things. They think that the world can begin again. (Of course, it must first be ended. . . .)

A revolutionary is a man who cannot bear to be a son. He wishes to travel "by his own name only."

But do not flatter the fathers. They cannot relieve you of yourself. All the origins in the world will not secure you against the reality of your individuation.

From one's descent, one's ascent.

It is pointless to oppose the world, and it is pointless to side with it.

You do not come from nothing, you go to nothing. And you can get there before you die.

Meir Katzenellenbogen's ruling was codified into law by his younger and more illustrious contemporary Moses Isserles: "A man whose father was an apostate is called to the Torah by the name of his father's father. He is not to be called by his own name only, so as not to humiliate him. This is the case only if he has never in his life been called to the Torah by his father's name [that is, if he is a boy thirteen years or older, who has just begun to be called to the Torah]; but if he is a grown man, and he is accustomed in that town to be called by his father's name, and then his father betrayed his religion, he may be called up by his father's name, so as not to humiliate him. And also so as not to enrage the apostate." The dignity of the Jewish individual and the security of the Jewish community: those are the grounds of Isserles' statute.

My sister had a dream. Our father was standing in her dining room. He was wearing a blue shirt and brown trousers, and he was criticizing me fiercely. She pointed her finger angrily at him and said: "Don't you dare attack my brother. You have no idea of what he's doing for you."

I was reading the Bible in shul this morning when somebody in the gallery opened a window. Instantly a beam of light sped toward my book and fell upon it. Dust danced in the beam, motes of matter without desire or direction; movement without will. The entropy looked beautiful above my book. It defied the teleology on my lap. For a few moments, the Bible was too bright to be read. All I could see was whiteness, and the unhallowed motion within it.

When they asked me to lead the prayers this morning, I did. When they asked me to lead the prayers this afternoon, I did. When they asked me to lead the prayers this evening, I didn't. I declined. It's too much. Too much for me, and too much for them. I shouldn't be their emissary, really I shouldn't. I want this to be over. I want this to be over. Is this a sign of solace? There were months when I wanted it never to end.

This evening again I couldn't bear the prospect of leading the prayers. Instead of racing from the office to the shul, I sat at a bar and drank a glass of wine. I didn't enjoy it almost at all, and I resented that, too.

The excruciations of the survivors of Spain and Portugal in the early decades of the sixteenth century were fiercely expressed in the sermons of the preacher Joseph Garçon, who suffered forced conversion and expulsion, and wandered in the Ottoman Empire before settling in Damascus, where he died in 1523. Garçon's homiletical vehemence is extraordinary. In Salonika in 1500, in a discussion of the sacrifice of Noah in the aftermath of the flood, the refugee rabbi preached: "Noah brought burnt offerings, it seems to me, because the burnt offering atones for a wayward thought. For it is well known that in the time of catastrophe everybody, even those who seem to the whole world like the most righteous people, rebels against God in their thoughts. How could He have produced this evil persecution? Since Noah witnessed the great catastrophe, then, he may have had a thought against God. It was to correct this, and to make his soul whole again, that he brought his sacrifice." In Damascus in 1507, the preacher told the congregation that "the ordinary people lack the stature to speak against God. They do not inveigh harshly against heaven, they fulminate more gently. . . . But the notables of the community speak against God with harsh words. . . . They fulminate against the Deity more furiously and say: We see that God is not just, for he is not avenging us upon the nations." Garçon was especially angry about the shattering of families by the conversions and the expulsions. In a sermon in Damascus in 1514, in the aftermath of a plague that ravaged an already ravaged community, he thundered: "Who is there, in this kingdom, who has a son who has survived? And if there is somebody whose son still lives, it is an even greater astonishment if he grows up to be righteous and learned, so that the son may acquit the father. . . ." Many Jews were dying without the hope of a kaddish. The panic of the parents: another mark of the people's wretchedness.

"I don't know about you guys," a fellow said good-humoredly in shul, "but my prayers get answered. If you're nice to me, I'll arrange for the assistance of a just God." We chuckled. And someone retorted: "So then everything that happens is your fault!" We chuckled again. A high level of banter, this morning. This guy jokes about the power of prayer, but his joke is exactly how the world is supposed to work, according to the tradition. The system makes no sense unless prayer is powerful, unless an intervention is possible. But it occurs to me that there is something more troubling than the inefficacy of prayer, and it is the efficacy of prayer. Who, really, would want the responsibility? What should be regretted is not our lack of cosmic influence. What should be regretted is our interest in cosmic influence.

In a new biography of Houdini I read that every year on the anniversary of his father's death he would seek out a house of worship and say kaddish. His diary is full of annual entries such as this one: "I went to Manchester to a temple early at

6 o'clock and said Kaddish. One man gave me a tallis and placed it on my shoulder." Some escape artist!

"I will begin the laws of the kaddish of mourners with the aid of the Father of Mourners." Thus does Benjamin Zev introduce his rulings on the subject. This is the first question that he addresses: "I have been asked by a friend, in the matter of the kaddish that was established, on the basis of that tale about Rabbi Akiva, to be said by those who mourn for their father and their mother, [what should be done] if there are other mourners in the house of worship, mourning for their brothers and sisters and sons and daughters, and they are claiming that they, too, should have a part, while the others, the mourners for their fathers and mothers, are disputing them, claiming that if they are given a part in the kaddish, then they will rob them of their part. My friend asked whether they should be given a part, so that one day these mourners recite it and the next day the others recite it, or not."

Those were the old days. All the mourners in the house of worship did not recite the kaddish together, as they do now. Instead a mourner was designated to lead the service and to say the kaddish, as sorrow's representative. Benjamin Zev was asked to adjudicate the claims of mourners who were vying for the appointment, for the opportunity to vindicate their dead. He rules for the orphans against the other mourners. The orphans have priority. He gives a number of proofs. The first is the founding legend itself: "From the legend about Rabbi Akiva, it would appear that the other mourners have no part in kaddish, only those mourning their parents. . . . [If it were otherwise], why didn't Rabbi Akiva arrange for the relatives of that man to say kaddish for him while his son was studying [and preparing himself to say kaddish], so that it would profit him? We must conclude from the fact that

Rabbi Akiva did not make such an arrangement that it would not have profited him [the dead man].” And, more ringingly: “The basis of this kaddish that was established was in the mourning for parents and not in other kinds of mourning, for this kaddish is warranted by no other relation than the relation of a son with a father and a mother.”

It is unwise, perhaps, to secure a law with a legend. The story of Akiva and the condemned man appears often in the legal opinions about the mourner’s kaddish. I wonder whether these medieval and early modern authors knew that this bit of folklore was not ancient. Would the history of the tale have lessened its authority in their eyes?

“This kaddish is not based on kinship,” Benjamin Zev continues. “It is based on the son’s righteousness, which is so great that the Name of Heaven may be sanctified by him, and in this manner the son acquits the father by demonstrating the merit of him who begat someone who sanctifies the Name of Heaven.” When the mourner appeals for God’s mercy for the deceased’s soul, this appeal is not made in the name of blood, it is made in the name of character. The mourner does not say: have pity on the soul of my father because he was my father. The mourner says: have pity on the soul of this man because he raised a man who stands before you and submits to your authority. There is nothing sentimental about the kaddish. (This will come as news to many Jews, for whom the sentimentality of the kaddish is almost the foundation of their faith.)

The kaddish is not a special pleading. It is a pleading according to the rules. The judge is not moved by the fact that the defendant was your father. What does blood have to do with character? No, the judge needs to know more. What kind of father was your father? In rising to say the kaddish, you have given an answer: he was the kind of father who taught his son to do *this.* And a man who directs his son toward truth deserves mercy. —I'm late to work. I won't be any good at work today. My mind belongs to the rabbis.

A man who directs his son toward truth deserves mercy. But the theology and the cosmology and the eschatology that are implied by the kaddish: is all this truth? I do not believe that it is. Still, I have no patience with people who treat it as nonsense. And I do not regret for a moment that I was taught to believe it. When they taught me what they believed to be the truth, they taught me to believe that there is truth. They spared me the dizziness of my contemporaries.

A wise old liberal once said to me, as he was drinking heavily, that the only people who have freedom of choice in matters of religion are people who were indoctrinated in a religion as children.

This morning, a strange development: when I rose to say the kaddish, I was seized by the fear that I had forgotten it.

Benjamin Zev pursues his point that kaddish is not essentially about kinship. "There is no kinship closer than that of a father for a son, and the concern of a father for a son is greater than the concern of a son for a father"—and yet the father is not required to say kaddish for the son. For "the father cannot acquit the son to the extent that the son can acquit the father. . . . We have never heard of a father reciting kaddish for his son in the house of worship when there are mourners for their parents present. If a father wishes to recite the kaddish for his son owing to his distress, this may be done only if there are no mourners for their parents present." The father may pray for his son, of course, as David prayed for Absalom, and in this manner he may "acquit him slightly," but the father's prayer for the son does not have the force of the son's prayer for the father. For the child is not responsible for the parent as the parent is responsible for the child. A father saying kaddish is showing what he feels. A son saying kaddish is showing what he was taught. The former is exemplifying love. The latter is exemplifying merit.

By way of showing that the kaddish is the inalienable duty of the son, Benjamin Zev considers also the case of "a community in which there was the custom of hiring the precentor or somebody else to say the kaddish in place of the son." Here is early evidence of this tasteless practice. Benjamin Zev is unequivocal about it: "I do not approve of this at all, except when the deceased has no son or when the deceased has a son who does not reside in the community permanently, since we are dispersed in this world for the sake of our livelihood." Again he gives the legend of Akiva as the grounds for his rejection of this custom: "Why didn't Rabbi Akiva hire somebody to say kaddish for that man and thereby release him from his suffering? Indeed, Rabbi Akiva preferred to leave him in his suffering until his young son grew up."

I came back from shul this morning and promptly fell asleep. But my slumber was troubled. I woke, or rather I rescued myself, from a grotesque dream. It was a dream in which I was tortured for the wasting of time. I don't remember feeling guilty about time before.

Sleep is the enemy. Look at the dead.

This morning I burned a small brick of incense on the old wooden table, and for a few hours the scent of juniper was in the air. Later I noticed the brick standing where I had burned it, except that it was ash. It had retained its form, but not its fragrance. It was upright, but ash.

It appears, from Benjamin Zev's responsum, that the competition among mourners for the recitation of the kaddish was fierce. And it appears that there were communities in which the hierarchy of grief was not honored. "If there is a community in which the mourners for other relatives are taking part even when mourners for a father or a mother are present, you might say [as the rabbis in the Talmud say in defense of local customs, that] every river runs its course, [and so justify this practice as the particular custom of this community]. Now, a custom supersedes a law if it is an ancient custom, but if it is not an ancient custom, it is a bad custom, and if such a custom is not a law it is not proper to follow it. . . . How, on the basis of a shaky custom, may the mourners for other relatives rob the mourners for their parents [of their recitation of the kaddish], when the prayer of the latter profits their dead and the prayer of the former does not profit them?"

The old way of reciting the kaddish, in which a designated mourner spoke for all the mourners, seems more orderly than the new way, in which all the mourners rise and fulfill their duty loudly and softly, swiftly and slowly, in all the corners of the room, their voices straying from one another in a cacophony of emotions and educations. The old way seems more orderly—and less true. Who wants a proxy for his or her grief? Let every sadness speak!

Benjamin Zev concludes his responsum with a report: "And I, Benjamin, am writing among the Ashkenazim in the holy community of Venice, where I have witnessed a worthy and lovely custom. When mourners for their parents are in the house of worship, they lead the worship . . . , or at the very least the precentor, when he nears the end of the worship . . . sits down, and the mourner completes the service. On the days when such mourners are not present, the precentor recites the kaddish differently and in a slight whisper for all the dead of Israel. And if the other mourners [the ones not mourning for their parents] had a right to the kaddish, why would they not have recited it in place of the precentor? But they don't here, and so they don't there [in the case before Benjamin Zev]. The conclusion, which is painfully obvious, is that orphans precede other mourners."

A cousin just back from Europe tells me that the old custom is still the custom in some places. He expected all the mourners to rise together and recite the kaddish, but when he opened his mouth in the back of the shul he was hushed. A designated mourner spoke the kaddish, and the other mourners followed along. I wonder when the system of the designated mourner broke down.

After dinner, I spend an hour with my books in search of clues. I don't come away empty-handed. For a start, I find a clear exposition of the old system in its details. It turns out to have been quite byzantine. In the responsa of Moses Mintz, a German Talmudist of the fifteenth century, there is an epistle on the mourner's kaddish. "I have observed," Mintz begins, "that in certain places residents and visitors are treated differently when it comes to reciting the mourner's kaddish and leading the prayers in the twelve months after the death of a parent. In some places, it is the custom that the resident has priority over the visitor in the saying of kaddish and the prayers, except for the first kaddish; and in other places it is the custom that there is one law for you and the stranger that sojourneth with you. And there are also other distinctions that are made, between the mourner in the seven days and the mourner in the thirty days and the mourner in the twelve months, and also the mourner on the anniversary of his parent's death. There are differences of opinion as to which of these comes first, and who precedes whom. For this reason I have been asked, by the congregation here in Bamberg, to put the matter in some order, so that there will be no quarrels. It is fitting and right that I should do so, because these divisions are always coming to the fore: this one says one thing and that one says another thing, and the view of one is not like the view of the other, one man claims that the custom is this and another man claims that the custom is that, and sometimes this makes the whole offering null and void." Mintz was the rabbi of Bamberg, in Bavaria, from 1469 to 1473. He proceeds to an extensive discussion of all the combinations of mourners and all their conflicting claims on the kaddish.

About the clash of the residents and the visitors, Mintz concludes that "it all depends on local custom," and he gives the reasons and the sources of both customs, citing his great predecessor Jacob Moellin, one of the early codifiers of modern Ashkenazic rites and rituals, who flourished in Germany in the late fourteenth and early fifteenth centuries. But Moellin "wrote at great length," Mintz remarks, "and the time has come to make it brief," to be practical. He notes that "it is well known that the custom here, in the holy congregation of Bamberg, and in the other congregations in these states, is that the native takes precedence over the stranger, though the stranger has the right to lead the prayers and to recite the mourner's kaddish once," but he does not suggest that the custom of Bamberg must be the universal custom. Yet this is hardly all that needs to be said. What if there are many kinds of mourners in shul, each demanding the privilege? Mintz states a general rule: "I do not believe that we should act on the principle that the strongest one wins, or that the first one wins, because this will lead to quarrels, and there will be conflict, and everything will be spoiled, God forbid. Our rabbis were very apprehensive about this, because they wanted social peace."

The rabbis concluded, in a Talmudic discussion of a similar competition about the presentation of sacrifices in the Temple, that the solution is a lottery. And so, "to establish order so that there will be peace in our palace, our holy sanctuary of worship, so that the obligation may be fulfilled properly, for the sake of heaven, without quarrels and altercations," Mintz launches into a comprehensive review of all the possible circumstances and outcomes of the kaddish lottery. The details are maddening. The machine is made of many parts. There are the different times of the day when kaddish is said; and there are natives and strangers; and there are various numbers of natives and strangers; and there are natives during the seven days, or the thirty days, or the twelve months, of their mourning, and there are strangers in the seven days, or the thirty days, or the twelve months of their mourning; and there is the individual who is commemorating the anniversary of a parent's death (he wins, since he has only one day on which to acquit himself of his obligation); and there are sometimes three or four or five individuals who are commemorating the anniversary of a parent's death; and there are the individuals who are commemorating the anniversary of a parent's death but fail to get to the house of worship on time; and there are siblings who are mourning for a parent, and only children who are mourning for a parent; and there are minors; and there are mourners who are competent to lead the service and to recite the kaddish, and mourners who are not competent to lead the prayers and to recite the kaddish (the kaddish is reserved for the incompetent and the young, because those who lead the prayers anyway have fulfilled their duty more brilliantly, since "prayer is commensurate with kaddish and is more praiseworthy," whereas "when it comes to the mourner's kaddish, all are equal," it is the lowest common denominator of sorrow in shul); and so on. In such a system, it seems, no mourner had the privilege of reciting more than a single kaddish a day. This is organized religion at its most organized. It is enough to make you forget why you came to shul.

The tortuous system that Mintz describes is premised, again, on the undemocratic practice of the designated mourner; and it is no wonder that this contraption eventually collapsed. But when did it collapse? Not for a long time. A hundred years later, Mordecai ben Abraham Jaffe, the maverick codifier from Prague who, after the expulsion of the Jews from Bohemia in 1561, eventually settled in Poland, admiringly reproduced Mintz's guide to the contingencies of the kaddish. Jaffe composed his code of Jewish law because he was frustrated by the elliptical character of the contemporary codes by Joseph Karo and Moses Isserles. "They present everything without any reasons, as if it had all been given to Moses at Sinai." Jaffe—who included treatises on astronomy, philosophy, and mysticism in his great work—felt a responsibility toward the reasons. About the *Shulḥan Arukh,* or the *Set Table,* of Karo and Isserles, he wrote: "They have set their table with sweets and with delicacies, with blossoms and with herbs, but the food is tasteless, because there is no salt. Scholars who eat this food will taste the flavor that is familiar to them. But how will needy people like ourselves find flavor in this tasteless, unsalted stuff? For a law cannot be considered without a reason, just as a dish cannot be eaten without salt." Jaffe prefers an unblind obedience. And his consideration of the mourner's kaddish is indeed a little salty. Writing of the Alenu prayer at the conclusion of the service, he instructs that "after this prayer the mourner's kaddish is recited, and even if a mourner in the year of his mourning is not present in the house of worship, it should be recited by another individual whose mother or father is dead. The reason is this: a kaddish must always be said after Scriptural verses have been heard, and there are also verses from Scripture in the Alenu prayer, and so it is required that a kaddish follow it. But there developed the custom of leaving this particular kaddish to a mourner whose father or mother died during the year, since there are young orphans—and even adult ones—who are incapable of being the emissary of the congregation and leading the service and the kaddish for the sake of their dead parents. From the story of Rabbi Akiva, after all, we know what a great benefit accrues to the dead if he has a son saying kaddish, especially in the first year after his death. And so it was instituted that this kaddish [at the conclusion of the service] will be put aside for mourners." And then Jaffe curtly adds: "For this is all that the mourners need, young or old." In the house of worship, mourning is not the main event. A few pages later, after he has cited Moses Mintz's responsa, Jaffe reports with irritation "a new custom that has become popular in these lands in my lifetime," according to which a medieval doxological poem that is recited at the end of the service on the Sabbath is divided into seven sections, and one section is said each weekday after the mourner's kaddish at the end of the service. Why this extension of the daily worship? "When I was young," Jaffe writes, "I heard that this was a custom without a reason, except that it had been established because sometimes there are many mourners, and in this way it would be possible for all of them to receive a kaddish." Jaffe does not approve of this multiplication of the mourner's kaddish. But he will not dare to annul a custom. "Now that it exists, let it be."

In Poland a hundred years later the traditional system of preferments still thrives, to judge by the influential legal commentary of Abraham Gombiner. Criticizing a lottery that was held to select someone to recite the kaddish, this seventeenth-century scholar writes that "this custom became widespread because they had not seen the responsum of Rabbi Moses Mintz, for it was not yet printed in those days. It was he, after all, who properly established the practices of kaddish"—though Gombiner then adds that, Mintz or no Mintz, "it is all according to custom." Gombiner proceeds to offer his own complications. What happens when a lottery of four or five mourners is cast, and two of them come out with the same high number? (Another lottery is cast by the two winners.) What happens when two or three mourners cast a lottery for that day's kaddish, and in the morning a third mourner appears? (A new lottery must be cast.) And so on. All this gambling on all this grief. It is mildly ridiculous. Hasn't a mourner had enough of luck for a while?

In Germany in the seventeenth century, I detect the beginning of change. In Joseph Schammes's compilation of the customs of Worms, things seem to be evolving in the direction of equality and simplicity. A system of rotation appears to have been introduced: "The mourners for their fathers or their mothers recite the mourner's kaddish in shul, one mourner after another mourner, in alternation. But a mourner at the conclusion of his first seven days of mourning has priority, and in his first appearance in shul he recites all the kaddishes [in the service]. And similarly, at the end of eleven months of mourning, when he stops saying the mourner's kaddish, he recites all the kaddishes." In the scheme described by Schammes, an order of recitation is arranged among the mourners, so that as many mourners as possible have the privilege of saying a kaddish publicly. Why not contrive, then, to add more recitations of kaddish to the service, and thus increase the mourners' chances, so that all may acquit themselves and their parents publicly? Interestingly, Schammes warns twice against the proliferation of the prayer. He even proposes to abolish an occasion for the mourner's kaddish near the end of the worship, arguing that a Biblical verse was appended to the ancient Alenu prayer in the years after its composition as a pretext for another mourner to say another kaddish. "It is best not to multiply the kaddishes," Schammes states.

A century later, rotation seems to have given way to participation, and the mourner's kaddish seems to have been democratized. And the democratizers came from outside the Ashkenazic world. In the annotated prayerbook that the stormy scholar Jacob Emden published in Altona in 1745, I find this comment on the mourner's kaddish: "About the different regulations of the Ashkenazim, in the matter of who takes precedence over whom in the saying of the kaddish and who defers to whom, I will not treat here, since this is entirely a matter of custom. (And how fine and fitting is the custom of the Sephardim, that when there are many mourners, they all have the privilege and say it all together. In a matter that is not essential or of primary importance, dissension and the toil of extracting the finer points of law are futile.)" In 1831, in a responsum written in Pressburg, or Bratislava, by Moses Sofer, the brilliant warrior against modernity, Emden's opinion is endorsed. Sofer remarks that "the Sephardim have a custom that all the mourners say the kaddish at all times together, and to all of them the congregation responds; and the sage Rabbi Jacob ben Zevi [Emden] wrote in his prayerbook that he would not treat of the laws of kaddish, since the custom of the Sephardim, that everyone says it together, was correct. Similarly, here in our hall of study, the young men who are in mourning say the kaddish that is said after study together, and in the house of worship, when there is an argument between two mourners, both of them say it. And what is wrong with that?" As for the problem of leading the prayers, which obviously cannot be led by all the mourners, Sofer writes that "I don't know how to arrive at a solution to the problem," except that the rabbi can establish another quorum for the afternoon and evening prayers. So the democratization of the kaddish appears to have been the work of the Sephardic communities, sometime between the sixteenth century, when Benjamin Zev was still coping with the problem, and the eighteenth century, when Emden was praising what was already an established solution to the problem. In the Ashkenazic world, however, the problem persisted into the nineteenth century, when Sofer had to find a way to satisfy the obstreperous mourners in his midst.

But democracy makes its own demands. There is the right to speak for oneself and there is the ability to speak for oneself. It turned out that there were mourners who wanted to recite the kaddish but did not know how to recite it; and they were glad to be reminded of the blandishments of representation. In 1849, in a polemic written in angry response to a conference of Reform rabbis four years earlier, the Galician rabbi Zvi Hirsch Chajes noted that "I have been told that in some places the practice has been instituted that the mourners do not recite the kaddish each on his own, but the leader of the prayers stands on the platform and recites the mourner's kaddish, and the mourners stand around him and repeat after him, word by word, whether they know the words or not. In my opinion this is a good reform, since it saves those who do not know the words from embarrassment."

Democracy comes with its own form of oppression. Its form of oppression is embarrassment.

Hold on. I am browsing through Sofer's decisions at the teahouse, and I find an opinion written in 1800 in which Sofer seems to think the opposite of what he thought three decades later! In 1831, he defended the group kaddish, citing Emden's precedent. In 1800, he reports Emden's comment that "the Sephardic custom, in which all the mourners say the kaddish together at the same time, is more comfortable and fitting," but in this earlier text he is skeptical. "It would seem that this is a legitimate custom; and the more people fulfilling an obligation, the better"—but if this is the best way to arrange matters, why didn't the masters of Ashkenaz arrange them this way? "We must wonder about our forefathers, who were in possession of the Torah as an ancient inheritance. . . . But how can we suspect them of spoiling and distorting the proper way?" Not that the merits of the Ashkenazic custom are entirely obvious. No, Sofer says, the tradition of the designated mourner, whereby the most wounded mourners have pride of place over the least wounded mourners, likewise "seems to require close analysis. . . . Imagine a business whose partners received a quantity of merchandise, and one of the partners said: 'I need the merchandise most, so give it only to me, and the rest of you have no share of it!' Surely the others would reply: 'What is it to us that you need the merchandise most? It belongs to us all and should be evenly shared!' Similarly, in this instance, the man in the first week of his mourning needs the kaddish more than the others, yet they are all partners. Why would the others renounce their share?" This would seem to clinch the case for the Sephardic custom, the group kaddish. But Sofer has a retort, based on a Talmudic source. Why would a man in the first month of mourning surrender his privilege to a mourner in the first week of mourning? Because it is in his interest to do so. The day will come when it is his own soul that is at stake, when the mourner in the first week of mourning will be his own son; and he will want his son to be given priority. The group kaddish may be in the interest of the mourners, but it may not be in the interest of the dead. And so Sofer concludes that the Ashkenazic tradition, the tradition of the designated mourner, should stand.

And it should stand for another reason, too. In this early text, Sofer offers an entirely different explanation for the efficacy of the mourner's kaddish. "The essence of the acquittal that the son secures for the father," he writes, "is to be found not in the son's recitation of the kaddish itself, but in the privilege that he provides the congregation for responding forcefully with their amens, and with their blessing of the Name of the Lord. It is by transforming himself into a go-between for the congregation that he acquits his father. In this light, the greater power of our own custom is clear. For, even if all the mourners recite the kaddish together, the decisive voice belongs to the one whose kaddish enables the congregation to respond; but then each of the mourners will try to grab the spotlight, so that he will be heard first and the congregation will respond to his words and not to the words of his fellow mourner." The mourner is a middleman between the congregation and their God, and his success in provoking the congregation to acclaim their God is the glory in which the soul of his father may bask. Only an individual mourner may play such a role. The mourners together, as in the Sephardic custom, will produce a din that defeats the kaddish. Sofer is proposing a kind of communitarian theory of the kaddish, in which the vindication of the dead is accomplished by the words of the congregation. And since the congregation is responsible, the congregation is rewarded. "The more the dead is in need of the congregation's response—to the mourner in the week after his death, and then the mourner in the month after his death, and then the mourner on the anniversary of his death—the greater is the reward for the congregation for its help to the dead."

How to explain the contradiction between Sofer in 1800 and Sofer in 1831? I don't know. Maybe the answer is that it is all a question of custom. Maybe I am looking for theories where there are no theories. Remember Emden's calming words: "In a matter that is not essential or of primary importance, dissension and the toil of extracting the finer points of law are futile."

This morning, when I led the congregation in the kaddish, it responded with vigor. I was a little startled. Are they reading Sofer over my shoulder? No, I know what happened. They are believers, and I said the right thing.

In 1831, when Moses Sofer was permitting the group kaddish in Pressburg, Akiva Eger was permitting the group kaddish in Posen. Akiva Eger was Moses Sofer's father-in-law, and an unflagging enemy of enlightenment and reform, and a rabbi of terrifying erudition. (Well, he has always terrified me.) Under the pressure of circumstance, Eger changed a custom: "In the month of Av in the year 5591, a plague of cholera began here, and there were many mourners who came to say the kaddish. I instituted the practice that the mourners should say the kaddish together, and thus it was done for a whole year. After almost a year had passed, on the first day of the month of Av in the year 5592, the plague abated, and I instructed that the kaddish should no longer be said in unison—except once a day, at the end of the morning service, when the kaddish would be recited by all the mourners together, but at no other time. In this way, at least, no mourner would be prevented from saying kaddish once a day. And so it shall be, and so it shall stand forever with the help of God." This is a fine example of the evolution of ritual. Jewish practice is compassionate, but it is not opportunistic. It adapts to the world, but it does not surrender to the world. A practice must justify itself not only before its circumstances, but also before its principles. Thus the modification of the mourner's kaddish ended when the plague ended, because the contingencies of history cannot furnish the legitimacies of law. The mourners of Posen reverted to the old system of delegating the kaddish, because history is not all that Jews need to know. But there was more to the story. They reverted incompletely. The group kaddish in Posen was only temporary, only an expedient; but the rabbi discovered in the temporary and the expedient an innovation that would be useful to his community also in plagueless days. And so a trace of the new custom was attached to the old custom. In this way the rabbi met the demands of the mourners and the demands of the principles, the needs of usual times and the needs of unusual times.

I looked up from my book, and through the window I saw some workmen laying a long cable in the street. They, too, were hard at work on the transmission of energy. —A cable running through time, not space.

In a remarkable exchange between two rabbis of the nineteenth century, a disagreement about the mechanics of the mourner's kaddish reaches to the very foundations of the custom. In 1854, Beer Oppenheim, the rabbi of Eibenschitz, or Ivancice, in Moravia, dispatched an opinion to Jacob Ettlinger, the rabbi of Altona, who published Oppenheim's opinion, and his opinion of Oppenheim's opinion, in a volume of his responsa. Oppenheim wanted Ettlinger's ruling on a reform that he had proposed. "This is what I was asked: A certain community used to have a large house of prayer and a small house of prayer, as well as other prayer quorums. When the large house of prayer became shaky and threatened to collapse, they razed it and built a grand and beautiful house of prayer that was big enough to house all the members of the community. They made an agreement that nobody would pray anywhere except in this house of prayer; and they also agreed that all the mourners, even those in the thirty days of their mourning and those who were commemorating a yahrzeit [the anniversary of a parent's death], would say the mourner's kaddish all together, at the same time. There were some who became alarmed by this, however, and who armed themselves with what Moses Isserles and Abraham Gombiner wrote in the code of law [that the mourner's kaddish must be recited by a designated mourner according to the old system of preferments]. But the community refused to institute the old system, responding that it would result in quarrels and altercations every day, since there is only one house of prayer. And they asked me whether they had done the right thing."

Oppenheim told them that they had done the right thing. The rabbi endorsed the change. "I responded to them that I saw a great and right reform in what they had done." He gives the reasons for his endorsement. One of them is a fine example of the time-honored technique of demonstrating a distinction between the cases so as to preserve the customs: "It is true that Moses Isserles wrote generally, and Abraham Gombiner after him wrote in detail, that some mourners have precedence in the kaddish; but they intended what they said to apply only to a town in which there were many houses of worship and houses of study, where it would be possible to fulfill all their stipulations about the priorities among the mourners, including the ones in their thirty days and the ones in their yahrzeits. In a town in which there is only one house of worship, however, many mourners in their thirty days and in their yahrzeits will be present every day, and so it is good that all of them say the kaddish together, at the same time, to lessen the likelihood of disputes. In this way, peace will be maintained." Peace, and all the authorities.

Oppenheim notes that some opposed this reform of the kaddish on general grounds: "There are those who sound the alarm and warn that it is forbidden to nullify a custom, because every custom has its gate in heaven and has its foundation in the sacred peaks [the ancient scholars]." Conservatism about custom, after all, was one of Judaism's strategems for survival. But Oppenheim has a short and noble retort: "I say that it is permitted to nullify a custom in order to put an end to conflict." Peace is a greater priority than authenticity. He cites a precedent in a responsum of David ben Zimra, the master of law and kabbalah in sixteenth-century Egypt, who cites an earlier authority that "we are not anxious about a custom that lightens the burden on the community"; and also that piety toward the past has its limits, since "we have only the judges who live in our own time." Oppenheim wants it known, moreover, that he is not exaggerating the danger of strife in the congregation in his own day: "There are often differing voices that give rise to conflict in the sanctuary. I know this with certainty, for I have myself seen that, as a consequence of the dispute about the kaddish, one man punched another man in the face."

Fisticuffs! So that is why we rise together in shul, all the broken-hearted men, and mourn our dead together. Otherwise somebody might get hurt.

This evening my prayers didn't amount to much. I couldn't get the mourners' brawl out of my mind. I'm sure that Oppenheim regarded the outbreak of violence in the house of worship as a tragedy. But the incident makes me smile. The comedy of profanity.

Oppenheim offers other grounds for his reform, and they are rather surprising. Indeed, they seem to strike at the heart of the mourner's kaddish. The reason that the kaddish may be organized in a variety of ways, Oppenheim asserts, is that the stakes are relatively low. The kaddish is not really that important. "For a start, we do not find the institution of the kaddish in either of the two Talmuds, or in Maimonides' code of law, or in Jacob ben Asher's code of law. All that we find is that Joseph Karo, in his commentary on Jacob ben Asher's code, reports that the *Kol Bo* copied the story of Akiva's encounter with the woodcutter from the holy *Zohar*; but in his own code of law Karo does not mention this practice at all, and it is mentioned only by Moses Isserles [in his supplement to Karo's code], who emphasized and secured it. . . . [If the kaddish is not found in ancient rabbinical law,] perhaps it is found in the midrash [ancient rabbinical legend]? But a recent book that is a collection of responsa and later rabbinical writings has concluded that the kaddish is not found anywhere in the midrash." Oppenheim also cites the late-fourteenth-century or early-fifteenth-century responsum by Isaac ben Sheshet Perfet, the one that helped me many months ago to track the history of the mourner's kaddish among the Sephardim, in which Perfet remarked that "this story [of Rabbi Akiva] is not found in the Talmud." This bibliographical survey is designed to demonstrate that the mourner's kaddish is not deeply rooted in the tradition. Worse, its basis in philosophy is as thin as its basis in history. Oppenheim makes a devastating comment on the legend of Akiva and the condemned man: "In truth, the actual story that appears in the holy *Zohar* has no explanation. Perhaps it came to somebody in a dream." The Moravian rabbi appears to have been a rational man.

And the Moravian rabbi continues his exercise in the demystification of the kaddish: "Moreover, if you consider the substance of the matter, then there is no reason that it should make a difference whether one mourner recites the kaddish or many mourners recite the kaddish. Indeed, the essence of the kaddish has been explained in *The Bequest* [by Abraham Horowitz], where it is written that 'the kaddish is not a prayer that the son prays for the father before God, that He raise him from the lower depths. It is, instead, a privilege and a good deed that accrues to the dead when his son publicly sanctifies the Name of God and the congregation responds . . .' If this is the case, then it is obvious that the more people who recite the kaddish, the more sanctified will be His Name." And so the old system may be abolished. Still, Oppenheim does not wish to replace an old consonance with a new dissonance. This is his recommendation: "The precentor should recite the kaddish, and the mourners should say it softly along with him, word by word. This is preferable to all of them saying it loudly at the same time, because the congregation would not be able to make out what they are saying and so it would not be able to respond." In fact, Oppenheim is not proposing a very radical change. It looks to me like a compromise. It eliminates only the undemocratic aspects of decorum.

Praying this morning was not like praying last night. This morning I was alive to every word. When I left the shul, I felt like a lit match.

Oppenheim knew that the abrogation of custom was a serious matter, and he attempted to defend his innovation by conferring the authority of Moses Sofer upon it. At the end of his ruling, he quotes Sofer's ruling of 1831 that, as Jacob Emden had observed approvingly, "the Sephardim have a custom that all the mourners say the kaddish at all times together, and to all of them the congregation responds . . . and similarly, here in our hall of study, the young men who are in mourning say the kaddish that is said after study together, and in the house of worship, when there is an argument between two mourners, both of them say it. And what is wrong with that?" But Oppenheim was not appealing only to Sofer's authority as a jurist. He was also appealing to Sofer's authority as a reactionary. It was Sofer, after all, who notoriously proclaimed that "the new is forbidden by the Torah"—who provocatively interpreted a Talmudic maxim about the impermissibility of using a harvest of grain until its first fruits had been presented at the Temple to derive "the principle that the new is forbidden by the Torah everywhere, and the old and very old is always more admirable." Thus Oppenheim concludes: "If the sage Rabbi Moses Sofer, who used to say that the new is forbidden by the Torah everywhere, and who hated innovations, said nonetheless that it is right that all the mourners should say the kaddish together, then it is surely right in this town, where there is only a single house of worship, that the custom of the Sephardim should be established, and anyway in a new house of worship new customs may be established."

Why the defensiveness about change? Because this rabbi was writing in a golden age of defensiveness about change. And the rabbi to whom he was writing owes his place in Jewish history to his resistance to change. The correspondence between Beer Oppenheim and Jacob Ettlinger took place a decade after the momentous conference of Reform rabbis in Brunswick in 1844, a synod of modernizing, even revolutionary, rabbis that horrified the traditionalists. Jacob Ettlinger was not only a respected legal authority, he was also one of the founders of what is now known as Orthodox Judaism, which was created to meet a new and unprecedented challenge to traditional Jewish life. The challenge was Reform Judaism. In significant numbers, and with intellectual sophistication, Jews were erasing their own tradition. (Among its many far-reaching revisions of Jewish practice, the assembly at Brunswick declared that "the marriage of a Jew with a Christian, and marriage with adherents of monotheistic religions generally, is not prohibited, provided that the laws of the state permit parents to raise the children of such a union also in the Jewish faith.") The traditionalists were provoked into a philosophical and historical defense of their Judaism. For their Judaism was no longer the only Judaism. A norm was becoming a denomination; the agonizing age of Jewish confessionalism had begun. Ettlinger was one of the architects of the Orthodox counter-offensive. "I don't know how to judge the sinners of Israel today," he wrote, with exasperation, about the public violation of the Sabbath. "The plague has spread to the masses." Ettlinger was a Talmudic prodigy who had also attended the University of Wurzburg, until the anti-Jewish riots of 1819 forced him to withdraw. In 1845, he established *The Faithful Guardian of Zion*, a journal of conservative ideology that was published in German and in Hebrew, and many of Ettlinger's responsa (including this one) originally appeared in its pages.

It is no wonder, then, that Ettlinger was distressed by Oppenheim's innovation. For the faithful guardian of Zion, the reorganization of the mourner's kaddish looked like the slippery slope to reform. "I am altogether astounded that my honorable colleague has described as 'a great and right reform' the revision of a Jewish custom that has been the custom of the communities of Ashkenaz and Poland for more than three hundred years, that the mourner's kaddish should be recited by every man individually [in his turn]. Instead he proposes to walk in the footsteps of the innovators of our time who have changed the liturgy and have also likewise instituted the practice that all the mourners should say the kaddish together." So the malevolent reformers in

Germany had emended the practice of the mourners in shul exactly as the benevolent traditionalists in Moravia had emended it. Did Oppenheim know this? Shame on him!

Having declared his general objection, Ettlinger declares his particular objections. They are philosophical, historical, and ritual. Philosophically, he is offended by Oppenheim's rationalism. "I would inquire of my colleague why he thinks that the story [of Akiva and the condemned man] 'has no explanation,' especially if it happened in waking life and not in a dream. Moreover, is it really surprising to find, in the sayings of our rabbis, that the spirits of the dead manifest themselves to the living, especially to notable individuals, and speak to them?" Ettlinger cites a number of ancient sources that portray a visitation of the dead to the living, and asks sarcastically "whether my honorable colleague would judge that these, too, were all dreams." Ettlinger denies that the story of Akiva appears in the *Zohar*—he is right, it does not appear there, and Oppenheim was also mistaken in suggesting that the *Zohar* served as a source for the *Kol Bo*—but he finds another tale in the mystical masterwork that demonstrates that "the dead would speak to the sages when they were awake." He notes that the story of Akiva does appear in the *Zohar Ḥadash*—in the passage that I pondered many months ago—and in that passage "it does indeed appear as if the incident took place in a dream. But really it does not matter whether it happened in a dream or in waking life. Since the midrash recounts the incident, it must be true, and not the stuff of dreams borne by the wind." Against Oppenheim's naturalism, Ettlinger insists on supernaturalism. In the rationalist reading of rabbinical legend, he detects the early stirrings of the impulse to tamper with rabbinical law.

Ettlinger turns next to the historicity of the mourner's kaddish, to prove that "the status of the kaddish is great and its foundation is in the holy of holies in [the tale of] Rabbi Akiva." He is indignant that "a great and exemplary scholar" such as Oppenheim "would contradict the word of Rabbi Moses Isserles, who wrote that it [the story of Akiva] is found in the ancient compilations of midrash." Ettlinger responds to Oppenheim's bibliography of the kaddish with a bibliography of his own. In Spain in the thirteenth century, he notes, Bahya ben Asher claimed that the story appears in a minor Talmudic tractate; and the same attribution to the same minor tractate was made by Isaac Aboab, the Spanish anthologist of ancient rabbinical teachings, in Spain at the end of the fourteenth century. (He notes that in Aboab's version of the story the mourner's kaddish is not mentioned, and the mourner fulfills his obligation by leading the congregation in a central prayer, "but this is no wonder, since the kaddish itself had not yet been established in Rabbi Akiva's days, but was established in Babylonia.") Ettlinger concedes that the story does not appear "in the texts [of the tractate] that we have." Still, "it is commonly known that we do not possess the complete texts of the minor tractates, and nonetheless it has never occurred to anybody to doubt Rabbi Moses Isserles and to deny that the story appears in any midrash." For the story appears, according to Ettlinger, in *Midrash Tanḥuma,* a canonical collection of rabbinical legends that originated in the Byzantine period in Palestine and underwent considerable development in the early medieval period. Yet Ettlinger concedes, this time in a parenthesis, that "this is not the same *Midrash Tanḥuma* that was published in Amsterdam." That is to say, he is unable to find the story of Akiva in the edition on his shelf (as I was unable to find it in the edition on my shelf).

Thus Ettlinger cannot himself vouch for the antiquity of the mourner's kaddish. Instead he relies on reports of its antiquity. But he strides on. He cites Perfet on the mourner's kaddish in fourteenth-century Spain (the same text that was cited by Oppenheim), and finally he announces his conclusion: "The custom of the mourner's kaddish is a custom that became widespread among the Jews in the days of the early authorities, more than six hundred years ago." More than seven or eight hundred years ago, more likely; but it is interesting to have Ettlinger's sense of the custom's history. (His survey of the sources is as incomplete as Oppenheim's.)

Even if he has not shown that the mourner's kaddish is an ancient prayer, Ettlinger has shown that it is a venerable prayer. This may suffice for his purpose, which is to pit the past against the present, to appeal to the venerability of the mourner's kaddish against those who believe that it lacks a long history "and therefore may be treated, in the hands of the rabbi, like clay in the hands of the potter, which may be shaped as he wishes." This, in his view, is the sort of willfulness that Oppenheim displayed when he allowed the mourners of Eibenschitz to recite the kaddish together. Ettlinger acknowledges Oppenheim's report of the dissension in the Moravian congregation, but he mocks it: "I am amazed to hear such words. Does custom really hinge upon a particular house of worship? What the members of the community have practiced until now: that is custom! When everybody is permitted to change as he wishes what the communities of Ashkenaz and Poland have practiced for hundreds of years, merely because there are a few sinners who resort to force in the house of worship—should we really dignify this by calling it a custom, a lenient custom? After all, it was about such people [the ruffians in the house of worship in Eibenschitz] that it was written [in Hosea], 'The ways of the Lord are right, and the just shall walk in them, but the transgressors shall fall therein." Why should the failure of a few individuals be permitted to distort the habitudes of the community? This much influence must not be conceded to sin.

Ettlinger stood firm against Oppenheim's realism. In this, too, he was a father of Orthodoxy. But what was he to do? He was a believer. For a believer, history has no power over truth. And that is the beauty of belief in a historicist age. In a historicist age, the aspect of eternity provides a standpoint for criticism.

Who needs a realist in a prayer shawl? There is nothing less edifying than a godly man who knows the score.

The world is always too worldly.

Ettlinger also denies that Oppenheim has read Sofer correctly. He points out that Sofer did not rule that the mourner's kaddish should be said by all the mourners together at all times, but only that a man who has been hired to recite the kaddish may recite it, once during the service, together with the mourner who is reciting it for all the mourners. I consult Sofer's opinion again; and while Ettlinger is correct about his ruling, Sofer's latitude about the collective recitation of the mourner's kaddish is unmistakable. It seems to me that Oppenheim's reading of Sofer was entirely plausible.

Ettlinger must deal not only with Sofer's opinion, but also with the precedent for Sofer's opinion, which is Emden's declaration that "how fine and fitting is the custom of the Sephardim, that when there are many mourners, they all have the privilege and say it all together." Ettlinger comments on Emden with a special authority. For Emden was Ettlinger's predecessor. The former was rabbi in Altona in the eighteenth century, the latter was rabbi in Altona in the nineteenth century. What, then, was the custom of Altona? This is Ettlinger's report: "It was here that Jacob Emden had his honored place and his own house of worship, and I have not heard that he changed the custom to permit the mourners to say the kaddish all together, even though he said that in his view the same practice among the Sephardim was correct." This is surprising. What rabbis say should be what rabbis do.

Then Ettlinger offers a nice excursus in Jewish anthropology: "As for the custom of the Sephardim: we have no way to know what is the basis of their custom. In any event, there is a huge difference between Sephardim and Ashkenazim. The Sephardim generally worship in unison, with one voice, without any worshiper racing ahead or lagging behind; and since they were accustomed to such a style of prayer, it is natural that when they said the kaddish, they would say it in unison. . . . But this is not the case with us, the Ashkenazic communities, who do not worship and declaim the prayers with one voice. Moreover, when many people worship together in unison, it is hard to hear the prayers and to concentrate on them. I know this well, because here the mourners are also accustomed to reciting the rabbis' kaddish together in unison, and it is a mockery and a farce, in which the strong one raises his voice and shouts for mastery, and his fellow screams to match him. The one starts the prayer when he wants, and the other finishes the prayer when he wants, and it is impossible to respond with an amen. I would long ago have prevented them from saying the rabbis' kaddish in such a manner, and certainly from instituting such a manner from the start, except that I am afraid to abolish a custom. As for the other kaddishes that appear in the service, not a single congregation in all the regions of Ashkenaz and Poland has been seen or heard to establish such a practice in saying them, except where a practice has been established by the propounders of reform, who do not value the customs of Israel." —I must hasten to shul. The kaddish is interfering with my study of the kaddish!

Finally Ettlinger makes an angry appeal to Oppenheim. "It seems to me, from the words of my colleague, that even he recognizes that it is not dignified to recite the kaddish all together, because many voices make it hard to hear what is said; and for this reason he has conceived a compromise, that the precentor recite the kaddish loudly and the mourners recite it softly along with him. But the truth is that this is exactly the custom that has been instituted by the propounders of reform, since everything about the kaddish is for them nothing but the stuff of dreams. They do not care whether the kaddish achieves its purpose, since their purpose is simply to appease those who ask to honor their parents with the kaddish. And so I would ask my honorable colleague, who does not share their view: is it not the aim of the kaddish, and is it not its greatness, that just as it provides an opportunity for many people to acquire the merit of publicly sanctifying God's Name, it also provides an opportunity for the father to acquire merit through [the son's] offices? And will this aim be accomplished if all the mourners recite the kaddish together and it is not heard? Surely their silence would be preferable to their speech, for their speech would seem false, a fraud."

How many times has my kaddish been a fraud?

Magnified and sanctified . . . Magnified and sanctified . . . Magnified and sanctified . . .

When my mother told a neighbor that I was scrupulously fulfilling my obligation to say kaddish, he said: "Good for your son, and good for your husband." She agreed that it was good for her son, but she wondered how it was good for her husband. I explained that her neighbor was expressing the traditional understanding of what I am doing, but she didn't seem impressed. My incredulous mother is right, of course. There is no proof.

In shul this morning we read about the Exodus from Egypt. I was startled by a word in a verse that I have read a hundred times—but never really, until today. "And it came to pass, when Pharaoh had let the people go, that God led them not through the way of the land of the Philistines, although that was near; for God said, Lest peradventure the people repent when they see war, and they return to Egypt." Thus the King James translation, which uses "repent" in the unloaded sense, to mean only a change of mind. God feared that the Jews, if they were confronted by the threat of war, would change their minds. But in the original the verse does not worry that they will "repent." It worries that they will be "consoled." Why consoled? And suddenly I see it, the primal meaning of the word that has tyrannized over this year of my life. To be consoled is to repent, that is, to change one's mind, to agree to have one's attention diverted from one's sorrow, to admit another object, another motive, another desire, into one's consciousness. For sorrow wants nothing but sorrow. It is the perfect example of single-mindedness.

The opposite of melancholy is not joy. The opposite of melancholy is many-mindedness.

My demons keep urging me to sleep. So I stay away from my bed. From the prayerbook I know that sleep is a death: "I thank you, living and eternal God," a Jew is supposed to say immediately upon waking, "for returning my soul to me." And a few moments later, "Blessed art Thou, who restores souls to dead bodies." Sleep frightens me, because I want it so much. In the mornings I hurry to shul, like a man in flight from a temptation.

Think again, think again. The sleeping are not like the dead. The dead are not sleeping. The dead are dead. They will not wake. —Well, I have just denied the resurrection of the dead, and thereby forfeited my right to a kaddish of my own. I have thought heretically. But truly I do not expect to see my father again. If death is not final, then we are being made fools. Is this a seditious spirit? Too bad. It is the only spirit in which I can pray for, or about, my father, in which I can continue with his kaddish.

Death is not a dying unto. It is a dying, period.

I am tired, I need a rest, or so I tell myself every morning after prayers. But it isn't that simple. I am not tired. I am weak. I have a sabotaging spirit. The fatigue about which I complain is really an excuse for the attrition in my alertness. I am in a war with myself and I am falling back. I am looking for mercies. I must stay away from my bed.

Despair strikes behind the eyes and bids me close them. I will not. Even in perfect darkness, one must keep one's eyes open. A darkness seen is an imperfect darkness.

A man is in a dark room. He sees nothing. Yet he is not blind. A man who sees nothing is not a blind man, if nothing is what there is to see.

XI

I'm not through with Benjamin Zev yet. There is still the mysterious responsum that he includes among his own responsa, to support his own analysis of the kaddish. "I have found an author who was asked about the matter of the kaddish," he writes in his introduction to this text, "and I have seen fit to append [his responsum] to mine to buttress my words." The responsum is signed "Ovadiah." Nothing more. Who is Ovadiah? His text refers to certain authorities of the fifteenth century, but I cannot identify him with certainty. It is decent of Benjamin Zev to give Ovadiah's discussion in its entirety, for it makes his own discussion seem highly derivative. Ovadiah, too, believes that "the merit of the relatives [of the dead] profits nothing, only the merit of the son for his father or his mother profits something"; and that the basis for the restriction of the kaddish to the children is "the legend of Rabbi Akiva that is familiar to all." Ovadiah confirms that orphans have priority in the synagogue over other mourners, and he reports that there is a universal consensus on this matter, including "Ashkenazic notables" who attended Rabbi Israel [Isserlein] and "informants from Spain and all the provinces." Ovadiah also makes an interesting observation about the creation of a special prayer for mourners. It is, he says, a concession to the realities of Jewish life: "In my humble opinion, it seems to me that, since not everybody is ready and competent to lead the service in its entirety, including the kaddish, and since not every individual has the knowledge or the ability to pray at all the proper times, the ancient sages established something that would be the same for everybody—the kaddish at the end of the service, which is easy and which everybody knows. Thus, an individual who has acquired knowledge should lead the afternoon and evening and morning services, for the more he prays and the more he multiplies the saying of kaddish, the better for the souls of the dead; and an individual who does not possess the strength or the knowledge to say all the prayers will say this kaddish, so that nothing will be lacking."

The history of Jewish literacy: now there is a delicate subject! It turns out that rabbis have been complaining for centuries that the book has too often been closed to the people of the book. (But my brethren in America should take no comfort from the history of Jewish illiteracy. They have broken new ground.)

In exploring the meaning of the kaddish, Ovadiah's responsum includes one of the most interesting formulations that I have found. It comes in his discussion of the exclusiveness of the mourner's kaddish, which is "only [the prayer of] the son for the father and the mother." What, then, of David's prayer for Absalom? Ovadiah is not the only writer to worry about this exception to the rule, but his solution to the problem is particularly illuminating, at least for me. His solution is that David's prayer for Absalom is not like the kaddish, because the kaddish is not a prayer. *The kaddish is not a prayer.* So what is it? Ovadiah explains: "David's prayer could benefit his son, for a man may ask for mercy for a fellow man even if he is not a relative. . . . But this kaddish is not a prayer that the son prays for his father, that God should raise him up from the lower depths. It is, rather, an ascription of merit to the father, that the father fulfilled his duty, in that one of his descendants will sanctify [*yakdish*] the great and exalted and awesome God before the entire congregation, and by this means God will be One and His Name will be One for the assembly, which will answer 'Amen, may the Great Name be blessed.' It is a great atonement for the soul of the father, since the flesh of his flesh and the bone of his bones has caused God to be sanctified in public. This, for me, is the reason for the kaddish of the son, and the reason that the son acquits the father: the son *is* the father, and the good deeds and fulfilled obligations of the son unfold and emanate from him."

In Ovadiah's view, the kaddish is not a prayer for something. It is a proof of something. The son does not request that his father be granted a good fate. The son demonstrates why his father deserves to be granted a good fate. The son is not the advocate, the son is the evidence.

I am the evidence!

Examine me and forgive him.

He taught me to be here, and here I am. It is the dead who are responsible for the kaddish for the dead.

If I am the evidence, then I am exempted from eloquence. What an unburdening! Eloquence is not inimical to truth, but insofar as it aims to please or to prettify, it is inimical to the spirit of truth, which must not be concerned with effects and consequences. When a statement that is true is expressed beautifully, is it the truth of the statement that persuades or the beauty?

Or rather, I may suffice with the eloquence of evidence. This is the eloquence that can dispense with art.

It defeats the purpose of a proposition about what is true and what is false for it to fascinate. Fascination is a surrender to charisma; a charmed collapse of thought.

If God could be seen, we would do nothing but look. We would squander our lives on the contemplation of God.

By light, light: so said Philo. But I don't think so. By light, what is in the light. Light never reveals only itself. For this reason, it is not an adequate metaphor for spiritual life in this world, which riddles us with objects and purposes.

Give thanks for light, because it reveals all the things for which we must give thanks.

A pure experience of light? Not with our eyes. For better and for worse, our eyes see more.

This is the teaching of Ovadiah: anybody may pray for anybody, and "if he is proper and fitting and worthy that his prayer be answered," the prayer will be answered, but the kaddish is not an utterance of this kind. It is not a petition, it is a demonstration of cause and effect. The effect has come to attest to the cause. For months and months, the child goes to shul to say—no, to show—who his or her parent was. The kaddish is not a prayer for the dead. It is an achievement of the dead.

So who was this Ovadiah, who gave me this gift? I send his text to Jerusalem, to an eminent historian of Italian Jewry. He writes back to say that he has consulted his files and has concluded that "I don't know." (When a learned man says that he does not know, you have learned something.)

The idea that the kaddish is not a prayer comes as a great relief to me. I have been uncomfortable all year with the notion that I am offering a prayer for the dead. I cannot offer such a prayer, because it is premised on a cosmos that I cannot accept. A prayer for the dead is a pious absurdity.

The kaddish, a prayer for the dead? Of course not. Just look at it! There is not a single mention of the dead in it. It is suddenly so obvious. The riddle of my early months of mourning is solved. The reason that I could not find any connection between the words that I spoke and the wounds that I felt is that there was none. I should have done what I was trained to do. I should have trusted the text.

But look again. The kaddish is not a prayer for the dead, but the kaddish is a prayer. It is a prayer for God! The mourner rises and prays that God be magnified and sanctified above all blessings and hymns and praises and consolations that are uttered in the world. I have been proving my father by praying for my Father! I understand that its familiarity and its frequency is what convinced the rabbis to attach the kaddish to the mourner; but suddenly the kaddish doesn't look easy at all. It looks like a wild metaphysical idea.

The idea that my living God needs me is even more incomprehensible than the idea that my dead father needs me. "Above all consolations": so God, too, is a mourner! The kaddish is a communication from one mourner to another. Every kaddish in the liturgy is the mourner's kaddish, and God is the mourner. In all this dailiness, a mystery.

And what does God mourn? I importune the rabbis of Ashkenaz. They have pondered the problem, of course. I find two interpretations of the consolations that are mentioned in the kaddish. Both these interpretations appear in the opening pages of the compilation of Rashi's rulings and customs known as Rashi's prayerbook. (It was substantially augmented by his students.) Rashi's first interpretation is literary. It is that "consolations" is another term for "hymns" and "praises": "In the theological pronouncements of the ancient rabbis, we have found it said that all of David's lauds in the Book of Psalms were designed for the eventual day of consolation. . . . Thus, when we say [in the kaddish] 'above all blessings and hymns and praises and consolations,' we mean: 'You will be praised more highly than in all the praises that were uttered by the prophets and by David for the eventual day of consolation.'" The consolation to which the kaddish refers is nothing more than a particular liturgical and homiletical form—the Biblical and rabbinical promises of comfort at the end of time, which are familiar from books and sermons and songs. The kaddish is a fantasy of worshipful excess, a dream of an unlimited language of praise. It proposes to shatter all the doxological forms; and the consolation is one of those forms. (This formal definition of "consolation" also appears in the Talmud. In a discussion of the arrangement of the prophetic books of the Bible, for example, the rabbis observed that "Jeremiah is entirely a destruction; and the beginning of Ezekiel is a destruction, and the ending of Ezekiel is a consolation; and Isaiah is entirely a consolation"; and they established the canonizer's rule that "destructions are placed next to destructions, and consolations next to consolations.") The object of these consolations is not the sorrow of God, but the sorrow of men.

But Rashi's second interpretation is not stylistic. It crosses the line into myth. In this reading, which "was heard from our master Rabbi Solomon," it is indeed the grief of God that the kaddish is designed to relieve. "These consolations are in accordance with what is stated in the Talmud: 'I heard a divine voice cooing sadly and muttering: "Woe is me, that I destroyed My Temple and burned My sanctuary and exiled My children among the peoples of the world!" Then the prophet Elijah told me that it is not just this once that the Divine Voice speaks this way—no, it speaks this way every day, three times a day [at the times of prayer]—more, when Jews come to the houses of worship and the houses of study and exclaim "May His great Name be blessed always and forever!" [in response to the beginning of the kaddish], God nods his head sadly and says: "Happy is the king whose children extol him in his own house! But woe to the father who banished his children, and woe to the children who have been banished from their father's table."' And this is why we say, in the kaddish, 'praises and consolations,' for He is in need of consolation for the anguish that He feels when He hears us respond."

In the opinion of Rashi, then, the kaddish lowers God's spirits and the kaddish raises them. For God, the prayer is a taunt. The exaltation that rises from the shul leaves Him dejected. It reminds Him of the old circumstances of exaltation, the unreduced circumstances that He reduced. (The nostalgia of God!) And so the kaddish must undo the damage that it has done, and console God with the imagination of an ultimate consolation. —A sweet fable.

An ultimate consolation for an ultimate grief.

Rashi's prayerbook does not give the beginning of this Talmudic tale. Here it is: "Rabbi Yose said: 'Once I was walking along a road and I went into a ruin, one of the ruins of Jerusalem, in order to pray there. The prophet Elijah appeared and waited for me at the entrance, until I finished my prayer. "Peace be upon you, my master!" he said to me, when I finished praying. "And peace be upon you, my master and my teacher!" I replied. "My son," he said, "why have you entered this ruin?" "To pray," I said. "You should have prayed on the road!" he said. "But I was afraid that I would be interrupted by the people passing by," I explained. "Then you should have prayed a short prayer!" he retorted. At that moment I learned three things. I learned that one should not enter a ruin; and I learned that one may pray on the road; and I learned that one must pray quickly when one prays on the road. Then Elijah addressed me again. "My son," he asked, "did you hear a voice in this ruin?" "I heard a Divine Voice cooing sadly like a dove and muttering: 'Woe unto My children, for whose sins I destroyed My house . . .'"'" The story of God's grief is stronger when it is set in the ruin. The prophet seeks to dissuade the rabbi from entering a ruin because the prophet does not want the rabbi to discover God's secret, which is that He is a mourner.

You see more in a ruin, because you see what is not there.

The history of Jewish civilization is the history of what can be accomplished in a ruin.

Rashi's interpretation of the consolation in the kaddish—I mean his second interpretation, the occult one, the outrageous one—appears in the commentaries on the kaddish that were subsequently produced in Ashkenaz. Solomon ben Samson of Worms in the eleventh century (or, according to a more recent attribution, Eliezer ben Nathan in the twelfth century) reproduces his contemporary's reading, but a few pages later there appears a phrase that suggests a certain philosophical discomfort with the idea that God is a mourner. The purpose of the consolations in the kaddish, he remarks, is "to console God, as it were." As it were, indeed!

The Perfumer, too, has a word of caution. "It is as if . . . ," he writes. As if what? "As if the Holy One is rueful when He hears the hymns and the blessings [that are said in the house of worship], and says: 'If only My temple were still standing, they would be singing and playing their instruments and offering their praises there!' And He regrets the destruction.

And so [in the kaddish] we say 'consolations' to refer to all the blessings and the hymns and the praises that used to be uttered, and will be uttered again." The kaddish, then, is a reckoning of God's loss. Elsewhere in his commentary on the liturgy, the Perfumer throws caution to the winds. "The emissary of the congregation who stands before the ark and leads the prayers must risk his soul, and pray with all the concentration of his heart." Passion is particularly appropriate to the kaddish. "When he says 'Magnified and sanctified,' he should train his eyes upon the holy ark, because the Divine Presence dwells in it." And, the Perfumer adds enigmatically, "the kaddish is the Song of Songs." (The kaddish, a lover's prayer?) As for the consolations in the kaddish, "its consolations are to comfort God for the exile, for God smites His hands together when He recalls His desolated city and repairs to the room known as 'the secret places' and lets out a lament from there." The Perfumer adds that this, too, is why the kaddish is recited mostly in Aramaic. The angels do not understand Aramaic, they understand only Hebrew, "and we do not want the angels in God's service to be aware of His pain, so we speak in Aramaic. . . . Otherwise they will ask: 'Why does the Divine Presence have need of solace?'" The Perfumer draws also a practical conclusion from this mystery. If God is a mourner whom we have come to console, then we must attend to the manner of our consolation. The offering in the house of worship must be beautiful. "We come to comfort the Holy One, Blessed Be He, who regrets the destruction [of the Temple]. If His Temple were still standing, He says, then His people would be praising Him with such pleasing voices. For this reason, when the leader of the prayers comes to 'consolations,' he must draw it out, thinking intensely in his heart that God will be consoled, and that He will console us, too, very soon."

As I was walking up the hill on my way home, I felt the need to stop and to bow my head. It is not only faith that humbles. Doubt humbles, too. (Actually, doubt humbles more than faith.)

Is there a god of inquiry? And how is a god of inquiry served—with questions or with answers?

There is another interpretation of the grief of God, a startling interpretation. It promotes the kaddish from an expression of longing for redemption into an expression of longing for apocalypse. I have run into this interpretation in a variety of medieval readings of the kaddish. In a fragment of a commentary on the kaddish, Hai Gaon, in Babylonia in the tenth and early eleventh centuries, refers to "the promises of the visionaries," and writes that God will be "glorified," as the kaddish says, "with the coming of the messiah . . . when the nations of the world gather to make war on the people of Israel, and Israel flees to Jerusalem . . . and the Holy One will reveal Himself to them in Jerusalem and make war"—and there the fragment ends. And in France, in *Maḥzor Vitry,* perhaps as early as the eleventh century, the apocalyptic reading of the kaddish is fully elaborated. (It is not found in the printed text of the work, but it is found in manuscripts in New York and Moscow, and has recently been published.) The passage begins by noting that the opening line of the kaddish—"Magnified and sanctified may His great Name be"—is based on a verse in Ezekiel: "Thus will I magnify myself and sanctify myself, and I will be known in the eyes of many nations, and they shall know that I am the Lord." This is the language of apotheosis, of eschatological climax. *Maḥzor Vitry* explains, a little curtly: "The text is referring to the war of Gog and Magog." Gog and Magog! In that final war, moreover, God will right an ancient wrong. He will avenge Himself for nothing less than the fracturing of His Name. When the Israelites left Egypt, remember, they were attacked by the Amalekites; and after the Israelites defeated the Amalekites in battle, God swore eternal enmity toward Amalek. Moses built an altar and proclaimed God's vow, taken with His hand on His throne, "that the Lord will have war with Amalek from generation to generation." But the Name of God that Moses invoked at that ceremony was a truncated name, an incomplete name. (Moses' word for "throne" was also truncated, incomplete.) Thus the kaddish, according to *Maḥzor Vitry,* is a prayer for the repair of God's Name, an affirmation of the hope that "the letters of God's Name will be rejoined, that is, the Name that was cut in half when He vowed to make war on Amalek." The basis for this is the spelling of the Aramaic word for "His Name" in the opening line of the kaddish, which makes it possible to read the phrase (I can give only a rough English equivalent) not as "may His great Name be" but as "may His Name be great," that is, larger than it has been until now, in the eon in which the war with Amalek is not yet won. In the desert, "God swore that in our time and on His throne His Name will never be complete until he avenges Himself on Amalek." And this is how the kaddish saddens God. It reminds Him of His own rupture in the desert.

"May His great Name be blessed." On these words in the kaddish, the anonymous author in *Maḥzor Vitry* has this to say: "It is imperative that the individual prolong the word 'great' with all his might, and while he prolongs it he must meditate in his heart on the legends [about Gog and Magog and Amalek] that we have just explained. For when the Holy One hears that the Jews deliberately come together to remind Him of the oath that He swore to wipe out the memory of Amalek . . . when He hears them proclaiming, with all their might, this language of praise [in which they hope for His Name to be made great], immediately He says: 'Woe to the children who have been banished from their father's table, and woe to the father who has distanced his children from his table and they praise him like this!' For this reason, the sorrow on high is great in that hour [when the kaddish is recited]. For it reminds Him of Amalek's outrage against heaven, which caused His Name to be divided, and so there is great sorrow on high. And when the angels hear and see this great sadness in the presence of the Holy One, they are rattled and shaken and stunned into silence, because they do not know why there is this sorrow in God's presence, since they do not understand Aramaic." But we understand Aramaic, and so we must console God for the fate that we have just recalled. We lowered His spirits, and so we must raise them. "Now we must provide Him with solace for His sorrow. . . . Be sure you understand the sense in which we speak [in the kaddish] of 'consolations' toward heaven. After all, there is no solace where there is no sorrow. But lo, the sorrow on high is huge, and it is this sorrow for which we provide solace. And that is why we speak in Aramaic: for the purpose of consolation."

The kaddish, banal? Not according to such a reading. Its subject is the restitution of the godhead! The liturgical trifle becomes a regular exercise in esotericism. Thus, near the conclusion of the kaddish, when God is petitioned that "a great peace from heaven—and life!—be upon us," the plea for life must be understood, according to *Maḥzor Vitry,* in the severe terms of the war at the end of days. "The blessing of life is called down upon Israel because there will be only a few survivors of that redemption, only one in a city and two in a family. Indeed, as it is stated [in the Talmud], 'let the messiah come, but let me not see him,' owing to the adversities that are fated to arrive in that time. For this reason, the blessing of life is wished upon [the Jews], so as to say, may His kingdom come for those who are still alive." The kaddish, a prayer for survivors.

Redemption is accompanied by atrocity. (The tradition calls it "the pangs of the messiah.") Speaking humanely, then, redemption *is* atrocity.

So who will redeem us from redemption? Only we can do this.

"May His kingdom come for those who are still alive." The kaddish, post-1945.

The pangs of the messiah: the pangs always arrive, the messiah never arrives.

In *The Book of the Orchard*, another volume in the Rashi literature, the apocalyptic reading of the kaddish is full and vivid. "'Magnified and sanctified.' But how may a mortal magnify and make greater the Name of the Holy One? As if, heaven forbid, it were lacking! But it *is* lacking . . ." In the oath to destroy Amalek, "only half the letters in the Name are mentioned." The kaddish is a supplication that the letters of the Divine Name be joined together. "We pray 'Magnified and sanctified,' as if to say, may it be the will of He who spoke and created the world that He rescue us from [the exile] among the nations and wipe out the memory of Amalek and sanctify His Name to make it whole." This will all transpire in the war of Gog and Magog. Indeed, "our own redemption depends upon the enlargement of the Name, for the Name will not be enlarged until the memory of Amalek is wiped out, and the memory of Amalek will not be wiped out until we are redeemed, and soon." (The text draws a surprising conclusion from this linguistic analysis of the fate of God's

Name, which is that "the Unique Name is an Aramaic word," and not a Hebrew word.) And the discussion of the angels and the kaddish in *The Book of the Orchard* is also noteworthy. The text notes correctly that the kaddish is a mixture of Aramaic and Hebrew, and that the words of praise in the kaddish—"blessed . . . praised . . . glorified . . . raised . . . honored . . . uplifted . . . lauded"—are not in Aramaic, but in Hebrew. "And if the angels understand these words, it is not important, because this is just praise." Not so the opening words of the kaddish. They are not praise, they are prayer. They hope for the healing of God. In this way, they are a confession of divine infirmity—and this information must not fall into the hands of the angels. "If a man should ask why the kaddish is recited in Aramaic, [the answer is that] it is so that the angels do not sense that the Name of the Holy One is lacking, lest they destroy the world." For the jealousy of the angels is murderous. They do not wish to share God with men. And it is only the fear of God that deters them—the fear of God, and our choice of language in the kaddish. Our Aramaic words prevent them from acquiring the knowledge that would provoke them to act against the world, the knowledge that there is a wound in God. And so we swing between Hebrew and Aramaic to thwart the uncherubic intentions of God's underlings. And we conclude the kaddish by imploring that "a great peace from heaven—and life!—be upon us and all Israel," "as if to say, let there be harmony in the celestial household, for if the angels do not understand what we have said, then there will be life upon all Israel."

The menace of angels, of all beings who fail to be human and fail to be divine.

"May His great Name be blessed always and forever!" *The Book of the Orchard* instructs that the congregation is to utter this response in the kaddish "like a man screaming loudly, who is reminding his hearers of things." Things that they had forgotten, and will forget again. Things that I had forgotten, and will forget again.

At the teahouse, the plot thickens. I am delighted to discover that the apocalyptic interpretation of the kaddish was soon rejected. The flight of the chiliastic imagination was thwarted by a rather homely consideration: it was not supported by syntax. "May His great Name be blessed": according to the apocalyptic reading, the congregation's response in the kaddish must be divided into two prayers, that His Name be great and that His Name be blessed. But this contradicts the Aramaic words in the text. The words do not say that His Name should be great and His Name should be blessed. The words say that His great Name should be blessed. Thus the apocalyptic interpretation of the kaddish makes no linguistic sense. In Ashkenaz this problem was pointed out only a generation or so later, when the glossators of the Talmud known as the Tosafists challenged the reading of the kaddish in *Maḥor Vitry.* They issued their challenge in a gloss on the story of Rabbi Yose's prayer in the ruin. The legend in the Talmud tells that "when Jews come to the houses of worship and the houses of study and exclaim 'May His great Name be blessed!' God nods his head sadly and says: 'Happy is the king whose children extol him in his own house! But woe to the father who banished his children, and woe to the children who have been banished from their father's table.'" The Tosafists observed that "on the basis of this, we may refute the interpretation in *Maḥzor Vitry* that the words 'May His great Name be blessed' are a prayer that we pray for the restoration of His Name. . . . From what the Talmud says here it is clear that these words comprise a single prayer, and that they intend to say not that His Name should be great, but that His great Name should be blessed."

Messianism? Not at the price of grammar.

The Tosafists' repudiation of the apocalyptic reading of the kaddish did not discredit it entirely in the French and German communities—the Perfumer mentions it glancingly in his commentary on the kaddish—but it seems to have migrated south. In Italy in the thirteenth century, Zedekiah the Physician records it with his brother Benjamin's interpretation of the kaddish. ("The kaddish is based on the future," Benjamin Anav succinctly remarked.) In Provence in the late twelfth and early thirteenth centuries, Asher of Lunel explains that the subject of the kaddish is "the age of the messiah, when the dead will live," and he, too, mentions the rupture of God's Name; but he ascribes the divine calamity not to the war with Amalek but to the exile. "In the exile," Aaron writes, "the Name is not complete"; and alluding to the Talmudic exegesis of the last verse in Psalms, he adds that "in the exile, the soul may praise only half the blessed Name." In Provence a hundred years later, Aaron of Lunel develops the apocalyptic reading of the kaddish at length, and quotes *Maḥzor Vitry* extensively. In Spain in the fourteenth century, David ben Joseph Abudarham, in his commentary on the liturgy, expands upon the apocalyptic analysis and its sources in Scripture. Indeed, Abudarham is commenting on the fuller Yemenite–North African–Spanish variant of the kaddish, which is explicitly messianic. In this rite, a few words are added to the first section of the kaddish: "May His kingdom come, and may He grow forth His redemption, and hasten the climax of His messiah, and restore His sanctuary."

In shul this evening I told a man who is saying kaddish for his mother that, according to Benjamin Anav, "the kaddish is based on the future." He looked at me sourly and said: "Not on my future."

In their discussion of the kaddish, the Tosafists pitted the clarity of language not only against apocalypse, but also against angelology. This wonderful passage—Jacob ben Asher, in Spain in the fourteenth century, identifies its author as the formidable Isaac ben Samuel of Dampierre, who was Jacob Tam's nephew and his heir in the development of Talmudism in France in the second half of the twelfth century—continues: "As for the popular view that the kaddish is recited in Aramaic because it is a lovely and greatly exalted expression of praise, and so it had to be formulated in Aramaic, since otherwise the angels would understand it and be jealous of us—this view is not plausible. After all, many beautiful prayers are in Hebrew [which the angels can understand]!" For the interpretation of the kaddish, Isaac is not in need of angels. This is especially striking in the light of Isaac's interest in the esoteric doctrines of the early pietists of Ashkenaz. It was even reported about him that "he ascended to heaven at night and received instruction from the angels." In Isaac's view, however, the angelological explanation of the kaddish is an instance of misplaced esotericism. "The reason [that the kaddish is said in Aramaic]," he observes, "is . . . that the kaddish used to be said after teaching and preaching, and there were ignorant people present, and they did not understand the Holy Tongue. Therefore the rabbis established the kaddish in the language of translation, so that everyone would understand it, for this was their language." Hebrew was "the Holy Tongue." Aramaic was "the language of translation," the language into which Scripture and rabbinical discourse was commonly translated in the ancient world. The diction of the kaddish was not designed to overcome the shortcomings of angels. It was designed to overcome the shortcomings of human beings.

"He ascended to heaven at night and received instruction from the angels." Maybe they told him that the kaddish is our problem, not theirs.

The trajectory of the apocalyptic interpretation of the kaddish may be seen in Jacob ben Asher's code of law, in which the traditions of the north collided with the traditions of the south. He cites the extravagant view that the reference to God's "great Name" implies that "the Name that is now not whole will be restored to its wholeness" as a consequence of "the wars of Gog and Magog." "There are those who interpret it this way," he writes. He also cites the angelological explanation of the Aramaic of the prayer ("so that the angels will not be jealous of us, that we offer praise as beautiful as this"). But then Jacob turns the screw one more time: "And Rabbi Isaac [of Dampierre] explained . . ." The scion of Ashkenaz living in Spain prefers the reading of his ancestors to the reading of his neighbors. And he clearly states the implication of Isaac's expulsion of the angels from the kaddish: "Its language must then be interpreted literally. The Aramaic is simply a translation of the Hebrew: 'May His great Name be blessed.'" —Not "may His Name be great" and "may His Name be blessed." Just "may His great Name be blessed." Instead of two mystical dreams, one unmystical dream. A vernacular dream.

A literal, unmystical, vernacular dream.

"Padding around the ancestral home," a friend writes, "I found this," and he encloses a gift. It is the text of a responsum by Solomon ben Abraham Adret that he has copied out of an old edition in his father's library. It is exactly like the text that I have in a newer and slicker edition of Adret's rulings. The late-thirteenth-century master of Spanish Jewry was asked about the Aramaic in the kaddish. He replied that "at the time, most people spoke only Aramaic. For this reason, the rabbis instituted the recitation of the kaddish in Aramaic, so that everybody would understand it and thereby sanctify His blessed Name." But Adret also reports a development in the linguistic history of the kaddish. "There are currently precentors [leading the congregation in worship] who translate [the Aramaic] into Hebrew . . . and they give no thought about reciting it in this fashion, even though it was originally recited in Aramaic." He notes also "the custom of different communities adding [to the text] as they wish, in Aramaic or in Hebrew—indeed, in any language that their hearts desire." Adret has no objection to this flexibility. "Nothing is lost," he writes. "Nor is there any reason to worry about the contemporary translation of most of the kaddish into the Holy Tongue, because in our day we no longer speak Aramaic. All languages are again the same to us." Languages rise and fall, especially among the Jews in exile. There is the Holy Tongue and there are the unholy tongues. The important thing is that those who say the kaddish know what it means. Like the rabbi in Dampierre, the rabbi in Barcelona explained the language of the kaddish immanently. It had nothing to do with angels. It was a concession to cultural realities. But Adret did not reject the apocalyptic reading of the kaddish entirely. He appends to his discussion of language a reference to the healing of God's Name when the oath against Amalek is fulfilled. "The Holy One will not enter into the heavenly Jerusalem," he writes, paraphrasing the Talmud, "until He has rebuilt the earthly Jerusalem."

"All languages are again the same to us." It is a question of convenience. Yet the reformers of Adret's day served the cause of convenience by translating the prayer into Hebrew. After all, who ever heard of a Jew who did not know Hebrew?

In Rome, Adret's contemporary Zedekiah the Physician records the interesting views of his brother and his teacher on the linguistic vicissitudes of the kaddish. "My brother Benjamin wrote that the kaddish was originally said in Hebrew . . . but in the days of persecution it was decreed that it was forbidden to proclaim 'May His great Name be blessed!' And so the rabbis established that it be said in Aramaic, so that the enemies would not understand the words." The kaddish, a crypto-Jewish prayer! Benjamin Anav's explanation is vague. Which ancient persecution does he have in mind? Anyway, that persecution has passed. Why not return the kaddish to Hebrew? He has an answer. "Even though the persecution is over, they did not wish to restore the matter to its original state in the Hebrew language, so that the miracles and the marvels [with which God saved His people from persecution] will not be forgotten, indeed, so that they will become widely known." The language of the kaddish is the commemoration of a redemption. The content of the prayer refers to salvation in the future, but the form of the prayer refers to salvation in the past. It follows from Benjamin's interpretation that the impact of these Aramaic words on the Jews is the opposite of their impact on God. God is disheartened by the sound of them, and so He needs to be consoled; but the Jews are heartened by the sound of them, the words are themselves a consolation of the Jews. Before it was appropriated for the mourner, then, the kaddish was a consolation. Not for the mourning of individuals. For the mourning of a people.

And Zedekiah's teacher, Meir ben Moses? "This was Rabbi Meir's interpretation: Why is the kaddish uttered in Aramaic? Because a sorrowing man exchanges raiments for rags." Zedekiah adds that Meir was speaking of the sorrow of God, but I will linger stubbornly at the literal meaning of Meir's words, and call this the year in which I exchanged raiments for rags.

Also the year in which I discovered the fine fit of rags. The silk in the sackcloth.

In a conversation with a friend about homosexuality and the Jewish tradition, I was reminded of the medieval story that I read months ago in the *Tana D'Be Eliyahu Zuta,* or *The Teaching of the School of Elijah, The Lesser Version,* in which the son prays for the release of his father's soul from the torments that he suffers for the sin of sodomy. When I went back to find the passage in the book, I found another passage that seems to combine the sorrow of God with the sorrow of the mourner, encompassing all the griefs that are treated by the kaddish. This passage appears in the "greater version" of the work: "In every generation the Holy One strikes His hands together [in grief] and places them over His heart, and then upon His arms, and weeps [for the exile of Israel and the destruction of the Temple]. He weeps privately and He weeps publicly. Why privately? Because it is demeaning for the lion to weep in the presence of the fox, and for the king to weep in the presence of his servants, and for the teacher to weep in the presence of his students, and for the proprietor to weep in the presence of the worker whom he has hired. As it is written [in Jeremiah], 'Oh, that my head were waters and mine eyes a fountain of tears, that I might weep day and night for the slain of the daughter of my people!' Is this verse really referring to Jeremiah? No, [since the Hebrew word for "slain" is similar to the Hebrew word for "violators of the law"]. It is referring to the Holy One, who divided His world according to two kinds of behavior—the righteous and the wicked.

Who is righteous? He who, from the age of thirteen, has studied Scripture and the teachings of the rabbis, and learned the fear of heaven and the performance of good deeds, so that these qualities accompany him all his life. When he dies, the Holy One is happy and comes to greet him, saying, 'If only such a father had a son or a grandson to fill his place!' And who is wicked? He who, from the age of thirteen, has studied Scripture and the teachings of the rabbis, and then deviates in the direction of ugly ways and abominable things. When he dies, God sighs and comes to greet him, saying, 'If only such a father had a son or a grandson to commend him in memory!' Thus the kaddish of the son consoles the father and the Father."

Perfection, grieving for imperfection. A sublime notion. But this is the God of the Jews: He is closed and He is open. His sufficiency is not sufficient. He wants to need.

The tears of the perfect, or perfect tears.

Yet the laughter of God would be hateful.

It is odd that Ovadiah's explanation of the kaddish, the one cited by Benjamin Zev, the declaration that "this kaddish is not a prayer that the son prays for his father," strikes me with such force. After all, I have encountered this explanation before. A few months ago, and again a few weeks ago, I read in Abraham Horowitz: "This kaddish is not a prayer that the son prays for the father before God, that He raise him from the lower depths. It is, instead, a privilege and a good deed that accrues to the dead, when his son publicly sanctifies the Name of God and the congregation responds."

A revelation must not only be given, it must also be received.

Was nothing said or was nothing heard? The fate of religion will be decided by the answer to this question.

If only it were possible to conclude with certainty that if nothing was heard, then nothing was said. Yet such a conclusion is not possible, because the senses are not our only source of knowledge. For this reason, the perplexity will never end.

God had spoken but the people had not heard! Or so the prophets thundered. But they enjoyed an unfair advantage: God had spoken to *them.* They did not appreciate the difference between a revelation and a report of a revelation.

Castigate the people for sin, but do not castigate them for doubt. Doubt is the candor of a discouraged mind.

When the eye does not see the object, it may be wrong to conclude that the eye cannot see or that the object does not exist. We need to know more about the circumstances of cognition, and its failures.

Mystics have always dreamed of the dissolution of the subject-object relationship. I do not understand such a dream. I dream instead of the renovation of the subject-object relationship. I do not wish to be what I see, I wish to see it clearly.

What if God had acceded to Moses' shocking request and had shown him His face? Moses would have seen the face of God only with his own eyes. Even in the presence of the unlimited, he would have been limited by his senses. The sight of God is still the sight of an object. It is not yet the transcendence of subjectivity. We would trust the subject's account, or we would not trust it. It, too, would have to be evaluated by philosophy.

A man may see God and still speak only for himself.

A world in which there are no obstructions between the subject and the object is a redeemed world.

Ovadiah, in Italy, and Abraham Horowitz, in Poland, protest that the mourner's kaddish is not a prayer for the dead. In Italy and in Poland: that is, in Catholic cultures, in which people prayed rampantly for the dead. Were these writers making a polemical point? They were certainly differentiating the Jewish commemoration of the dead from the non-Jewish commemoration of the dead. Perhaps they worried that their brethren would see the kaddish in an alien light.

I have been living this year almost entirely in a single idiom. Of course, I have done many things that have nothing to do with Judaism, that are neither clouded nor clarified by it. But the strong feelings, the large thoughts, the deep experiences: this year my tradition is there to snatch them up and to transpose them into its key. I am not complaining that it is airless. There is plenty of air in my tradition. It's not more air I want, it's different air.

Tonight, and last night, and the night before last, we almost failed to get a quorum, and the regulars were angry about it. There are too many truants, they grumbled. It shouldn't have to be so hard. There were some harsh words. There were some practical suggestions for increasing the attendance. And in the corner stood an elderly man in a hat and a coat, lost in prayer.

The common English translation of the Hebrew name for what I have been reciting in shul is the "mourner's kaddish." Now, after all this time, I see that this translation is wrong. This is the *kaddish yatom:* it is not the "mourner's kaddish," it is the "orphan's kaddish."

Elsewhere in Benjamin Zev, another responsum about the kaddish. This one is really interesting. It is provoked not by an inquiry, but by an observation. "Since I have observed people being strict, when there are mourners for their parents in the synagogue, not to say kaddish on the New Moons and the Sabbaths and the holidays during the year of mourning, I have attempted to find proof that they are wrong and support for those who say kaddish on New Moons and Sabbaths and holidays." So the old contest between joy and sorrow in Ashkenaz in the eleventh century, the controversy between the funeral customs of Mainz and the funeral customs of Worms, survived in the form of a disagreement about the appropriateness of the orphan's kaddish on the days of joy! Benjamin Zev does not approve of the view that denies the mourner the fulfillment of his duty on those days. He cites custom against it: "How splendid is the practice of the Ashkenazim that I have seen here in the congregation of Venice, this city of sages, who, in the matter of kaddish, make no distinctions between the ordinary weekday and the Sabbaths and holidays and New Moons! This, in my humble opinion, is how it should be done." And he cites a text. A text that is, for my purposes, a treasure.

The text that Benjamin Zev cites is a responsum "that I have found" by Isaac of Corbeil. Isaac's responsum is a brief review of the custom of the mourner's kaddish—when it should be said, which mourners have priority in the saying of it, and so on. I am thrilled to discover this responsum because Isaac lived in France in the thirteenth century—he was the author of the so-called *Sefer Mitsvot Katan*, or the *Small Book of Commandments*, a work that influenced many medieval and early modern jurists. Isaac's responsum, in other words, is one of the earliest discussions of the orphan's kaddish. It is certainly the earliest responsum on the subject that I have discovered. What is so striking about this early text is its tone of familiarity with the kaddish and its problems. "As for the case of a man who had one son and another man who had two sons—every single son is obligated to honor his father, and after his [father's] death as well. Thus it is fitting that the task be shared, so that the son of the first man may recite [the kaddish] for his father, and the son of the second man may recite [the kaddish] for his father." Isaac writes of the kaddish as if it is already an institution. This impression is confirmed later in the text, when he tells of "an old man [who] told me that he had commanded his sons that after his death they should pray and say the kaddish." This old man must have acted according to the custom of his fathers—more evidence that the kaddish has come to me from the twelfth century.

Isaac makes it clear that the orphan's kaddish is a short and expedient prayer—an abbreviated version of the "full kaddish" that appears elsewhere in the worship—that was established for minors. Adult mourners, by contrast, can acquit themselves with the full kaddish elsewhere in the service, and with all the other prayers. After all, he writes, "prayer is the equal of the kaddish and is more splendid than it." And here is the part of Isaac's responsum that interests Benjamin Zev: Isaac has "heard that there is an erroneous popular view that the kaddish that is said on the Sabbath or the worship [that is said on the Sabbath] does not avail the dead as much as the kaddish that is said by boys on weekdays. But if the abridged kaddish [that is said by boys on weekdays] profits the dead, then surely the full kaddish [that is said by the man leading the prayers] profits them even more." This is Benjamin Zev's proof that "we are not to be overly strict about not saying the kaddish, and certainly not about [having the mourner lead] the prayers, on Sabbaths and holidays and New Moons, exactly as it is said on ordinary days, because it profits [the dead] on those days as it does on the other days." Benjamin Zev has found his answer.

In his little miscellany of considerations on the kaddish, Isaac of Corbeil stresses the needs of young mourners. "Indeed, those men who recite the abridged kaddish are stealing from the minors, since they can [fulfill their obligation] with the full kaddish and the rest of the service. And to this day, when the anniversary of the death of my father and my mother arrives, if it falls on a weekday I lead the prayers until the abridged kaddish, and I leave this portion to the boy, since it is his." This is the earliest mention of the yahrzeit, and of the obligation to recite the mourner's kaddish on that day of commemoration, that I have come across. Three centuries later Benjamin Zev adduces the prevalence of the yahrzeit as further proof that the kaddish must be said on Sabbaths and holidays. "We see everywhere that every year, on the anniversary of the death of a father or a mother, people mortify themselves and say the kaddish for their sake in the house of prayer. But if it were true, as some say, that the kaddish is not to be said on Sabbaths and holidays and New Moons, since the dead are relieved from their torments on those days, and if they say kaddish they would be comparing the dead to the wicked [whose torments do not end when the year of mourning ends], then it would be necessary to prevent them from fasting on the anniversary of the day that their parents died, since the days of judgment have passed, and this custom would not be legitimate. But from the fact that it is practiced without interference, we must conclude that it is proper to say the kaddish on Sabbaths and holidays and New Moons, even though the dead rest on those days." This is a fine illustration of the authority of custom in Jewish jurisprudence. The rabbis do not only argue from principles to practices. They argue also from practices to principles.

"An old man told me that he had commanded his sons that after his death they should pray and recite the kaddish beyond the seven days of mourning, a full thirty days, on weekdays and on the Sabbath. And so I myself commanded my sons to do when their mother died. And I have heard that this was the ruling of the Perfumer." Isaac of Corbeil's testimony about the early history of the custom is very valuable. And here is more proof, for Benjamin Zev, of the precedent of not excluding the mourner's prayer from the Sabbath service. Still, the old man's injunction is a little puzzling. Why did he limit his request to thirty days, when contemporary sources in Ashkenaz prescribe the orphan's kaddish duty for a full year? And that is not all that puzzles me in Isaac's text. He makes a remark about the kaddish that I have seen nowhere else. The kaddish should be said, in his opinion, "for twelve months and ten days"—so much for the old man's restriction on its duration—"as against the year of the Flood." Isaac hastens to add the familiar qualification that the twelve months should be abbreviated to eleven months, "so that no one equates his father with the wicked of Israel, even if his judgment takes twelve months"; but it is the reference to the Flood, and the additional ten days that are added to the kaddish to commemorate the Flood, that is so peculiar. Why the Flood? Why ten days? Isaac makes a calculation of the duration of the Flood, based on a comment by Rashi on Genesis and an astronomical consideration, to the effect that the deluge lasted a year. So the year of mourning is linked, in Isaac's mind, to the year of the punishment of the world by water. Why? He does not say. Because one death broaches all death? Because a grieving man sometimes has trouble keeping his head above water?

For five years now I have hung on the refrigerator in my kitchen a postcard that was sent to me by a friend, a much older man, and one of the handful of people I have known who possessed a spiritual temperament of their own. "It's sad about your domestic situation," he wrote, to fortify me in a time of trouble. "I find prayer efficacious if not spent too much time on my knees." He died last year, too.

On an autumn day in 1521, Benjamin Zev and two colleagues certified that a fellow named Moses Sousi was dead. "On Wednesday, the eighth day of the month of Ḥeshvan in the year 5281 . . . Rabbi Samuel ben Solomon appeared before us. He testified that one day he was sitting in the doorway of his house, when a Turk approached him and said: 'Samuel, would you sew such and such a linen garment for me?' (It was the sort of garment that Samuel customarily made for him.) Samuel replied: 'I don't have time right now. I have too much work. I will make it for you later.' The Turk also said to him: 'None of you has heard anything from Moses Sousi, have you?' Samuel said: 'No.' The Turk said: 'Then know that a certain Turk has murdered him.' Samuel also testified that on the day that it was rumored that Moses Sousi had run away, he [Samuel] encountered a Turk from outside the city. 'Have you seen Moses Sousi?' Samuel inquired of him. 'He is said to be somewhere in your orchard.' And the Turk turned on him angrily, and almost drew his sword. And when we heard these testimonies, we recorded them in the records of the community." The consequence of Benjamin Zev's acceptance of Samuel's testimony was that the wife of Moses Sousi was permitted to marry again. The rabbi ruled that she was not an *agunah,* a woman who is forbidden to marry a second husband because the evidence of the death of her first husband is not conclusive. But no sooner had Benjamin Zev released his lenient ruling about the wife of Moses Sousi than all hell broke loose. Moses Sousi was sighted in Salonika. Moses Sousi was sighted in Egypt. And David ben Hayyim Ha'Cohen of Corfu challenged Benjamin Zev's ruling, on evidentiary and other grounds. "I tried to vindicate you in any way possible," David wrote to Benjamin Zev, "but what can I do? My Father in heaven said that I am not to be intimidated by any man. . . . I hereby inform you that very unpleasant things are being said about you—that you have permitted forbidden women—and it is a terrible charge. I advise you, if you do not wish to get yourself into such situations, not to rely on yourself. Consult with the scholars of our generation, who are all around you." The controversy between the rabbi of Arta and the rabbi of Corfu lasted a decade, and bitterly divided the authorities of Italy and the Levant. A hundred pages in Benjamin Zev's reponsa are taken up with the texts of the dispute. (He prints the opinions of all sides.) There is a great deal of politesse in these harsh and learned exchanges, but I'm not sure that it was entirely insincere. For I have found the rabbi of Corfu collegially citing the rabbi of Arta in a responsum about the orphan's kaddish.

David ben Hayyim of Corfu spent the last year of his life in Adrianople, where he died in 1530. Most of his works were destroyed in a fire in his son's house, except for thirty responsa. The son published them in Constantinople in 1537. (The title page of the second edition, which appeared in Ostrow in 1834, recounts that "the son's property was consumed but the book was saved, even though the fire was large and it burned all around, and there were only two rulings that were not singed by the flame; but the book survived, it was a miracle.") David's thirtieth responsum treats this perplexity: "One of the apostates who left the religion of Israel for the religion of the Baal-worshipers, under the pressure of the decree of the government that in the ancient days decreed that Jews must reject their religion in favor of the religion of the Baal-worshipers—this apostate was murdered on the road by robbers, and the robbers left his flesh for the birds of the heaven and the beasts of the field. Now his son wishes to say kaddish for the repose of his father. But there are other mourners in the house of worship, whose fathers were Jews when they died. Do they have priority in the recitation of kaddish, or may this mourner whose father died an apostate recite the kaddish in the regular manner, as one of them?"

The "apostates" were the marranos, the "Baal-worshipers" were the Christians, and "the ancient days" were not ancient at all. In this responsum, the drama of mourning is once again set in the context of the Iberian drama of the fourteenth and fifteenth centuries. (David may have disguised the heresy and the history to fool the censors.) Like the rabbi of Arta, the rabbi of Corfu has been asked to allow the grieving son of a Christian who was a Jew to honor his tormented and murdered father with the kaddish. And David's ruling is ringingly clear: "I am always uneasy about making decisions, but in my humble opinion, and at a glance, this case does require a great authority to decide it. It is obvious that this mourner whose father was killed in his apostasy must recite the kaddish as one of the mourners." And David provides the principle on which he has based his ruling: "Even though he sinned, he is a Jew."

"Even though he sinned, he is a Jew": this is one of the most momentous sentences in the history of the Jews. Its source is the Talmud, in its discussion of the sin of Achan, of the tribe of Judah, who "took of the accursed thing," causing Joshua's army to be routed by the army of Ai. When Joshua rent his clothes and fell to the ground and beseeched God to inform him of the reason for the defeat of the Israelites, he was told that "Israel hath sinned." Achan subsequently confessed and was stoned to death, and "the Lord turned from the fierceness of his anger." In the Talmud, Rabbi Abba bar Zabda sees a fine point in God's words to Joshua. "'Israel hath sinned': Rabbi Abba bar Zabda said: Even though it sinned, it is still Israel." Israel's guilt has not erased Israel's identity, Israel's sanctity. Sinning Jews are still Jews. And Rabbi Abba continued: "As people say, a myrtle that is found among the reeds is still a myrtle, and it is still called a myrtle."

For the rabbis, the perdurability of the myrtle was not only a matter of solace, it was also a matter of law. In the Middle Ages, the principle that "even though he sinned, he is a Jew" became Jewry's great resource against the ravages of forced apostasy in Ashkenaz (where Rashi adapted the Talmudic statement to the aftermath of the First Crusade) and in Spain. It appears again and again in the wake of the cross. Converts could be welcomed back if conversion was not really defection. For even in the depths of Christian society, where they lived as Christians, they were Jews. (This comes perilously close to a racialist definition of Jewishness, I know; but what was perilous for these people was not Jewish racialism, but anti-Jewish racialism.) So I am not at all surprised to find the rabbi of Corfu, a small island that received exiles and *conversos* from Spain and Portugal, invoking this principle of rescue to allow the kaddish to be said for the apostate who was murdered. "For even though he sinned, he is a Jew," David writes about the dead man. "As it says [in the Talmud], 'Israel hath sinned': Rabbi Abba bar Zabda said: Even though it sinned, it is still Israel. And as people say, a myrtle that is found among the reeds is still a myrtle, and is still called a myrtle. After all, as it is taught in the same passage, Achan transgressed against all five books of the Torah, but he was nonetheless referred to as 'Israel.'"

"Even though he sinned, he is a Jew." The Jews save themselves with definitions.

"Even though he sinned, he is a Jew." For ancient Jews and medieval Jews, there was no escape from Jewishness, and this was their happiness. Can modern Jews understand such happiness? For modern Jews, who are everywhere escaping, "even though he sinned, he is a Jew" does not sound like an instrument of compassion. It sounds like an instrument of enforcement. Modern Jews do not fear oppressive Christianity. They fear oppressive Judaism. (Some of them, of course, escape their tradition guiltily. For these Jews, "even though he sinned, he is a Jew" might be received as a kind of fail-safe, as the Talmud's premonition of the easy ethnicity in which they sooner or later seek refuge.)

"Even though he sinned, he is a Jew." This is a manifesto of involuntarism. It takes Jewish identity out of the hands of Jews. (They are not to be trusted with it.)

The voluntarism of modern Jewish identity was one of the great revolutions of Jewish history. Like all revolutions, however, it exaggerated. It made foolish Nietzschean demands of ordinary men and women. But most people do not invent themselves. Most of them choose to be what they already are. This is a kind of honor, too.

Freedom is not expressed in self-hatred. Indeed, self-hatred is a form of unfreedom.

Do you wish to subtract what you have been given? Well, you can't. But there is something you can do. You can add.

The additive nature of human existence: on this dazzling fact all orthodoxies and all heterodoxies come to grief.

We are various, and variety confers responsibility. Variety is an ethics, not an aesthetics; a doctrine of fidelities.

If you are many things, then there are many things for you to learn, to develop, to protect.

The more you cherish, the more you work.

"Even though he sinned, he is a Jew." Fine. But what else is he?

The orchids on my desk died last night. And in the morning there were white and pink flowers strewn over my books, as if my books had died.

"There is much more to be said on this matter," David of Corfu writes, "but there is no time. So I will be brief and say that the son [of the murdered apostate] acquits him [with a kaddish], for the son acquits the father, as the Talmud says." But the rabbi is anything but brief. He proceeds to an extended justification of his ruling. Some of his reasons and his prooftexts are familiar to me. Against those who would argue that "since the son is required to honor his father and mother in death as in life, and since there is no greater honor than the son's vindication of his parent [by means of the kaddish], then we must give precedence in the recitation of the kaddish to the mourner whose father died a Jew, on the grounds that he is more obligated to honor his father than the mourner whose father was an apostate to Baal," David responds that this is nonsense, that the filial obligation of the one is not greater than the filial obligation of the other, and he cites Maimonides to prove his point. David's summary of the Maimonidean view is that "the son is obligated to honor the father even if the father was wicked, and even if he committed adultery and did not repent, and even if he is guilty of other transgressions, and maybe even if he was an apostate and an idolator with an intention to outrage." David concedes that there are differences of opinion about the latter case, but "in a case such as this one, in which the apostate was killed by robbers, everybody would agree that the son is obligated to honor the father and to recite the kaddish for the repose of his soul, because his murder was his absolution." David also adduces the precedent of Hezekiah, the king of Judah, who dragged his wicked father's bones to burial to atone for his wickedness, and the sages concurred that he did the right thing: "Whatever the son can do to earn merit for the father, he must do, even if the father was an idolator with an intention to outrage, as Ahaz [Hezekiah's father] was. . . . If Hezekiah's action had not benefited his father, he would not have done it, and the sages would not have concurred."

Not that the marranos are as evil as Ahaz. Quite the contrary. David hastens to add that a man like this murdered apostate is not "an apostate with an intention to outrage," he is merely "an apostate for his own benefit," which is a lesser kind of villainy. Indeed, David states categorically about all the crypto-Jews of Spain and Portugal that "all of these apostates are only apostates for their own benefit." By their benefit, he means their survival. Their Christianity is not principled, it is pragmatic. They cannot be condemned, because they are the victims of circumstance. "If they commit transgressions, if they eat forbidden foods, they do so practically, not provocatively. . . . [They are] apostates by force, who abandoned their faith under compulsion. . . . If they remain where they are and do not flee, it is because it would be harmful to do otherwise. And if they appear to take part in the service of Baal, it is because they are coerced to do so, for if they did not, they would be killed." David then cites the opinion of Asher ben Jehiel, who fled the atrocities of Germany in the early years of the fourteenth century and went to Spain. "Asher ben Jehiel was asked whether such people are like apostates who eat forbidden things with an intention to outrage, and he said no, they are to be considered as those who have been forcibly taken prisoner by idolators, and they do what they do for their own survival."

David also reveals that he knows more about the facts of this case. It turns out that the man for whom he is permitting the kaddish to be said was not merely murdered in his apostasy. He was murdered also in his repentance. He was on his way back. This is the extraordinary conclusion of David's opinion: "All the more must this apostate who was killed not be regarded as an apostate who eats forbidden things with an intention to outrage, because I have heard that he came as far as Arta for the purpose of returning to Judaism, but there he was robbed and all his money was stolen, and he returned to his country [Spain or Portugal] to earn some more money. Later he made it back to this place, and he was on his way to Arta when he was captured by robbers who took everything he had. So there is reason to believe that this poor man remained in his country all that time only for his own sake, and it was his intention to return to Arta to become a Jew. Obviously he is no worse than those apostates from whom the Talmud permits us to accept sacrifices. When he was murdered, moreover, he found atonement. So it is entirely fitting that his son recite the kaddish for him among the mourners. May God remove the sin of the serpent from upon us and send us our redeemer and save us from errors, amen.

Thus has David ben Hayyim Ha'Cohen spoken, who is burdened by the convulsions of his time."

What an unlucky man! In David's account, though, he was not only a victim, he was also a hero. And on the next page of the book that is open before me, I learn why David found it necessary to explain why his hero "remained in his country," and endured his double life, for as long as he did. The Ostrow edition of 1834 prints as an appendix the texts of four responsa that were censored from the Constantinople edition of 1537, and the first of the censored responsa begins with this stringency: "It is perfectly plain that a Jew who is compelled by the ruler of the city to worship idols, and has the ability to leave the realm of that evil ruler and go to another realm where he can worship his Creator, but does not do so—such a man is considered an idolator not by accident but by design." An idolator by design: in Jewish law, this is a malediction. But it does not fall upon the brave and loyal son of Israel struck down by the highwayman of Arta. He must have his kaddish!

David's text reminds me of a remark by a Portuguese marrano of the seventeenth century who was tortured and imprisoned by the Inquisition and eventually made it to Amsterdam, where he became a great defender of Judaism. Looking back on his dangerous and divided life in Portugal, he explained: "I showed a Christian face because I am fond of living." When I came across this statement years ago, I was pleased by its sardonic tone. It is not a tone that you hear much in the medieval and early modern literature of the Jews; but they earned it.

Today is the first day of the eleventh month, the final month of kaddish. I thought that this would bring me cheer. When I left shul this morning, however, I was anxious. Suddenly the kaddish felt like a farewell, and I did not want it to end. For as long as I have been organizing my life around the kaddish, I have been organizing my life around my father. When kaddish is over, he will be gone. My strict observance of the year of mourning has had the consequence of delaying the return of a normal life. I have lived in a state of suspension, shielded from a fatherless world by a fatherful practice. The Jewish way of mourning has turned an absence into a presence. Perhaps this is not so brilliant, I mean psychologically. As the end of the kaddish nears, I am scared. An absence is an absence. There is no point in pretending otherwise.

You do not relieve a man's sadness by making it into his distinction.

A man walked into shul this afternoon who had buried his son this morning, and we all gave way before his grief. He led the prayers, as he will lead them for a while; but he will say kaddish only for thirty days, for the father does not acquit the son. My duties as the emissary of the congregation may be over. (Though on the last day of my father's kaddish I will have one last turn at the head of the flock.) I had a father, he had a son. There is something nastier than the natural working of the world, and it is the unnatural working of the world.

I was checking a reference in the sharp little digest of the laws of the kaddish by Ephraim Margolioth, the early-nineteenth-century rabbi and businessman of Brody whose misogyny annoyed me months ago; and Meshullam Finkelstein of Warsaw, whose misogyny annoyed me even more, remarks in a commentary on Margolioth's text that "the pains of hell are not a sixtieth of the pains that the sinful soul suffers before its entry to hell, and it is written in the kabbalistic books that for this reason it is fitting, even after the twelve months of mourning have concluded, that the son have the countenance of his father etched before him, and that he imagine it crying bitterly, 'Deliver my soul from the sword; my darling from the power of the dog!' " Just as I suspected: the saga of me and my father's soul will never end! Once a mourner, always a mourner. Here is Jewish lachrymosity at its best.

But who is this Finkelstein to sentence me to a lifetime of metaphysical worry? I must say that his authority is not enhanced in my eyes by the asterisk with which he concludes his citation from Psalms, which refers me to some mystical inanity of the sixteenth century about the eschatological significance of dogs. (Since the dog is sentient even in its sleep, it guards the road to heaven, so that the soul seeking to avoid the thirty thousand roads to hell cannot sneak by.) And the macabre Meshullam is not yet finished. Even the son of a righteous man is not relieved of his duties after twelve months, he says. "Even if he believes that his father is a righteous man and his soul delights in the abundance [of heaven], he should imagine that he is providing his father with the delicacies that his father loved, for Torah and good deeds and charity for the soul of his father are his father's delicacies." Your father may have been a saint, but he will require you forever. In the Jewish family, neediness does not end at death. You must eternally write, you must eternally call!

Indeed, Finkelstein suggests that the far-sighted parent provide for himself: "A man should command his sons to commit themselves for their lifetime to the fulfillment of a particular commandment, and if they fulfill it, this will be valued more highly than the saying of kaddish." And he concludes: "This is an excellent device for those who have no sons but only daughters." This was Abraham Horowitz's splendid suggestion a few centuries earlier; and it somewhat qualifies my view of Finkelstein's indifference to the sorrow of Jewish women. It is always nice to find a rabbi concerned about the women. Finkelstein's morbidity is egalitarian, and I admire him for it. If Jewish sons cannot get away, neither can Jewish daughters. This is what the enfranchisement of women in Judaism means: a more equitable distribution of the burden.

A person who has known death is not like a person who has not known death. But henceforth death is not all that such a person knows.

It snowed this Sabbath morning, and when services were over and we stepped outside, there were some who gasped at the beauty of what they saw. A great whitening had taken place. I went for a walk in Rock Creek Park. My eyes struggled to keep faith with the forms. The snow repeated every curve and every plane, so that each branch and each rock was a lighter version and a darker version of itself. Every object came with a shroud. But the sight was not saddening. It was the picture of a refinement. This, too, was a test of the quality of my attention. Here were patterns of light and dark that were not patterns of good and evil.

XII

It is getting near the end of my father's kaddish, and the friend with whom I am sharing mourner's duties at the shul, whose father died a few weeks after mine, suggested that we consult the calendar to determine the date of the last kaddish. We sat down with the rabbi and looked at the calendar. I received a shock. It appears that I miscalculated. My eleven months ended a month ago! I have said kaddish for my father, in my innocence, in his innocence, for twelve months. It is over.

I was shaken by the news. I told the rabbi that this is unacceptable, that I cannot simply stop, that I must have a last day with the kaddish. We agreed that it will be the day after tomorrow.

In his innocence, Lord of the Universe, in his innocence. I have recited the kaddish thirty more days for him, in his innocence.

All this study, and I failed to arrive at the most elementary grasp of my situation! I hate the calendar and its indifferent, inexorable numbers. It is the coldest piece of paper in the world. In the early months I thought that it would be vulgar to know when the kaddish would be over, as if I were eager for it to end; and as the months wore on, I did not want the kaddish to end, and so I stopped marking time. I outwitted myself.

Or maybe I didn't. In my error, I honored my father excessively. My father always thought that he should be honored excessively. I imagine him bragging to the others about his kaddish: "Eleven months? Big deal! My son—maybe you've heard of him?—for twelve months my son . . ."

I told a friend what had happened and she said: "Your lucky father. His son can't count, but he can pray."

I called my mother to tell her what I had sworn to myself that I would one day tell her: that I had done it, that it is done. My voice trembled. This is the day on which she has the proof of my love.

My father's kaddish ends as my father's kaddish began, suddenly.

But wait. Surely the Hebrew anniversary of my father's death cannot fall so far short of the English anniversary. The whole thing seems too swift. I ask my mother to check the documents in her possession. She reveals that I was mistaken. I confused the day of my father's death with the day that I stop praying for him. For my kaddish ends a month before the anniversary of his death, so as not to impute wickedness to him. In fact, my kaddish ends—today!

My kaddish, his kaddish: which is it?

I call the rabbi and we have a little laugh. We agree that we will stick to our schedule, that I will conclude my kaddish tomorrow.

I confused the day of my father's death with the day that I stop praying for him. The psychology of my failure to establish the date properly is obvious, and boring. I prefer the poetry of it. I prefer to think that my soul has been spinning out of time. Chronological time is not the same as spiritual time. The calendar establishes only the external stops and starts of religious life. But the internal motions . . .

So my father does not get the gift of another month of kaddish, he gets the gift of only a few more days of kaddish. Come to think of it, this is exactly the way it used to be. He wanted the most, and I gave him only more.

In his innocence, Lord of the Universe, in his innocence. I have recited the kaddish two days more for him, in his innocence.

So back to the drill. Morning, afternoon, evening. The last day. But the drill was diversified this afternoon. The lobbyists' office from which I lobby for my father's soul is across the street from a cathedral. When I turned the corner onto Rhode Island Avenue, the red brick of the church glowed in an unexpected winter sun, and hundreds of people poured down the steps and onto the street, where they were greeted by priests in lavender vestments. It was Ash Wednesday and a mass had just concluded. I liked the spectacle of these urbane men and women marked by ash. They, too, had interrupted their business for a godly dolorousness. I was moving against the crowd, as a Jew should move in a Christian crowd; but I felt also a sensation of solidarity. Together we were raising the avenue out of its profanity. In this city, not a small thing.

It is the last day of kaddish. At home after the evening prayers, I feel a need not to speak. I think of my father, strongly but serenely. I have a few sips of grappa. From the window of my kitchen, I see the moon in a black sky, a sliver of light in the shape of a comma. The celestial punctuation of terrestrial toil. I wash a few dishes, and watch the water scatter the remains of a meal and rinse away the stains, until the white plates are clean.

This last morning I shared the task of leading the service with the man whose son died. The thoughts that distracted me from the prayers were all the appropriate ones—my father, my tradition, my father, my tradition, my father, my tradition—but they were distractions all the same. Just pray, I said to myself. Just pray.

This last morning I would have wished to make a beautiful sound, to sing with a voice that finds favor, but it was only the sound of my own voice that I heard. There were moments of release along the way to the kaddish. "Hear, our God, our prayer . . . and do not return us empty from your presence": those were my father's favorite words in the prayerbook. And in the psalm of the day, I was heightened by this verse: "I am the Lord thy God which brought thee out of the land of Egypt, open thy mouth wide and I will fill it!" At the crossroads of belief and appetite: there I will live. And then came the kaddish, which I recited softly, almost in a whisper, not like a man making an argument, but like a man taking his leave. Magnified and sanctified . . . After the service all the company gathered round to raise the customary glass to the soul whose kaddish has concluded. "For the soul an ascension, for the Jews a redemption": the man with the resonant voice recited the pithy couplet, and we all downed our drinks. A few friends came up to me and wished my father's soul a fine fate and went off to work. I took a deep breath. Only the afternoon kaddish remained.

It went quickly. The Talmud stood on the shelf before me as I prayed, and as I uttered the last words of my father's kaddish I rested my hand on the Talmud, almost as if I were taking an oath. "He who makes peace in His high places, may He make peace on us and on all of Israel, and all say amen!" And all said amen. I was done. There were no eruptions. I was not plunged into despair and I was not lifted into joy. Time kept beating.

I kept my promise.

I took the rest of the day off and drove around town. Grand streets, gutted streets: a city of pomp and ruin.

Eventually I made my way to Rock Creek Cemetery, to my sanctuary in the city, the figure of cowled contemplation by Saint-Gaudens that marks the grave of Henry Adams and his suicide wife. I do not know a more universal corner or a more concentrating sight than this Western figure in an Eastern spirit, beyond believing and beyond not believing. It is mute in a manner that makes other statues seem to chatter; it would not speak if it could. I come here often, and never without reciting to myself what Adams once wrote about the meaning of this obscure place: "The most dignified thing for a worm to do was to sit up and sit still." Sitting up and sitting still was what I needed today. The snow had not yet melted from the polished granite bench. I cleared a seat for myself and for an hour I sat. Nothing significant was thought or felt. Instead I rested in the precincts of seriousness. Then I walked back to my car down the muddy slope, on straw that had been scattered to provide a surer footing on the slippery ground.

I drove around the city some more. I stopped to buy some fruit. When I returned home, an abandoned crutch was lying in the alley behind the house.

It is my first morning without the kaddish. Now I am a mourner without an instrument.

No, I have an instrument. I took to the teahouse a compilation of rulings, customs, and homilies by Joseph Hahn Nordlingen, rabbi of Frankfurt, that he completed in 1630. I recall the book from my study of the persecutions of the Jews, since it is a vivid source for the Fettmilch riots of 1616, in which a guild leader named Vincent Fettmilch incited violence against the Jews of Frankfurt, who were forced to flee the city. Hahn records that the emperor arrested Fettmilch, and hanged him and his followers, and invited the Jews to witness the hanging, "and when the people of the city saw the deference with which the imperial officials treated us, they dared not speak against us, but instead they helped us to clear the rubble from our quarter." All this occurred in the month of Adar, the month of Purim, and so Hahn records that the Jews of Frankfurt established a new Purim, "Purim Vincent," on the twentieth day of the month, to celebrate their salvation from the "new Haman." But this is not what interests me now. I have found in Hahn's work an arresting comment about the orphan's kaddish.

"It is known that [the kaddish] raises the dead from hell, and to this end it is best to pray every prayer as best one can," Hahn writes. And he adds: "But this regulation is designed only for the ignorant." The kaddish, in Hahn's view, is a concession to the coarse realities of Jewish religious life, to the intellectual incompetence that he describes rather witheringly earlier in his book, where he writes that "whoever has it in his heart to understand [the prayers], but owing to his laziness has not troubled to understand them—such a person is a sinner, since he does not wish to direct himself to the proper intention. In my eyes, he is almost like someone who introduces an idol into the sanctuary. . . . The duty to study the prayers and to explain the prayers precedes any other study in the world."

So, then, what is the proper way to accomplish the objective of the kaddish? Hahn has an emphatic answer: "The study of Torah profits sevenfold more than all prayer, and by means of it the dead may be admitted to Eden. If the son breaks new ground in the study of Torah, there is no measure to the credit that accrues to his father in the session [literally, the yeshiva] above. . . . And so every mourner for a father or a mother should strive to make the utmost effort to study as much as possible according to his capacity."

I like Hahn's priorities. If the son's study is preferable to the son's prayer, then my father is headed for heaven. Anyway, kaddish is over. Study is all that remains for me. Hahn's suggestion is perfectly timed.

In Judaism, the antinomy between prayer and study is ancient. I remember this passage from the Talmud: "Raba observed Rabbi Himnona prolonging his prayers. He said: 'They abandon the life that does not pass for the life that passes.' He believed that the time for study should be kept apart from the time for prayer. Rabbi Jeremiah came before Rabbi Zera and busied himself with study, and when the hour for prayer was nigh, Rabbi Jeremiah hurried to finish, whereupon Rabbi Zera adduced against him the verse [from Proverbs], 'He that turneth his ear away from hearing the law, even his prayer shall be an abomination.'" In the Jewish tradition, prayer and study have often denoted different religious ideals, different spiritual styles. Not least because I have fared poorly with the one and nicely with the other, my own preference has been clear to me for a long time.

The difference between study and prayer is the difference between thinking and feeling, between knowing and wanting, between what is within our power and what is beyond our power, between toil and arousal, between the life that does not pass and the life that passes.

The beginning of the twelfth month. I am still a mourner. It is only an eschatological technicality that forbids the kaddish to be said for the twelve months of mourning. For the final month of my mourning, therefore, I will attend shul faithfully, except that I will not recite the kaddish, I will merely respond to the kaddish. For the other mourners, I will be there to say amen, and may the Name of the Lord be blessed for ever and ever, and may these other sons and daughters acquit those other fathers and mothers. Tonight, in my new role, I said amen, and may the Name of the Lord be blessed for ever and ever. The others smiled at me, as if I were the lucky one who got away. But I didn't get away.

And a fine, banal evening in shul it was. There were the usual jitters about the quorum. Pointing to the local Jewish newspaper on the table, one man said: "Maybe we should read the obituaries and see who the mourners are." Where there's death, there's hope. Another man looked at him and asked: "Are you in trusts and estates?" We all agreed that the shul should not have to depend for its services on its mourners. Death is a poor foundation for community. (But it helps.) Eventually there were ten and I said amen.

When the others rise to say kaddish, I also rise, but I stand silent. I am with them but I am not of them. I am a mourner on his way out of mourning, a man in the halfway house of grief, whose release from death's company has at last been granted.

"Amen." The tiny Hebrew word denotes faith, hope, enthusiasm, finality, belonging, the answerability of man. In the Talmud they speak of an "orphaned amen." An orphaned amen is an amen uttered after a blessing that you have not heard. An orphaned amen is forbidden. "He who says an orphaned amen—his sons will be orphans," the second-century sage Ben Azzai icily warns. So there is an orphaned amen and there is an orphan's amen. After a while you start collecting these things, like butterflies.

"Amen." It is not a natural utterance. You must learn to say it.

"All of a sudden, a voice, behind us." So begins a chapter in Jorge Semprun's memoir, which arrived in the office today. "A voice? More like a bestial moan. The inarticulate groaning of a wounded animal. A bloodcurdling wail of lamentation." Semprun is recalling the events of April 14, 1945, three days after the liberation of Buchenwald, where he was interned. "'You hear that?' [his friend Albert asks him about the voice]. 'What is that?' 'Death,' I told him. 'Who else?' It was death that was humming, no doubt, somewhere between the heaps of corpses. The life of death, making itself heard. . . . Albert's face went livid. He strained to hear, and suddenly became frantic, squeezing my arm painfully. 'Yiddish!' he shouted. 'It's speaking Yiddish!' So, death spoke Yiddish. . . . We take a few steps down the center aisle, and stop. We listen hard, trying to determine where the voice is coming from. Albert is panting. 'It's the prayer for the dead,' he whispers. . . . Two minutes later we have extracted from a heap of corpses the dying man through whose mouth death is singing to us." As I read this, my blood freezes. It was not Yiddish that was sounding, it was Aramaic. A Jew was saying kaddish in a quorum of corpses. For himself? For the others? For the universe? This is the most terrible kaddish there ever was.

But then Semprun almost ruins it for me. "We carry the man out in front of the hut, into the April sunshine. We lay him down on a pile of rags that Albert has collected. The man doesn't open his eyes, but he hasn't stopped singing, in a rough, barely audible voice. I have never seen a human face that more closely resembled that of the crucified Christ." Come again? "Of course, Christ on the Cross does not usually intone the Jewish prayer for the dead, but this is a minor detail. There is nothing from a theological point of view, I presume, to prevent Christ from chanting the Kaddish." This disgusts me. It reminds me of the painting that Chagall painted to protest the fate of the Jews in Europe, the one that hangs in the museum in Chicago, in which a bearded Jew is hung on a cross. A Christian civilization was exterminating the Jews, and the Jewish painter portrays the Jews as Jesus! This is not paradoxical, it is dishonorable. And here is Semprun, writing similarly of "my Christ of the Kaddish."

I flew to New York and met my mother and my sister at the cemetery, to make the final arrangements for my father's monument. A concrete foundation for the stone had been sloppily laid. I stood at the spot, the acquitting son. I thought of the wooden box buried a few feet beneath my boots. I was not moved by the thought. It is not my father who lies in the cold ground, it is the physical remains of my father. No, my father is to be found elsewhere. He is to be found in retrospection, or not at all.

The difference between the living and the dead is the difference between the remembered and the forgotten. To be alive but forgotten, or neglected, or denied: is that not a kind of death? And to be dead but remembered, or studied, or missed: is that not a kind of life?

My mother and my sister joined me at the spot. The sun was at our backs and threw our shadows on the grave. I saw three shadows and a shade. We agreed to plant ivy, and we left.

When the last person who remembers my father dies, then my father will no longer be alive. He will not be memory, he will be history. In America, to be history is to be over. "He is history": the phrase means that there is no sense in which he continues to exist, to engage the living. Here history is a kindly oblivion. (It is not the Potomac that flows through this city. It is the Lethe.) But Jews despise oblivion. And yet we must not gloat. Often we take our historical consciousness too far. We are idolatrous about history. But there are things more lasting than history.

History is the Baal of modernity.

Back in Washington. Green shoots are breaking through the thawing ground and I am getting sick of symbolism.

I can't get Semprun's story out of my mind. When I mention it to a friend, he refers me to a volume of documents about the fate of religious Jews in the Holocaust. I think I have the book somewhere on my shelves. Yes, I do. I open it and read about the fate of the Jews in the town of Szydlowiec, in central Poland. In September 1942, thousands of Jews were deported from Szydlowiec to Treblinka. I read: "In the second car [of the train that was carrying them to the death camp], the philanthropist and communal leader Isaac Steinman took candles out of his pocket, and as he lit them he said: 'Jews! Since nobody will be left behind to say kaddish for us, let us fulfill our final obligation and say kaddish for ourselves!' They all jumped to their feet and with burning tears and fathomless devotion said 'Magnified and sanctified be His great Name. . . .'"

And I read about the inscription found on the wall of the shul in the town of Kovel, where the Jews were herded as they waited to be taken to the cemetery and shot. One of them scrawled: "I, Yeruham ben Shlomo Ludmirer, was here on the fifth day of Tishrei, 1942. If any of my relatives survives, I request that they say kaddish for me."

And I read about a certain Rabbi Yeruham, who addressed his parishioners when they came to Treblinka: "Our journey through life is at an end. We have been brought here for destruction, fathers and mothers and their children, not a soul will remain. And so I say to you: let us say for ourselves the kaddish that in normal times our sons and our relatives would have said for us." And a witness later reported: "The great kaddish was heard."

All this buries me.

In this week's reading of the Torah, Moses is instructed to command the Israelites "that they bring thee pure olive oil beaten for the light, to cause the lamp to burn always." What is always? My edition of Scripture cites an ancient rabbinical observation: "Always, even on the Sabbath. Always, even in impurity." The rabbis were referring to the ritual requirements of the Tabernacle and the Temple, but I understand their statement more generally. Always is not a measure of time. Always is a measure of range. It is not necessary to burn every minute of every day. It is necessary to burn in all one's modes. The pure, the impure: there are no realms in which the flame should not flicker.

In an absence of mind, I started to say the kaddish at the end of the afternoon service today. There I stood, a mourning machine.

In religious life, habit is essential. In spiritual life, habit is shameful.

The light this morning looked like a new light. In the streets of Georgetown, perfect nightlessness. The shul looked as if it had been gilded a thin white gold, like an illumination in the margins of a manuscript.

Yesterday my kaddish-mate, whose period of mourning for his father roughly coincided with my own, said his last kaddish, and this morning was the first morning in more than a year that the prayers were not led by a mourner. The congregation seemed a little wistful. They will miss their mourners. Still, as one of them said, life was returning to normal. I'm not so sure. In a gathering without grief, human experience is inadequately represented.

I sat at the teahouse and watched people rushing places, and I decided that nothing will ever destroy the world. The children of parents are the parents of children. The students of teachers are the teachers of students. It will not end. When I opened my book, a compilation of the customs of the medieval Jewish communities of Austria and Germany, I had the same sensation of indelibility. The tradition is like the world. It is larger than everything in it. There is not one of us that has the power to bring it all down. It exists to endure. We are born into a being that loathes non-being, and this is our comfort.

Jacob ben Moses Ha'Levi Moellin died in Germany in 1427. He was a jurist, a teacher, an astronomer, a cantor. The yeshiva that he founded in Mainz in 1387 produced some of the greatest rabbis of Germany, Austria, and Bohemia, and he was their master. His practices were recorded and widely disseminated in a compilation by a student named Zalman of St. Goar—"a lowly shame of a man called Zalman," as he described himself in the introduction to the book. (Zalman was his nickname. He was born Eleazar ben Jacob.) Zalman included in his book some of Moellin's homilies for the holidays, and also Moellin's oral and written pronouncements on legal matters, as well as a record of the customs of some of Moellin's teachers. Moellin's ways, as his amanuensis explained, were exemplary: "I have observed and searched out the conduct of this man of God . . . because it is fitting to act as he did, who received the traditions from our great rabbis and was very careful to follow their customs." In these pages, Jewish life in Central Europe in the Middle Ages jumps to life. It is a book without philosophy, which is why I like to browse in it. It delivers me to a rough and vital culture of obedience, so strange and so familiar. Moellin leaves me marveling at the muscle of tradition. Now I have returned to him for a look at his ways of mourning. Fine new editions of his customs and his responsa have been produced in recent years in Jerusalem, and my bookseller in Brooklyn has sent them along.

Near the end of the chapter on mourning, I find a very touching account of his wife's death in 1426. Here it is (the words in brackets are interpolations from various manuscripts): "When Rabbi Moellin's wife died, a year before his death [in the year 4186, which was a year before he was summoned on high in the month of Elul, 4187, he in Worms and his wife in Mainz] [and when she died, he went into a room and wept loudly, and said: 'You wives and women, help me to mourn my wife, the crown that has fallen from my head'], her husband the rabbi walked at the head of the procession and carried the bier, and his son was with him. He instructed those who carried the bier with him to walk slowly and not to hurry. They placed the dead in the house in which the dead are cleansed and purified on the ground, [and the rabbi put down] the bier, and his son and his daughter sat by their mother and wailed for her. The rabbi went off to inspect the coffin, so that it would be made according to his wishes. In a loud voice he said the blessing that justifies the judgment, and his son stood to his left and said it with him, and the entire congregation gently with them. Then, as before, the mourners at the head of the procession carried the dead to the gravesite, and they placed the dead on the ground and they took their places at her head. The rabbi took a knife and cut all his outer garments, [and he cut all the garments of] his son, except his shirt. And he said to him that he should further rend each of them with his own hands, until he exposed his heart, and he performed the act of rending from the right, from his collar. [And he ordered the women to rend his daughter's clothes.] He ordered his children not to look into the coffin [and see the body lying there] when it was opened to lay the dead properly down in it. When they lowered the dead into the grave and began to cover it with dirt, the rabbi and his son repaired to the house in the cemetery, and it was still two hours before noon and the rabbi prayed the Eighteen Blessings prior to the arrival of the congregation from the gravesite. When they arrived, they washed their hands. His son began [to recite the kaddish for his mother] to say the rabbis' kaddish. His father did not recite it with him. Nor did the rabbi sit among the congregation. They went and tore grass and tossed it behind them. The rabbi walked in his shoes, and his son [and his daughter] walked without their shoes. And when he went to his house from the courtyard of the synagogue, the entire congregation escorted him, and the rabbi instructed them to pray there [in a quorum of ten] all the prayers [without omissions] exactly as they pray in the synagogue."

The story of Moellin's grief continues: "On the eve of the Sabbath [that fell during his seven days of mourning], when it was time to begin the evening prayer, the sexton went to summon the [mourning] rabbi. Nobody else went with him, and on that Sabbath he did not bless the children or his relatives [as he was accustomed to do on other Sabbaths]. As he left the house of worship in silence and went on his way, he did not say 'good Sabbath' to anybody, as was his custom to do every Sabbath, when he would stand for a while in front of the house of worship and greet strangers [ask strangers for news] and say 'good Sabbath' to the entire congregation. On the morning of the Sabbath he brought the *Four Pillars* to the synagogue, as he always did on the Sabbath, and I assume [I don't know for sure] that he studied the laws of mourning, for the mourner is forbidden to study during shivah [the seven days]. After the Sabbath [when it grew dark], the rabbi and his son stood [in the courtyard of the house of worship near the door] until the evening prayer was done, and then they went home. And on that same Sabbath the son of Rabbi Zalman Runkel was present. He had come to say the orphan's kaddish on the anniversary of his father's death. The custom in Mainz was that the orphan's kaddish is not said every day, but only three times on the Sabbath. Rabbi Moellin instructed his son to say kaddish for his mother on the Sabbath evening and on the Sabbath morning, and the son of Rabbi Zalman Runkel to say the kaddish at the conclusion of the Sabbath, otherwise his son would have to go home. And so he instituted the practice that when somebody appears to say kaddish on the anniversary of the death of a father or a mother, and there are local mourners present, he says it only once. And if there are no other mourners present, he says it the full three times."

For the modern reader, the legalistic details with which this narrative concludes may seem extraneous to it, a casuistic anticlimax; but they are the climax. The modern reader of medieval texts must beware. The modern reader kindles to the human particulars in the text, but the human particulars are there for the sake of the ritual particulars, to explain their origins and to establish their occasions. In this case, to explain Rabbi Moellin's ruling about Rabbi Runkel's son. In writings such as these, the historical imagination is the unintended beneficiary of the ritual imagination.

"The custom in Mainz was that the orphan's kaddish is not said every day, but only three times on the Sabbath." Should I conclude that as late as the fourteenth century the mourner's kaddish was only a rite of the Sabbath, as it was in its beginning? I'm not sure.

In the pages preceding the account of the exequies for Moellin's wife, Zalman recorded the master's customs regarding death and mourning. Moellin "taught that one mourns for a parent for twelve months, and in a leap year, too, no more than twelve months. But the orphan must lead the prayers and say the orphan's kaddish only for eleven months, so as not to portray them as sinners. But during the twelfth month he must nonetheless follow all the customs of mourning, and not attend happy gatherings." Pretty standard—but then Moellin adds a detail. "He should wrap his cloak over his neck [to cover his head], in the manner of the mourners who live in the region of the Rhine." Moellin instructs "that in the region of the Rhine the mourner wraps himself in his *mitron* above his neck. All seven days of mourning he would sit wrapped in this manner, swaddled in his garment, wearing his mantle, for it is forbidden for a mourner to go around with his head uncovered. And if he does not cover himself in this way, then he is considered to have an uncovered head. On the Sabbath, too, during the seven days, when he sits with his family at table, he should wrap himself thusly, and the shoes that he wears for the

Sabbath will suffice to show that he has reduced his mourning for the honor of the Sabbath. And it is the custom of the Rhinelanders, when they mourn for those other than their parents, to cover themselves [with the *mitron* that they wear around their necks] in the synagogue for thirty days, and when they mourn for their parents, for the full twelve months. In Poland [and Saxony], however, it is not the custom to wrap the *mitron* around the neck, [but they act] in the manner of those places where mourners do not wrap themselves in this way [even when they mourn for a father or a mother]. Once it happened that a young man from Poland was studying in Rabbi Moellin's yeshiva in Mainz, and it fell to him to mourn for his mother, and the rabbi instructed him to wrap himself in his *mitron* in the manner of the Rhineland, but to stay unshaven for all the twelve months, as was the custom in his country [for it is proper to impose upon oneself the stringency of one's own place]."

The *mitron,* or *matran,* was a small cloak, or a cowl, or a hood from which there fell a tail of cloth that could be draped on the shoulders or wrapped around the neck. It could also cover the eyes. I consult a history of Jewish costume on my shelf and learn that it is "a *chaperon* whose great importance derives from the fact that it serves as a covering of both the head and the eyes so that the worshipper was entirely wrapped at the time of prayer." (A *chaperon* is a hood.) I remember this wrap from early modern German woodcuts that depicted Jews in the house of worship. And I like this interest in the mourner's attire. It is appropriate to the drama. When life has isolated you, a sign of your isolation may be useful as a communication to others that they must not expect to encounter you whole. The ripped garment in which the mourner returns from the funeral is such a device, and so, too, is the mourner's wrap, the covering of the mourner's head. The visible presents the invisible.

Across the road I saw a beautiful woman with a deformed foot, haughty and hobbling. An emblem of truth.

XIII

I have retreated to my room and built a wall of books around me, and I am tracking the mourner's headwear through the tradition. Here are the results of my little exercise in the history of religious fashion. The story begins in the Talmud, where such a story usually begins. There the rabbis state in one passage that "he is required to cover his head" and in another passage that "the mourner is required to wrap his head." They derive this injunction from Scripture, from the twenty-fourth chapter of Ezekiel, which includes a verse from which the rabbis deduce a great deal about the practices of mourning: "Son of man, behold, I will take away from thee the desire of thine eyes with a stroke; yet neither shalt thou mourn nor weep, neither shall thy tears run down. Forbear to cry, make no mourning for the dead, bind the tire [covering] of thine head upon thee, and put on thy shoes upon thy feet, and cover not thy lips, and eat not the bread of men." For the rabbis, this is a statement of implied opposites: if the prophet must not cover his lips because he is forbidden to mourn, then the mourner must cover his lips. In Leviticus, moreover, there appears this ordinance about the leper: "and he shall put a covering upon his upper lip." The canonical translation of the Bible into Aramaic, made by Onkelos in the second century, renders these words as: "And he shall cover his upper lip like a mourner." In the third century, the sage Samuel furnishes an important detail: "Any covering that is not in the manner of the Ishmaelites is not a covering." And Rabbi Nahman adds: "All the way down the sides of his beard." Including his chin? The Jerusalem Talmud infers from the verse in Ezekiel that "he must cover his mouth," and prudently adds that he wrap it "from below," so that (as Rabbi Hisda explains) "people will not say that he has a pain in his mouth." People must not fail to see that a mourner is a mourner. Sherira Gaon, the great authority of Babylonian Jewry in the tenth century, observed—according to the eleventh-century Italian lexicographer Nathan ben

Jehiel—that this wrapping should cover the face, along the cheeks and down to the mustache, and "it should be above the nose. To this day there are Ishmaelites who wind some of their turbans around their mouths and above their noses." In Babylonia in the tenth century and the eleventh century, mourners wrapped their heads, as Hai Gaon's description of the custom of "demanding the reason" shows. In Kairouan, in North Africa, in the early eleventh century, the pioneering Talmudist Hananel ben Hushiel explains that "the manner of the Ishmaelites" means that "he veils his mustache and his beard and his nose in his turban or in his shawl. The Arabs call this *al'mana.*" Hananel notes that "on the Sabbath he is required to uncover his nose and his mustache and his beard that he covers when he is mourning, because there is no mourning on the Sabbath," and then he adds: "but it is not necessary for him also to uncover his head." In his Talmudic commentary, the mysterious Solomon the Son of the Orphan, who appears to have lived in southern Italy in the eleventh century, and was extensively familiar with Jewish life in the orbit of Islam, notes that "the Spaniards, the people of Granada and Cordoba and their environs, ordinarily leave their heads uncovered, whereas in most of the world people cover their heads in the style of the Ishmaelites, that is, they cover the entirety of their faces except for their eyes, which they leave exposed." So that was the look. The mourner had literally to hide his face. Isaac ibn Ghiyyat, in eleventh-century Spain, ruled that the mourner "must grow his hair wild, and he must not cover it with his hat and his mantle and the like, and he must wrap in the style of the Ishmaelites." For Maimonides' code of law, composed in the twelfth century in Egypt, the practice of wrapping is mandatory, and the sources given are Ezekiel and Onkelos. In a compendium of customs written by Abraham ben Nathan of Lunel, the Provençal scholar of the late twelfth and early thirteenth centuries, the mourner "covers his head in the style of the Ishmaelites, until the tip of his beard. If he covers only his mouth, according to the literal meaning of the verse [in Ezekiel], then the others will infer only that he has some trouble with his mouth, and is not eating." Moses of Coucy, the French scholar and preacher of the thirteenth century, repeats Samuel's ancient assertion that this swaddling is in the Arab style and adds, ethnographically: "I saw this practiced in Spain." Nahmanides, in the thirteenth century in Spain, says that "the meaning of this wrapping is that the head should be covered. . . . He must be covered around his head and his beard, down to his chin"; and Nahmanides then reproduces Sherira Gaon's stipulation that "this covering is to be above the nose, and to this day there are Ishmaelites who wind some of their turbans around their mouths and above their noses, which they call *al'litham.*" Nahmanides writes also that the mourner must be swaddled in this way "all day long, but when others come to console him he lifts his covering to reveal his head, out of respect for the public, until he enables them to acquit themselves [of their duty to console him]," at which point he goes under again. Nahmanides also establishes, in the name of the ninth-century gaon Mattathias bar Mar Ravi, that a scarf and a shawl will do equally well. In Spain, the great Talmudic commentator Yom Tov ben Abraham Ishbili, of the late thirteenth and early fourteenth centuries, declares that "the essence of this wrapping is that the head be covered," and rejects the variation on the custom practiced in some communities where "they place a piece of cloth over their mouths and their beards, but they do not cover their heads." He seems to care less about the Talmudic requirement that the chin be covered, though he notes interestingly that the purpose of this requirement is so that "the lips be sealed," almost as a symbol of silence. (Silence and abridged speech are prescribed for the mourner, based on the injunction to Ezekiel: "Groan silently. . . .") Now, all these authorities lived in or near the orbit of Islam, in regions in which such swaddling was a sartorial commonplace. In Ashkenaz, however, things were different. Rashi, in Troyes in the eleventh century, explains in his commentary on the verse in Leviticus that the "covering upon his upper lip" means "like a mourner"; and in his commentary on the Talmud he notes that "the dimples on the chin below his mouth" must also be covered. But Rashi was recording what he imagined, not what he saw. Indeed, for Rashi the proper interpretation of the ancient descriptions of the mourner's head was not a practical matter, for in the Rashi literature the obligation of the mourner to cover his head was simply annulled. Thus we read: "Mourners are required to wrap their heads for seven days, day and night. But there are many people who do not practice this, because the gentiles mock them, and even those in their own household mock them, and in this manner they become objects of scorn, and are disgraced in the eyes of the others. As it says [in the Talmud]: 'A mourner should not hold a baby in his lap, because this might lead to levity, and he would be mocked by the others.'" Some generations later, in a commentary on a passage in the Talmud, the Tosafists observed that "the contemporary custom no longer to cover the head and no longer to turn over the bed [another ancient requirement for mourners] is based on the statement in the Jerusalem Talmud that 'a traveler [who is in mourning] is not required [when he lodges at an inn] to turn over the bed, so that it will not be said that he is a sorcerer,' that is, a practitioner of witchcraft. We, too, are found among the gentiles; and we have manservants and maidservants [who watch us]. . . . And there is another reason for [the abrogation of] the wrapping of the head, and it is that it would result in laughter, since it is in the manner of the Ishmaelites." Moses of Coucy, having testified to the prevalence of the custom in Spain, testifies also that "in these kingdoms [northern France] this was not the custom, because it would provoke the derision of the gentiles and the manservants and maidservants in our midst." (A few generations later, the Spaniard Ishbili records without comment Moses' view that the custom is no longer practiced "because they live among the gentiles, who would otherwise make fun of them.") In northern France, a cold climate and a Christian climate, people did not dress like Arabs. Nor in Germany: there were no Ishmaelites along the Rhine. Jews who walked around with their faces buried in rags would have been derided, and the danger of ridicule was reason enough to suspend the practice. The Jews did not wish to seem too alien. The political arrangements of their life among the Christians were too fragile. In Italy, in the thirteenth century, Zedekiah the Physician reproduces Rashi's annulment of the practice, and testifies that "it is also our custom not to wrap the head." I suspect that this marked a change in the Italian custom, a change that took place under the influence of the Ashkenazic revision of the practice, since in the eleventh century the Roman lexicographer Nathan ben Jehiel, in his dictionary of rabbinical words and concepts, lists "wrapping" matter-of-factly, with no indication that it had been discontinued. But the story gets still more complicated. In Germany in the late twelfth and early thirteenth centuries, Eliezer ben Joel Ha'Levi twice reproduces the Talmudic injunctions about covering the head, but without any indication that they were obsolete. Perhaps they were not obsolete in all of Ashkenaz. In Germany, it seems, Rashi's abrogation of the practice was not altogether accepted. When the requirements of security collided with the requirements of authenticity, there were those who were not prepared to surrender the ancient custom to the present danger. Thus in Worms, the Perfumer (Eliezer ben Joel's almost exact contemporary) states that "the mourner is required to wrap his head, as in our time, when the hat is pulled over the eyes. And on the Sabbath [when the public display of mourning is suspended] this is done discreetly and not in public." The tilt of the Perfumer's hat was a sly compromise. There was nothing conspicuous or Ishmaelite about it. The Jews would see a sorrow, the non-Jews would see a hat. Such are the encryptions by which minorities sometimes live. The hat to which the Perfumer refers may have been the famous pointed hat that Jews were required to wear as a sign of their subaltern status, the notorious hat in which non-Jews expected to encounter them. And it may be that the Perfumer's tipped hat also enjoyed a basis in the Talmud: after Samuel ruled that the mourner's head must be unveiled on the Sabbath, since there is no public mourning on the Sabbath, his great rival Rav ruled that the unveiling of the mourner's head on the Sabbath is optional; and the Tosafists, the Perfumer's contemporaries in Germany and France, in their commentary on Samuel's dictum that "any covering that is not in the manner of the Ishmaelites is not a covering," suggest that Rav differed more generally about the definition of this practice, and "held that a covering that is not in the manner of the Ishmaelites is still a covering." The Tosafists add that "generally, when there is [a disagreement between] Rav and Samuel, the law is according to Rav." So the inflection of a hat will do. In Provence, many views seem to have been honored. In Perpignan, in the late thirteenth and early fourteenth centuries, Menahem Ha'Meiri records this: "A mourner is required to wrap his head—that is, he must not stand with an uncovered head, but instead he must wrap it in a manner that covers some of his face, that is, his eyes and, lower down, his mouth, so that he gives the appearance of a shattered and surrendered man. . . . In any event, there are those who maintain that the cloaks we wear, which cover the eyes and the beard, make the obligation moot. There are also those whose custom is to wear the wrapping beneath the cloak. And according to their custom, the mourner is required to do this even on the Sabbath if the people who have come to console him are present, for a mere covering of the head is not a sufficient sign of mourning; but a complete covering in the manner of the Ishmaelites, which covers the entire face, is forbidden on the Sabbath." And in Lunel, in the early fourteenth century, Aaron ben Jacob Ha'Cohen also records the existence of different practices. He notes that a person who has heard a report of the death of a member of his family thirty days or more after the death occurred may fulfill his mourner's duties with only a single day's mourning, and need only (this is Nahmanides' ruling) take off his shoes and not wrap his head, but "a person who has no shoes on his feet wraps his head for an hour and thereby acquits himself of his obligation." And then Aaron states the general principle: "What is necessary is that he act in a way that is peculiar to mourning, so that his mourning will be publicly known." A few pages later he writes more generally that "the mourner is required to wrap his head all seven days, night and day, but there are many people who do not maintain this practice, since the gentiles mock them." So in Aaron's day there are those who wrap and there are those who do not wrap. Perhaps this flexibility was owed to the political turbulence of Aaron's day. (The Jews were expelled from France in 1306, and Aaron fled to Majorca.) Aaron of Lunel also records another interesting variation, in a comment by Asher ben Saul of Lunel, his precursor in Provence a century earlier: "In *The Book of Customs,* he explained that the wrapping of the head is the same as the unkemptness of the head, that is, the mourner is required to refrain from anything that makes the hair or the beard attractive, which is why women, upon the death of their husbands, used to remove their kerchiefs, and upon the death of their other relatives, they used to let their hair fall from the baskets on their heads." This really is clever: the Talmud forbids a mourner to cut his or her hair for a time, so that the unkemptness of one's appearance will illustrate the disorder in one's life—and the wrapping of the head, too, is an expression of indifference to one's appearance, and a way of marking one's temporary expulsion from the run of things. What is important is that the mourner be somehow branded. Yet a century or so later, in Germany, the Perfumer's compromise is not accepted, and the millinery of mourning is worn. It is reported of Israel Isserlein that "all seven days of his mourning he sat in the cloak that the gentiles call a mantle and in the *mitron* that the gentiles call a cape, and on the Sabbath he would remove the former and sit in the latter. During the rest of the days of the year he always wore his great hat at home, and it was only when he was away from his house or when he was at the yeshiva or in his winter room, that he wore his cloak and his *mitron*." What was constant in Isserlein's mourning dress, then, was the covering of his head. Again, the *mitron* was a cowl, or a hood from which there fell a tail of cloth that could be draped on the shoulders or wrapped around the neck. (The "winter room" was the largest room in the house of the master of the yeshiva, the room in which he studied with his students; it owed its name to the fact that it was the only room in the house that was heated by a fireplace.) Jacob Moellin reports that "in the region of the Rhine the mourner wraps himself in his *mitron* around his neck. All seven days of mourning he would sit swaddled in this manner, and wearing his mantle, for it is forbidden for a mourner to go around with his head uncovered," and so on. And an interpolation in a manuscript concludes the sentence with these words: "He [Moellin] considered the hood on our *mitron* equivalent to an exposed head," and so it was not satisfactory. The drape of the cowl had to be wrapped around the mourner's neck and onto his head. It could not be allowed merely to fall on his shoulders, which was the look of an ordinary man, not of a man who had been stricken by a death. But Moellin's custom was not universal; he notes that in Poland the mourners did not wrap their heads. And yet he instructed a mourner from Poland who found himself in the Rhineland to defy his native custom and to cover his head. Moellin lived in a time of widespread anti-Jewish violence, but unlike his predecessors he did not recommend caution. In a short responsum on the subject of mourning on the Sabbath, his student Jacob Weil, the rabbi of Augsburg in the early fifteenth century, whose rulings became enormously influential in the early modern centuries, speaks matter-of-factly of the covering of the head, as if the practice was common: he says that in his time it was done during the first thirty days, and in earlier times during the first seven days. Meanwhile, in North Africa, there is evidence of a plurality of practices. Isaac ben Sheshet Perfet, the great Spanish jurist who fled the persecutions of 1391 and became the head of the rabbinical court in Algiers, prescribed that a mourner who leaves the house of mourning to pray at the house of worship on the Sabbath "must cover his mustache, so that everybody will recognize that he is a mourner and may seek to comfort him." Perfet's view is reported by his student and successor Simeon ben Tsemaḥ Duran, the foremost religious thinker and legal scholar in North Africa in the first half of the fifteenth century. In one of his responsa, he gives a portrait of the mourner's head in his day: "Those who leniently rule that the wrapping of the head need not be practiced at night, since there is no grief at night, are acting unbecomingly and trespassing against the words of the ages. . . . It is possible, though, to forgo the covering of the head when one moves among the gentiles, so as to avoid their ridicule. And the head covering is removed in the presence of those who have come to console the mourner, out of respect for them." So wrapping was practiced, but there were extenuating circumstances. A century later, the old distinction between the orbit of Islam and the orbit of Christianity, between the customs of the Sephardim and the customs of the Ashkenazim, reasserts itself in the rulings of Joseph Karo and Moses Isserles. They rule differently and paradigmatically. In Safed, Karo declares that "the mourner is required to cover his head, that is, he should wrap his head in a shawl or a scarf and wind its edge above his mouth and his nose, and this covering must be worn all day, but when people come to console him he reveals his head out of respect for them." In his commentary on Jacob ben Asher, Karo elaborates. Referring to the concern in the Jerusalem Talmud that a man in mourning not be mistaken for a man with a toothache, Karo observes that "it appears from the Jerusalem Talmud that those who wrap a scarf around their chins are in error, for it is not clear that this is a sign of mourning, and he could be taken for a man who feels a pain in his mouth. In fact, this was what happened the first time that I saw somebody who was covered in this way. I thought that his mouth hurt, until I later learned that he was a mourner." Was it one of his Ashkenazic brethren whom Karo had seen? Moreover, citing Moses of Coucy's warning (it was originally Rashi's) that the hostility of the gentiles should not be risked by an outlandish costume, Karo writes haughtily that "we have not seen or heard of anybody who made an exemption from such covering on the basis of such an argument." In the Ottoman Empire, after all, a person smothered in fabric would arouse no suspicion. In Poland, however, Isserles animadverts upon Karo's ruling: "There are some who say that in these countries we do not practice wrapping, and this is the common custom, and we must not be so stringent as to alter what our forefathers practiced." So had the practice disappeared from Ashkenaz? Not exactly. Isserles himself reveals that the Perfumer's old compromise was still sometimes observed; he comments, about Karo's statement that only public expressions of mourning, such as wrapping the head, are suspended on the Sabbath, that "this is the case when the wrapping is in the style of the Ishmaelites, but the partial wrapping that is practiced in some places for thirty days" is not suspended on the Sabbath, owing presumably to its relative discretion. In the late sixteenth and early seventeenth centuries, Mordecai Jaffe, the student of Isserles and his critic, records the tradition that he inherited: "In these realms it is not the custom to wrap the head, because it provokes much laughter among the gentiles, and it is forbidden to be stringent and to deviate from the practices of our ancestors." A half a century later, however, Shabbetai ben Meir Ha'Cohen, who chronicled the pogroms of 1648 and fled for his life from Vilna seven years later, was unwilling to discard the custom for reasons of security. Commenting on Isserles' statement that the custom should be left to the oblivion to which the forefathers consigned it, Shabbetai retorts: "Be that as it may, the proper practice is a partial covering. That is, to pull the hat down over the eyes." This is the Perfumer's old stratagem, revived for a new time of terror. In his compilation of the customs of the community of Worms in the middle decades of the seventeenth century, Joseph Schammes writes that "the mourner sits [at home] with his *mitron* wrapped around his neck onto his head. He sits in silence, and the others offer him condolences all seven days, after the morning service and after the evening service, as he sits on the floor mutely, his *mitron* around his neck. And when the consolers leave, he may unwrap his *mitron*, if he wishes, and wear it in the ordinary way." This is like Isserlein: out of respect for his visitors, he must cover his head. And Duran and Karo were like Nahmanides: out of respect for his visitors, the mourner must uncover his head. This difference was owed, I assume, to larger cultural differences in manners and dress. In a gloss elsewhere in Schammes's book, his younger contemporary Yair Hayyim Bacharach notes that "on every [Christian] holiday, when he does not go into town, or on every occasion that he appears in public, at a funeral or whatever, the mourner must appear among the others with his *mitron* wrapped around his head in the usual manner, not in the manner of mourning." Safety first. (Mourning must be public, but it is in public that trouble begins.) In 1630, documenting the practices of the Jews of Frankfurt, Joseph Hahn Nordlingen writes: "The old custom is that the mourners wrap themselves in the courtyard of the cemetery [before the funeral], but after they have said the Justification of the Judgment they remove their shawls, so as not to taunt the dead, and the people [at the cemetery] who were wrapped, such as those wearing capes, do not remove them from their heads until they get home. The obvious purpose of all this is to ensure that people do not gather in the cemetery without covering themselves." And he continues, reiterating the old scruple that the sartorial demands of Jewish law not interfere with the safety of the Jews: "It was the custom in Worms on their [the Christians'] holidays, when Jews do not leave their quarter, that mourners go around wrapped in their *mitron*—in German it is called a *kappe*—all day long. Let no man alter this custom of our forefathers. And for the same reason they [the mourners] wrap themselves in the courtyard of the house of worship, according to custom." The odd thing about Hahn's report is that he seems to be referring to the use of the mourners' prayer shawls for the purpose of their wrapping prior to the funeral, though they remove them in accordance with the prohibition against wearing phylacteries and prayer shawls in the graveyard, so as not to "taunt the poor." Interestingly, in Cracow at the same time, Joel Sirkes makes a point of distinguishing the mourner's wrap from the prayer shawl "in which we are accustomed to wrap ourselves all year round, which is not a wrapping in the style of the Ishmaelites, and its sole purpose is the dignity and the splendor [of the ritual] as it is reflected in the [ornamented] collar that is worn on it, in the custom of the Ashkenazim." Sirkes makes this observation in his commentary on the fourteenth-century legal code of Jacob ben Asher, who preferred the appearance of the mourners in Spain to the appearance of the mourners in Ashkenaz and stated, without a hint of the controversy, that "the mourner is required to wrap the head." But Sirkes gives a report of the controversy about the mourner's wrap (and also about the propriety of wearing one's prayer shawl in the early days of one's mourning). Adducing the innovation of the Performer, Sirkes relates that the mourners "in our country," in Poland, "lower their hats below their eyes," and "this is called wrapping"; though he has heard that in Jacob Weil's day, two hundred years earlier, the obligation was fulfilled by "a garment called a *kappe.*" Yet on the Sabbath, when public mourning is prohibited, the hat must be worn in the house of worship "in the way that ordinary people wear it." By the end of the nineteenth century, however, the wrap has disappeared, and so has the hat. In Belorussia, Jehiel Mikhel Epstein observes in his code of law that "the wrapping of the head is no longer practiced among us," and cites Isserles. Yet Epstein has an anxiety: "In that case, there is no outward sign of mourning." This is not acceptable. A correspondence must exist between the inward and the outward. And so "for this reason it has been the custom that immediately after burial the mourners remove their shoes." But I will not step into the history of the shoes. It is enough that I have wrapped myself in the history of the wrap.

XIV

Tradition is a shawl. It is not a shroud. In a shroud, you are pure. In a shawl, you are warm.

I know how my ancestors thought. I want to know how they looked.

And what about the women? What did the bereaved women wear? Of all the writers that I have scoured, only Joseph Schammes writes explicitly about the women. "A woman in mourning goes around with her head covered, in what is known as a *storz,* and wrapped in her shawl around her head, all thirty days, and all twelve months if she is mourning for her father or her mother, in shul and wherever she may be." Schammes then describes the proper dress for various female relatives of the dead; and he notes that "they also have a custom that they do not wrap their head in the *storz* in the year after their wedding, even on the anniversary of their parent's death . . . and not even upon the death of their relatives—except upon the death of those whom they are obligated to mourn completely [that is, upon the death of a parent], in which case all the laws of mourning apply to them, even in the year after their wedding." It sounds altogether fair. But then Schammes somewhat spoils it. "There are many such customs that pertain to the women," he writes. "They are known to the women. There is no need to write them all down." Schammes has more important things to do, such as writing down the customs that pertain to the men.

The Lord told Ezekiel that his wife was to die yet he was not to mourn. Why not? Because he was to exemplify to the people that, in the aftermath of the punishment that was to be visited upon them, they, too, were not to mourn. "And you shall do as I have done: ye shall not cover your lips, nor

In the most extensive discussion of the practices of mourning in the Talmud, the equivalence between the mourner and the pariah is frequently considered. The mourner and the pariah are representatives of a dissolution, and so they are figures of the periphery: the shattered and the shattering who are barred from participation in the ordinary activities of the community. (Or, in the case of the mourner, barred from participation in the ordinary way.) Evil, impurity, death: these are the radical ruptures, the unassimilable heterogeneities. A society must mark them, control them, banish them.

I was a pariah until I became a mourner. Well, not exactly. I was never expelled from the center; but for many years I expelled myself from the center, and lived richly in a periphery of my own devising. (The center is the shul. This is one of the elementary facts of Jewish history.) Then I was faced with a duty that I refused to shirk, and I was brought near. This has the ironic consequence that I cannot experience mourning as marginality, as it is supposed to be experienced. For me, it has the aspect of a homecoming. An inevitable reunion with an unexpiring essence.

A person who has left home before will leave home again. He has learned how to live at home away from home. He is not unfaithful. He has a different system of fidelity.

Essences are portable.

There are nomads who travel heavy.

"May He who dwells in this house comfort you," they advised the mourner. "May He who dwells in this house incline your heart to heed the words of your fellows, so that they may bring you near," they advised the pariah. Thank you very much for the advice to the mourner, but it is the advice to the pariah that I can use.

Back to my Rhenish forefathers. Judging by a passage in Moellin's book of customs, the competition to recite the kaddish publicly in the house of worship was intense. "Rabbi Moellin was asked about the orphan's kaddish when there were three brothers and a stranger" present in the house of worship and demanding the privilege. Moellin's answer was that the matter should be decided by lots. (Or as we would have said in Brooklyn, they should flip for it.) Yet that did not resolve the dispute entirely. "The stranger asked if he had to cast lots against each of them, or would it suffice to cast lots only once to be done with all of them." A clever stranger! But Moellin didn't fall for it. "He replied that he must cast lots against each one of them, for the merit of their father stands him in good stead for having many sons." Still, a principle of fairness is quickly enunciated, so that there will be no misunderstanding: "For the orphan's kaddish, a stranger has the same standing as a citizen of the town, and the poor man is like the rich man, and the child is like the adult, and the ignorant is like the learned." Grief, like death, is a great leveler. And so lots may be cast.

Perhaps Moellin worried that the competition to represent the congregation before God would be decided on the basis of social or economic status. In a shul? Imagine!

Having thus democratized the kaddish, Moellin turns to the liturgical predicament of young children in mourning. They may be equal, but they are not equipped. "If the orphan is a child [who does not yet know how to read, Rabbi Moellin said that] they read it with him, word for word." It appears that in medieval Mainz little boys rose to acquit their dead parents. And one manuscript suggests that in Paris, too, they were patient: "Rabbi Isaac used to demand that they wait for the small boy who is just learning to read, until he put the kaddish together letter by letter and with all its vowels, and the congregation in Paris, may their Rock and their Redeemer look after them, used to wait." I have no idea who Isaac of Paris was, bless his soul.

This evening I was the tenth man.

There is an interesting entry about the efficacy of prayer in Moellin's book of customs. It concerns the bizarre statement in the Talmud that "he who hastens to return to prayer after he took his three steps backward [thereby concluding his prayer] is like a dog that returns to its vomit." I am not the only one who is flummoxed by this parable. "Rabbi Moellin said that a dispute has broken out and is widespread about the proper manner of resolving this parable. It seemed to him that it should be resolved in the light of the statement, which appears in a number of places, that he who repents must feel as if he has never sinned, since he is sure that he has been completely forgiven. He must not [say: what good will my repentance do me, for I have sinned and transgressed and done ill in the eyes of the Lord, and so my prayer may not be accepted], and think that perhaps his sins have not been forgiven. No, he should be resolute in his mind never to sin again. And here, in this case, when a man concludes his prayer and takes his three steps backward, he must remain standing in silence and imagine that his prayer has been accepted, that he is forgiven and absolved of everything. If he returns immediately to prayer, it seems as if he is hurrying to pray and to make his supplication because he will sin again [and also as if it is not certain that his first prayer was accepted], like the dog in the parable, who is so full of the food he ate that he is disgusted by it and spits it out, and then returns to it, and it tastes for him as sweet as honey, and he eats it."

Moellin wishes to banish doubt about prayer. A man who does not stop praying is a man who does not believe in—what? The suggestion in the text differs from the suggestion in the interpolation to the text. The former suggests that the man forever in prayer is not sure of himself, and therefore he will not desist. The latter suggests that the man forever in prayer is not sure of God, and therefore he will not desist. There is a basis in experience, surely, for both of these uncertainties. We will all sin again. We will all find our prayers greeted by silence. Between the sin and the silence, it is no wonder that there are petitioners who do not wish to leave their posts.

At the teahouse with two volumes of Moellin's legal opinions. One of the volumes is a collection of "new" responsa, that is, responsa that were not included in the original edition that was published in 1556. Among these fugitive texts, there is one of the clearest discussions of the orphan's kaddish that I have discovered. Moellin received a simple inquiry from two rabbis in Landshut: "Why is it is called the orphan's kaddish? And why may minors say this kaddish, since it is a matter of sanctification [for which a quorum of men is required]?" Basic questions. Moellin responded with basic answers. "This kaddish was established [to be recited] after 'Rabbi Eleazar said in the name of Rabbi Hanina' [a Talmudic passage in praise of scholars that appears a number of times in the Sabbath service] and the Song of Ascent [a series of Psalms in the liturgy for Sabbath afternoon] and after preaching and teaching." In other words, the kaddish, textually and historically, has nothing to do with mourning. Its association with mourning, Moellin continues, is a practical matter. "Orphans recite it because they cannot recite

'Bless the Lord' [a central prayer in the morning and evening services] until they are adults, for one cannot acquit others of an obligation that one is oneself not obligated to fulfill," and the obligation of the man who leads the service is to acquit all present of their obligation. Thus the orphan's kaddish is an expedient that will permit orphans who are minors to stand and attest to their parents, without interfering in the business of the congregation. Moellin's point is that the kaddish was chosen as the mourner's text owing to its relative insignificance. "All the instances of kaddish are regulations of the rabbis," that is, they do not enjoy a basis in Scripture. "This kaddish is not something that is compulsory, and therefore the young may utter it."

Moellin alludes to the legend of Akiva and the condemned man, and continues: "For this reason, it seems to me, adults, too, are more punctilious about the orphan's kaddish than about the other instances of kaddish and about 'Bless the Lord,' though this kaddish is an addition to the service and not an obligatory part of it. They believe that they give satisfaction to their parents [by reciting this one] rather than the others." In Moellin's time, then, two hundred years or so after the invention of the orphan's kaddish, it already commanded a disproportionate amount of attention. In his view, the orphan's kaddish owes its centrality not to law, but to feeling. Speaking legally and liturgically, it is a small thing that looms large.

Indeed, it looms too large. Moellin is frankly troubled by the prestige that the orphan's kaddish has acquired in Jewish life. (And this was five hundred years ago!) He is, it turns out, a critic of the kaddish—more precisely, a critic of the cult of the kaddish. "But I am not in agreement with them on this matter. Quite the contrary. One who fulfills a duty that he is obligated to fulfill is greater than one who fulfills a duty that he is not obligated to fulfill." Kaddish is not the main event. Worship is the main event. (Moellin's last sentence is a famous Talmudic dictum.)

Already in the early fifteenth century, Moellin wishes to restrain the enthusiasm for the orphan's kaddish. It is nice to learn that the distortion of religion by sentimentality is not a new development. Here is one of the great medieval rabbis insisting upon the priority of law to feeling. Prayer, he scolds, is a particularly exigent kind of self-expression. In spiritual life, there are objectives more lofty than the articulation of human needs. Moellin is an early enemy of psychology. (Or so I will picture him.)

How, then, to account for the cult of the kaddish? Moellin remarks upon the sudden increase in its popularity: "It is the custom in many places to recite the orphan's kaddish more frequently." He gives two reasons for this development, both of them historical. One of them concerns the decline of religious competence in his time. "Adults are no longer so accustomed to stand before the ark" in the house of worship and to lead the congregation in prayer. That is to say, adults in mourning, like children in mourning, have come to rely on the shorter and less strenuous kaddish. It is the best that they can do. Moellin's comment puts the incompetence of my own contemporaries in perspective. (It is always good to be robbed of golden ages.) But the other historical reason that Moellin offers for the popularity of the kaddish has the opposite effect. It makes me grateful for coming so late in the history of my people. If there are places where the orphan's kaddish is heard more often, Moellin writes, it is because "in a time in which the wrath in the world has increased, they cannot suffice with [the orphan's kaddish that is said] on Sabbaths and holidays."

The wrath in the world? Near the end of his life, Moellin witnessed the ravaging of the Jews by the Hussite wars. Here is the text of an epistle that he sent from Mainz to the Jewish communities of Bohemia in 1420: "We, the lowly and the lambs, have seen the great atrocities that are erupting throughout Ashkenaz. Only yesterday we received letters from our brethren and our rabbis in Cologne, Eger, Nuremberg, Erfurt, and Meissen, that they are all in fear and in trembling, for atrocities have already taken place on the roads, and in Neustadt near Nuremberg too, and also other things that are not to be spelled out in writing. It is our opinion that we must rely only on our Father in Heaven, even though the people of our locality, the council and the populace, are standing with us, God be praised, and they are still providing for our security, as in other places, God be praised. Still, vain is the help of man. So we have thrown our distress upon the Lord, may He be blessed, and seized upon the artful practice of our forefathers, and taken upon ourselves, in a unanimous decision, the members of this holy congregation and all those pray with us, that after this Sabbath, the Sabbath of [the reading of the beginning of] Genesis, there will be a fast for three days, night and day, that applies to everybody twenty years old and older, men and women, except for the sick and the wayfarers and the women who are nursing." The fast took place in the early days of October, 1420; and the worst did not come to pass. Moellin's contemporaries attributed the good fortune of the German communities to his spiritual agitation. The pioneering historian Joseph Ha'Cohen, in *Emek Ha'Bakhah,* or *The Vale of Weeping,* a chronicle of Jewish adversity that appeared in 1558, reports that "many of those who went to war [against the Hussites] took an oath that if they returned home safely, they would do with the Jews as they pleased. The Jews experienced a great fear and were terrified, and among them was the pious Rabbi Moellin, and they decreed fasts and they fasted for three days and nights in the month of Ḥeshvan, and they prayed the prayers of Yom Kippur, and God saved them." The wrath in the world.

But that was not all. Moellin and his contemporaries also had the memory of the recent past with which to contend. They presided over a Jewry that was recovering from other attempts to obliterate it. The Black Death in 1348–1349 unleashed a century or so of anti-Jewish violence, in which the Jews were regularly accused (in the words of an anti-Semitic writer of the time) of "planning to exterminate Christendom by poisoning the air," and the wells, too. In Germany alone, atrocities occurred in 1348, 1357, 1382, 1397, 1401, 1424, 1448, 1453, 1472, 1475, 1501, 1541, and 1543. Folded into one of my books I find the yellowing copy of a page from the old *Jewish Encyclopedia,* a horrifying page of small print that lists the German towns of the fourteenth century in which the persecutions took place: there are 333 towns on the list. The wrath in the world. Thus Moellin, referring to an earlier authority, wrote that he "lived before the persecutions, when it was known that there were sages in the land. But we are an orphaned generation, without anybody who knows the difference between right and left." The acute sense of decline that appears in the writings of Moellin and his contemporaries was owed in part to the fact that they were ministering to a blasted community, to "an orphaned generation." There were so many dead. The conventions of mourning could not accommodate the occasions of mourning. Liturgically, the solution was simple. The more death, the more kaddish.

I have taken the text of Moellin's letter of 1420 from one of the most crushing works of Jewish historiography. It appears in the second volume of Simon Bernfeld's *Sefer Ha'Dema'ot,* or

The Book of Tears, a three-volume anthology of historical and literary sources on the persecution of the Jews, from the Seleucid Greeks of the second century B.C.E. to the Ukrainians in 1768. For the student of calamitology, these books are indispensable. And their pathos extends to themselves. Bernfeld's volumes appeared in Berlin, between 1923 and 1926. They appeared, that is, at the climax of their own story. The saddest sentences in these books may be Bernfeld's own, at the conclusion of his long introduction: "One essential thing, and it is the foundation of our understanding of Jewish history, has been made sufficiently clear: the Jewish Question will find its proper answer only in the answer to the human question. The road is still long." I have the original edition of Bernfeld's work, with its dark brown wrappers and its gorgeous fonts. My copy is badly beat up. I found it many years ago, at the bottom of a box of old books, in Mr. Stein's dusty bookshop in Jerusalem. Mr. Stein warned me that the books were almost too frail to use. "They look like they were saved from a fire," he said. "They *were* saved from a fire," I said. When I see them on my shelf, I see the fire.

Tonight I was gripped by the fear that my bookcases would fall over and everything would be destroyed by my books. This is crazy. My books are my least likely source of ruin.

Moellin's demotion of the kaddish must not be misunderstood. The kaddish may be an institution of custom rather than an institution of law, but Jewish custom is one of the foundations of Jewish law, and Moellin owes his place in the history of Jewish law not least to his advocacy of Jewish custom. He prized the ritual diversity and the liturgical diversity of Jewish life, and argued ardently for its legitimacy. "All the laws of the twelve months of mourning," he states in a responsum, "are implemented differently in different places, according to local custom." He concludes another responsum, this one about the kaddish, with these vigorous words: "Do not rely upon me. The important thing is custom, and so you should inquire into it. There is no need to say more." And so, in his reply to the rabbis of Landshut, Moellin repeats that the orphan's kaddish is not "a [legal] obligation and a statute of the rabbis, but a custom"—and yet, in the event that there are no orphans in the synagogue, "far be it that the orphan's kaddish be canceled. Quite the contrary, the kaddish must always be recited after learned discourses and the verses of Scripture," and he cites Maimonides for support. Duties have many sanctions. One is bound by the lesser sanctions as well as by the greater sanctions.

Custom is lovable in a way that law is not. Custom is so unpristine. It has fingerprints all over it. It asserts the reality of practices against the ideality of principles.

The story of law is a story of rationalism. The story of custom is a story of humanism.

You can destroy objects, you cannot destroy geometry. But you cannot touch or taste geometry.

"At home, we used to . . .": there was never a holiday in our household when my father or my mother did not begin a sentence with those words, and describe the manner in which the occasions were observed in their corner of the Carpathians in the 1930s, before the apocalypse. They were proud not only that their families had preserved the tradition, they were proud also that they had inflected the tradition. They boasted about the vanished usages, as if to say: See how much there was!

Custom differs from law also in its vulnerability. Since it lives in the individuals and the communities that practice it, it dies with them, too. Custom may be wiped out. The burgeoning "customs literature" of Moellin's era was owed in part to the fear that customs would be wiped out. (The religious diligence of my parents was owed to a similar fear.)

The preservation of custom is not an anthropological imperative. It is a moral imperative. My parents taught me this. With these particulars, we prove that we are alive and that we are free. When, on the eve of Passover, I chop apples and walnuts and cinnamon with wine precisely as my parents, and their parents, chopped them, I mark the defeat of our enemies. In our kitchen, empires fall again.

From custom I learned about the power of detail, not from art.

Law, or the glow of necessity; custom, or the glow of contingency.

In Moellin's pages, the discussion of the kaddish, and of the variety of customs associated with it, brushes up against a matter of political theory. What are the privileges of the stranger compared to the privileges of the citizen? Moellin notes a divergence of practices in this regard. "In the case of visitors who appear in the house of worship in their twelve months [of mourning] and wish to lead the prayers and to recite the orphan's kaddish, the custom in Austria is to let them do so, for in this matter the townspeople have no priority over visitors; but Rabbi Meir Segal [Meir ben Baruch Ha'Levi of Fulda, a jurist of the fourteenth century] established the custom in his own house of worship that the regulars are preferred, and on his authority this custom was followed by Rabbi Abraham [Klausner, Moellin's teacher, who authored an influential anthology of practices]. And that is our custom in this town, too, that the inhabitant of the town trumps the visitor, unless the visitor has come to the house of worship to say kaddish for the first time or on the anniversary of his parent's death."

This appears to be another illustration of the mysterious divergence of ritual traditions between the communities of Germany and the communities of Austria, between *minhag Rheinus,* "the custom of the Rhine," and *minhag Ostreich,* "the custom of Austria," in the late medieval centuries. In this instance, the Austrian custom and the German custom seem to be based on different notions of community. The Austrian custom treats the obligation to say the orphan's kaddish as a universal Jewish obligation, and it recognizes no distinction between any of the orphans who appear in a shul. Membership in the Jewish people is all that is required for membership in the Jewish community. The stranger is an equal. For the German custom, by contrast, the stranger is not an equal. Membership in the community is what matters. All kaddish is local. So how does Moellin adjudicate between the inclusive Austrian way and the exclusive German way? "Every river runs it own course," he writes, citing the Talmudic formula for religious diversity, "and I am not worthy to adjudicate between them." Since neither of these customs is contradicted by the law, the proper attitude is tolerance.

But there is more. (There is always more.) Moellin's expression of respect for the varieties of Jewish experience is immediately embellished by his enthusiasm for his own tradition. His humble conclusion that "I am not worthy to adjudicate between them" is followed by this: "Still, our custom seems slightly more plausible." And he proceeds to explain why. "After all, all the needs of the house of worship fall upon the community, such as hiring a cantor or a quorum, if they must, or purchasing a Torah scroll and its garments, and the building of the house of worship—all of this comes out of the wherewithal of the community, for the members of the town compel each other to build the house of worship and to purchase the Torah scroll and to hire a [few men to complete the] quorum for the High Holidays . . . and it is not within their power to compel the visitor to contribute anything for all of this, or to any of the expenses of the house of worship. . . . This is the reason for the custom in certain communities that a member of the town actually displaces a visitor from his seat in the house of worship, and that only a member of the town is called to the Torah on holidays—though on Sabbaths they are accustomed to honor their guests [by calling them to the Torah], and the townspeople do not stand on pride, for on all the Sabbaths of the year many people may be called to the Torah. . . . Even somebody who dwells in town but does not have business there has priority over somebody who is visiting, owing to his presence and to the benefits that the community derives from his presence. And so in this case, too, the members of the congregation may prevent strangers from assuming the privilege of fulfilling this duty, since they do not share the burden of the synagogue." Help the stranger, but honor the citizen.

Still, Moellin does not wish to seem callous. And so he concludes his discussion with a point of information, which puts those rights and those responsibilities in perspective: "In Austria it is also their custom to say the orphan's kaddish regularly even on weekdays, and perhaps that is why they are not fussy [about the difference between strangers and citizens].” The difference, then, is not only philosophical or political. It is also practical. In Austria, there were more opportunities for the expression of grief.

And so, in this single text, I have been taught to appreciate inclusiveness for reasons of principle, exclusiveness for reasons of principle, inclusiveness for practical reasons, and exclusiveness for practical reasons. Such is the rabbinical imagination. It must picture all the eventualities. To know the right answer, it must know the world.

“Every river runs its own course.” In this way the Talmud validates all the communities and their customs. And into this river you can step twice. Indeed, you must step twice into this river. You must step into it regularly. This river is not the Heraclitean river. Its difference from itself does not impair its sameness with itself. It is subject to change, but it is not only flux.

You cannot step into the same river twice: that is the statement of a sullen monist. Every river runs its own course: that is the statement of a busy pluralist.

In another responsum, the one to the rabbis of Landshut, Moellin writes somewhat more succinctly about strangers and citizens. “I have observed that in Austria no distinction is made between a resident and a visitor. They are treated equally, even the strangers who come from a distant land. But Rabbi Meir Segal instituted the custom in his house of worship and in his house that the kaddish is not recited except by the regulars who go there always. And Rabbi Abraham [Klausner] followed his custom. And it is also the custom in this town, that residents bar strangers from reciting the kaddish and leading the prayers, and it is my impression that such is the custom in all these regions, a simple custom. . . . The orphan's kaddish belongs to the townspeople, and outsiders have no right to it." So far, this text is like the other text. In this one, though, Moellin gives another reason for the difference between the customs. It is a ghastly one: "In those places where they make no distinction between residents and visitors, it may be that they made a decision to overlook the difference owing to the throng that was there. For a huge number of people were present there in the hour of wrath, and so the townspeople made the concession." The strangers were not visitors, the strangers were refugees. They came to the shuls because they had nowhere else to go. And so they were permitted to lead a congregation that was not their own.

In support of this custom that is not his own, Moellin reaches for a distant text from the Talmud: "And in this matter we invoke the general principle that 'the poor themselves are pleased [to make the concession].'" Moellin is referring to a discussion of gleanings in a field. According to the Talmud, a minor has no right of possession to things that he finds. Why, then, are children permitted to glean a field after their parents? After all, they will carry away what should belong to the poor. The sage Rabba proposed an extenuation of the children in the fields: "The rabbis chose to treat one who has no right like one who has a right. Why? Because the poor themselves are pleased [to make the concession], so that when they work in the fields their own children will also be permitted to glean after them." Moellin, then, is making an ominous point. He is saying that the citizens permit the strangers to recite the kaddish because one day the citizens may be strangers. One day they, too, may straggle into a shul far from home and ask for the right to mourn their parents or their children.

Moellin has found a basis in history for the Austrian practice of inclusion. The German practice of exclusion, it would seem, is a practice for a time of peace. Yet in Austria it was not always a time of peace. I am puzzled. Indeed, in Germany, too, it was not always a time of peace, as Moellin himself observed. Why, then, didn't the German communities accept the practice of the Austrian communities? The shuls of Germany, too, were often filled with refugees. Yet the German custom remained the German custom. And that is the point. You run with your river. Thus Moellin concludes his opinion: "The custom of a place is its custom, and I will not dispute our own customs. . . . And you decided rightly, all the more so because the custom of our ancestors in this land, whose custom is Torah, supports you. And this is how I have already responded to the community in Augsburg."

So the other responsum went to Augsburg! The Jewish historian leaps at such revelations. The observant Jew yawns at them.

This morning I brought a contemporary of Jacob Moellin's to the teahouse. He is Isaac of Tyrnau, the Austrian author of a popular anthology of customs. (And the subject of an extraordinary legend, according to which the crown prince of Hungary fell in love with Isaac's beautiful daughter, and converted to Judaism, and secretly studied with Isaac, until he was discovered by Catholic priests and burned at the stake.) "Since my youth," Isaac remarks, "my heart has been given over to the customs." His book is nothing more than a manual, he tells the reader, written in "simple language and for everybody, even those who are not scholars. For this reason, I have been brief about proofs and reasons . . . so that the reader may race through it, according to the need of the hour." Isaac's brief description of the state of Austrian Jewry confirms the picture of devastation that Moellin painted: "As a consequence of our sins, the number of students and scholars has dwindled. And in Austria people of faith and learning and good deeds have been lost and decimated, so that I have seen a settlement or a community in which there are not two or three people who know the true customs of their own town, not to speak of the customs of other towns." And so Isaac put pen to paper. In Jewish history, writing is often a form of rescue.

The final chapter of Isaac's manual is called "Laws of the Orphan's Kaddish," and it is devoted in its entirety to the conflicts between mourners in the house of worship. "In the matter of the orphan's kaddish," Isaac begins, "there are communities in which it is the custom that the resident has priority over the visitor, and there are communities in which they are equal, and every river runs its own course." Isaac then proceeds to a calculation of the rights of citizens and the rights of strangers, of mourners in the first week, in the first month, and in the year of mourning, in various situations on Sabbaths and on weekdays. He notes that in the case of a mourner in the first week of mourning, "the resident has no priority at all over the visitor." When right conflicts with right, he recommends lots. Isaac discusses the yahrzeit, or the anniversary of a parent's death, when kaddish must also be recited, at greater length than I have seen it discussed in the texts of his time. He remarks that "if people from many different places come to a new town and wish to establish a custom, it is proper that the same custom be established inside the house of worship and outside the house of worship." And he discloses more about the nature of membership in the community: "If the sons of the deceased live in another town, and they come to this town [as a consequence of their father's death], they are not considered residents merely because their father is buried here. Only those who live in the community are considered residents, and they are the ones who pay taxes or serve the community. But even the poor people of the town, who have permanent residence there, are counted among the residents." And "if a man establishes his dwelling in the community, he is considered a resident from the moment that he is required to carry the burden with the other dwellers in the community, and not when he completes a tax assessment with the nobleman [that is, the local Christian magnate], though he is required to pay taxes to the nobleman." If the house of worship retains a teacher or hires a sexton for a period of time, "if he is unattached, and has no wife and children, then he is considered a resident, but if he has a wife and children in another place, he is considered a foreigner."

The Jews of the medieval world had a genius for community. Later this was transformed into a genius for politics. But the Jews paid a price for their entry into politics. Their self-understanding was politicized. I have often maintained, to the dismay of certain Jewish friends who believe that politics is among the highest ends of life, that in the history of the Jews the communal impulse was not identical with the political impulse. The Jews did not have a political system of their own, and look what they accomplished! They had a moral system of their own, a religious system of their own, a legal system of their own, a social system of their own. For the purposes of a significant life, they did not need politics. Oh, happy Jews. But no, that isn't right. Finally they were not happy, they were not happy at all. It transpired that they needed politics in order to survive. (But only in order to survive.)

The Jewish culture in which I was raised was a survivalist culture. It was still dazed by the destruction in Europe. "I used to be highly critical of Jewish philosophies which seemed to advocate no more than survival for survival's sake," a Jewish philosopher wrote in the 1960s. "I have changed my mind." He went on to make his reputation by proposing to add to the 613 commandments of the Torah one more commandment, "what I will boldly term the 614th commandment: the authentic Jew of today is forbidden to hand Hitler yet another, posthumous victory." In its day, this spiritualization of the disaster did not seem grotesque. But it was not long before I began to hear critical voices claiming that survival is not the end of the subject. Survival for what? Survival as what? When I was young, I was excited by such questions. They pried me away from the permanent commemoration in which I lived. And they were good questions. Still, I know better now. The antinomy is not acceptable. Even in extremity, there was no such thing as survival for survival's sake. There is no survival without meaning, and there is no meaning without survival. My parents understood this. I am the son of survivors who were not survivalists.

Today I was estranged from everything.

Yohanan ben Mattathias Treves was a contemporary of Jacob Moellin, and the chief rabbi of Paris. When his authority was challenged by the scholar Isaiah Astruc, one of the great quarrels in rabbinical history ensued. "Look down from the heaven of your study," Yohanan beseeched a prominent Spanish rabbi for support, which he was granted. The quarrel ended abruptly in 1394, when the Jews were expelled from France. (The argument about authority was settled by power.) Only a few of Yohanan's responsa survive—some of them in Moellin's responsa, and one of them in Joseph Karo's commentary on Jacob ben Asher's code of law. The subject of this fugitive opinion is the orphan's kaddish, and it expounds a truly idiosyncratic solution to the problem of the priority of the mourners in the house of worship. Here is the case that Yohanan was asked to adjudicate: "One of the residents of the town was saying kaddish for his mother, who had died in the town; and a hired teacher in the town was also saying kaddish for his mother, who had not died in the town and had not lived in the town; and an old woman in the town died without leaving children, so her relatives hired someone to say kaddish for her soul." In the distribution of the kaddish in the house of worship, who comes first? "This has nothing to do with the payment of taxes," Yohanan begins. "If one has no money, but resides in the town, even if one is only a hired laborer, then one has a portion [in the recitation of the kaddish]. Generally, if one resides in the town, even if one is only a hired laborer, then one has a portion." A fine egalitarian rule. And then Yohanan introduces a peculiar idea: "If the kaddish is said for a person who died in the town, then one has a portion by right of the dead, and if one resides in the town, even as a hired laborer, then one has a portion by one's own right—and so this comes to two portions. But if one does not reside in the town, and the dead [for whom one is saying kaddish] did not reside in the town, then such an individual has no portion at all [in the recitation of the kaddish]. This is how I construed the law, and this is how I established the practice where I live." It strikes me that the consequences of Yohanan's ranking of mourners are absurd. By his logic, an orphan away from home must yield before a local stranger hired to say kaddish for a local stranger. This flies in the face of the tradition's hierarchy of sorrows. About the rights of the living, Yohanan is fair. But he believes that the dead, too, have rights. There is the citizenship of the living and the citizenship of the dead! How could rootedness have mattered so much to a rabbi who was himself a victim of expulsion? Yohanan's responsum is a fantasy of stability. But the Jews moved around often because they were often moved around. The mourners were near and the dead were far.

What is a refugee? A person who does not honor his dead where they lived.

If the dead have rights, then the dead have responsibilities! But there were rabbis who believed that, too. . . .

As I was walking on Wisconsin Avenue in the evening, a big old black car drove by. On its fins were painted the words "Living Proof." The orphan's chariot!

"Living Proof": the more I thought about the phrase, the more it irritated me. About the important matters, surely, the distinction between living proof and dead proof is not interesting. Proof is proof. Either you have it or you don't. Anyway, all proof is living proof. That is why the dead prove things, too; that is why the dead live.

One last text by Moellin. (I will miss him.) It is the most melancholy text of all. He received a query: "Would my master enlighten me about something that I heard in the name of Rabbi Meir of Rothenburg—that he taught and instituted that the kaddish is not to be recited for a father who was killed for the Sanctification of the Name. Might the reason for this be what is written in [the Talmud] that as a consequence of his martyrdom his sins were forgiven, and so he is not to be considered a wicked man [and therefore his soul is not in need of the kaddish]? But surely the blemish on the family [that would result if the kaddish was not said for the father] suggests that we should be stringent [and say the kaddish]! And I have heard it reported in the name of my master

[Moellin] that he mandated that it be said." The tradition refuses to impute wickedness to a man who died for the tradition. The righteous may or may not be martyred; but the martyred are righteous. Such sacrifices are all you need to know. Yet the idealization of the martyr would seem to make the kaddish moot. Surely a son need not present evidence on behalf of such a father. The manner of his father's death is evidence enough. Why worry about a verdict if there has been an acquittal?

The rabbi who addressed the question to Moellin has heard that Moellin rules differently. And Moellin confirms that this is so. "In the matter of the kaddish of the orphans of the martyrs," he begins his response, "I have not heard what the gentleman reports in the name of our holy rabbi [Meir of Rothenburg], but I have heard that others have this opinion [that the kaddish should not be recited for a martyr]. I have not bothered with these opinions, since it seems to me perfectly plain that kaddish should be recited." Moellin cites as his authority a responsum of the late thirteenth century by Hayyim ben Isaac, the son of the great Isaac of Vienna, who "wrote that it is required to mourn for martyrs, and responded at length and concluded that he who asserts that martyrs are not be mourned is himself in need of atonement."

Having adduced a legal precedent, Moellin proceeds to a historical precedent. "I have heard from my teachers that such was the case during the persecution in Prague, when there were some who did not want mourning to be observed for the martyrs, but in the end the sages of those days agreed to mourn." This probably refers to the assault on the Jews of Prague in 1389. And then Moellin proceeds to the reasoning behind his ruling: "This seems to me right on substantive grounds. Even though [the martyrs] are holy at the highest level, and no creature is worthy to be counted in their company, who can be sure, really, that there are no sins that deserve to be punished by unnatural deaths and the pangs of the grave, as Rabbi Simhah wrote? Nahmanides, too, wrote that there are some sins whose punishment, in this world and in the next, is a premature death. For if we believe otherwise, then no kaddish would be said on behalf of a father who was renowned for his learning and famous for his lifelong piety! Moreover, death is said to cleanse one of one's sins, and there is also the cleansing of Yom Kippur and repentance, and sometimes an individual must avail himself of all these [and yet we say kaddish for such an individual]. We cannot be certain that he [the martyr] did not reject the atonements, and we have other anxieties as well. We have seen it stated [in a rabbinical legend] that Jesse died as a consequence of the serpent's counsel [to Eve, that is to say, Jesse owed his death not to any sin of his own but to the fact of human mortality], and yet [it is also stated that] he was killed [by the king of Moab, according to another rabbinical legend]. Somebody as smart as you will find this easy to understand. Job will be the proof. And also Saul and his sons: they waged the wars of the Lord, but they nonetheless needed reassurance [by Samuel, conjured up by the witch of Endor] that 'tomorrow shalt thou and thy sons be with me.'"

Moellin's responsum is profound. It teaches that the way you die does not absolve you of the way you live. A holy death does not denote a holy life. For Moellin, the idealization of martyrdom reaches its limits at morality: even the martyr, the Jewish man or the Jewish woman murdered for being Jewish, does not escape ethical judgment. The martyr, too, may have sinned.

There is nothing ugly about such a presumption. Moellin's notion of the universal likelihood of sin certainly should not be mistaken for a notion of original sin. In the Jewish tradition, the serpent's counsel did not make the descendants of Adam and Eve guilty. It made the descendants of Adam and Eve finite. (The confusion of finitude with guilt had distorted an entire tradition of modern thought, from Heidegger to Levinas.) The descendants of Adam and Eve are only the imperfect creatures, the creatures with the interest in evil, the free creatures, the creatures stained and staining.

The medieval rabbi seeks a reason for the kaddish to be said for the righteous because he does not want righteousness to be mistaken for innocence. There is no ideal of innocence in Judaism. There is only an ideal of goodness. So utter the kaddish, and save a soul from hell with your skepticism about it. Open your eyes to the one you loved and rise to pray.

In insisting that the kaddish be said for the soul of the martyr, Moellin is insisting that the jurisdiction of morality is broader than the jurisdiction of history. The fact that you have been visited by evil does not make you good. You never escape your own worth. Many years ago I was struck by the remarkable absence of historical extenuation from the moralistic literature of the Jews. The hideous circumstances in which so many Jewish writers and Jewish communities found themselves do not figure prominently, or at all, in their articulations of how they should live. They did not relax their expectations of themselves because the world had treated them unfairly. History offered them an alibi, and they refused it. Moellin's responsum falls into this heroic tradition. In the midst of persecution, he rules that persecution is not all that matters.

But why would one "reject the atonements," as Moellin worries that this martyr may have done? The answer is, because one can. Since we are free beings, we may reject good as well as evil. Moellin's phrase is remarkable. It broaches the question of human perversity.

It is not precisely the case, as the religious existentialists and the philosophers of a tragic view of life and the theologians in the age of totalitarianism have all asserted, I mean the Jewish ones, that the Jewish tradition is "immanent," and enamored of finitude, and unburdened by the belief in the perfectibility of man. No religious system or moral system can do without the belief in the perfectibility of man. The moralists in the Jewish tradition, too, insist on compliance with the highest standards of conduct, and they base those standards on metaphysical absolutes, and they scold harshly. What else are they to do? Values do not wink. Finitude is not an exemption. Quite the contrary: only finite beings may be ethical beings.

Forgiveness, not forgivingness.

The task is to distinguish between human perfectibility and human perfection, and to recognize that perfectibility is a greater condition than perfection. The animals are perfect, insofar as they are always what they must be; but we are never what we must be. We are the ones from whom more may always be demanded.

Either perfection or transcendence. —Except that it is not really a choice. We do not have the power to transcend our power to transcend. And that is our perfection.

Transcendence is not accomplished only by mystical visions. It is accomplished also by common thoughts. Think a thought, and you have detached yourself from yourself. Think a thought, and you are a pilgrim.

Perfect beings cannot live in time, and human beings cannot live out of time. So what is the perfection of beings who live in time? Perfectibility.

The infinite is the inhuman. That is its attraction. I will not pretend that I am immune to its attraction. The adoration of the human is an idolatry. Why *not* seek the infinite? Seek it, then. But do not think that you will find it; and if you find it, do not think that you can be it. (But you want to be it . . .)

And after ecstasy, what?

Contradictions are the most clarifying things in the world! But they may also clarify excessively. I must always remind myself of this. The thirst for dichotomy is a thirst for simplicity. For the world is full of notions and entities that do not go together but also are not opposed. Reality is not so easily ordered. For this reason, patience is the surest sign of thought.

"Nothing Jewish is alien to me." Scholem liked to say that. We argued about it many times. I objected that a great deal that is Jewish is alien to me (and to him, too). Also that this is as it should be. In a tradition that includes all the varieties of spiritual life, there must be varieties that one rejects; or else one is tribal and not spiritual.

I am browsing in Biegeleisen's bookstore, surrounded by black hats and black beards and black caftans, when suddenly I feel that I must never leave this musty place again. Here in this room, arranged on tables and shelves, is what I need. Here is what the millennia were for. I feel tiny and happy. The books plead: stay, stay, stay. I am quivering, like the willing victim of a seduction. At the last minute, I pay my bill and get away. (At the last minute before what?)

The right response to tradition is vertigo.

Shalom of Neustadt was Jacob Moellin's teacher, and there is a new edition of his "laws and customs" in Biegeleisen's shop. Shalom was a jurist in Vienna in the latter half of the fourteenth century, and eventually he established himself in his ancestral town of Neustadt. (Not too gladly, it seems. "A man must always live where his father lived, according to the rabbis," Shalom is reported to have said. "Otherwise I would have pulled up my tent and left Neustadt a number of times already.") Shalom's "laws and customs" are the most clipped and undiscursive that I have read. The book consists of very brief reports of his sayings and his practices, and it is almost completely devoid of legal or theological explanations. In Shalom's rulings and rituals I see the origins of Moellin's rulings and rituals; but the interest of these snapshots of this rabbi's life is not just scholarly. Here are a few of the snapshots:

—"In the matter of a Jewish woman who was murdered in the persecution, Rabbi Shalom said that her relatives should rend their garments and mourn for her as they would mourn for any other dead."

—"It happened once that a [Jewish] maiden in Austria left the faith, and died in her wickedness, and was buried in their [Christian] obscene graveyard. Many years passed, and the local Jews came to collect her bones and throw them upon their charnel mound, according to their law and their custom; but her flesh had not been completely consumed. Astounded, they came to the saintly Rabbi Shalom of Neustadt and asked him what this meant. He pushed them away. To his students, however, he said that as long as the flesh was not consumed, she was still being judged, and her sin had not yet been forgiven. This could be deduced, he said, from the statement in the Talmud [in the discussion of the burial of criminals executed by the court] that 'if the flesh has been consumed, he may be buried with his fathers,' where Rashi explains that 'in that case he is like a righteous man, but as long as his flesh remains he is still considered a wicked man, and the righteous are not to be buried with the wicked.' . . . And do not be perplexed about the righteous whose bodies are intact in their graves long after their death. This is owed to their character and their goodness. For the righteous die with a divine kiss, and their bodies survive until an hour before the resurrection of the dead."

—"In Austria, there occurred an incident involving an apostate who was killed. More precisely, the apostate was badly wounded for his wickedness, and he was mortally ill in bed for three days before he died, and in that time he did not recant. Rabbi Shalom wanted to permit the man's relatives to mourn for him, since the man had suffered such serious wounds, and the terrible manner of his dying could count as his atonement. But Rabbi Moellin responded to him: '[According to Talmudic law] a dying man is like a living man in all respects, and this man all the more so, since he lived for three days after he was wounded and he had the opportunity to repent, but he persisted in his bitterness, and so his relatives are not required to mourn for him. In the case of a man who was struck down and died instantly, we certainly say that he made a reckoning and repented before he died, and so his death may count as his atonement. In the case of this man, however, we saw with our own eyes that he made no reckoning.' Rabbi Shalom conceded that he was right."

"A man must always live where his fathers lived": no, dear teacher, not if a man is an exile. In exile, a man must live where he can live a significant life safely. And he must not mistake the land where his fathers lived for the land of his fathers. Shalom's remark is a perfect example of the axiom that Jewish nationalism came into being to repudiate.

The spiritual conditions of exile are precious—behold the medieval civilization of the Jews! But its spiritual conditions are not to be confused with its physical conditions. The Torah travels.

In what appears to be a report of a ruling, Shalom is said to have explained "why there are places in the Rhineland where the orphan's kaddish is not said on weekdays." His explanation was that in those places the Alenu prayer at the end of the service did not conclude with the Biblical verse—"the Lord shall reign for ever and ever!"—with which it commonly concludes, "and so the kaddish would not follow Scripture," and therefore cannot be said. The orphan's kaddish, too, must meet the general requirement of the kaddish, to conclude a recitation of Scripture and study. I am interested to learn that in Austria in Shalom's time, in the two centuries or so after the invention of the orphan's kaddish as a feature of the liturgy for the expiration of the Sabbath, it had not yet become a universal feature of the liturgy for all the days of the week.

Oh, the sweetness! This is the reminiscence of Joseph Ostreicher, who compiled the chronicle of Shalom's customs: "I saw Rabbi Shalom's wife, in the time of her mourning, singing to her granddaughter to quiet her, and Rabbi Shalom was with her and said not a word. I assume that he told her that it was all right." Song is forbidden to the mourner, insofar as it is an expression of joy; but the rabbi ruled in favor of the lullaby.

Remember, always remember, the creatureliness of the teachers.

"An infant a year or two old who was baptized together with his mother [and died]—according to the rabbis, there is mourning for him, though obviously there is no mourning for an adult [who apostatized and then died]. But according to Our Master Tam, there is no mourning for him." This, from a brief responsum by Meir of Rothenburg in the thirteenth century, reporting on the ruling a century earlier by Jacob ben Meir Tam, Rashi's grandson and one of the most forceful rabbinic minds of the Middle Ages. I am struck by one of the explanations that Meir provides for Jacob's opinion. "Our Master Tam used to give as his reason [for ruling that there must be no mourning over the death of a baptized infant] that there must be rejoicing over his death. For if the child had lived, he would certainly have ended up an idolator." Rejoicing over the death of a child! Meir reports that the rabbis took issue with Jacob's ruling and Jacob's reasoning ("a child, who doesn't know the difference between his right hand and his left hand . . . ?"), but Jacob refused to budge. "Be that as it may," Meir reports, "Our Master Tam declared that it is the custom not to mourn the death of such children, but to rejoice and be happy." This is sickening. But I have to say that the reality in which Jacob produced his opinion was also sickening. In his chronicle of the Second Crusade, Ephraim of Bonn writes that in 1147, "on the second day of the festival of Shavuot [Weeks], the wayward rabble in France descended upon Ramerupt, and burst into Rabbi Jacob's house and plundered everything that was inside it. They tore a Torah scroll in his face. They seized him and took him to a field, where they disputed with him about his faith. Then they fell upon him murderously. They inflicted five blows on his head, exclaiming: 'You are the leader of the Jews, and so it is upon you that we will avenge ourselves for the one who was crucified. You wounded our Lord five times, and we will wound you the same way!'" Jacob would have perished on the spot, except that "Our Creator took pity upon him for his learning, and caused a great nobleman to pass through the field. The rabbi bribed the nobleman with [the promise of] a horse. The nobleman took custody of the rabbi from the mob. 'Leave him with me,' he told them, 'and I will talk to him. Perhaps he will be seduced away from his faith and we will succeed in persuading him. If he refuses, I will return him to you.'" And so the rabbi survived to rule that Jews must rejoice over the death of a child who would have been lost to the Christians. The narrative of the near-martyrdom of Our Master Tam concludes: "The rabble relented, and in this way the evil hour was averted. Thus did God, in his compassion for His people, have mercy upon the man who propagated His law among them."

I worked late into the night and got lucky. I found the source of Meir of Rothenburg's report of Jacob Tam's unpleasant ruling about the baptized baby. Meir's source was his teacher, Isaac of Vienna. Isaac gives a somewhat fuller account of the dispute between the twelfth-century rabbis of Ashkenaz. (Against Jacob Tam, the rabbis asked: "A child who was put into the water—what can this add to him or take away from him?" The baptism of a Jewish infant, they are defiantly suggesting, is a cruel but futile act.) Isaac carries the discussion back to its Talmudic beginnings. And his conclusion? He does not have a conclusion. He is clear about the apostate parent, but he is not clear about the apostate child. At the end of his consideration of rites (or the lack of them) for those who died guilty of a capital crime, Isaac remarks: "Based on what I have explained earlier, that there is no mourning where there is no atonement, I declare that I, the writer, do not know how I would rule in the case of the death of the child of a wicked individual." The jurist is defeated by the tragedy.

I have located the responsum by Hayyim ben Isaac about mourning and martyrdom, the one cited by Jacob Moellin, and I am very glad. Law, history, and religion are beautifully joined in this opinion. (The text was put together from a number of sources by Hayyim's son Isaac.) Hayyim begins: "There has appeared before me my kinsman and my friend Nahman the son of Rabbi Shemaryah, who showed me a letter from Rabbi Moses the son of Rabbi Meir, may the memory of the righteous be a blessing, according to which our teacher Rabbi Shemaryah the son of Rabbi Hayyim ruled that there is no mourning for the martyrs." "The martyrs": this seems to refer to the particular victims of a particular atrocity. Hayyim is incensed by this ruling. "From the character of this man," he retorts, "I might conclude that he never set foot in the hall of study! I declare that he is himself in need of atonement and forgiveness for what came out of his mouth."

Hayyim proceeds to cite a Talmudic dispute as it was explicated by his father, Isaac of Vienna, on the question of whether death brings forgiveness to a man who died in his wickedness—that is, who died guilty of a sin whose punishment is death, and without repentance. Since we do not mourn the wicked, is such a man mourned? Isaac was clear about his own opinion: "It seems right to me, the writer, Isaac the son of Moses, that a man who commits a sin whose punishment is death, and then dies before he has repented, is not to be mourned." (This is the text that I was reading the other night.) The proper response to the death of a man executed by a court, Isaac notes, citing the Talmud, is not mourning but grief, "for grief is only in the heart," and it is not expressed in ritual. And then the dialectics commence. A distinction is drawn between a sinful man who died naturally and a sinful man who was put to death. The latter is certainly mourned. Then a distinction is drawn between a sinful man who was put to death legally, that is, by a Jewish court, and a sinful man who was put to death illegally, that is, by a non-Jewish government. The latter is certainly mourned. Eventually Isaac concludes that "a man who died in his wickedness, having committed a sin that carries with it the punishment of death [and having not repented of it]—all the authorities [in the Talmud] agree that he is not to be mourned. But if, in his wickedness, he was executed by gentiles, everybody agrees that he is to be mourned." Martyrdom cleanses a sinful soul.

Hayyim presents his father's reasoning and then launches into his own criticism of the ruling that martyrs are not mourned. If we mourn for Jews who were guilty of a capital crime and were executed by non-Jews, then surely we mourn for Jews who were guilty of nothing and were slaughtered in the persecutions! Hayyim rules with a fury: "Thus it is all the more the case, from now until the end of the world, that we mourn [a Jew] who was murdered in his righteousness by gentiles, such as these martyrs who were murdered at the hands of gentiles, and thereby sanctified the Name of God and were made holy [by the manner in which they attested to] the uniqueness of His Name. Whoever said that there is to be no mourning for them demeans them, in suggesting that, heaven forfend, they are like those who died in their wickedness. Such an individual himself is in need of atonement and forgiveness!" Hayyim writes passionately, and it is no wonder: he fell heir to the memory of many martyrs. And the danger had not passed.

Hayyim is aware of the severity of his criticism. No sooner has he delivered it than he offers a few words of apology for his insolence: "Now, I have not come to chastise, for who and what am I, my life is mere dust and worms, I am a lowly student, and Rabbi Shemaryah the son of Rabbi Hayyim is the master. But my kinsman [Rabbi Nahman the son of Rabbi Shemaryah] writes me often, and so I have not restrained myself from expressing my opinion, and what is in my heart." And then the lowly student rises to his previous pitch of indignation: "And if he took heed of my opinion, it seems to me that he would take it upon himself, as a consequence of what he said, to fast every Monday and Thursday until Rosh Hashanah." Hayyim concludes with a prayer and a peroration: "May the Holy One, Blessed Be He, unify our hearts to love His Name and to fear it, and return us to His Presence in penitence, and incline our hearts to a complete repentance before Him, and as a reward for this may He send us our Redeemer speedily and in our own days. And peace be upon my teacher and his teaching and his yeshiva, and upon the entire community of Regensburg, and may God have mercy upon them and upon us and upon all of Israel swiftly and soon, and defeat our enemies and shatter and rout all who rise in evil against us, amen and so may it be His will."

Hayyim's reasoning is the opposite of Moellin's reasoning. (Maybe that is why Moellin cites the intensity of Hayyim's responsum but not its analysis.) Hayyim believes that the martyr is to be mourned because he has been purified of his sins by the manner of his dying. Moellin believes that the martyr is to be mourned because we cannot be sure that he was pure. The one regards the martyr idealistically, the other regards the martyr realistically. Both come to the same compassionate conclusion.

I am not sure that I understand Hayyim's reasoning. What is the point of mourning a cleansed soul, when the purpose of mourning is precisely to assist in its cleansing? It is the deplorable soul, the fallen soul, the wicked soul that requires the services of a son.

I am also not sure that I correctly understand the Talmudic discussion upon which Hayyim's decision is based. Again and again I am bothered by the shallowness of my knowledge of Talmud. I should study it, I should study it, I should study it. But it is too late—not too late to study it, but too late to believe that the study of it is what finally matters.

Hayyim's text concludes with a powerful passage that Hayyim's son discovered in a compilation of writings by Hayyim's father: "Whoever is killed for the unity of the Name and the sanctification of the Name, in a time of persecution or not in a time of persecution, in a circumstance in which he is told, 'serve the strange god or I will kill you,' and he delivers himself to death and is slain or hung or burned for the sanctification of the Name—all Jews are required to mourn for him, since he sanctified the Name with his soul and his body, and they are required to rend their garments, and to eulogize him in the houses of worship and the houses of study, and his wife must never marry again, out of respect for heaven and respect for him." In a word, he was a hero.

Driving down Connecticut Avenue, I pondered the fate of the wicked who do not have the good fortune to be martyred. The ones whom we are forbidden to mourn: how do they find forgiveness? When I got home, I had another look at that page in the Talmud, and Rashi explained it to me. The rabbis state that we may grieve for a man executed by a Jewish court, but we may not mourn for him. This is the fundamental distinction in Jewish law between the emotional response to death and the ritual response to death. A murderer who has been executed for his crime is denied the rites that are owed the dead, since giving him those rites, as Rashi notes, would constitute "a lack of respect to the murdered," that is, to the victim of his crime; but he cannot be denied the feelings that are owed the dead. As for atonement, "his disgrace will be his atonement." The shame of his exclusion from the decencies of mourning will do the work of the decencies of mourning. If grace won't do the trick, disgrace will.

I am beginning to think that in this tradition it is almost impossible not to find forgiveness. There is nobody for whom there is not a way home. The ingenuity of the unredeemed.

An affecting responsum by Jacob Weil, the German authority of the fifteenth century, written to instruct and to comfort a certain Rabbi Simeon, who mourned for his brother but wondered whether his mourning was proper. The facts of the case are unclear, except that Rabbi Simeon's brother had been executed for a crime. "You did well that you mourned for your brother," Weil writes, "since he was not executed according to the law of the Sanhedrin." He cites Maimonides' ruling that mourning is not denied those who are killed by the state, even if they are guilty of the crime with which they were charged and deserving of the sentence that they received. In Weil's view, there is no significant difference between martyrdom at the hands of non-Jews and capital punishment at the hands of non-Jews. In both cases, non-Jews spill Jewish blood. Yet it is clear from Maimonides' language—"all who are executed by the state, even though they were executed according to the law of the king and the Torah has provided the authority for such executions . . ."—that he has in mind not a death penalty carried out by a non-Jewish state, but a death penalty carried out by a Jewish state. How, then, does this support the mourning of Rabbi Simeon, whose brother was executed by Christians in Germany? Weil argues *a fortiori:* if we mourn for a Jew who was legitimately killed, surely we mourn for a Jew who was illegitimately killed.

And then the merciful rabbi furnishes his grieving correspondent with a list of reasons to believe that his brother did not forfeit his right to be mourned, in the way he lived or in the way he died. Weil reminds his anguished correspondent that his brother was "killed by gentiles in a strange style of execution, and he was subjected to terrible suffering not according to the law of the Torah," and it is well known that "suffering cleanses." Also, "he did not fall into the category of those who separate themselves from the community [who are denied the rites of mourning]," he merely committed a crime. Also, "in such a case it is assumed that he confessed his sins and repented, as you wrote," and the Talmud states that "all who confess have a place in the world to come." Also, "he willingly gave himself up to the executioner, as you wrote, when he was told 'go outside of your own free will and turn yourself in, so that you will have atonement for your sin,' which he did; and since he delivered himself to his death so that he would be granted forgiveness, surely he was granted forgiveness." Weil concludes with the ancient tale of the son of the sage Yosi ben Yoezer, who "did not behave properly" and "imposed upon himself the four death penalties" of Jewish law, at which point a voice was heard to say that a place in the world to come awaited him. (Weil relates the tale imprecisely. In the ancient text, the penitent scoundrel was not Yosi's son but his nephew; and his "improper behavior" included apostasy and the taunting of his uncle as he was about to be martyred by the Greek authorities; and the voice that promised him eternal life was the voice of his uncle, expiring at the end of the hangman's rope; and he executed himself in a horrible contraption that hung him, stoned him, burned him, and ran him through with a sword. Perhaps Weil did not wish to torment Rabbi Simeon with the violent details of this analogy to his brother.)

The crime of Rabbi Simeon's brother is not in question. What is in question is whether the punishment for this crime may come from outside the tribe. No, say these sources. Guilty Jews are still Jews. The murder of a Jew by a non-Jew must never be treated as normative.

I think that I have detected a conflict between Maimonides and Rashi. (An amateur Talmudist's dream!) It occurs in the interpretation of the Talmudic phrase "those executed by the state." For Rashi, "the state" refers to "idolators," that is, to non-Jews; and so the statement that these poor souls find forgiveness refers to the victims of a non-Jewish government. For Maimonides, "the state" refers to a Jewish government, and to its victims, since "the Torah has provided authority for such executions." Maimonides, then, must have another reason for absolving the guilty with the manner of their death. And what is the Maimonidean view of the execution of Jews by non-Jews? May the guilty victims of a non-Jewish executioner be likened to the guilty victims of a Jewish executioner? I should follow the matter further into the conceptual thickets, but to do so I would need someone to study these texts with me, and I have no one. (This is my fault.) So I will make do tonight with a historical conclusion. It is that the orbit of Islam was much less unkind to the Jews of the Middle Ages than the orbit of Christianity. In Cairo, Maimonides might have permitted himself a comparison between Jewish justice and non-Jewish justice. In Troyes, such comparisons looked more and more outrageous. When Rashi hears of executions by the state, he hears the cries of martyrdom.

Guilty Jews are still Jews: I was raised on this attitude, and sometimes it vexes me. For guilty Jews are also still guilty. Why should identity matter to justice? I understand that, historically, identity did matter to justice—or more precisely, to injustice. Many more Jews were murdered because they were Jewish than because they were guilty. The Jewish suspicion of non-Jewish justice is not exactly fanciful. But I want to consider the matter not only from the standpoint of what is real, but also from the standpoint of what is right. (In their analysis of moral problems, the rabbis never stopped at history.) So I return to Isaac of Vienna's statement that "a man who died in his wickedness, having committed a sin that carries with it the punishment of death [and not having repented of it]—all the authorities agree that he is not to be mourned. If, in his wickedness, he was executed by gentiles, everybody agrees that he is to be mourned." Why? Is it not an ancient axiom of the rabbinical tradition (the idea goes back all the way to Jeremiah) that, in civil matters, "the law of the state is the law"? If a Jew commits a capital crime against the state, and the state responds with capital punishment, is this really a variety of martyrdom? To promote it into martyrdom seems like the tribal exoneration of a guilty man. If he was an evil man, why should I care that he was one of us?

I have been wandering through my books in search of an answer to my question, and I have found something. It is a legal opinion by Moses Sofer, who relates that on a Friday in the summer of 1811 "there was brought here the body of a righteous man who was killed by a gentile murderer. The name of the man was Rabbi David Secherles, may God avenge his blood. He was buried the day after his murder. Since the elders and the heads of the burial society had gone to the marketplace in Pest, and those who remained here were not proficient in the customs of the burial society, they came to me with the question of whether it was right to bury him in the tomb of his fathers, or should a separate spot be set aside for his grave. For they had heard it said that the four death penalties [of the Sanhedrin] have not been abrogated [despite the fact that the Sanhedrin is no more], and that a person who is deserving of [one of] those penalties is not to be buried with his fathers. I thoroughly searched the books of the early authorities and the code of law, and I found nothing to support this. Still, I told them that I would not interfere with the custom of the members of the burial society if they were present; but such a ruling will certainly not be issued by me. The man is to be buried with his fathers in accordance with the respect that is due him."

Sofer objects to the assumption that a Jew who was killed by a non-Jew deserved to die, in the sense that he must have been guilty of a capital crime, and so his murder was really his punishment. Sofer resents this reasoning from death to guilt. "There is nothing of substance in what those people said. The statement that the four death penalties were not abrogated means that whoever deserves to die by the sword is delivered over to the state. Let us grant that. But if we were also to say that whoever is delivered over to the state deserves to die by the sword, then we would have to conclude generally that whoever dies at the hands of gentiles is deserving of [one] of the four death penalties—and how, then, will we explain [the martyrdom] of Rabbi Akiva and the victims [of the Romans] at Lydda? No, our sages took care with their language. They said that whoever deserves to die by the sword is delivered over to the state. They did not say that whoever is delivered over to the state deserves to die by the sword. And all the more so is this true in the case of someone who was killed by a murderer lying in wait for his blood. Therefore we regard this man [David Secherles] under the rubric of righteousness and worthiness and holiness."

Sofer, then, stands my question on its head. The problem for law—and for theodicy—is not the unhappy fate of the guilty, but the unhappy fate of the innocent. Sofer takes it as given that the guilty find their punishment. It is not the reality of justice that exercises Sofer, but the reality of injustice. Later in his responsum he deduces from the consideration of the Talmudic passage that I have been studying that "someone who is murdered by gentiles is forgiven immediately, even before the torments of the grave begin." Surely this, too, is just!

The prayers this morning went too fast. They were over before I could ready myself for them. This irritated me. The de-acceleration of life is one of my reasons for returning to shul. I cannot imagine anything more revolutionary than to slow things down.

A rainy afternoon. Hail is falling from the sky. And I have come upon an instance of continuity in the Jewish tradition that shatters me. I found it in a work called *She'elot U'Teshuvot Me'Ma'amakim*, or *Responsa from Out of the Depths*, by Ephraim Oshry.

From 1941 to 1944, Ephraim Oshry was a rabbi in the ghetto of Kovno. He taught Talmud in that charnel house, and the devout Jews who shared his captivity often sought his opinion about the ways in which they could continue to observe Jewish law in their obscene circumstances. After the war, Oshry came to New York and served in a shul on the Lower East Side. (I prayed there a few times during my college years.) Between 1959 and 1976, he published his Holocaust responsa in four volumes. In the second volume, I find this: "Question: On the eleventh day of the month of Heshvan, on the third day after those master butchers the Nazis, may their name be blotted out, removed more than ten thousand people—men, women, and children—from the Kovno ghetto and transported them to their slaughter in the Ninth Fort—where they were murdered in bitter and excruciating and horrible ways, with a terrible cruelty that it is hard to describe—a refugee from the valley of slaughter appeared before us. He was a young man who had managed to escape, and he related all the details of that fearful event. The cursed Germans ordered the doomed to undress and to leap into the pits that had been prepared for them, and then fired upon them with machine guns; and when they completed the murderous deed they covered the pits with earth and buried them all—the living and the dead together, for many of those martyrs still had the breath of life in them, and had only been wounded by the bullets. There was not a house in the ghetto where there were not some dead. Here a man wept bitterly for his brother, and there a man lamented his wife; here a man wailed over his children, and there a woman howled for the husband of her youth. 'Oh, papa!' a man cried. 'My son, my son!' a woman cried, pouring out her pain. The inmates of the ghetto who survived were covered in sorrow and agony, and they were full of mourning and lamentation. And there came before me Bertchik the glazier, the treasurer of the burial society of Kloyz, and he asked me whether we are required to mourn the martyrs and to recite the kaddish for them."

This is what Bertchik needed to know! In the *anus mundi*, a point of law. (This, too, is "Jewish resistance.")

The rabbi knew what the glazier needed to know. "Answer: In the responsa of Rabbi Jacob Moellin, number 99, it was asked whether it was necessary to recite the kaddish for those who were killed for the Sanctification of the Name. The inquirer wished to suggest that there is no mourning for martyrs, and Rabbi Moellin replied: 'I have heard from my teachers that such was the case during the persecution in Prague . . .'"—and Oshry gives Moellin's ruling that the martyrs are to be mourned, the very ruling that I studied not too long ago. Oshry adds to Moellin's view a reference to Moellin's contemporary Isserlein, and he concludes: "On the basis of these sources, I instructed the inquirer that there is to be mourning for the martyrs of the Ninth Fort, and kaddish is to be said for them. Indeed, it was an awesome and terrifying sight to see, when the congregation that survived in the ghetto said kaddish together, with one voice, for those dear to their hearts. May He who heals the broken of heart bind up our sadness and hasten the rescue of His people and send them salvation and save them forever."

There were about thirty thousand Jews in the Kovno ghetto. The atrocity that Oshry describes took place on October 28, 1941. It was known as "the big *Aktion*." The Ninth Fort was one of a chain of forts that were built around Kovno in the nineteenth century. Nine thousand Jews, half of them children, were taken there and murdered. And to make sense of what happened—to deny the Nazis the attainment of their objective, which was not only the extinction of the Jews but also the extinction of Judaism—the survivors of 1941 consulted the survivors of 1389!

1389, 1941: the generations live and die together.

1389, 1941: remember not only the dead, remember also what the dead remembered.

1389, 1941: our enemies are dust, they are the dust on our ashes, they are the dust on our books. . . .

The Jews of Kovno responded to the slaughter with a question about the kaddish! Oshry's text puts me in mind of some of the most savage lines in Hebrew poetry, Hayyim Nahman Bialik's imprecation upon the survivors of the pogrom in Kishinev in 1903. He describes men crawling out of their hiding places after the rape of their wives, and running to the shul and blessing God for saving them—and then the priests among them rush to the rabbi with an inquiry: "Rabbi! My wife, what is her status? Permitted or forbidden?"

The poet detests them for this. Their fidelity to their way of life seems blind and cowardly (and indifferent to the suffering of their wives and daughters). They seem almost complicit in the calamity. The poet prefers revolt. If the fate of the Jews must change, then the Jews must change, too. Bialik was right: the time had come for the Jews to act against their own wretchedness, and no such action was possible without a rejection of the old quietism. Survival demanded a measure of spiritual self-immolation. And yet the anger in Bialik's poem reflects also an exasperation of another kind. The modernist had come up against a faith that would not be moved. It seemed beyond the reach of reason or experience. Before such unworldliness, the worldly can only seethe.

"Rabbi! My wife, what is her status? Permitted or forbidden?" The question is not only ridiculous, it is also sublime. The revolutionaries spoke only half the truth. The whole truth is that the Jews must change and the Jews must stay the same. I do not see a way out of this wildly undialectical situation, except to live strenuously by both its terms. I see glory in the poet in Kishinev and I see glory in the rabbi in Kovno.

Oshry has a few other responsa about the kaddish from out of the depths. This, from his first volume: "Question: After the accursed Germans, may their name be blotted out, on the third and fourth days of the month of Nisan, carried out the mass murder of Jewish children that they called the *Kinderaktion*, and exterminated twelve hundred babies and sucklings whom they snatched from the bosoms of their mothers and sent to the slaughter, I was asked by the crushed parents whether the obligation to recite the kaddish for their young children is incumbent upon them, and if it is not, then how young must a child be to require a kaddish?" And this is Oshry's response: "Answer: It is written in Isaac of Vienna . . ."—no, I can't stand it. This material hurts. Suffice it to say that Oshry marshals a remarkable array of inconsistent authorities on the subject of the age at which a Jewish child is legally significant, and the bereaved parents are told to recite the kaddish. My hand shakes as I turn Oshry's pages. I loathe the reality out of which those pages emerged. Enough! The sun is high. I'm going for a walk.

Surely it is foolish to hate facts. The struggle against the past is a futile struggle. Acceptance seems so much more like wisdom. I know all this. And yet there are some facts that one must never, never accept. This is not merely an emotional matter. The reason that one must hate certain facts is that one must prepare oneself for the possibility of their return. If the past were really past, then one might permit oneself an attitude of acceptance, and come away from the study of history with a feeling of serenity. But the past is often only an earlier instantiation of the evil in our hearts. It is not precisely the case that history repeats itself. We repeat history—or we do not repeat it, if we choose to stand in the way of its repetition. For this reason, it is one of the purposes of the study of history that we learn to oppose it.

If you have made peace with the human world, you should be ashamed of yourself.

In an anthology of Jewish apocalyptic texts that was published in Israel in the apocalyptic year 1943—"it is the hope of our generation that we are the last to experience the longing for redemption and the first to experience redemption," writes the editor, Judah Even-Shmuel, in his preface—I was checking a reference to *The Book of Zerubbabel,* the esoteric text from the seventh century that I consulted many months ago; and in Even-Shmuel's notes I stumbled upon Hayyim Nahman Bialik's understanding of the orphan's kaddish. The editor notes the recitation of the kaddish in heaven by Zerubabbel—as it is reported in *The Alphabet of Rabbi Akiva,* the seventh-century work with which I began my research into the orphan's kaddish—but he fails to note its purpose properly. In the pseudo-Akivan text, Zerubabbel recites the kaddish so that the souls of the dead may be given a reprieve from hell. Yet Even-Shmuel remarks that Zerubabbel's kaddish, and the orphan's kaddish generally, was "the prayer of martyrdom, which binds all the generations of Israel." Never mind that the kaddish that appears in *The Alphabet of Rabbi Akiva* is not the orphan's kaddish, which had not yet come into existence. "Since the essential foundation of Jewish education is the training of every Jew in readiness for martyrdom," Even-Shmuel explains, "the kaddish became accepted as a commemoration of the fathers. The hidden link, it would appear, is this: 'Your teaching, O my fathers, is preserved in me, and so I am ready and willing to sanctify the Name.'" What a peculiar view of the kaddish! And it turns out to have been the view of the kaddish that Even-Shmuel learned from Bialik, who had an enormous influence upon him. "The conjecture that the kaddish is the martyr's prayer I have taken from Hayyim Nahman Bialik, may his memory endure forever! [Bialik died in 1934.] In his opinion, the prayer was composed (in its Hebrew version) in the days of Bar Kokhba [who rebelled against the Romans in 132], perhaps by Rabbi Akiva [who supported Bar Kokhba's revolt and considered him a messianic figure]. In this prayer, the martyrs mentioned the redemption and the messiah, and assured the crowd that stood around them and wept that in their own lifetimes and in their own days the redemption would come and the messianic age would appear." Conjecture, indeed! Such a view of the kaddish is not supported by the text of the prayer or by the history of the prayer. (What is the "Hebrew version" of the kaddish?) This reading is bizarre. But it may not have seemed bizarre in 1943, when every day was a day of martyrdom. In 1943, when my grandparents and my uncle were gunned down in a ravine called Bronica, where wildflowers grow.

XV

It is the beginning of the final week of my year of mourning. My sleep last night was ruined by care. I know why. This was the year of my life, the only year of my life, about which I can say with certainty that there was never a day without an untrivial moment.

The Jewish ideas about sorrow include the idea that sorrow has limits. The end of mourning is an essential part of the tradition of mourning. Ancient and medieval authorities are adamant that it is not to exceed the period of a year. There must be no wallowing. The temptation to nestle with nothingness must be resisted. The world has not died; only someone you love has died. The world awaits your return. There is work to be done in the world.

"Rabbi Judah said: Rav said that he who mourns for his dead too stubbornly weeps for some other dead." This Talmudic comment about the obsessive character of sorrow goes deep. If one's life is not to be reduced to the life of a mourner, it is not only because there is more happiness in it. It is also because there is more unhappiness in it. The orphan's sorrow is never his sole sorrow. When my father died, it was already a season of gloom. As I said kaddish for him this year, I remembered sometimes a friend who died in London two years ago and sometimes a friend who died in New York last year, and I grieved for them, too. Waxing griefs, waning griefs. So, says Rav, one must get one's sorrows in order. Know which is which. Do not confuse the one with the other. And do not grieve generally. Grieve only in the particular.

Since death is final, grief is final. Since death will never end, mourning will never end. That is why the tradition must intervene to end it.

Sorrow is not a worldview. It is a pain, and the world will certainly dull it. And feeling is not thinking. A man who has never known pain can still believe that existence is painful. He may be right or he may be wrong, but his own experience will not settle the matter.

The Talmudic text continues: "A woman lived in the neighborhood of Rav Huna, and she had seven sons. One of them died, and she wept over him too much. Rav Huna sent a message to her: 'Do not do this.' She took no heed. He sent another message: 'If you harken to my warning, fine; and if not, prepare shrouds for your other sons.' And they died. She cried endlessly. Finally he sent another message to her, telling her to prepare a shroud for herself, and she died." The story of a woman who mourned to death.

There are many circumscriptions of grief in the tradition. The deadline of twelve months—a deadline, indeed—is only the last of the limitations of mourning. The rabbis in the Talmud interpret the verse in Jeremiah, "Weep ye not for the dead, neither bemoan him," to mean: "Weep ye not for the dead too much, neither bemoan him disproportionately." And they draw practical conclusions about the days immediately after the death. "How, concretely, is this done? There are three days for weeping, and seven days for lamentations, and thirty days in which one may not wear new clothes and cut one's hair." After thirty days, the mourner returns to sartorial and tonsorial normalcy, but the rest of the year remains, with its restrictions. The ritual regulation of grief is based on the recognition of its gradual diminishment. And then mourning is over, whether or not it is spent.

A broken heart, too, must show a sense of measure.

The Tosafists cite a fearful passage from the Jerusalem Talmud: "All seven days, the sword is drawn; until thirty days, it wavers; and after twelve months, it returns to its scabbard." Those are the inward stages of mourning to match the outward stages of mourning. And where is the threatening sword for the remaining eleven months of the mourner's year? Hanging steadily over my head, I presume. It is true: the disappearance of a father or a mother is experienced as a danger. And what is grief, if not an overwhelming sensation of the vulnerability of life? They die, you die. Life does not grow less fragile. What changes with time is not life's fragility, but one's power over one's intuition of life's fragility. Slowly you acquire a standpoint from which to offer resistance to your sorrow, until your sorrow becomes just another of your parts. It is not erased, it is conquered; and it is conquered when it is contextualized. Context is another name for consolation.

The sword may be back in its scabbard, but death is never disarmed.

The Tosafists did not quote the entire passage from the Jerusalem Talmud. The rest of it is even more ominous: "For the entirety of that year, judgment is aimed at the entire family." (He always did entangle us in his affairs!)

Maimonides handles the sword this way: "For the first three days of mourning, he should see himself as if a sword were resting on his neck; and from the third day through the seventh day, as if it were lying in a corner; and thereafter as if it were stalking him in the street. All this so as to exercise him, so that he will stir from his sleep and repent. For it is written [in Jeremiah] that 'thou has stricken them, but they have not grieved,' and from this we must conclude that one must wake and be moved."

People sometimes speak about mourning for themselves. I dislike such talk. The imagination of a standpoint beyond mortality weakens me in my attempt to think lucidly about my mortality. It is impossible to mourn for oneself. You cannot pretend, or imagine, or report, that you have died. Until you die, you live. It really is that simple. You want to mourn for yourself? Then it is not grief that you feel, it is regret. But regret differs from grief significantly. It has an ethical dimension. Grief is helpless. Regret is not helpless. If the way you have lived has brought you to grief, then live differently. (No matter how you live, though, you will die.) With respect to yourself, sorrow is never all that remains for you. There is also contrition.

Every intimation of immortality is an evasion of mortality.

Mourning for yourself? This is regret without responsibility.

Mourning is not like morality. It owes its force to the fact that nothing can be done. Death cannot be corrected.

A few years ago I learned about a soldier who died in the battle at Cold Harbor in 1862. They found his journal near his body, and in it he had written: "I was killed here."

The passage about mourning in the Jerusalem Talmud does not make do with the analogy of the drawn sword. It moves to another analogy. "What is this like? It is like a vault of stones: when one of the stones is rattled, all of the stones are rattled." Another fine discrimination. Mourning is not an event with repercussions. The repercussions *are* the event.

I have spent an entire year in an aftermath.

Elsewhere in the Talmud, the rabbis consider the man who runs into his friend and discovers that he is in mourning.

"During the twelve months, he may offer him words of consolation, but he may not inquire about his well-being." Sometimes "how are you?" is a sadistic thing to say. And the passage continues: "After the twelve months, he may inquire about his well-being, but he may not offer him words of consolation, though he may do so indirectly." I like that little loophole. And the passage continues: "Rabbi Meir said: What does the man resemble, who after twelve months of mourning encounters his friend and is offered words of consolation? He resembles a man who broke his leg, and his leg has healed, and then he encounters a doctor who says to him: 'Come to me and I will break your leg and then heal it, so that you will admire my medicines.'"

Happy is he who comes too late to console.

My sister phones. The gentleman at the cemetery wants to know if the ivy should be planted in time for the unveiling of the grave this month. She thinks that he should wait. If he plants it now, there will be nothing left to do. It will be over. I tell her that it *is* over. She knows this, but she wants "to prolong the finality."

To prolong the finality! If I have heard a finer articulation of Jewish morbidity, I don't know what it is. Maybe that was always my quarrel with my tradition's enthusiasm for exequies. I don't see any reason to prolong the finality. The finality is quite long enough.

Menasseh ben Israel concludes *The Soul of Life* with a remarkable analysis of the limits of mourning. His subject is the first anniversary of the death, the end of the year of the kaddish. "Finally," he writes, "it is the common custom to eulogize the dead and to mourn them at the conclusion of the period of a year, and the reason for this custom is given [in the Talmud], where it is written that [after death] the body lasts for twelve months and the soul ascends and descends, and after twelve months the body is gone and the soul ascends and no longer descends." I remember this Talmudic legend from months ago. But Menasseh is disturbed by the physicalist implication of the passage. It seems to conform the period of mourning to the fate of the flesh. "On what basis did they decide to limit the time to twelve months in all instances? Experience demonstrates, after all, that the disappearance of bodies is determined by the precise mixture of their composition and by the place of their burial, whether it is moist or dry, whether it is rock, soil, or sand." No, says Menasseh, the limits of mourning are fixed not by the vicissitudes of the body, but by the vicissitudes of the soul. "The truth is that souls are desirous of their bodies, and so they linger over them with ardent desire, until little by little they forget them. And this happens to the souls after twelve months, for even the most exemplary love will go this far and no further."

Does love really quit after a year? Menasseh proceeds to parallels from Jewish law. From the laws of marriage: "And so He who knows human hearts placed a limit of one year on the time in which a groom may celebrate his happiness with his wife, as is written [in Deuteronomy], 'When a man hath taken a new wife, he shall not go out to war, neither shall he be charged with any business, but he shall be free at home one year, and shall cheer up his wife that he hath taken,' for love at its most powerful lasts a year." From the law of torts: "The period during which one must publicly declare that one has found a lost object is twelve months, for after that it is assumed that the owners have despaired of recovering it." From the laws of blessings: "This is why the rabbis said that he who encounters his friend after an absence of twelve months must say 'Blessed are Thou who raises the dead,' for surely he had forgotten him after twelve months." And so Menasseh concludes: "In this way we may understand the intention of our sages in saying that for twelve months the body subsists and the soul ascends and descends. They were not really making this point about the body, for the loss of the body is due to its composition and to the earth in which it is buried, as I have said. Their point was rather that the force of the soul's desire for the body exists at all times during the twelve months, and after twelve months the force of its desire for the body is spent, and then the soul ascends and no longer descends. . . . It was to convey the pain that the relatives experience at the separation of the dead from them, in all and every aspect, on the day of the soul's final ascension to the heights of heaven and its departure from them, that mourning and an expression of the relatives' grief were established, for it is as if they were giving up on it, and despairing of ever seeing it again."

Menasseh was not a romantic. He expected heat to cool. He foresaw the end of passion, and he prepared for it. And yet the tale that he tells is profoundly romantic. In his story, the soul lingers after death because it loves the body. It cannot quit what it loves. The period of mourning is the year in which desire has not yet been defeated by death. When twelve months are over, and death defeats desire, the soul will be gone. And the son will be back.

"Rav said: The dead are not forgotten for twelve months." And he has a prooftext, from Psalms: "I am forgotten as a dead man out of mind, I am a broken vessel." How did Rav infer a year's time from this verse? I'm not sure. The "broken vessel" of the King James translation is a "lost vessel" in the original, and it is possible that Rav was thinking of the laws of torts, of the lost object that is abandoned after twelve months.

"I am forgotten as a dead man out of mind." This is not the end of desire. This is the end of memory. An awful prospect, especially for Jews. We don't mind not being wanted. We mind not being remembered. Anyway, what is desire without memory?

When his judgment is over, he is forgotten. That's it: when Jews stop worrying, they stop remembering. But they never stop worrying, so their tradition is safe. For many years I have thought about the collective memory of the Jews, and wondered what makes it work. Now I know. Worry makes it work! In its way, worry is a sense of history; it is an acknowledgment of all the adversity that did happen, that could happen, that must not happen. Worry, the engine of Jewish civilization. (And the answer was in front of me all the time, right there in my parents' house.)

"Blessed art Thou who raises the dead." I happen upon a delightful comment on this blessing by Mordecai ben Hillel, the scholar and martyr of Nuremberg in the late thirteenth century. Citing an ancient authority, he observes that one must recite this blessing upon seeing an old friend, but "only if one is fond of his friend and happy to see him." Mordecai is right! It would be unfair to demand that everybody be delighted to see everybody. In this respect, the end of days will be a nightmare. The resurrection of the dead means the return of one's least favorite people.

I should know better than to joke! I found this in the Perfumer this evening, while I was looking for something else: "Two persons who hated each other while they lived are not to be buried next to each other, because even in death they will have no rest." (He reports that this gem of rabbinical dourness was "copied from *The Book of Glory* that was created by the great man Rabbi Judah the Pious.")

Today, a short and suggestive text by Jacob Weil. It is a responsum "in the matter of the woman who commanded her daughters not to wear the [mourner's] cloak [after her death]." Here is more evidence that the wrap was still worn; but this woman was insisting that her daughters flout the custom. Her request poses an interesting problem. If her daughters honor her wish, then they dishonor her; and if they dishonor her wish, then they dishonor her. Can a parent command a child to mourn less, or not to mourn at all? Here is Weil's answer: "Reason determines that her daughters should fulfill her request—as in the case of the man who asks that his property not be used to pay for the funeral [for him by his children], about which [the rabbis ruled] that he must be obeyed, because the ceremonies are designed for the respect of the dead, as it is stated [in the Talmud]. So in this case, too, from the end of the thirty days to the end of the twelve months, this is about the respect of the mother, and since she renounced her honor, her honor is renounced." What about the first thirty days of mourning? Weil is not sure. It is only for parents, remember, that mourning lasts a year. For the other dead, it lasts only thirty days. "It is not clear to me," Weil writes, "whether the thirty days, during which people mourn for their other dead [and not only for their parents], are about the honor of the living, and so they cannot be renounced, or about the honor of the dead, and so they can be renounced." But Weil does not wish to be misunderstood. Whatever one decides about the thirty days, "it is certain that mourning itself cannot be renounced, since in that case the laws of mourning would be nullified."

May a father ask that his son not say kaddish for him? (And may his son disobey him?)

Weil is referring to the discussion of the Talmud about the proper motivation for the rites at the funeral. "The rabbis asked: Is the eulogy for the respect of the living or the respect of the dead?" The distinction is not theoretical. The rabbis are pursuing a practical distinction. "What practical difference does it make if he says that he wants no eulogy spoken for him?" If a eulogy is designed to respect the living, then the deceased had no authority to dispense with it; and if it is designed to respect the dead, then the heirs have no authority to dispense with it. And there is another practical difference: "Also, so as to extract [the costs] from the heirs." If a proper burial is designed for the respect of the dead, then the heirs must pay for it, regardless of their wishes. If it is designed for the respect of the living, then grudges and greed may prevail. The Talmudic passage proceeds to a series of Biblical examples that seem to suggest that the honor of the dead precedes the honor of the living, but on closer inspection they fail to clinch the case. Finally a determination is made on the basis of this statement by Rabbi Nathan: "It is a good sign for the deceased that he is punished [in this world] after death. If a dead man is not eulogized and is not buried, or if he is dragged along by a wild animal, or if rain falls lightly on his bier, it is a good sign for him." His sins, in other words, will be forgiven. And so the rabbis rule: "We conclude from this that [the rites are] for the respect of the dead." For if they were for the respect of the living, why would the degradation of the poor man's body save him from the consequences of his sins?

So mourning looks to the dead, not to the living. (Again the tradition reveals an admirable indifference to psychology.) But all this leaves Weil with a worry. If the rituals of grief are designed to honor the dead, then the dying may have the right to dispense with them, as the woman in the question that was posed to Weil wished her daughters not to swaddle their sobbing heads. And so Weil declared that "it is certain that mourning itself cannot be renounced, since in that case the laws of mourning would be nullified." Splendid! Your father cannot absolve you of your mourning for him, because your mourning for him is not merely a matter of obedience to him.

When you mourn for your father, you serve things larger than him. Mourning is mandated by more than its object and by more than its occasion. It is mandated by one's location in a family, in a tradition, in a world.

Is there anything more subjective than sorrow? Yet sorrow is objective, too. It is ordained by a cosmos in which you have a position. The kaddish is one of the entailments of that position.

The objectivity of sorrow.

You do not mourn only because he died. You mourn also because you are commanded to mourn. There is your heart, and there is the Torah.

Your father cannot forbid you to mourn him. And your father cannot forbid you to love him. And your father cannot forbid you to forgive him. And your father cannot forbid you to leave him. The limitations of your father's power are what make it possible for you to respect him. You could not respect a force that could compel you completely. All you could do is fear it, and run.

Your origins cannot retract you.

women and death. (I read this passage a few months ago in the Perfumer.) The passage records a difference of opinion about the proper order of the funeral procession. There are those who say that the women walk ahead of the bier and the men walk behind them, and there are those who say that the men lead and the women follow. The reason given for the latter view is "to protect the honor of the daughters of Israel, so that nobody will stare at the women." The reason given for the former view is not so solicitous. The women walk at the head of the procession because "they brought death to the world." These ancient rabbis were thinking of Eve, whose sin made us mortal; but in this ruling I detect also a terror of women. Women, the mothers of death? But they are the mothers of life!

And Meir had another observation: "Our predecessors banned the bringing of water from the river, because it happened once that the gentiles pronounced a libel and killed Jews there."

And another observation: Meir recounts the custom of tearing up grass after the burial, and explains that this is a symbolic reference to the resurrection of the dead, and then notes that there are some who throw the torn grass over their shoulders. Why do "they throw it backward and not forward"? He has an answer. "I have seen it written . . . that the soul accompanies the body of the dead as far as the grave, but it does not have permission to return to its place until those who have gathered [at the grave] give it permission, and the throwing of the grass backward is a sign of their permission [for the soul to go back], as if to say, go to your rest." But what if you do not want this soul to depart? What if you cannot acquiesce in a world without this soul? Meir would say that you are cruel, that the soul deserves a rest. But I would say that the death of a father is also cruel,

If, as Rabbi Nathan says, atonement comes to the dead who are not interred, who are savaged by the beasts, who are swept by the rains, then atonement came to my grandfather and to my grandmother, to my aunt and to my uncles, to my cousins, to all my brethren whose bodies were left in the fields and the ravines and the pits and the forests, in this time and in the other times. Rabbi Nathan's beautiful provision for the corpses of the centuries.

A crow outside my window won't stop squawking. What's the matter? Oh, I see. It is almost seven o'clock. I must get to Georgetown. I have been summoned to prayer by a bird!

Meir ben Baruch of Rothenburg was not only the supreme Talmudist of his time, he was also a figure of romance. In 1286, when thousands of Jews were fleeing Germany, owing to the renewal of the blood libel, and owing to Rudolph I's unjust policy of taxation and his expropriation of Jewish property—"the Jews, collectively and individually, in their capacity of serfs of Our Chamber, belong to us with their persons and all their property. . . . It is right and proper that if any such Jews become fugitives and, without Our special license and consent as their master, render themselves beyond the seas and thus alienate themselves from their true lord, that We, as the lord to whom they belong, may freely enter into all their possessions, objects, and property . . ."—when the Jews were fleeing this definition of their status, Meir was among them. But he never made it out. In Lombardy, the rabbi was recognized by an apostate Jew, who informed on him to the local authorities, and they imprisoned him. The Jewish community amassed a vast sum of money with which to ransom their leader; but when the emperor, hoping to extort from the Jews a validation of his view of their status, insisted that they were paying not a ransom but a tax, the deal collapsed. Seven years later, Meir died in prison. (Fourteen years later, his body was ransomed and he was buried in the Jewish cemetery in Worms.) In his confinement, however, Meir did not stop working. The captive had an uncaptive mind. Sometimes he had pen and paper, sometimes he did not. And in the tower at Wasserburg, he had the company of a devoted student named Samson ben Zadok. Samson produced a book in which he recorded his indomitable teacher's thoughts and practices, and included some of Meir's responsa and other texts. "Our teacher Rabbi Meir of Rothenburg was accustomed always to have his meal on the Sabbath eve at sunset, and not wait until it was really night": this is how Samson's prison book unceremoniously begins, and it proceeds through all the obligations of Jewish life as his teacher commented upon them, including the obligation to sanctify God's Name in martyrdom. (Samson records Meir's famous observation that "when a man resolves to sanctify the Name and to sacrifice his life for the Sanctification of the Name, and they stone him or burn him or bury him alive or hang him—whatever they do to him, he feels no pain. . . . Many deliver themselves to the fire and the killing and they do not cry woe, woe.") Finally Samson gets round to the laws of mourning. His notes are a vivacious supplement to Meir's own treatise on the laws of mourning, which is the only one of his extended works to have survived.

In Samson's notes, I find a few magical lines about the verse from Psalms that I have been pondering, "I am forgotten as a dead man out of mind." Meir has two interpretations of the verse. Both of them are based on numerology. The first interpretation is legal. "In these three words there are twelve letters, and from this we learn that the dead is forgotten after twelve months and a lost object is despaired over after twelve months." As simple as that. The second interpretation

is lyrical. "There are also those who point out that [the numerical value of the letters in the words] 'I am forgotten as a dead man out of mind' is equal to [the numerical value of the letters in the words] 'except for the bride of one's youth.' Oh, how she is adored! From this we learn that the adored bride of one's youth is never forgotten and is never out of mind." Meir was arrested when he was attempting to flee with his family. As he sat in his cell and glossed this verse about oblivion, was he thinking about his wife, the bride of his youth whom he would never see again? I have never thought of the great rabbi in this way. A knight of law, a knight of love.

When I say that Samson's lines are magical, I mean magical. His pages about the living and the dead describe a spectral universe, a world in which men and women traffic with spirits. In this respect, Meir of Rothenburg perfectly exemplifies the paradox of his culture: he was at once ratiocinative and superstitious. In his work, the logical is bundled with the supernatural. Thus, Samson records a story that his master told him: "A person died in a house, and one of the people in the house drank the water that was in the house at the hour of death. When the sage saw this, he rebuked him and said that one must not drink at the hour of death. A short while later, the person who drank the water died. They asked the sage: 'Why did you rebuke that man?' And he said: 'I saw the angel of death polishing his knife in the water in that house after the death.'"

Meir had another observation about the customs of mourners. When they leave the cemetery, he told Samson, "the women must return to their homes first, because the angel of death and Satan take their hands and dance with them in the cemetery." Perhaps he had in mind the awful passage in the Jerusalem Talmud about the special relationship of

even if his soul deserves a rest. So stand at the fresh grave, I say, and tear up the grass, but throw it forward, not backward, and the fury with which it travels toward the horizon will be your fury. For you are yourself traveling in that direction, fatherless toward the horizon.

I wonder what became of Samson after the death of his master. He must have missed those years in prison. I imagine that he did not experience them entirely as an imprisonment.

"A Jew asked a question of Rabbi Meir of Rothenburg, may he live long. The question was whether the man is in need of atonement for having slaughtered his wife and his four sons on the day of the great killing in Coblenz, the city of blood. For they had beseeched him to do this, when they saw that God had brought forth His wrath and the enemies had begun to murder the children of the living God, who were dying for the Sanctification of the Name. He intended to kill himself, too, so that he would die with his family, but God saved him through the intervention of certain gentiles." This terrible inquiry must have been addressed to Meir around 1265, when the massacre in Coblenz occurred. And this was the rabbi's reply: "I do not know very well how to rule in this matter. It is certain that he who is prepared to die for the Sanctification of the Name is permitted to destroy himself. But to slaughter others? This requires careful scrutiny as to whether a proof may be found that will permit it. . . . We have heard and we have found that many notables slaughtered their sons and their daughters. Rabbi Kalonymos also did so [in Mainz in 1096], as we know from a poem of lamentation—and surely anyone who suggests that he was in need of atonement slanders our pious predecessors. Since his intention was to do the right thing, out of the magnitude of his love for our Creator, he struck and put his hand to his life's delight; and his children also beseeched him to act in this way. This situation is not to be compared to the situation described in the Talmud [in its discussion of damages for personal injury], where it is decided that [a man who is beseeched to] 'blind my eye and break my leg' is nonetheless liable [for damages if he does as his victim requests]. Here, in this case, surely we forgive him, because he acted out of the love of God, and he is not to be treated stringently at all."

Meir's leniency toward the miserable man is not surprising. I am stirred especially by the opening words of his reply: "I do not know very well how to rule in this matter." Who would? A blessing on the authority who confesses to the limits of his authority.

The martyrological materials of Ashkenaz are the most moving documents in the medieval history of my people, but they must be resisted. I must honor the martyrs, but I must not admire them. A proposition is not true because somebody has died for it. Does this seem callous? Then I will put it another way. A proposition is not true because somebody has killed for it.

There is altogether too much certainty in all these narratives of holy killing and holy dying. Still, who cannot admire the martyrs for their courage? A definition of martyrdom: imaginable courage in the service of unimaginable certainty.

The martyrs terrify me with the consequences of the love that we share.

I came early to shul this evening and looked in the digest of Meir of Rothenburg's opinions on mourning that appears in Mordecai ben Hillel, his great student, who died a martyr five years after Meir died. What leaps out at me this evening is Meir's adamancy about the limits of mourning. He cites his predecessor Eliezer ben Joel Ha'Levi, the sage of Bonn in the eleventh and twelfth centuries, and the author of one of the basic works of Jewish law in the Middle Ages (I remember him as the rabbi who was forced to dictate a responsum because his vision was damaged by his tears for his brother, who was martyred in 1216): "Rabbi Eliezer ben Joel wrote that it is said that a mourner for a father or a mother should not attend a house of merriment until twelve months have passed, so that [we may infer that] in a leap year [in the Jewish calendar, a year of thirteen months] we suffice with twelve months. That is why the text speaks in terms of months and not in terms of a year." And later in Mordecai's text it is reported that "our Rabbi Meir" made a point of noting that the judgment of the dead takes twelve months, "and even if he was a wicked man, he receives his sentence twelve months after his burial, so [after this period of time] the mourner is never again to mourn for his father or his mother, except in the case of one [who learns of his parent's death more than twelve months after it happened, and such an individual] mourns for a single hour, but otherwise absolutely not."

"Absolutely not": Why look back at a year of looking back? Nostalgia is bad enough. Nostalgia for nostalgia is ridiculous.

It may be ridiculous, but it may also be our lot. How long will it be before we find ourselves pining not only for the past, but also for our pining for the past? People will remember the days when they remembered. They will commemorate their commemorations.

It is a commonplace that modern life has been unkind to memory. And having damaged memory, we idealize it.

Guiltily we promote it into more than it is, and confer upon it an authority that it does not deserve. Memory is the most fallible of our faculties. It is always in need of correction.

Memory is essentially partial. That is its strength. It does not preserve everything. If you cannot forget, you cannot remember. The retrieval of tradition is partial, or it is useless. But then the historian arrives, to care for all the precious things for which memory did not care.

Memory is admired for its immediacy and for its authenticity. But immediacy is the antithesis of authenticity. We cannot instantly be what we must be. We cannot instantly be even what we are.

The only authenticity that is immediately ours is biological authenticity. Therefore it is morally insignificant.

Authenticity, or living vicariously through one's own ancestors.

For many years I encouraged my father to commit his memories of his murdered world to tape. He never got around to it, and I do not altogether regret it. His memory endures in my memory, his version of him in my version of him. I do not doubt that he got some of the story wrong, and that I get some of the story wrong. I will never mistake my memory of my father for my knowledge of him. But I am his heir, not his historian.

I cannot say the same about my tradition. I am its heir *and* its historian. I must remember it *and* I must know it. I must be faithful *and* I must be doubtful. I must be near *and* I must be far.

I am always gathering myself up and carrying myself to where I am.

People without secrets cannot understand people with secrets. It is not a question of honesty. People with secrets are not dishonest. They are unhappy. They want to be loved but not to be known. —A thought about my father.

Is secrecy compatible with the fullness of life?

Tonight is the beginning of the last day. When I came to shul, I almost fell to my knees. I listened desperately to the kaddish. I drove one of our elders home. As I left the shul, there were people busy inside, preparing food for a local shelter for the homeless.

This morning I dreamed a terrible dream. There were ancient bowls. A big man was trying to shatter them, and I was trying to save them. He was trying to shatter them because I was trying to save them, so as to torment me for my love of them. We came to blows, again and again. I rescued the ancient bowls, and the ones that were beyond my ability to rescue failed to break, and this was a miracle.

The big man was my father. I woke in fear. This was another one of my wrathful dreams about him. I used to have them a lot. But now, a year after his death? I guess the unconscious hasn't heard the news.

A chilly morning. The very last one. The leather straps that I wrap around my arm and my head remind me of the steel that reinforces concrete. I can use the reinforcement.

The worship ends with the psalm of the day: "I removed his shoulder from the burden."

In a fourteenth-century work I have found a short essay against the mentality of mourning. The work is *Tsedah La'Derekh,* or *Provision for the Way,* and its author is Menahem ben Zerakh. A digest of religious laws and religious concepts, Menahem's book was produced for the upper class of the Jewish community of Toledo, for "owing to the turbulence of the age and the coveting of titles and superfluous things, they grow steadily more delinquent in the fulfillment of the religious duties that they are required to fulfill, especially those who travel and those who serve at the royal court." Menahem's introduction is famous among intellectual historians for the account that it provides of the development of the tradition from the beginning to his own day; but it also contains a brief but unforgettable memoir. When Menahem remarked upon "the turbulence of the age," he was speaking from experience. "I, the author of this book, the lowly one in my family, Menahem son of the holy Rabbi Aaron ben Zerakh, was born in the land of Navarre. My father was one of the exiles from France, who were banished from there in the year 5066 [1306] in the month of Av. When I was sixteen, I married. . . . In the year 5088 [1328] God became angry at His people, and the king of France, who ruled over Navarre, died, and the mobs rose up and conspired to destroy and to murder and to exterminate all the Jews in the kingdom. In Estella and in the rest of the land they killed approximately six thousand Jews. My father, my mother, and my four younger brothers sanctified God's Name and were killed. Only I escaped from my father's house. I was severely injured and in great agony, because twenty-five villains beat me and wounded me, and I was left naked among the dead, where I remained from dusk until midnight. It was the twenty-third day of Adar. At midnight there appeared a knight who was a friend of my father, and he took me out of the dead and brought me to his house, and he treated me kindly. When my wounds finally healed, I resolved to go to Toledo to study Torah. A new king arose in Navarre, and we children of the dead cried out to him to avenge the spilled blood of our fathers, but it was useless. I studied for two years with my teacher Rabbi Joshua ibn Shouaib. And then in the year 5091 [1331] I came to this place." Menahem proceeds to the details of his studies—the Talmudic methods of Ashkenaz had been introduced into Spain, and Menahem joins them to the methods of the Spanish school—and he moves from Toledo to Alcalá, where he will succeed his teacher at the academy; but it is not long before his vocation is violently disrupted. Henry of Trastámara and Pedro the Cruel engulf the place in a fratricidal war. In 1368, Henry lays siege to Toledo, and when Pedro arrives to lift the siege he is killed by his brother, who ascends to the throne. "In those days of fighting, when there was chaos everywhere and every man did as he wished and the common people pillaged and plundered the Jewish communities of Spain, the people of Israel were sorely reduced, and for the Jews in the kingdom of Castile it was a time of trouble the like of which they had not seen since they came there in their exile. The holy community of Toledo suffered doubly because of the siege, until they came to eat the flesh of their sons and daughters. About eight thousand Jews died in the siege, the great and the small, from starvation and deprivation. Only a few survived, and the king imposed a tax upon them, until they had not even a morsel of bread for themselves. I, too, was left destitute of all that I had, for they plundered and stole from me, and they smote me and wounded me and took my mantle from me, and nothing was left to me from all my labors except my books and my house and my land." Menahem is rescued from Alcalá by the courtier Don Samuel Abravanel ("an intelligent man and a lover of scholars . . . who is eager to study the works of writers and philosophers when the pressure of time permits"), who resettles him in Toledo, where "the surviving notables, who knew me from before, beseeched me, and I agreed to live among them, so that God would perhaps grant a saving remnant." (Six years after Menahem's death, in the wake of the anti-Jewish riots of 1391, Samuel Abravanel converted to Christianity and became Juan Sanchez de Sevilla, but later he fled with his family to Portugal and returned to Judaism.)

Menahem ben Zerakh was, as we would say, a survivor. (That is one of the honorifics of our time.) And this survivor, this man who lost everything twice, who was pulled from a pile of corpses—this man delivered a warning against mourning. He chose as the text for his little sermon against morbidity the verses from Ecclesiastes that seem to suggest the opposite: "It is better to go to the house of mourning than to the house of feasting" and "The heart of the wise is in the house of mourning, but the heart of fools is in the house of mirth." The author of these verses, says Menahem, "was precise in his language. He said 'to the house of' and 'in the house of.' He did not say that it is better to go to mourning, and he did not say that the heart of the wise is in mourning. For the truth is that the heart of fools is in mourning, because anger lingers in the hearts of fools. Mourning is one of the evil qualities that detracts from the perfection of man, since wisdom and inspiration depart as a consequence of mourning."

Menahem illustrates the impoverishing effects of mourning with the example of Jacob's mourning for Joseph, whom he falsely believed to have been killed. Jacob "was perfect to the height of perfection," and yet "the Spirit of God did not rest upon him all the time of his mourning, and it was therefore hidden from him for much of his life." Menahem makes his implication clear: "If such a perfect man suffered such a great deficiency owing to his mourning, how much more likely it is that [this will happen to] an ordinary individual who mourns too much." Menahem does not mean to be unfeeling. He understands that mourning is human. "Scripture does not at all forbid weeping," he writes, "for it is natural that one will be stirred to tears by the parting from loved ones, even when they are alive. . . . The sages do not deny nature, and it is in the nature of man to cry when he is parted from his loved ones, and all the more so when he has no expectation of seeing them again." But the natural is the beginning, not the end, of human life. The natural awaits the spiritual. The rabbi acknowledges the truth of feeling and then he seeks the mastery of feeling. Even grief demands discipline.

"The true wisdom," Menahem continues, "is to know that mourning for the dead is neither an expression of wisdom nor an expression of proper faith." Those are strong words. In what way is mourning an interference with faith? Menahem's answer is a little startling. It is that excessive mourning is a sign of excessive love. What interferes with faith is not the mourning for the loved one, but the love for the loved one. This is what Jacob did not understand. He mourned for his son in a manner that distorted the purpose of his paternity. "There is no reason for the righteous to have sons," Menahem asserts, "except to serve the Lord with them."

Well, no, there are other reasons. We have children, Menahem notes, because we are animals: there are those who "have the will [to reproduce] because they are imprinted with the nature of all living things that do not have the power of thought and the power to create with their hands, and they desire to have children and to raise them, and they rejoice in their toil with them, and when their children die they mourn because all their toil and effort is gone. He who mourns in this way is not different from the animals. His grief is like the grief of a cow bellowing upon the loss of a calf, and there shall arise contempt and wrath." There are also those who desire children, Menahem writes a little opaquely, for "an evil reason": so as "to have their help and to be vain about them toward their neighbors and their relatives." These scheming parents mourn their children as the commander of an army would mourn the loss of his army, "and it would be best if these people did not produce children, because the loss will be held against them as a sin." Yet there are also those who grasp the higher purpose of human reproduction, "whose intention in giving birth to children is that they learn to walk in the ways of the Lord and to serve Him, and those who are on this path deserve to rejoice in reproduction, and they will give thanks and give praise when they [their children] are taken away from them." In this respect, Abraham succeeded where Jacob failed, when he prepared himself to sacrifice his son, "and he did not ask to be unburdened of this commandment, the hardest of hard commandments in the natural order of things." What Abraham understood was that human love must rise above animal love. The difference is in the detachment. A man's children are not his children, they are God's children. Menahem (relying upon a famous Talmudic tale about the death of Rabbi Meir's sons) suggests an analogy from the laws of torts. He likens a child to an object that has been deposited with somebody for safekeeping. The object is not his property, and his purposes are not its purposes. "When the owner comes to collect what belongs to him, is it proper that the person who was keeping it for him should be crestfallen? This would reflect an unkind heart, and it is useless."

Menahem's argument against the tyranny of love is powerful, not least because it appears in a discussion of the laws of mourning. Three days for weeping, seven days for lamentations, and so on: to explain the diminishing protocols of Jewish grief, Menahem gives a defense of detachment. I say that he is right. I am not only an animal, and I am not only a son. My soul surpasses my ancestry. My father imbued me with my purposes, but my purposes carry me beyond my father. In the heart of the family, there must be a wise alienation, a standpoint stricter than the standpoint of love. In the heart of the family, a spiritual wedge.

A father, a mother, a son, a daughter: they, too, can be idols. Idolatry may be nothing more than too much love.

Reading Menahem, I am struck by the narcissism of grief. A year ago my father died. But is that really the most precise description of what happened? Of course not. A year ago *this man* died. Just as I am not only his son, he was not only my father. So forget that he was my father. Who was he? What did he do? Forget that he was my father, and mourn him.

What, then, is the objective of mourning, in Menahem's view? He is quite straightforward: "There is nothing for an intelligent man to mourn over and to grieve over except his sins." It has taken me a year to feel the force of this idea. Sorrow as a form of remorse. Remorse as the essence of sorrow.

Menahem adds his voice to the chorus of thinkers for whom there is an essential connection between mortality and morality. The mourner is a man whose reflections on the reality of death disabuse him of his dependence upon the material world, who "sees that the body of a good man is destroyed like the body of an evil man, and so the living man will truthfully scrutinize his own life." In such a view, mourning takes place on this side of metaphysics. Mourning is a process of remoralization. In sorrow is the seed of change.

If the son can prove that there is merit in the father, then the son can prove that there is merit in the son.

The moral energy of mourning: when I encountered this idea in Nahmanides in the early months of this year, I rebelled against it. I was in no mood to be preached at. I was offended by the idea that my father's death was the occasion for a reckoning with how I live. My grief was not a struggle with values, it was a struggle with facts. It was the world that had to explain itself. But on this day, the last day, I see what I am supposed to see. Let the facts drift dumbly and the world repeat itself forever. But I am a man who will die, the son of a man who has died, and I can exceed myself. I am the gap in the world, since I can exceed myself.

The world is choking on nature.

The last day, the last day. I worked quietly at the office and walked quietly to the afternoon prayer, and then I started to crumble. I watched the fellow from the government agency, the sweet man of hard faith, stand and pray. His lips moved slowly. His imploring arms drew arcs above his motionless figure. I noticed that as he got nearer to God, he got farther from us. This is as it should be. The sight of him steadied me. The service came and went. "Our Father, our King, favor us and answer us, for we have no deeds. Treat us charitably and kindly, and save us." As I left the lobbyists' office, a friend put his hand in mine, as if to congratulate me on the completion of the course. The servant of God in the corner was still making his address.

On my walk back to work I pause at the little plaza with the statue of Longfellow. It is no more than an island in the traffic, but an island in the traffic is what I want. The old poet sits sternly above me. His right hand has dropped over the side of his chair, and it holds a book. He is considering what he has just read, or forgetting it. I sit under a naked tree, on a wooden bench that shows its winters, and I watch the pigeons. My head empties out. I am beyond reasons. I am aware only that I am aware. I know only that there is something rather than nothing. This is the rustle of being. It passes quickly and I return to work.

In Maimonides' code of law, I read: "A man must not mourn excessively for his dead. As it is written [in Jeremiah], 'weep ye not for the dead, neither bemoan him.' That is to say, weep ye not too much, for this is the way of the world, and a man who anguishes about the way of the world is a fool."

The world does not explain. That is its special, inhuman privilege.

I am at home. The light has begun to move in the direction of my release. The sun will soon set on my mourning. I sit at my desk, but I cannot work. I can only stare through the window and watch the throes of the day, and measure its concluding moments by the changes in gold and gray.

It is dusk. My duty is done.

It is dusk. I give up his ghost.

It is dusk. He is judged.

It is dusk. I am judged.

These are things for which I am too small.

Will night never fall?

Night fell. I went to shul. The air was full of the fragrance of fireplaces. My mourning for my father slipped out of the world like my father. I passed my hand over my sorrow's eyes.

When my cup is full, I study it. When my cup is empty, I drink it.

I am in a mind to bless. Blessed be the book, the page, the verse, the word, the letter. Blessed be the great names and the ungreat names. Blessed be the velvet that is the color of wine, and the wine. Blessed be the particle in the light, and the light. Blessed be the shoulder and blessed be the burden. Blessed be the calendar. Blessed be the clock.

XVI

I am no longer a mourner. That is to say, my mourning is all mine now. For a year, private was public. In accordance with the requirements of my tradition, and sometimes thoughtfully, I exposed the condition of my heart. But that rite has now expired. The public no longer has any claim on the private. I need not show anything anymore. I am alone again with the purities and the impurities, his and mine.

What is happening to me now is nothing like what Americans call "closure." What a ludicrous notion of emotional efficiency! Americans really believe that the past is past. They do not care to know that the past soaks the present like the light of a distant star. Things that are over do not end. They come inside us, and seek sanctuary in subjectivity. And there they live on, in the consciousness of individuals and communities.

An empiricist account of tradition cannot be given.

The soul does not heal as the body heals, because the soul is improved, and even enchanted, by its wounds.

"Closure" is an ideal of forgetfulness. It is a denial of finality, insofar as finality is never final. Nothing happens once and for all. It all visits, it all returns. But "closure" says: once and for all. This is a misunderstanding of subjectivity, which is essentially haunted.

From an essay on death, by the most dedicated rationalist I know: "A man's life may include much that does not take place within the boundaries of his body and his mind, and what happens to him can include much that does not take place within the boundaries of his life. These boundaries are commonly crossed by the misfortunes of being deceived, or despised, or betrayed. (If this is correct, there is a simple account of what is wrong with breaking a deathbed promise. It is an injury to the dead man. For certain purposes it is possible to regard time as just another type of distance.) A man is the subject of good and evil as much because he has hopes which may or may not be fulfilled, or possibilities which may or may not be realized, as because of his capacity to suffer and enjoy." Is this not a theory of immortality?

The rationalist explained that you can hurt a dead man. I rose in the mornings to say the kaddish. It is the same thing.

A rationalist's theory of immortality!

Above the entrance to a building near the Mall, I notice a clock that has no hands. If there is a clock in paradise, this is it.

Sometimes the work of students elevates me more than the work of masters. I am bored by the worship of greatness. There is so much that can be accomplished on this side of greatness. And so I have been reading Joseph ben Moses, known as Yossel. He was a disciple of Israel Isserlein, the greatest authority in Germany in the generation after Jacob Moellin. In 1475, Yossel completed a digest of his master's laws and customs in which he recorded anecdotes as well. Yossel reminds me of Zalman, Moellin's faithful student and scribe, except that he is more charming. He writes that he is not brilliant—"many of these matters came to me after great toil, I had to request explanations of my master and of the students three times until I understood"—and not resourceful—"I was unable to cut a quill with which to write, and also I cannot write quickly, and sometimes it was a burden for me to buy paper and ink with which to write this book." He is a humble man, and a little embarrassed by his project: "I must explain how it occurred to me to write this book, since I have not yet accomplished what is necessary to be called a rabbi or a fellow of the academy, and I am already forty years old." (Isserlein's colleagues and students insisted that he write it.) Yossel's discussion of mourning, not surprisingly, discloses the circumstances of his own bereavement. About the death of his father: "When I heard that my father had left this life while in the middle of his journey to the Holy Land, and I did not know whether or not the news had reached me twelve months after his death, he [Isserlein] told me to say a single kaddish that would suffice until I learned the date of his death, even though there were other orphans in mourning in the synagogue [who had the right to say the kaddish at that service], and I did not have to rend my garment." (The perplexity of a child who is uncertain about the fate of a parent is discussed extensively in Jewish law.) About the death of his mother: "I remember that when my mother, Mistress Feyga, left this life, I was not yet [the age of] bar-mitzvah. She was buried in the lower cemetery in the town of Augsburg, because my father lived for twenty-eight years in the settlement of Hoechstadt on the Danube River, and there I was born. My father used to pay taxes to the duke of Fuerth and followed the customs of Augsburg, such as not to eat the butter of non-Jews. Thirty days after the death of my mother, my father sent me to the community in Augsburg to study Torah and to say kaddish. And there was present there a mourner who already was a bar-mitzvah and was a young man and was engaged to the daughter of one of the members of the congregation, and he did not want me to recite the kaddish, since I was a stranger and not yet a bar-mitzvah, but Rabbi Jacob Weil ruled that he should allow me to recite the kaddish twice a week."

Yossel's pages on mourning touch on familiar themes: the casting of lots to determine the priority of mourners in the house of worship (he describes a rather elaborate system of such godly gambling); the custom "in most communities that a stranger in mourning says the kaddish just like a local in mourning"; the disqualification of the mourner from representing the congregation in prayer on holidays ("he [Isserlein] did not want to hear a mourner, he wanted to hear a cantor who would sing joyously or a cantor who would take care with the words," and mourners were also forbidden to lead the prayer for rain). And he tells a delicious tale: "I recall that once there were two relatives who hated each other. When the one died, the other refused to mourn for him. Rabbi Jacob Weil ordered him to mourn against his will."

It is in Yossel's conscientious jottings that I find a reference to my own situation. "For the period of mourning, the month of a leap year counts toward the twelve months, and there is no need to mourn for thirteen months [when the anniversary of the parent's death is finally reached]. Still, he [Isserlein] instructed that [the mourner] observe a difference [during the thirteenth month]—for example, he should not sit in his father's place until the anniversary of his father's death." I, too, have mourned for my father in a leap year. Having mourned for twelve months, I now must wait another month for the anniversary of my father's death, for the yahrzeit. So I am in a limbo. From Yossel, in the name of his teacher, I learn that I must mark this little limbo with "a difference," a twist.

I like the idea. But what twist? I could stop going to shul, but then I would dishonor what I am attempting to honor. I could keep going to shul, but then I'm supposed to be going to shul anyway. (This entire melodrama of my kaddish was premised on my delinquency. When religious Jews mourn, they merely add a short prayer to the service at which they are already to be found.) I do not aspire to my father's place, so Yossel's suggestion that I not sit in his place is useless. I never imagined that I would have difficulty in designing a twist. I was once the master of twists.

Yossel concludes his discussion, and his book, with this tale: "I recall that I asked the sage Rabbi Isserlein: 'An old man such as yourself—what pleasure can you have in the messiah?' And he answered: 'Oh, that I should see the messiah only for half an hour, and then I would willingly die.' And I was too slow to ask him for his reason." Poor, plodding Yossel! But his master's reason is not hard to guess. The sage had lived a life in expectation. The pleasure that he would gain from the coming of the messiah was the pleasure of knowing that he had not been deceived. The hour of proof—the half an hour of proof—was all it would take. Yossel had asked a young man's question.

Hail Yossel, hail Zalman, hapless heroes of a deathless tradition!

Oh, for half an hour of proof.

It is almost over. But it is not quite over, and so I must open a book. There has arrived from Brooklyn a new edition of the rulings of Hayyim ben Isaac of the late thirteenth century, the son of Isaac of Vienna and the student of Meir of Rothenburg. I pondered his responsum on martyrdom and the kaddish a little while ago. In the new volume, I find this: "If there are two mourners, each mourning in his own house, the one should leave his house and visit the other, even during the first three days of mourning." A mourner during the first three days (and in our time, during the first week) is not supposed to leave his house; but the obligation to mourn is here superseded by the obligation to console. Hayyim reports on another practice in thirteenth-century Germany, of which he obviously approves: "In Speyer, it is the custom that a mourner, before the days of his mourning are over, leaves his house to join the funeral procession of another dead and to bury him, though this should [only] be done after the first three days." It would seem cruel for an individual just back from one funeral to be hustled out to another funeral; but in truth it is not cruel, it is an exercise in social responsibility. The mourner, too, has a social responsibility. His experience has conferred upon him an expertise that others need. Grief must not impede the specialist in grief.

The disconsolate are the masters of consolation. They offer sympathy without illusion.

In Brooklyn, for the unveiling of my father's grave. My sister gave me a lift to shul in the morning. "I had a peculiar dream last night," she said. "I dreamed that he was a lumberjack. He was carrying wood." She was talking about our father. I was too taken aback to tell her about Akiva and the dead man condemned to carry wood. Maybe Akiva wanders the graveyard in Elmont, too. As I walked into shul, I imagined running into Akiva in the graveyard at Elmont, and saying to him: I know, Akiva, I know. I must vindicate him. But I have vindicated him. I have said the kaddish and I have studied the Torah. My father saw to it that your services would not be required.

Bless my father, Akiva, bless my father.

The old shul was in the throes of a quarrel, ugly even by its standards. I think I know which side my father would have taken.

It is the seventh day of Adar. This is no ordinary date in the Jewish calendar. On this day Moses died. After the service in shul, I devote a short while to study, on the subject of the seventh of Adar. This is my text for the morning, from the Talmud: "When the lots that Haman cast [to set the date for the destruction of Persia's Jews] fell on Adar, he rejoiced, saying: 'The die has been cast for the month in which Moses died.' He did not know that Moses had not only died on the seventh of Adar, but was also born on the seventh of Adar." The point of this passage is that the merit of the fathers—in this instance, the merit of Moses—stood the Jews in good stead, and saved them from their enemy. It is a good sign, or so I would say if I believed in signs, that we are unveiling a tombstone that boasts that "they did cry out and God heard them and delivered them from all their troubles" on the date that defeated Haman. After all, my father made Haman's acquaintance.

But how did the rabbis determine that the seventh of Adar was Moses' day? Rashi performs the extrapolations from the Biblical verses, correcting for the Israelites' proper period of mourning for their leader. The Israelites' proper period of mourning! Even then? Yes, even then. It is an axiom of rabbinic culture that a Jew is a Jew is a Jew. If we are like our ancestors, then our ancestors are like us. Anachronism is one of the instruments of identity.

Rashi is struck by the fact that Moses died on the same date that he was born. This requires explanation. "So that the birth will atone for the death," he explains. This is not the first time that I have encountered the notion that death is a matter for atonement. In what sense, exactly? For what must the dead be forgiven? For their iniquity, or for their mortality?

Is death itself a sin? Twenty years ago, in an English writer of the seventeenth century, I came across this sentence: "I am not so much afraid of death, as ashamed thereof." I found it shocking then, and I do now. Here was a man for whom human mortality was a contradiction to human dignity.

It is a mistake to be embarrassed by finitude, but it is a gorgeous mistake.

The bay across from my mother's house was not troubled and it was not untroubled. The waters were in a condition of mild, infinite motion. They preached the permanence of impermanence. I heard them clearly. Small boats passed back and forth, to and from the sea.

The car came to a stop on the unpaved lane at the back of the cemetery. Car doors opened and closed. Arms were taken in arms. There were whispers. An indescribable sobriety. And there stood facing us the strangest thing I have ever seen: a stone that said WIESELTIER.

More cars pulled up. Cousins mainly, and a few of my father's friends. All of a sudden a winter wind arrived, out of season, for this moment. It blew bitterly. The rabbi summoned us to begin. I read a psalm: "And he shall be like a tree planted by the rivers of water, that bringeth forth his fruit in his season; his leaf also shall not wither." My sister read a psalm: "As for man, his days are as grass; as a flower of the field, so he flourisheth. For the wind passeth over it, and it is gone." The rabbi said a few words about my father, all of them true. People were shivering in the cold. I asked a younger cousin to recite the memorial prayer that beseeches a merciful God to "devise a right rest" for the departed, and he recited it in a breaking voice. The rabbi commanded my mother to remove the cheesecloth that covered the footstone that bears my father's name, and the names of his brother and his sister. She did, and the names were revealed. Finally my mother had buried somebody she loved.

My father, my father, buried and unveiled.

It was not the sight of my father's grave that caused me to lose control of my sadness. It was the sight of the old men huddled against the wind, the old men in their caps and coats, who had come to bury one more of their own, to harken to one more prayer for one more dead, the firm, selfless old men with the accents and the histories, my exhausted and inexhaustible elders, unmoved again by the gusts. They are getting to their end, I thought; and I loved them; and I wept.

I was bursting with descent.

The living and the dead, I miss them all.

Then the rabbi instructed me to read another psalm. "The Lord is my shepherd; I shall not want." I chose to sing it, in the sweet, sepulchral manner in which it is sung on Sabbath afternoons. I stepped closer to the grave and sang, and as I sang I broke away from my dread. I sang to the death of wailing. My song grew, as if to make room within it for all the true and punished people who gathered around it, to shield them with its splendor and to seal them with its peace. Lean on my time, lean on my heart, lean on my fire. I will not bend beneath your load, I will not bend. "Surely goodness and mercy shall follow me all the days of my life; and I will dwell in the house of the Lord forever."

The living and the dead, I miss them all.
I will dance with them at the mourner's ball.

Then I said the kaddish. I stood in the ashes of fury and spoke the sentences of praise. Was that voice my voice? It was no longer the effusion of woe. Magnified, I said. Sanctified, I said. I looked above me, I looked below me, I looked around me. With my own eyes, I saw magnificence.

ACKNOWLEDGMENTS